The Granite Garden

THE GRANITE GARDEN

Urban Nature and Human Design

ANNE WHISTON SPIRN

Basic Books, Inc., Publishers

NEW YORK

Library of Congress Cataloging in Publication Data
Spirn, Anne Whiston, 1947–
    The granite garden.
    Bibliography: p. 290
    includes index.
    1. City planning—Environmental aspects. 2. Human
ecology. 3. Landscape architecture. I. Title.
HT166.S638 1984   363.7'009173'2   83-70767
ISBN 0–465–02699–0 (cloth)
ISBN 0–465–02706–7 (paper)

Cities have often been likened to symphonies and poems, and the comparison seems to me a perfectly natural one. They are in fact objects of the same kind. The city may even be rated higher since it stands at the point where nature and artifice meet. A city is a congestion of animals whose biological history is enclosed within its boundaries, and yet every conscious and rational act on the part of these creatures helps to shape the city's eventual character. By its form as by the manner of its birth, the city has elements at once of biological procreation, organic evolution, and esthetic creation. It is both a natural object and a thing to be cultivated; individual and group; something lived and something dreamed. It is *the* human invention *par excellence*.

Claude Lévi-Strauss
Tristes Tropiques

CONTENTS

PREFACE

NATURE pervades the city, forging bonds between the city and the air, earth, water, and living organisms within and around it. In themselves, the forces of nature are neither benign nor hostile to humankind. Acknowledged and harnessed, they represent a powerful resource for shaping a beneficial urban habitat; ignored or subverted, they magnify problems that have plagued cities for centuries, such as floods and landslides, poisoned air and water. Unfortunately, cities have mostly neglected and rarely exploited the natural forces within them.

More is known about urban nature today than ever before; over the past two decades, natural scientists have amassed an impressive body of knowledge about nature in the city. Yet little of this information has been applied directly to molding the form of the city—the shape of its buildings and parks, the course of its roads, and the pattern of the whole. A small fraction of that knowledge has been employed in establishing regulations to improve environmental quality, but these have commonly been perceived as restrictive and punitive, rather than as posing opportunities for new urban forms. Regulations have also proven vulnerable to shifts in public policy, at the mercy of the political concerns of the moment, whereas the physical form of the city endures through generation after generation of politicians. In the United States, the Reagan administration of the 1980s reversed the environmental policies of the 1970s, dismantled the institutional framework that had been constructed to implement those policies, and undermined the achievements of the previous decade. Regulations controlling the emission of air pollutants may be altered, but the urban form designed to disperse those pollutants will continue to do so regardless of changes in policy.

This is a book about nature in cities and what the city could be like if designed in concert with natural processes, rather than in ignorance of them or in outright opposition. It reviews comprehensive strategies for sweeping change most readily implemented in rapidly growing cities, as well as incremental solutions more appropriate to the gradual redesign of existing urban cores. Its concentration on the look and shape of the city, especially the open space within which buildings are set, reflects the fact that its author is a landscape architect and environmental planner, not an economist or a student of government policy.

The issues explored in this book have been personal concerns for as long as I can remember. I never learned to doubt that the city was part of nature. For years, a tiny plot of trees in a nearby vacant lot was a wilderness whose mysteries I never wholly unraveled. This woodlot of little more than 5,000 square feet, set in a meadow of high grass, provided ample space for childhood fantasies. Several blocks away, a creek disappeared into an underground culvert large enough to accommodate two small adventurers armed with candles and matches, seeking the stream's mouth. Later, downtown Cincinnati, a fifteen-minute bus ride away, afforded nature of a different sort: flocks of pigeons in Fountain Square; the wide, brown waters of the Ohio River; hilltops overlooking the river and city beneath; and parks whose creekbeds were littered with stone twigs and shells—the fossil remains of ancient plants and animals. Maps and books now augment my investigation of urban nature and the urban form that has evolved within it, aids to the eyes and imagination.

I first learned about the field of landscape architecture while studying art history. The letters and writings of Frederick Law Olmsted gave me a new appreciation for the social values of nature in the city, which extended far beyond the aesthetic, intellectual, and spiritual pleasures it afforded. From the close of the Civil War to the end of the nineteenth century, Olmsted forged a role for urban parks which was bound up in the alleviation of the nineteenth-century city's social and environmental problems. In the process he helped transform the American city. Through the design of parks and parkways, he sought to improve the city's climate, to alleviate air and water pollution, to mitigate floods, and to provide a naturalistic counterpoint to the city's buildings and bustling streets. Olmsted was a social reformer who exploited nature to nurture America's growing urban population. The issues he addressed and the approaches he advocated seemed very modern to me. I left art history to enter a profession that promised to permit a synthesis of nature, city, and art.

As a landscape architect and environmental planner, I was trained to design new communities that accommodate both human purpose and natural processes. However, it seemed contradictory to be so concerned with the integration of nature and human activities at the edge of the city and so little concerned with the reclamation of damaged land at its center. Why concentrate on mitigating damage to land that might not need to be developed were the central city more wholesome and attractive? Couldn't urban design also exploit the opportunities that nature afforded and respect the constraints it posed? Why not produce some of the environmental amenities of the countryside within the inner city—clean air and water, a garden plot, contact with other living organisms, and access to woodlots and meadows—while simultaneously exploiting mineral resources, protecting water resources, and mitigating natural hazards? Professional wisdom then held that, although theoretically it might be beneficial to design the city in concert with nature, either too little nature existed downtown or too little was known about it for such an approach to have practical results. The form of cities was seen as forged largely by social and economic forces in which nature played little role, except to embellish man's creation with street trees and parks.

Later, I discovered that a wealth of information about urban nature did exist, sequestered in specialized scientific journals, in conference proceedings, and in technical reports. This book arose out of my frustration in failing to find a volume that summarized that knowledge and applied it to urban design. Rooted in my experience as a landscape architect and planner, the book evolved with a growing appreciation for the crucial role that those outside the design and planning professions play in molding the city's form. The result is a book for all concerned with the fate of the city and of nature: policy makers and public officials, journalists and community activists, designers, planners, and citizens.

The literature on the natural environment of cities is far-flung and fragmented, falling within many disciplines. I owe much to the many specialists who generously assisted my research. A year's fellowship at the Bunting Institute was indispensable to my immersion in the literature, an overview of which constitutes the book's bibliography. I relied upon personal knowledge of the projects, such as the Dayton Climate Project, the Woodlands New Community, and the Toronto Waterfront Study, in which I was directly involved, and upon published descriptions of other case studies.

I have been fortunate to have fine teachers and colleagues. Ian McHarg, Narendra Juneja, Frederick E. Smith, and Carl Steinitz have all influenced this work both directly and indirectly. I am indebted to Heidi Cooke with whom I first explored many of these issues a decade ago. Many people provided important information: Fred Bartenstein, Jim Bockheim, Andrew Euston, Al Fein, Richard Forman, Mollie Hughes, Phil Lewis, Richard Nalbandian, Jim Patterson, Jim Prince, Elliot Rhodeside, Carl Steinitz, and Frank Vigier. I am grateful to Fred

Bartenstein, Blanche Linden-Ward, Mollie Hughes, and Fred Smith for commenting on specific chapters, and to Carl Steinitz and Paul Spirn for reading the entire manuscript.

A project fellowship from the National Endowment for the Arts helped pay for illustrations and for a portion of the time spent writing. Dean Gerald McCue and the Graduate School of Design provided support for typing and research assistants. I am particularly grateful to TenBroeck Davison, Jane Emens, Willa Reiser, and Donna Viscuglia for facilitating the production of the manuscript from rough to final draft, and to Randy Palmer for his dedication and talent in producing the final drawings. Many research assistants have provided valuable aid: John Burkholder, Laurel Raines, Elisabeth Miller, David Johnson, Dana Brown, Lynn Wolf, and Mark Goldschmidt.

My editor, Jeannette Hopkins, who first challenged me to write this book rather than a more technical version, has been a source of relentless, incisive criticism, inspiration, and sound advice for the past three years. The enthusiasm Jane Isay of Basic Books showed for the idea from the beginning, and the encouragement she offered all along the way, helped shape the book and promote its progress. Judith Greissman provided welcome suggestions and support during the final throes of writing and production; and Sheila Friedling facilitated the production process with skill and patience.

To Paul Spirn, my toughest critic and most wholehearted supporter, I owe a profound debt of both the heart and the mind, and to my son, Sam, renewed hope for the future.

ANNE WHISTON SPIRN
Cambridge, Massachusetts, 1983

The Granite Garden

Prologue

The Granite Garden

SEEN FROM SPACE, the earth is a garden world, a planet of life, a sphere of blues and greens sheathed in a moist atmosphere. At night, lights of the cities twinkle far below, forming constellations as distinct and varied as those of the heavens beyond. The dark spaces that their arcs embrace, however, are not the voids of space, but are replete with forests and farms, prairies and deserts. As the new day breaks, the city lights fade, overpowered by the light of the sun; blue seas and green forests and grasslands emerge, surrounding and penetrating the vast urban constellations. Even from this great distance above the earth, the cities are a gray mosaic permeated by tendrils and specks of green, the large rivers and great parks within them.

Homing in on a single constellation from hundreds of miles up, one cannot yet discern the buildings. But the fingers and patches of green—stream valleys, steep hillsides, parks, and fields—swell and multiply. The suburban forest surrounds the city; large lakes and ponds catch the sunlight and shimmer. Swinging in, now only a few miles up, the view is filled by a single city. Tall buildings spring up toward the sky, outcrops of rock and steel, and smaller homes poke up out of the suburban forest. Greens differentiate themselves into many hues. Silver ribbons of roadway flash across the landscape, and stream meanders interrupt and soften the edges of the city's angular grid.

Flying low, one skims over a city teeming with life. The amount of green in the densest part of the city is astonishing; trees and gardens grow atop buildings and in tiny plots of soil. On the ground, a tree-of-heaven sapling is thriving in the crack between pavement and building, and a hardy weed thrusts itself up between curb and sidewalk. Its roots fan out beneath the soil in search of nutrients and water. Beneath the pavement, underground rivers roar through the sewers.

The city is a granite garden, composed of many smaller gardens, set in a garden world. Parts of the granite garden are cultivated intensively, but the greater part is unrecognized and neglected.

To the idle eye, trees and parks are the sole remnants of nature in the city. But nature in the city is far more than trees and gardens, and weeds in sidewalk cracks and vacant lots. It is the air we breathe, the earth we stand on, the water we drink and excrete, and the organisms with which we share our habitat. Nature in the city is the powerful force that can shake the earth and cause it to slide, heave, or crumple. It is a broad flash of exposed rock strata on a hillside, the overgrown outcrops in an abandoned quarry, the millions of organisms cemented in fossiliferous limestone of a downtown building. It is rain and the rushing sound of underground rivers buried in storm sewers. It is water from a faucet, delivered by pipes from some outlying river or reservoir, then used and washed away into the sewer, returned to the waters of river and sea. Nature in the city is an evening breeze, a corkscrew eddy swirling down the face of a building, the sun and the sky. Nature in the city is dogs and cats, rats in the basement, pigeons on the sidewalks, raccoons in culverts, and falcons crouched on skyscrapers. It is the consequence of a complex interaction between the multiple purposes and activities of human beings and other living creatures and of the natural processes that govern the transfer of energy, the movement of air, the erosion of the earth, and the hydrologic cycle. The city is part of nature.

Nature is a continuum, with wilderness at one pole and the city at the other. The same natural processes operate in the wilderness and in the city. Air, however contaminated, is always a mixture of gasses and suspended particles. Paving and building stone are composed of rock, and they affect heat gain and water runoff just as exposed rock surfaces do anywhere. Plants, whether exotic or native, invariably seek a combination of light, water, and air to survive. The city is neither wholly natural nor wholly contrived. It is not "unnatural" but, rather, a transformation of "wild" nature by humankind to serve its own needs, just as agricultural fields are managed for food production and forests for timber. Scarcely a spot on the earth, however remote, is free from the impact of human activity. The human needs and the environmental issues that arise from them are thousands of years old, as old as the oldest city, repeated in every generation, in cities on every continent.

The realization that nature is ubiquitous, a whole that embraces the city, has powerful implications for how the city is built and maintained and for the health, safety, and welfare of every resident. Unfortunately, tradition has set the city against nature, and nature against the city. The belief that the city is an entity apart from nature and even antithetical to it has dominated the way in which the city is perceived and continues to affect how it is built. This attitude has aggravated and even created many of the city's environmental problems: poisoned air and water; depleted or irretrievable resources; more frequent and more destructive floods; increased energy demands and higher construction and maintenance costs than existed prior to urbanization; and, in many cities, a pervasive ugliness. Modern urban problems are no different, in essence, from those that plagued ancient cities, except in degree, in the toxicity and persistence of new contaminants, and in the extent of the earth that is now urbanized. As cities grow, these issues have become more pressing. Yet they continue to be treated as isolated phenomena, rather than as related phenomena arising from common human activities, exacerbated by a disregard for the processes of nature. Nature has been seen as a superficial embellishment, as a luxury, rather than as an essential force that permeates the city. Even those who have sought to introduce nature to the city in the form of parks and gardens have frequently viewed the city as something foreign to nature, have seen themselves as bringing a piece of nature to the city.

To seize the opportunities inherent in the city's natural environment, to see beyond short-term costs and benefits, to perceive the consequences of the myriad, seemingly unrelated actions that make up daily city life, and to coordinate thousands of incremental improvements, a fresh attitude to the city and the molding of its form is necessary. The city must be recognized as part of nature and designed accordingly. The city, the suburbs, and the countryside must be viewed as a single, evolving system within nature, as must every individual park and building within that larger whole. The social value of nature must be recognized and its power harnessed, rather than resisted. Nature in the city must be cultivated, like a garden, rather than ignored or subdued.

PART I

City and Nature

CHAPTER 1

City and Nature

IN THE NEXT DECADE important decisions will be made concerning the future of cities across the globe. These decisions will have consequences for millions of people for many years to come. The deteriorated infrastructure of older cities—their water supply, storm drainage, and sewage systems, especially—must soon be renovated or repaired. In Asia, Africa, South America, and the Middle East, rural emigrants swell urban settlements, straining local capacity to provide the most basic necessities of life: food, shelter, water, and safe waste disposal. The central cores of large, older North American cities are shrinking in population, but many of those fleeing the core and the inner suburbs are shifting no further than the outskirts of the old metropolis; while in the densely populated countries of Europe there is little remaining wilderness and countryside to settle. Cities in southern and western parts of the United States with populations under one million are booming, but are finding it increasingly difficult to secure adequate water and to reconcile the growing conflict between transportation and pollution.

The rewards of designing the city in concert with nature apply equally to all cities, old and new, large and small. The investment required to upgrade the infrastructure of older cities will require billions of dollars in North America alone. The opportunities for a fresh approach to resources and waste are enormous, and the potential for costly blunders is equally vast. The challenge facing growing, smaller cities and new towns is to learn from the mistakes of older cities and to design the city from the outset to exploit the opportunities of the natural environment. This challenge is particularly acute in fast-growing cities where entire new districts are springing up seemingly overnight.

Disregard of natural processes in the city is, always has been, and always will be both costly and dangerous. Many cities have suffered from a failure to take account of nature: Los Angeles and New York suffer poor air quality three days out of four, the result of both urban form and transportation modes; Mexico City has subsided twenty-five feet because it failed to recognize the relationship between water and ground stability; Los Angeles and Hong Kong are plagued by massive landslides, many of them triggered by urban development; Houston is devastated by floods caused by urbanization upstream, and Harrisburg by construction on the floodplains within the city; Boston and Detroit can no longer afford to maintain their parks and street trees; Niagara Falls is poisoned by its own accumulated wastes. The cost of disregarding nature extends also to the quality of life. The newer parts of cities—across continents, climates, and cultures—are everywhere acquiring a boring sameness. The potential of the natural environment to contribute to a distinctive, memorable, and symbolic urban form is unrecognized and forfeited.

More fortunate are those few cities that have adapted ingeniously to nature: Stuttgart, West Germany, which has deployed its parkland to funnel clean, cool air into its congested downtown; Woodlands, Texas, a new town whose private and public open spaces function as an effective storm drainage system, soaking up floodwaters and preventing floods downstream; Boston, where wetlands upstream of the city were purchased for flood storage at a fraction of the cost of a new dam; Zurich and Frankfurt which manage their urban forests for timber production as well as recreation; Philadelphia, which has transformed sewage sludge into a wide range of useful products. These cities have each dealt in a comprehensive way with at least one urban problem.

But comprehensive solutions are not the only means of improving the city. There are ingenious small projects as well: a tiny downtown park that provides a cool, calm retreat in the midst of Manhattan; plazas in Denver that detain stormwater to prevent floods; a project that has transformed the degraded South Platte River into a resource for urban recreation and flood protection; parks in Delft, the Netherlands, that have exploited both the energy and the beauty of wild landscapes. Incremental change through small projects is often more manageable, more feasible, less daunting, and more adaptable to local needs and values. When coordinated, incremental changes can have a far-reaching effect. Solutions need not be comprehensive, but the understanding of the problem *must* be.

Although many of the environmental challenges facing cities are more substantial than ever before, the understanding and the tools available to meet them are far more sophisticated. They need only be applied. Nature in the city must be cultivated and integrated with the varied pursuits and purposes of human beings; but first it must be recognized, and its power to shape human enterprises appreciated.

Urban Nature and Human Design

In the natural environment of every city, there are elements of both the distinctive and the common. It is to the distinctive features of their natural environment that many cities owe their location, their historic growth and population distribution, and even the character of their buildings, streets, and parks. Most cities occupy the sites of ancient villages, selected by the original inhabitants for ease of defense, access to supplies of water, fuel, and building materials, and proximity to transportation routes. The site of Washington, D.C., for example, was not selected by chance.[1] The falls of the Potomac at Georgetown mark the limit of navigation from the sea and the boundary between two physiographic regions, the piedmont and the coastal plain. These two physiographic regions, each with characteristic topography, building materials, and scenic qualities, bisect the city. The transition from steep hills to flat plains, from narrow rapids to broad rivers, and from rock quarries to clay pits delineates the boundary.

The flat coastal plain of northeastern and southern Washington, easily farmed and built upon, was settled a century before the hilly district of northwest Washington. L'Enfant laid out the capital's formal avenues across the level plain, siting monuments and major buildings on the higher elevations within it. Many of the earliest houses were built of brick from the abundant clay, but the poor drainage of the same clay soil eventually made that land undesirable and relatively inexpensive. Small row houses and large apartment complexes dominate this part of the city today, in contrast to the expensive, detached homes and mansions of northwest Washington. The erosion-resistant, metamorphic rocks of the piedmont give northwest Washington its distinctive character of steep slopes, incised stream valleys, and hilltops with views. Settled later than the coastal plain, it is now an area of large homes and embassies. Many of the houses are built from the rocks of the region—mica, schist, and gneiss.

Washington is not unique; many cities in the eastern United

States, from New Jersey to Georgia, straddle the boundary between coastal plain and piedmont. Most of the major East Coast cities between Trenton and Macon and the railroads which connect them are on the "fall line"—Philadelphia, Wilmington, Baltimore, Washington, D.C., and Richmond; and the same pattern of urban development recurs again and again. Like Washington, the oldest part of Philadelphia lies on the flat coastal plain where brick row houses are the dominant house type. The piedmont was settled later with larger homes built from the local schist.

Respect for the limitations imposed by nature and exploitation of its resources have led to memorable urban form. The ancient Greeks, for example, were masters at matching the buildings, squares, and streets of the city to its topography. The urban form of Jerusalem enhances its spiritual significance. The entire city is composed of the local limestone; important monuments are sited atop the ridges and high points of the landscape, their silhouettes against the sky visible from afar. New York City owes the distinctive skyscraper skyline of Manhattan Island to the strength of the underlying bedrock and its proximity to the surface. The Manhattan schist that forms the spine of the island and provides the foundation for its tall buildings outcrops in Central Park. Further south, in midtown Manhattan at Thirtieth Street, the bedrock plunges hundreds of feet below the ground, then rises again to within forty feet of the surface at the island's southern tip. Two clusters of skyscrapers, one in midtown between Thirty-fourth and Sixtieth streets and the other in the financial district near the tip, testify to the proximity of bedrock for foundations.

The resources afforded and the difficulties posed by each city's natural setting comprise a constant that successive generations in that city must address again and again, each in accordance with their own values and technology. Civilizations and governments rise and fall; traditions, values, and policies change; but the natural environment of each city remains an enduring framework within which the human community builds. A city's natural environment and its urban form, taken together, comprise a record of the interaction between natural processes and human purpose over time. Together they contribute to each city's unique identity.

Despite their differences, all cities have transformed their environments in a similar fashion: certain urban natural features are as characteristic of ancient Babylon and Rome as they are of modern Boston and Chicago. The human activities that modify the natural environment are common to all cities: the need to provide security, shelter, food, water, and the energy to fuel human enterprises; the need to dispose of wastes, to permit movement within the city and into and out of it; and the ever-escalating demand for more space. The ancient cities of Asia and the Mediterranean and the old cities of Europe transformed nature into a characteristically urban environment many centuries ago. The younger cities of North America are equally urban, but the transition from wilderness to city took place more recently over the past three centuries. The process continues today as new towns spring up in the countryside throughout the world and as existing cities expand onto adjacent farmland, forest, and desert.

The natural environments of London, Tokyo, and New York—all large cities with a temperate climate—have as much in common as each has with its own rural outskirts. All cities, by virtue of density of people and buildings and the combustion of fuel, alter the character of their original climate and pollute the air. The excavation and filling of the land necessary to secure abundant level ground for building, to find firm building foundations, and to exploit mineral resources transform the original landforms. The profusion of paved streets, sidewalks, and parking lots, and the storm sewers that drain them short-circuit the hydrologic cycle and change the character of streams and lakes. The disposal of wastes contaminates both surface water and groundwater, making the ever-increasing demand for clean water more difficult to satisfy. Fertilizers, herbicides, and pesticides applied to lawns and gardens, along with salt dumped on icy streets, further contaminate groundwater and diminish its value as a resource. Demand for water leads cities to seek resources many miles distant and has thus changed the water balance of entire regions and nations. Native vegetation is cleared and new plants are introduced (both intentionally and inadvertently), with the result that cities throughout the world with similar climates harbor virtually the same plant species.

All these interactions between human activities and the natural environment produce an ecosystem very different from the one that existed prior to the city. It is a system sustained by massive importation of energy and materials, a system in which human cultural processes create a place quite different from undisturbed nature, yet united to it through the common flow of natural processes. As cities grow in size and density, the changes they produce in the air, earth, water, and life within and around them trigger environmental problems that affect the well-being of every city resident.

Boston, Massachusetts, has evolved from wilderness over a mere three-and-a-half centuries. In that short span of time the original natural environment has been transformed almost beyond recognition into a characteristically urban nature. Although vastly altered, the natural setting continues to pose a constellation of opportunities and constraints. Some of these are special to Boston and others are shared by all cities; some have elicited successful response, others have been ignored. As with all cities, Boston's form has evolved within this framework, molded by the interaction of human pursuits with the features and processes of nature. In Boston's story are lessons for every city.

Boston: A Natural Environment Transformed

The colonists of the Massachusetts Bay Colony sailed into Boston Harbor in 1630 and found a propitious site for the future city: a readily defensible peninsula connected to the mainland by a narrow neck, capped by several hills, and already cleared of forest; a broad, protected harbor; and an abundant supply of fresh spring water.

The shape of the land was the work of both violent and gradual forces over millennia. The peninsula on which the town was founded lies in the approximate center of a semicircular basin ringed by hills to the north, south, and west, and bounded on the east by the Atlantic Ocean. Millions of years ago, earthquakes shook the region, as they have many times since; the encircling granite hills were thrust up along fault lines, and the basin fell. The framework of rim and basin remain, but most of the land forms in the basin itself—its hills and ponds and the course of its rivers—are remnants of a glacier which covered the entire region more than ten thousand years ago. As the sheet of ice moved southeast across the basin, it obliterated ancient river valleys and hillsides and dumped massive quantities of sand and gravel, remolding the land. Many of the hills within the Boston basin, including most of the Boston Harbor Islands, are drumlins—elliptical hills formed by the glacier and aligned along its path of movement. Slowly the land of the basin sank, and the sea flooded the valleys, forming long, broad bays. Boston Harbor is a drowned landscape; construction workers tunneling eighteen feet below present sea level found an Indian fish weir, a testament to the rise of the sea within human history.[2]

Ten thousand years of gradual landscape change, eroding hills and rising seas preceded the settlement of Boston by the Massachusetts Bay Colony in the seventeenth century. The Indians with their fishing weirs and limited agriculture made little impact on the land, but the transformation of the natural setting accelerated after the founding of the new town. The shoreline and topography of Boston have been altered more by man's activities over the past 150 years than by natural processes in the preceding ten thousand. The story of that transformation is the story of Boston: the demand for harbor facilities, building space, and an adequate supply of water, food, and fuel; and the need to protect its citizens' health, safety, and welfare. In providing for these needs, citizens of Boston assumed a role as geologic agents, with a force equivalent to ice, water, and wind.

Today Boston has a radial shape. Downtown Boston, on the original peninsula, is the hub. The city's transportation network—its highways, bus routes, and railways—fan out from this center along the rivers and peninsuli. An early ring road connecting the northwestern suburbs runs atop the ancient fault lines along which the hills of the Boston Basin were thrust up; the more recent circumferential highways are out beyond the edge of the basin. Downtown Boston lies at the center of the basin; the wealthier suburbs, with few exceptions, are outside the basin, arrayed around its rim. Today the boundaries of metropolitan Boston, Providence, and Worcester nearly touch. Residents of the urban fringe may commute to any one of the three.

Boston's protected harbor gave the city an early importance as a major colonial port; but its small peninsula became a liability in the nineteenth century when it impeded municipal growth. It constricted the city as surely as the fortified walls of continental European cities, leading to an extremely dense settlement within the old core. Shallow tidal flats and a ready supply of fill from gravelly hills permitted expansion of the peninsula onto the adjoining rivers, marshes, and harbor. Today the original peninsula is surrounded by an apron of flat, filled land upon which nineteenth- and twentieth-century urban designers have deployed their art. Although Boston's Trimountain (Beacon Hill, Mount Vernon, and Pemberton Hill) was mined nearly level, many of the city's hilly, glacial land forms remain, landmarks upon which Bostonians built monuments and institutions: the Bunker Hill Monument; hospitals atop Parker and Powderhorn hills; schools atop Orient Heights and Telegraph Hill. The drumlins that form the islands in Boston Harbor, long used for garbage dumps and unwanted institutions like prisons and asylums, are now part of the Harbor Islands State Park and provide a cool, breezy park system.

There is a surprising amount of undeveloped land within the city of Boston, land that was too difficult or too expensive to build upon. This land—tidal marshes, swampy meadows, steep, forested slopes, and boulder-strewn woodlands—reveals a distinctive character that is missing from more manicured parkland.

Most of the oldest buildings in Boston are brick, a fire-resistant material readily available from the area's many clay pits. Stone buildings were rare until the nineteenth century, when construction of a railroad near Quincy Quarry enabled stone to be transported more easily. Granite curbs became mandatory and now line all of Boston's streets, a clue to the abundant snowfall—granite will stand up to the snowplow far better than concrete or asphalt.

NEW LANDFORMS

Even though nature has profoundly influenced the growth and form of Boston, its original settlers would scarcely recognize the city's topography and shoreline today. The land forms of contemporary Boston, though composed mainly of sand, gravel, clay, and stone, are also the product of human activity. Formed artificially, they are nevertheless as vulnerable to the natural processes of ero-

---

FIGURE 1.1
Boston in 1806, on the eve of great expansion. Within eighty years, tidal flats at the base of Mount Vernon (a), the Mill Pond (b), and Back Bay (c) were filled and built upon.

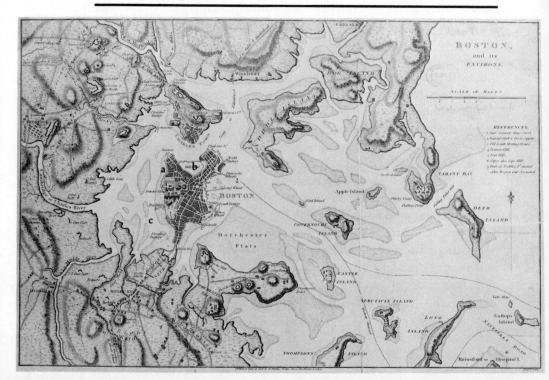

sion and sedimentation as any natural hill or outcrop. They may now even appear as "natural" as features formed solely by the processes of nature, as do the rocky outcrops of an abandoned quarry in Roxbury or the banks of the Muddy River, both of which were fashioned intentionally for human purposes.

The colonists first settled the flat plain between the harbor and the Trimountain. A road ran across the long, narrow neck of the peninsula connecting this initial settlement to the mainland. Boston prospered, a consequence largely of its success as a port, and by 1690 it was the largest city in the North American colonies, with a population of 7,000.[3] The early merchants built their wharfs on the waterfront, beginning a modification of the shoreline that has never ceased (figures 1.1 and 1.2). In 1641, one merchant carved a town cove from the tidal flat in Bendall's Cove, now the site of Faneuil Hall. Within two years settlers had dug out a second cove and shortly thereafter, in 1643, built still another.[4] By the early eighteenth century, the North End and the area around the town cove were densely settled and the shoreline bristled with wharfs. The longest, built in 1710, was over one thousand feet in length and lined with shops and warehouses.

FIGURE 1.2
Filled land in Boston, 1982. Much of Boston, like other coastal cities, is built upon filled land. Landfill provides opportunities for expansion, but leaves a legacy of problems.

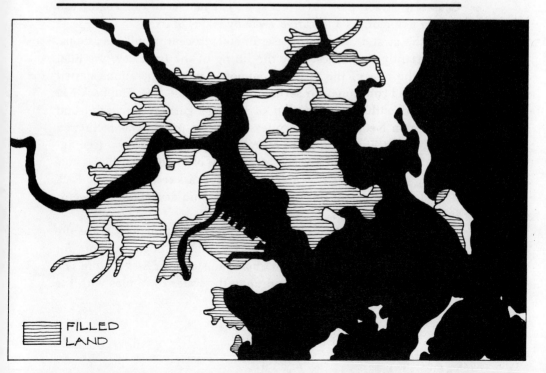

FILLED
LAND

It was in the nineteenth century, which brought rapid growth in population and wealth, that Bostonians changed their landscape most radically. Between 1790 and 1825 the city's population had more than tripled, increasing from 18,320 to 58,277.[5] Remaining vacant lands were soon filled, and land on the peninsula was at a premium. In 1799, the Mount Vernon Proprietors bought John Singleton Copley's property on the Trimountain, at the time mainly upland pasture; four years later, the Mount Vernon Proprietors had fifty to sixty feet sliced off the top of Mount Vernon, carted down the hillside in a gravity railroad, and dumped in the water at the base.[6] Thus, they not only made level building sites on the hill, but also converted tidal flats at the base to new land. The new, fashionable residential section they created includes much of what is now known as Beacon Hill.

Other ambitious gentlemen hastened to follow the example set by the Mount Vernon Proprietors. Mills had been operating along the Mill Pond since it was dammed in 1643. In 1804, the mill proprietors established the Mill Pond Corporation and proposed to fill the pond to create fifty acres of new land for buildings. In 1807, John Hancock's heirs agreed to excavate their property on Beacon Hill to provide the necessary fill. By the time they had dug sixty feet below the original level of their land on Beacon Hill, they had undermined both the Beacon Hill Monument and a house on an adjacent lot in Bowdoin Street (see figure 1.3).[7] The last summit of the Trimountain was lopped off in 1835 to create eight new acres of land north of Causeway Street. Sixty-five feet were cut off the top of Pemberton Hill in five months and carted away by teams of oxen.[8]

But the most dramatic of these nineteenth-century fill operations, and certainly the largest, was the filling of the Back Bay, the tidal flats at the base of the Boston Common. Landfill operations started in 1858 and continued for several decades (figure 1.4). The Back Bay was filled with a combination of Boston's garbage and sand and gravel from Needham, nine miles away. The project was facilitated by two recent inventions: the railroad and the steamshovel (see figure 1.5). "Land fill progressed at the rate of almost two house lots per day, a train of thirty-five loaded gravel cars arriving in the Back Bay on the average of once an hour, night and day, six days a week, for almost forty years."[9]

Filling operations have proceeded nearly continuously since the creation of the Back Bay (see figures 1.1 and 1.2). Logan Airport, for example, lies upon the former harbor and islands of East Boston. The inevitable encroachment of land upon the water continues with the

constant search for new space and a place to dispose of garbage. But the filled land is not without problems. Much of the land is quite low and susceptible to flooding. Extensive areas have a saturated soil whose fluctuating water level can damage building foundations. Buildings on filled land are particularly vulnerable to earthquake damage, when ground shaking may liquify the saturated soils under their foundations. Land filled in the nineteenth and early twentieth centuries is densely settled, packed with buildings constructed before earthquake-resistant provisions in building codes. An earthquake would wreak far greater damage in these areas than in adjacent parts of the city underlain by more stable soils. Although Boston is not prone to as frequent earthquakes as San Francisco or Tokyo, it is at similar risk to earthquakes of great magnitude. In 1638, in 1727, and again in 1755 major earthquakes shook Boston. Damage caused by the 1727 earthquake was considerable. Chimneys toppled, roofs caved in, and some brick buildings cracked and col-

FIGURE 1.4
View of Boston, 1870. Building construction on the newly created land in Back Bay is proceeding rapidly.

lapsed. An earthquake of similar magnitude today could be catastrophic.

The proportion of downtown Boston that lies on filled land is not extraordinary. One-third of San Francisco Bay has been filled and built upon since 1849, as has much of Tokyo Bay.[10] (Not surprisingly, the greatest damage in the Great San Francisco Earthquake of 1906 occurred on these saturated soils.) In the Netherlands, the scale of land reclamation is unequaled; today, the Dutch are constructing new towns on vast, flat expanses of land newly reclaimed from the sea, just as many of the older Dutch cities, like Amsterdam, were built in the past.

CHANGING THE COURSE OF TIDES AND RIVERS

Bostonians have long used water for power and for waste disposal. Within thirteen years of their arrival, the settlers of the Massachu-

FIGURE 1.5
Steam-shovel loading fill onto train bound for Back Bay, ca 1859. Two steam-shovels did the work of two hundred men, loading a thirty-five-car train in ten minutes. This steam-shovel was among the first produced in the United States.

setts Bay Colony had harnessed the power of the tides to operate the mills that ground their corn. The Mill Pond, created by a dam across a natural cove, maintained a grist mill, a saw mill, and a chocolate mill, until it was filled in the nineteenth century. The citizenry also depended upon the action of the tides to carry off their wastes. Not until the nineteenth century did the conflict between the tides as a source of power and as a cleansing agent become critical. During the eighteenth century, Boston had begun an ambitious street-paving program in which most newly paved streets were built with a crown in the middle and gutters at the side. An extensive subsurface storm drainage system was constructed through private initiative.[11] These early storm drains were so effective that considerable filth from wastewater and streets was emptied onto the tidal flats. The degree to which the tides were able to flush out the wastes to sea depended on uninhibited tidal flow. Producing power from the tides, on the other hand, necessitated controlling them and restricting their flow.

The issues of water quality and public health were central to a nineteenth-century controversy surrounding a proposal for a new mill dam in the Back Bay. The promoters estimated that the project could provide power for eighty-one mills, including "six grist mills, eight flour mills, six saw mills, sixteen cotton and eight woolen mills, twelve rolling and slitting mills, as well as many others for turning cannon, making anchors, scythes, grindstones, grinding paints, and heaven knows what now else."[12] Opponents of the proposal foresaw the consequences of limiting tidal flow in the Back Bay, and one opponent predicted in a June 10, 1814, letter to the *Daily Advertiser* what would later become self-evident to the most undiscriminating nose:

Citizens of Boston! Have you ever visited the Mall! Have you ever inhaled the Western breeze, fragrant with perfume, refreshing every sense and invigorating every nerve? What think you of converting the beautiful sheet of water which skirts the Common into an empty mud-basin, reeking with filth, abhorrent to the smell, and disgusting to the eye? By every god of sea, lake, or fountain, it is incredible.[13]

But the scheme was approved, the Mill Dam completed in 1821, and the fate of the Back Bay sealed.

The water contamination predicted by the Mill Dam's opponents was rapidly realized. Both the Muddy River and the Stony Brook emptied into the Back Bay Basin; so did all the sewers of Roxbury. Tidal action was impeded not only by the dam but also by the two railroad causeways that crisscrossed it. By 1849, the Boston Health Department, demanding that something be done about the Back Bay, described its condition as "one of nuisance, offensive and injurious to the large and increasing population residing upon it."[14] In the 1870s, when the Back Bay residential district was nearly complete, the Back Bay was described as "the foulest marsh and muddy flats to be found anywhere in Massachusetts without a single attractive feature; a body of water so foul that even clams and eels cannot live there, and a place that no one will go within a half mile of in the summertime unless absolutely necessary, so great a stench was there."[15] The situation was exacerbated by the efficient storm drainage system and the vulnerability of adjacent areas to flooding. Floodwaters and the sewage with it were carried back into the low-lying streets of Roxbury.

In the 1880s, Frederick Law Olmsted proposed a plan for the remainder of the Back Bay that addressed both sanitation and flooding (see chapter 7). Its central feature was a park called the Fens, created by dredging the tidal flats into a bowl and landscaping them with plants tolerant of periodic changes in water level. The Fens was designed to store stormwater temporarily without flooding the adjacent neighborhood. A tidal gate controlled the flow of the tide into and out of the Fens, providing for a cleansing water circulation. A new subsurface sewer intercepted sewage from Stony Brook and diverted it directly into the Charles River. Thus were the Back Bay tidal flats transformed into an attractive park. The Fenway became a fashionable address, lined with homes and the new buildings of old Bostonian institutions. Olmsted's solution was both effective and very "modern"; similar techniques still represent the state of the art today. In fact, in 1977, when the Army Corps of Engineers began to purchase thousands of acres of wetland upstream from Boston for their capacity to retain flood waters, thereby preventing flooding in downtown Boston, that action was considered innovative (see chapter 7).

Although construction of the Back Bay Fens reduced flooding and improved the water quality of that area, the tidal flats of the Charles River still remained a health hazard, especially at low tide when combined storm and sanitary sewers continued to empty their filth. Finally, in 1910, a dam was built across the mouth of the Charles River, converting it to a freshwater pool; the shallow flats along the river's edge were filled to create the Charles River embankment, whose shape now bears no resemblance to the wide bays of the original tidal river. Boston has never dealt adequately with its sewage. Most of the city's sewers contain a combination of sanitary and storm sewage. The city's sewage treatment plants are overburdened and outmoded, and raw sewage is routinely dumped into the harbor during storms and increasingly frequent breakdowns. Combined sewers and deteriorated treatment facilities are problems shared by most cities of the northeastern United States and many older cities of Europe. In these cities, increased flooding leads to increased water pollution.

IMPORTED WATER AND DROWNED VALLEYS

Local water supplied by springs and wells was sufficient for Boston's water needs through the end of the eighteenth century. In 1794 Thomas Pemberton remarked that most inhabitants were supplied with pure water from wells in their own yards.[16] By 1825 when the population had tripled, however, an adequate supply of uncontaminated water could no longer be provided by private wells or even by a municipal water source within the city. An 1834 survey of the city's wells revealed that many were contaminated, and that the overall water supply was insufficient. The water in nearly one-quarter of the wells was undrinkable. Only seven wells out of a total of 2,767 yielded water soft enough to wash clothes. Surveyors discovered forty or fifty pumps that were chained and padlocked with keys furnished by owners for an annual fee. Some streets had no wells at all.[17] The study concluded with a recommendation that the city tap the water of ponds fifteen miles away in Framingham and Natick.

In 1846, after debates continuing over more than ten years, construction began on an aqueduct from Long Pond in Natick to Boston. Sixty miles of iron pipe were laid within two years.[18] On October 25, 1848, the first water from Long Pond, renamed Lake Cochituate, was celebrated in a grand event on the Boston Common (figure 1.6). A crowd of between 50,000 and 100,000 attended the Water Celebration. The Mayor declared a school holiday, and the new fountain in the Common gushed all day. The celebration was premature, how-

FIGURE 1.6
The Water Celebration on Boston Common, October 25, 1848, inaugurating the new water supply with bands, parades, cannon, and gushing fountains. Cause for celebration was short-lived. Within five years, water use exceeded expectations, and Boston again faced a water crisis.

ever, for water use increased much more rapidly than anticipated. Public fountains were built in parks and squares, and water closets and bathtubs introduced into homes. Within five years, the average daily consumption exceeded all expectations. By 1869, only twenty years after the Water Celebration, the Lake Cochituate water was insufficient. The city of Boston has been casting its eyes on water further afield ever since.

As early as 1895, the city began to lay the political groundwork for the Quabbin land grab of 1928, in which it appropriated the 186-square-mile watershed of Quabbin Valley, sixty-five miles to the west, as a reservoir. The houses, churches, schools, and cemeteries of four towns were moved out of the valley before it was flooded. The Quabbin Reservoir has been the major source of Boston's water ever since. Fifty years later it is still possible to walk on a road through the Quabbin Reservation and follow it to the water's edge where it disappears, bound for the underwater site of a drowned town. By 1974, the Quabbin Reservoir provided water for nearly two million people in thirty-two cities and towns within a fifteen-mile radius of downtown Boston. The pollution of wells that originally forced Boston to tap a water supply far outside the city limits continues. One by one, the wells of outlying suburbs are contaminated by toxic wastes, forcing those communities to tap into the Metropolitan Water District, further increasing the population it must serve. Many towns have joined the district, not out of necessity, but simply for convenience. Ironically, several of these towns—Canton and Norwood, among them—are situated on the Neponset aquifer, a potential source of supplementary water for the city of Boston. These communities, however, have no incentive to protect the quality of water in the ground beneath them, and the aquifer is currently threatened by industrial development and waste disposal. Today the city of Boston, ever water short, is looking west again to the Connecticut River, scheming to capture the water on its way to the Long Island Sound and divert it by pipe to Boston. No longer is the battle for water merely between city and countryside; it now pits city against city.

Boston's predicament is no exceptional case: all major cities are forever on the lookout for new sources of water. The problem may be most acute in cities of semiarid and arid regions, for example, Denver, Los Angeles, and Phoenix. But even cities in regions with abundant rainfall (New York, Baltimore, New Orleans) are finding it increasingly difficult to secure adequate supplies of uncontaminated water.

DOMESTICATION OF FLORA AND FAUNA

The Massachusetts Bay Colonists founded the city of Boston on an unwooded peninsula. Its vegetation probably consisted of the flora typical of saltwater marshes and low-lying swampy areas, as well as of scrubby shrubs and some trees. Although the colonists used the tides to power their mills, wood was the only source of fuel during the seventeenth century, and wood for fuel was constantly in short supply.[19] Nearby woodlands were stripped to provide the growing city with fuel; wood was brought by sleds from the mainland in the winter and by boat from islands in the harbor during the other seasons.[20]

The colonists brought fruit trees and garden crops with them from Europe, and in 1728 the first row of trees was planted on the Boston Common as a shady promenade.[21] Many trees planted in eighteenth- and nineteenth-century Boston were imported European species; Lombardy poplars, lime trees, and English elms were all popular. The fashion of planting exotic species peaked in the nineteenth century when botanical gardens were planted in Boston and in other cities throughout the United States and Europe. The result is today's cosmopolitan flora. Trees on Boston's city streets have mixed origin; the honey locust is native to the central United States, the Norway maple and little leaf linden to Europe, the gingko to eastern China. The Kentucky bluegrass in private yards and parks is not a native of Kentucky, but an asiatic transplanted to North America by way of Europe.[22]

Between 1880 and 1895, Bostonians created great new plantations of trees and meadows within the city—Franklin Park, Arnold Arboretum, Jamaica Pond. These were man-made landscapes shaped by teams of horses and troops of workers, part of a general movement in North American and European cities, in which large, pastoral parks were created for the growing urban population. Like Franklin Park in Boston, the landscape of New York City's Central Park was entirely remodeled and replanted with more than four thousand new trees and shrubs. Most of the work on Central Park was accomplished within a period of five years. The project employed as many as 2,500 workers per day, who created hills and valleys, ponds and marshes, moving boulders and uprooting mature trees. These pastoral parks, designed as an idealized form of nature derived from British country estates, require an enormous amount of maintenance. Today, many of them are in decline and badly in need of renovation.

Not all plants were imported for agricultural or ornamental purposes, or even planted intentionally. Some plants found their own
way—stowed in travelers' baggage, caught in axles or the hooves of
livestock, mixed with commercial seed, or embedded in the dirt on
packing boxes. Among these were plants that had attached themselves to man thousands of years before. They have been fellow
travelers ever since, cropping up in abandoned agricultural fields
and city lots, along roadsides, and in garden plots. They thrive on
bare soil—one of the most common man-made habitats. *Plantago lan-
ceolata*, or ribgrass, is among man's most ancient camp followers.
First associated with early Neolithic farmers, it is now common in
lawns, parks, roadsides, and sidewalk cracks in Boston and many
cities on both sides of the Atlantic.[23]

Remnants of native plant communities still abound in forgotten
and neglected spots throughout the city. In most places, however,
the hardiest plants mingle with naturalized aliens, forming a cosmopolitan community found in cities of temperate climate all over the
world. An abandoned quarry in Boston thus harbors many of the
same plant species as the rubble of an old railroad station in Berlin,
that was destroyed in 1945: tree-of-heaven (*Ailanthus altissima*), black
locust (*Robinia pseudoacacia*), Norway maple (*Acer platanoides*), and
quaking aspen (*Populus tremuloides*).[24] These "urban wilds," so expressive of nature's regenerative powers, and so poignant a counterpoint to dense city streets, are now becoming recognized as a resource in Boston, as they are in Germany and the Netherlands (see
chapter 9).

The colonists brought with them cows, sheep, pigs, and dogs.
Cows and sheep grazed in the Common, supervised by a cowkeeper,
but pigs and dogs ran wild. "Hogs roamed the streets at will, serving
a useful purpose as scavengers, but making passage of the thorough-
fares dangerous for man and horse. Constant attempts were made to
abolish this nuisance. In 1634, Bostonians voted that swine should
not be allowed to run at large, but should be 'kept up in yards', and
two years later chose Richard Fairbanks as hog-reeve with power to
impound all strays."[25] Stray dogs were also a nuisance in seventeenth-century Boston, as they still are today. The town attempted to
solve the problem in 1697 by forbidding anyone below a set minimum income to own a dog. Stiff fines were imposed for letting a dog
run free, and anyone was permitted to kill a stray. In modern North
American cities, estimates of the dog population average one dog
per seven people. Free-ranging dogs are still a nuisance in American
cities, and in cities of Japan and Great Britain as well.

The alteration of Boston's plant communities and the increasing density of the human population triggered corresponding changes in the city's wildlife. Most native animals, deprived of habitat and food sources and preyed upon by domestic dogs and cats, retreated to the city's outskirts. Over time, alien species have filled the niches created by man—building eaves and ledges, warehouses, and gardens. These aliens—English sparrows, starlings, pigeons, rats, and roaches—now abound in most cities. Along with adaptable native scavengers like sea gulls, they comprise the bulk of Boston's wildlife community today. Yet Boston's large, urban parks and reserves, like Mt. Auburn Cemetery, harbor abundant and diverse wildlife species, as do Rock Creek Park in Washington, D.C., and Regent's Park in London (see chapter 11).

THE ALTERED AIR

Boston's original situation, open to sea breezes and with little predisposition to inversions, protected it from the air pollution experienced by colonial cities in less fortunate locations, such as the Spanish colony of Los Angeles. Wood smoke from the city's seventeenth- and eighteenth-century chimneys was probably blown quickly away. In fact, Boston rivals Chicago for the title "Windy City," a fact widely appreciated in the past decade after the construction of the Prudential Center Tower, the Hancock Tower, and numerous office towers downtown that catch the wind and send it swirling down to the street. The filling and building operations of the nineteenth century must have produced a marked change of climate in certain parts of town. Where tidal flats were filled and built upon, winds were slowed at ground level. The Common, which had been open to the unbroken force of winds blowing down the Charles River was, by the 1870s, protected by the new residential development on Back Bay. But the wind still blows, barely abated, along the shoreline and on exposed hilltops. Tall buildings constructed since 1965 aggravate the city's natural wind problem, creating uncomfortable, even dangerous conditions on some street corners. Boston's long, cold winters increase the city's demand for fuel and impose a hardship on urban pedestrians, especially in large, open, windswept spaces. When the Prudential Center office tower and shopping mall opened near Copley Square, stores anticipated a booming business. The harsh wind conditions created by the tall tower wrecked that promise, and much of the mall was subsequently enclosed. The open portion of the shopping plaza is still uncomfortable even in summer, when the winds kick up grit, throwing it at shoppers. The mall has never achieved its predicted economic potential.

There is abundant evidence of ongoing natural processes in modern Boston. The tides rise and fall in salt marshes and along docks and sea walls. On a calm day, a stiff breeze blows into the downtown off the ocean. Muddy river water after a storm testifies to erosion upstream. Plants colonize the bare soil of vacant lots within weeks. Tree seedlings invade lawns, and the forest is kept at bay only by repeated mowing. The natural environment of Boston—its sea breeze, its drumlins, rocky outcrops, and harbor islands; its rivers, ponds, marshes, and buried brooks; its parks; and even its wastelands and city streets—is no less "natural" than the intensely cultivated landscape of the countryside or the shady streets and tended gardens of the outer suburbs. Less pastoral, perhaps, but no less a part of nature. Seeing nature in the city is only a matter of perception.

The Search for Nature: Park, Suburb, and Garden City

However blind they may have been to natural processes, city dwellers have cherished isolated natural features and have sought to incorporate those features into their physical surroundings. This search for nature has been evidenced, over the millenia, in garden plots, parks and promenades, suburbs, and utopian proposals for garden cities. In the seventh century B.C., Sennacharib built a park for the citizens of Ninevah; in the nineteenth century, cities set aside huge tracts of woods and meadows for the edification, health, and enjoyment of their residents. Philosophers in ancient Athens gathered their students in gardens with groves of trees; residents of seventeenth-century cities strolled along tree-lined promenades. Citizens in medieval European cities tended abundant gardens within city walls, just as city gardeners today cultivate tiny plots on penthouse terraces and in vacant lots.

So long as the city remained relatively small, it was not divorced from the countryside. Most residents of ancient Mesopotamian cities, even craftsmen and tradesmen, cultivated their own fields or those of others.[26] Most of this acreage was outside the city walls, but some land for crops and grazing lay within the walls, a precaution

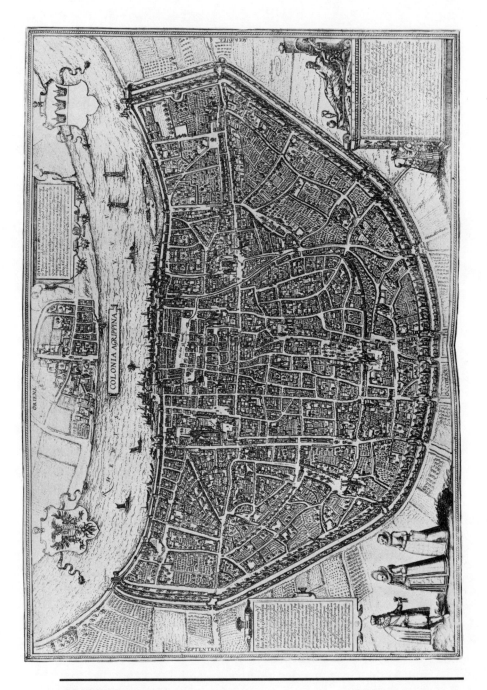

FIGURE 1.7
Map of sixteenth-century Cologne, Germany. This plan illustrates the close relationship between city and countryside, typical of many cities in medieval Europe. Note the gardens and street trees within the city wall, the tree-lined path along the moat, and the agricultural fields just outside the wall.

against siege. Thousands of years later, in medieval Europe, agricultural and rural pursuits, like fowling and fishing, formed a part of daily urban life. The city and countryside were still interconnected. Vegetables were brought into the city, and refuse and dung carted out to fertilize fields in surrounding rural villages. In sixteenth-century Cologne, an important European city, most houses had a large back garden. The new market was a large square filled with trees, as were the six streets that marked the sites of former city walls (figure 1.7). A wall, a moat, and a tree-lined path encircled the city. The wall and moat, rather than presenting a barrier to the countryside, created a pleasant place for strolling and recreation: "Outside the city," reads an inscription in a contemporary atlas, "there are two hills and a broad moat, shaded by green trees, which serve as playing grounds in summer, and are used for the recreation of the students and all other kinds of sport and pastimes."[27]

As cities grew larger and more congested, distance from the countryside and nostalgia for nature increased, while complaints about city life—particularly the smoke and the stink—multiplied. This was as true of first-century Rome as it was of sixteenth-century London and twentieth-century New York. By the seventeenth century in Europe, a garden of one's own and easy access to the countryside, formerly the privileges of every townsman, were outside the reach of the common citizen. Where backyard orchards and gardens had once been, houses were now built, served by dark alleys behind the main streets. By the eighteenth century, the many gardens of Cologne and most other European cities had disappeared. City dwellers have been trying to recapture nature ever since. As early as 1516, when Sir Thomas More published *Utopia*, many of the amenities of smaller medieval cities like Cologne had already disappeared in the major urban centers of London and Paris. More's description of the imaginary capital of Utopia, with its abundant and flourishing backyard gardens and its surrounding green belt of countryside, fits the Cologne of his era. Later utopian authors have again and again echoed More's themes of limited city size, cultivation of gardens within the city, and the integration of city and countryside.

Those who introduced nature into the civic landscape in the form of parks, trees, and gardens sought to create a small piece of utopia where they lived. "Here or nowhere is our utopia," maintained nineteenth-century civic reformers who argued for the realization of the ideal city latent in every town.[28] The crowded conditions and polluted water and air created by the growing size and density of the nineteenth-century city precipitated a sanitary reform move-

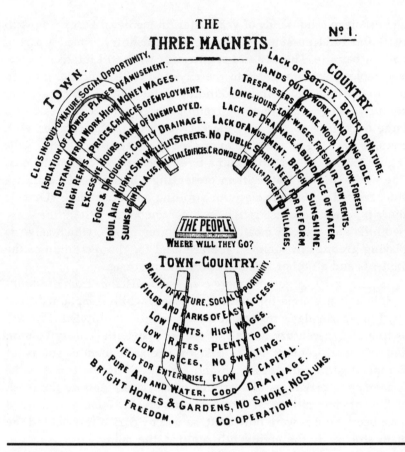

FIGURE 1.8
Ebenezer Howard's summary of the ancient debate on advantages of city versus country life. Howard proposed to combine benefits of both in the Garden City.

ment that provoked massive investment in civic infrastructure and landscape, an investment whose magnitude is little appreciated today. During that period, most cities in the United States ripped open their streets to install new sewer and water lines. Large public parks were built in cities across North America and Europe, intended as "lungs of the city," part of a comprehensive effort to improve the health, safety, and welfare of city residents through the alteration of the physical environment. When these enterprises harnessed the forces of nature and when projects such as parks, the drainage of streets, and the treatment of sewage were perceived and designed as related enterprises, they achieved memorable success, such as that of Olmsted in the Boston Fens. All too often, however, they focused on

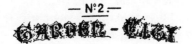

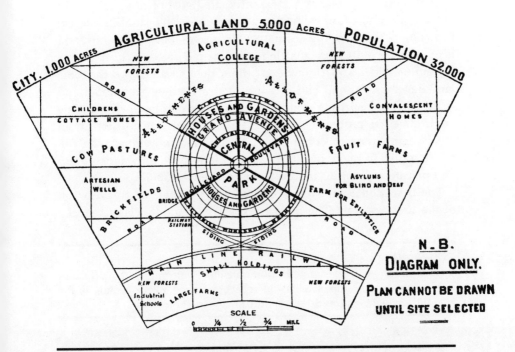

FIGURE 1.9
The Garden City, as envisioned by Ebenezer Howard in 1902, recalled many aspects of Thomas More's Utopian city. Aspiring to the integration of nature and city, the garden city and the new towns and suburbs it inspired incorporated the trappings of nature, but failed to address underlying natural processes.

the delightful, but superficial, manifestations of nature and ignored the underlying natural processes.

But others rejected the old city in favor of suburbs or new "garden cities." In 1902, Ebenezer Howard described his ideal city, a city where industry and commerce would be integrated with homes, gardens, and farms (figure 1.8).[29] Apart from the addition of modern industry and railroads, his "garden city" bears a striking resemblance to Thomas More's description of the Utopian city. Each garden city, surrounded by a green belt, was to be one of a constellation of garden cities, each with population limited to 30,000, separated from each other by countryside (figure 1.9). Garden cities were in fact built both in Britain (Welwyn and Letchworth) and the United

States (Greenbelt, Maryland, and Radburn, New Jersey) and provided the impetus for a new town movement still influential today (Reston, Virginia, and Columbia, Maryland). Although the integration of nature and city is a frequently cited goal of new towns and an implicit one of suburbs, most new towns and suburbs merely incorporate the trappings of nature, like trees, lawns, gardens, and lakes, but are built with as little regard for the processes of nature as were the old cities. With few exceptions, they have utilized the same land development and building techniques. As they grow older and as urbanization spreads around them, they exhibit many of the same environmental problems as earlier cities. They may at first be an ideal combination of country and city for the individual who can afford to live in them, but in the long run they are only a temporary and private solution to the problems of the metropolis.

The first suburb probably appeared shortly after the construction of the first city wall. The mass exodus of the middle class from the

FIGURE 1.10
View of the United States at night from satellite. Photographs from airplanes and remote sensing from satellites have revolutionized our perception of the world. Here, lights of the cities form urban constellations.

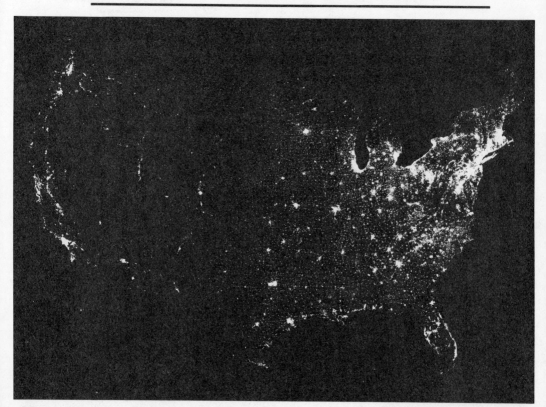

city to the suburbs, however, dates from the nineteenth century and the invention of new modes of transportation. The street car and then the automobile made it possible to work in the city and live outside. For the first time, many could afford to "create an asylum, in which they could, as individuals, overcome the chronic effects of civilization while commanding at will the privileges and benefits of urban society. This utopia proved to be, up to a point, a realizable one: so enchanting that those who contracted, failed to see the fatal penalty attached to it—the penalty of popularity, the fatal inundation of the mass movement whose very numbers wiped out the good each individual sought for his own domestic circle."[30] The magnitude of the nineteenth- and twentieth-century migration to the suburbs eventually brought the environmental problems of the city to the countryside, and created a massive wall of privately owned property between those who lived within the inner city and the rural precincts beyond, a wall even more effective in separating the

FIGURE 1.11
Urban constellations delineated by Philip H. Lewis, Jr., from satellite image, most surrounding a large wilderness area.

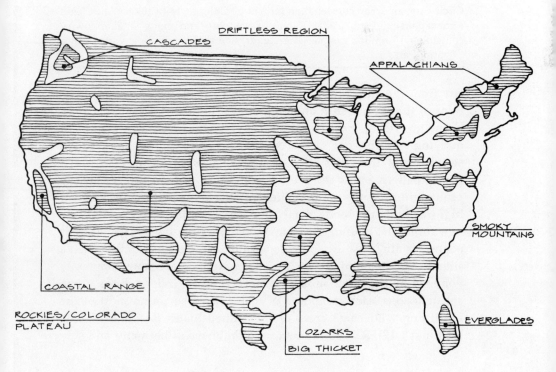

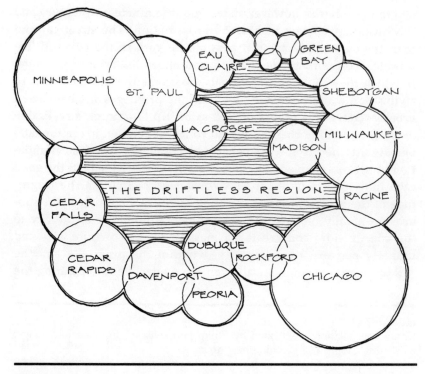

FIGURE 1.12
Circle City, an urban constellation formed by Chicago, Milwaukee, Eau Claire, Minneapolis-St. Paul, Cedar Rapids, Davenport, and many smaller towns, containing 15 million people. The countryside in the middle is Circle City's "Central Park."

city from the surrounding countryside than the extensive fortifications of the seventeenth and eighteenth centuries.

The growth of most twentieth-century cities has been mainly in outlying suburbs, not in the central core. Urban populations have swept out of the city's core in successive waves, setting in a dispersed pattern across the countryside—a pattern encouraged by the proliferation of the automobile and the construction of efficient highway systems. Modern metropolises have taken on an entirely new form. The boundaries of many older cities now overlap at their edges, forming vast urban fields with multiple centers, rather than a single core. Remaining patches of countryside are now commonly bounded by the outer suburbs of several cities. Indeed, huge urban constellations, each composed of many cities, surround most of the remaining wilderness areas of the United States (see figures 1.10, 1.11, and 1.12). Real solutions to the problems of both city and suburb can now be achieved only through understanding the place of each within the larger region and by viewing city, suburbs, and countryside as a single, evolving system linked by the processes of nature and the social and economic concerns of humans.

City dwellers have demonstrated a sustained interest in nature throughout history. Today that interest has been heightened by a growing consciousness across society of the costs to health and welfare exacted by continued environmental degradation. It is time to expand what has been a romantic attachment to the ornaments of nature into a commitment to reshape the city in harmony with the workings of nature. Knowledge of those processes and the application of new technology can provide that means.

PART II

Air

CHAPTER 2

Dirt and Discomfort

ON A CLEAR DAY the bright blue sky overhead shades to leaden gray around the city; in summer the skyline shimmers with heat. The image is commonplace, no copy for headline news, yet the everyday impact on health is pervasive and deadly. The very old, the very young, and those with heart and lung disease suffer city dirt and heat most intensely, but over the years dirt and discomfort take their toll on healthy people, too. The impact of air pollution on children is the most insidious and long-lasting.

The air in New York City and Los Angeles, cities that contain almost 8 percent of the nation's population, fails to meet U.S. ambient air quality standards most of the time; three days out of four in New York and seven days out of ten in Los Angeles.[1] When the air is "very unhealthy" (one in four days in New York and one in three days in Los Angeles),[2] many people may cough, feel drowsy, or suffer a mild headache, but officials warn the elderly and those with heart and lung disease to remain indoors and limit physical exertion.

Even when overall air quality is deemed "adequate," carbon monoxide and poisonous dust on sidewalks and playgrounds may reach dangerous levels. Increased lead poisoning among inner-city and suburban children is now linked more to the lead in urban dust than to paint, and loss of physical coordination from carbon monoxide inhalation has been cited as a cause of accidents in heavy traffic.

In summer, the further insult of heat is added to dirt. The city, especially its dense core, is both hotter and less ventilated by winds than the outlying countryside. The city's added heat load increases summer discomfort and the energy required for air conditioning day to day, and during heat waves contributes to more deaths than occur in the cooler suburbs.

Problems of dirt and comfort are linked. Automobiles, power plants, furnaces, and factories poison and heat the air. Dense buildings block the wind, preventing the dispersion of dirt and heat. Valleys and street canyons trap pollutants. Stone and concrete absorb heat and store it during the day, then give it off at night. Together, these factors produce a city climate distinct from that of the surrounding countryside. Urban activities, forms, and materials, and the manner in which they are combined, account for the wide variation in microclimate and degree of air pollution from spot to spot within the city. The characteristics of city climate (see table 2.1), its causes and effects, are well known, but that knowledge is rarely exploited.

TABLE 2.1
Characteristics of Urban Climate

Element	Compared to Rural Environs	
Contaminants:		
Condensation nuclei	10	times more
Particulates	10	times more
Gaseous admixtures	5–25	times more
Radiation:		
Total on horizontal surface	0–20%	less
Ultraviolet, winter	30%	less
Ultraviolet, summer	5%	less
Sunshine duration	5–15%	less
Cloudiness:		
Clouds	5–10%	more
Fog, winter	100%	more
Fog, summer	30%	more
Precipitation:		
Amounts	5–15%	more
Days with less than 5mm	10%	more
Snowfall, inner city	5–10%	less
Snowfall, lee of city	10%	more
Thunderstorms	10–15%	more
Temperature:		
Annual mean	0.5–3°C	more
Winter minima (average)	1–2°C	more
Summer maxima	1–3°C	more
Heating degree days	10%	less
Relative humidity:		
Annual mean	6%	less
Winter	2%	less
Summer	8%	less
Wind speed:		
Annual mean	20–30%	less
Extreme gusts	10–20%	less
Calm	5–20%	more

SOURCE: Helmut E. Landsberg, *The Urban Climate* (New York: Academic Press, 1981).

All too often, the builders of cities—government and corporate officials, engineers, architects, landscape architects, and city planners—are oblivious to the effects they have on urban climate and air quality. Air pollution, discomfort, and energy consumption are treated separately when they are addressed at all, not as the interrelated whole they represent. Attempts to solve one problem often create several new ones.

Poisons in the Air

Pollution, illness, and cities have an ancient association. In A.D. 61 Seneca complained of Rome, "As soon as I escaped from the oppressive atmosphere of the city, and from that awful odor of reeking kitchens which, when in use, pour forth a ruinous mess of steam and soot, I perceived at once that my health was mended."[3] London was known for foul air as early as A.D. 852.[4] The first smoke abatement law, enacted in London in 1273, prohibited the use of coal as "prejudicial to health,"[5] but it was short-lived, undermined by the lack of a cheap alternative to bituminous coal. London's air pollution problem grew with the city, and by the sixteenth century the air of London was notorious. In 1661, John Evelyn complained, "Whilst these [chimneys] are belching it forth their sooty jaws, the City of *London* resembles the face rather of *Mount Aetna*, the *Court of Vulcan, Stromboli,* or the *Suburbs of Hell,* than an Assembly of Rational Creatures, and the Imperial seat of our incomparable *Monarch* . . . the weary *Traveller,* at many Miles distance, sooner smells, than sees the City to which he repairs."[6]

A London physician, Harold Des Veaux, coined the term "smog" (smoke plus fog) in 1905 to describe a phenomenon that by then had been known for centuries.[7] Londoners had long associated smog with illness, but in the nineteenth century, when officials began to tally "excess deaths" during particularly severe episodes, 650 excess deaths were documented during a two-day episode in December 1873 and 1,176 during a three-day period in January 1880. This trend continued into the twentieth century, culminating in the infamous incident of December 5–9, 1952, when "killer smog" caused the deaths of more than 4,000 people.[8]

Five air pollutants—sulfur dioxide, nitrogen oxides, ozone, carbon monoxide, and total suspended particulates—are monitored in most metropolitan regions in the United States as indicators of air pollution. The primary sources and effects of these pollutants are indicated in table 2.2. Sulfur dioxide (SO_2), a primary ingredient of London smog, finds most of its victims among patients with chronic respiratory and heart diseases. Long-term exposure to even low levels of atmospheric sulfur dioxide has been implicated as a cause of emphysema and chronic bronchitis. John Evelyn's words in 1661 remain a classic description of sulfur dioxide pollution: "this is that pernicious Smoake which sullyes all her Glory, superinducing a sooty Crust or Fur upon all that it lights, spoyling the moveables, tarnishing the Plate, Gildings, and Furniture, and corroding the very Iron-bars and hardest Stones with these piercing and acrimonious Spirits which accompany its Sulphure; and executing more in one year, than exposed to the pure *Aer* of the Country it could effect in some hundreds."[9] Sulfur dioxide corrodes steel and destroys stone buildings and statuary. Cleopatra's Needle has deteriorated more in the ninety years it has been in New York City than during its previous three thousand years in Egypt. The burning of sulfur-bearing fuels, such as coal and oil, account for most sulfur oxides. Sulfur dioxide pollution has declined in the past decade, but it may emerge again as a major problem if coal burning increases.

Sulfur dioxide and dust, for centuries the major urban air pollutants, have recently been displaced by photochemical smog and carbon monoxide. The proliferation of the automobile and the switch from wood and coal to oil and gas fuels account for this shift. Photochemical smog, the Los Angeles type, arises when nitrogen oxides and hydrocarbons—products of automobile exhaust and petroleum refining—are exposed to intense sunlight and undergo a photochemical reaction, producing ozone and other chemically reactive

TABLE 2.2
Sources of Major Air Pollutants

Source	Source Type	Percentage of Emissions from Each Source by Pollutant[a]					Percentage of All Emissions
		CO	SO_2	TSP	HC	NO_2	
Transportation	Mobile (line)	83.5	3.0	8.8	40.7	39.6[b]	55.8
Road vehicles alone	Line	(75.2)	(1.3)	(6.6)	(34.9)	(29.0)	(49.0)
Fuel combustion	Stationary (point, area)	1.1	81.8	38.7	5.4	56.1	22.1
Electric utilities alone	Stationary (point)	—	(64.2)	(27.0)	(0.3)	(30.6)	(14.6)
Industrial processes	Stationary (point)	8.0	15.2	43.8	35.6	3.1	14.8
Solid waste disposal	Stationary (point)	2.6	—	2.9	2.6	0.4	2.0
Miscellaneous		4.8	—	5.8[c]	16.0	0.4	5.3

SOURCE: Statistics from U.S. Bureau of Census, *Statistical Abstracts of the United States, 1979*, originally from U.S. Environmental Protection Agency, *National Air Quality and Emission Trends Report, 1977*.

[a] Figures are U.S. totals for 1977 and include both metropolitan and nonmetropolitan areas.

[b] The sum of this column is less than 100 percent due to rounding off.

[c] The construction industry accounts for most of this category (U.S. Environmental Protection Agency, *Environmental Outlook*, 1980).

compounds. It is for this reason that cities like Los Angeles, Denver, and Mexico City, with intense sunlight and congested traffic, are plagued by severe photochemical smog. The dirty brown haze of photochemical smog reduces visibility, irritates eyes and noses, and causes coughing and headaches. On bad days, some people with bronchitis, emphysema, and heart disease have difficulty breathing.[10] Unlike other pollutants, photochemical smog is often worse in the suburbs than in the city center. The transformation of nitrogen oxides and hydrocarbons emitted in morning rush hour traffic into smog occurs six to ten hours later, when the polluted air mass has moved away from the center.[11]

Carbon monoxide, an odorless, invisible killer, is most concentrated at the city center where cars, trucks, and buses clog narrow streets flanked by tall buildings, and most severe on weekdays during morning and afternoon rush hours. Breathing the carbon monoxide commonly found at major intersections, inside cars commuting in heavy traffic, and in tunnels and street canyons can cause headaches, drowsiness, and dizziness.[12] Policemen, taxi drivers, people working in open shops, and others who work on busy streets for extended periods flirt with carbon monoxide poisoning daily.[13] Cigarette smokers are especially vulnerable; smoking produces elevated carbon monoxide levels in the blood, so that even a moderate increase in atmospheric carbon monoxide affects smokers.[14] Heart patients are at greater risk of angina attacks in cities with carbon monoxide problems.[15]

Since gasoline-powered vehicles are the primary source of carbon monoxide, cities that rely mainly on the private automobile for transportation are prone to carbon monoxide pollution. In Los Angeles, for example, 97 percent of carbon monoxide stems from vehicle exhaust,[16] and high concentrations of carbon monoxide permeate extensive sections of the city daily. A Los Angeles commuter driving two hours a day in morning and afternoon traffic is exposed to enough carbon monoxide to elevate carbon monoxide blood levels to a "serious" level, a level of exposure sufficient to impair alertness, vision, and physical coordination.[17]

City dust is more than common dirt. Particles of lead, arsenic, asbestos, and cadmium are blown about in city air and breathed into the lungs. Many particulates, not necessarily poisonous in themselves, are host to toxic vapors adsorbed on their surfaces. Although automobile exhaust produces a relatively small proportion of the total suspended particulates in the ambient air above the city, these particulates have a substantial impact on health. They are not only emitted at breathing level but are also small and easily inhaled, and embedded in the lung. Thirty percent of lead particles inhaled, for example, are absorbed and retained.[18]

The character and severity of air pollution problems varies from city to city. Tables 2.4 and 2.5 compare cities on the basis of the Pollutant Standard Index (PSI), the values of which are defined in table 2.3. New York has the worst carbon monoxide pollution in the United States.[19] In 1977 carbon monoxide reached unhealthy levels there nearly seven days out of every ten. Carbon monoxide is also the predominant air pollution problem in Denver, Chicago, Detroit, Philadelphia, Seattle, and Portland, Oregon. In Los Angeles, the carbon monoxide problem is overshadowed by the ozone in photochemical smog. Total suspended particulates are Buffalo's biggest problem; sulfur dioxide, Toledo's. A city's major industries, the types of fuels used to generate heat and electricity, and transportation patterns influence which specific pollutants predominate. A city's regional climate, physiographic setting, location of major pollution sources in relation to other land uses, and urban form all influence the distribution of air pollution within the city and help determine whether it is concentrated or dispersed. Los Angeles, for example, owes much of its air pollution problem to its sunny climate and its location between ocean and mountains. Its intense sunlight promotes the formation of photochemical smog; inversions and prolonged periods of high-pressure weather limit circulation. In New York City, where heavy traffic penetrates narrow street canyons, the carbon monoxide problem is primarily a consequence of transportation patterns and urban form.

Inversions and Stagnant Air

The most infamous air pollution episodes, those that kill thousands and make headline news, are invariably caused by inversions. Normally air pollutants are borne up and away from the city on currents of warm air rising into cooler air above. Occasionally, the normal pattern of temperature stratification may be "inverted," with cooler air below and warmer air above: when a warm air mass moves in over a cooler one; when warm air flows over a colder surface; or when the air near the ground is cooled from below at night. The cooler air, unable to rise into the warmer air above, is trapped near

TABLE 2.3

Definition of Pollutant Standard Index (PSI) Values

PSI Index Value	Air Quality Level	Pollutant Level					General Health Effects	Cautionary Statements
		TSP (24-hour), $\mu g/m^3$	SO_2 (24-hour), $\mu g/m^3$	CO (8-hour), $\mu g/m^3$	O_3 (1-hour), $\mu g/m^3$	NO_2 (1-hour), $\mu g/m^3$		
500	Significant harm	1000	2620	57.5	1200	3750		
400	Emergency	875	2100	46.0	1000	3000	Premature death of ill and elderly. Healthy people will experience adverse symptoms that affect their normal activity.	All persons should remain indoors, keeping windows and doors closed. All persons should minimize physical exertion and avoid traffic.
300	Warning	625	1600	34.0	800	2260	Premature onset of certain diseases in addition to significant aggravation of symptoms and decreased exercise tolerance in healthy persons.	Elderly and persons with existing diseases should stay indoors and avoid physical exertion. General population should avoid outdoor activity.
200	Alert	375	800	17.0	400[a]	1130	Significant aggravation of symptoms and decreased exercise tolerance in persons with heart or lung disease, with widespread symptoms in the healthy population.	Elderly and persons with existing heart or lung disease should stay indoors and reduce physical activity.
100	NAAQS	260	365	10.0	240		Mild aggravation of symptoms in susceptible persons, with irritation symptoms in the healthy population.	Persons with existing heart or respiratory ailments should reduce physical exertion and outdoor activity.

SOURCE: U.S. Council on Environmental Quality, *Tenth Annual Report*, 1979.

[a] 400 $\mu g/m^3$ was used instead of the O_3 Alert Level of 200 $\mu g/m^3$.

TABLE 2.4
Ranking of Standard Metropolitan Statistical Areas (SMSA) Using Pollutant Standard Index (PSI) Air Pollution Data, 1975–77

Severity Class	SMSA	Number of "Unhealthful" Days (PSI over 100)		Number of "Very Unhealthful" Days (PSI over 200)	
		Three-Year Average	Minimum–Maximum Annual Days During Three Years	Three-Year Average	Minimum–Maximum Annual Days During Three Years
I (More than 150 days of PSI readings above 100)	Denver	157	143–182	30	20–37
	Cleveland	225[a]	228–229	41[a]	12–59
	Los Angeles	264	253–272	132	117–142
	Louisville	150	104–185	20	14–31
	New York	273[b]	—	87[b]	—
	Riverside	193	174–224	106	88–122
II (100–150 days of PSI readings above 100)	Anaheim	120	95–134	38	17–58
	Chicago	139	81–195	21	14–31
	Philadelphia	103	79–143	12	7–19
	St. Louis	123	97–141	21	13–33
	Washington, D.C.	110	74–147	16	7–26
III (50–100 days of PSI readings above 100)	Baltimore	64[a]	49–79	18[a]	10–25
	Houston	54	48–64	9	4–12
	Jersey City	74[b]	—	8[b]	—
	Nashville	59	39–76	3	1–5
	Portland	78	70–83	7	3–13
	Salt Lake City	82	61–110	18	9–25
	San Diego	59	45–74	6	4–9
	San Jose	58	42–81	8	0–21
	Seattle	86	73–95	5	4–5
IV (25–50 days of PSI readings above 100)	Buffalo	41	31–51	7	3–11
	Cincinnati	41	20–63	2	1–4
	Dallas	26	18–35	1	0–2
	Dayton	33[a]	29–37	1[a]	1–2
	East Chicago	29	27–31	—	—
	Hartford	34	25–41	6	3–8
	Indianapolis	33[a]	17–49	2[a]	1–3
	Milwaukee	35	32–40	8	7–8
	Sacramento	26	19–38	1	0–3
	San Francisco	33	24–45	1	0–2
V (0–25 days of PSI readings above 100)	Akron	14[b]	—	0[b]	—
	Grand Rapids	3[a]	1–8	0[a]	0
	Honolulu	0[a]	0–1	0[a]	0
	Kansas City	12	5–23	3[a]	0–8
	Memphis	24	19–24	3	0–7
	Norfolk	13	9–16	1	0–2
	Oklahoma City	11[b]	—	0[b]	—
	Rochester	5	2–8	0	0
	San Antonio	10[a]	8–11	0[a]	0
	Syracuse	6	5–7	1	0–2
	Tampa	11	5–19	1	0–1
	Toledo	21[a]	14–25	1[a]	1–1

SOURCE: U.S. Council on Environmental Quality, *Tenth Annual Report*, 1979.

[a] Based on only two years of data. [b] Based on only one year of data.

TABLE 2.5
Frequency of Unhealthy Air Quality in Four Cities (1977)

| | Number of Days Pollution Standard Index (PSI) Exceeded[a] | | | | | | | | | | | |
| | New York | | | Los Angeles | | | Denver | | | Chicago | | |
Pollutant	100–200	200–300	300+	100–200	200–300	300+	100–200	200–300	300+	100–200	200–300	300+
CO	165	82	0	69	21	0	109	18	0	89	1	0
O₃	21	3	0	66	96	0	6	0	0	18	5	0
TSP	0	1	1	1	0	0	7	2	1	13	10	1
NO₂	—	—	—	—	—	—	—	—	—	0	1	0
SO₂	—	—	—	—	—	—	—	—	—	3	0	0
SO₂ + TSP	—	—	—	—	—	—	—	—	—	0	1	0
Total[b]	186	86	1	136	117	0	122	20	1	123	18	1
Total[c]	273			253			143			142		

SOURCE: U.S. Council on Environmental Quality, *Tenth Annual Report*, 1979.
[a] PSI 100–200: "unhealthful"; PSI 200–300: "very unhealthful"; PSI 300+: "hazardous."
[b] Number of days within each category.
[c] Total number of days PSI exceeded 100.

the ground for hours or even days and all the city's poisonous emissions with it. The longer the inversion persists, the higher the concentrations of air pollution within the city. Inversions are occasional and brief events in all cities, and frequent or prolonged ones in cities with a topographic or climatic predisposition. Inversions can form at the scale of an entire metropolitan region, or at the scale of a street canyon (see figure 2.1).

Inversions are most pronounced in clear, calm weather, and common and prolonged in cities like Los Angeles and Tucson with climates characterized by frequent, stable high-pressure systems. Like London, Los Angeles has an air pollution problem as old as its settlement by humans. Juan Rodriguez Cabrillo named Los Angeles "the Bay of Smokes" in 1542 after observing the smoke from Indian fires trapped by an inversion.[20]

Inversions are common in valleys and in valley cities like Cincinnati or St. Louis. Valley inversions form on clear, calm nights, when dense, cool air pools on the valley floor and the air temperatures remain up to 10° Fahrenheit warmer on adjacent hillsides,[21] and although frequent, usually lift by midday. In Stuttgart, West Germany, an industrial city in the Neckar River valley, inversions occur on the average of 247 days per year.[22] When an industrial city is located in a valley, the valley becomes a pollution basin. One of the most famous air pollution disasters in the United States occurred in Donora, Pennsylvania, a small city of steel mills and blast furnaces in a valley surrounded on all sides by steep hills. In 1948, a thermal inversion put a lid over the valley for three days. By the end of the third day,

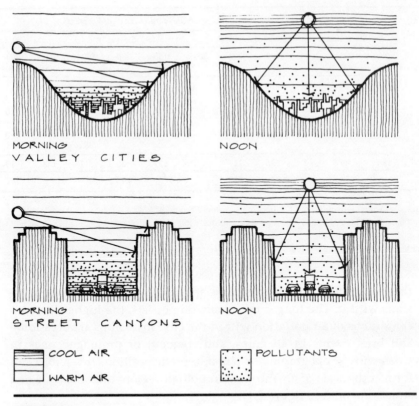

MORNING
VALLEY CITIES

NOON

MORNING
STREET CANYONS

NOON

COOL AIR

WARM AIR

POLLUTANTS

FIGURE 2.1
The formation of inversions in valley cities and street canyons, both a result of the same processes.

nearly 6,000 people were ill, including more than 60 percent of the elderly residents, and 20 people were dead.[23]

To ignore air pollution considerations when designing cities that experience frequent inversions or periods of stagnant weather is irresponsible. Yet in Tucson and Los Angeles, work and home are widely separated, and both cities are poorly served by public transport, necessitating heavy automobile traffic. New factories and freeways are often located in valleys, instead of on higher elevations where they would be better placed. Planners frequently locate new industries on the basis of prevailing wind directions rather than wind directions under inversions, with the result that pollutants may be swept back over the city when an inversion does occur. In Baltimore, for example, 52 percent of all winds are from the southwest to northwest, but during stagnation periods, 41 percent of the winds come from the east to south.[24]

Gusts and Lulls

Winds determine whether the poisons at street level are rapidly dispersed and diluted or linger to concentrate to dangerous levels. Contrary to the subjective experience of city dwellers, buffeted daily by gusty turbulence, the city is actually less windy than the surrounding countryside. Most gusts felt by urban pedestrians are swirling masses of stationary air which trap and concentrate pollutants, rather than dispersing and diluting them.

The city presents a rough surface to the wind. Building peaks and street canyons, with their abrupt changes in shape, height, and orientation, place a frictional drag on the layers of air closest to the city's surface, slowing them down (figure 2.2). Whether regional winds dip below roof level to penetrate the city depends on the orientation and continuity of open spaces and streets. Indeed, the precise pattern of air flow through and within an individual city is unique and complex. Winds accelerate along streets oriented parallel to the direction of the wind; eddies are created in streets running at right angles to the wind; and calms persist at the bottom of deep courtyards and other small, confined spaces. Gusts and lulls, eddies and jetlike winds, occur simultaneously within several hundred yards of one another or from one second to another in the same

---

FIGURE 2.2
Reduction of wind speed over city and suburb, expressed here as percentage of gradient winds, those winds uninfluenced by surface friction. Winds, slowed by the complex building surface in cities, may be half as strong at ground level as in level countryside.

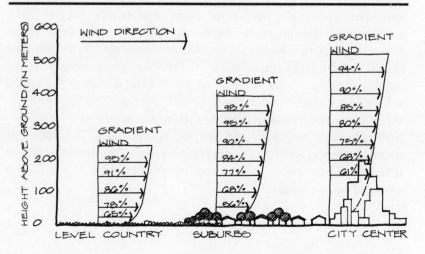

place, a product of the interaction of changing regional wind speeds and directions with surface topography, the aerodynamic shapes of nearby buildings, the size and shape of the space surrounding them, and the form of the city upwind.

The overall form of a city that is laid out without regard to wind patterns not only increases the likelihood that air pollutants will concentrate, but also intensifies the discomfort of city residents by permitting the formation of a phenomenon known as the urban heat island.

The Urban Heat Island

The city is hotter than the surrounding countryside during part of the day and much of the night. Summer nights bring little relief to the city, even when the surrounding suburbs have lost the day's heat. After sunset on a clear night, the temperature difference between city and suburbs is frequently 9° F and may reach 20° F.[25] The results, in hot weather, are higher air conditioning bills, greater discomfort, and in a prolonged heat wave, more strokes and death. The densest parts of the city are the hottest; temperatures fall as density decreases and drop sharply at the limits of continuous urban development.

The urban heat island is a universal characteristic of city climate, clearly visible on a map of nighttime temperatures for any metropolitan region (see figure 2.3). Several factors account for the urban heat island. In the city, concrete, stone, brick, and asphalt replace the natural plant cover of the countryside. These materials absorb heat more quickly and store it in greater quantities than the plants, soil, and water that make up forests, fields, and ponds. All day long, pavement, walls, and roofs absorb and store incoming solar radiation as heat. Although plants and water absorb solar radiation also, much of that energy is expended in evaporation and transpiration—resulting in heat loss rather than gain. City activities are also a source of heat; much of the heat results from combustion, which is the mainstay of transportation, and from the activities of manufacturing, heating buildings, and generating electricity. The combined metabolic processes of all the people who live in the city adds to that total, a phenomenon appreciated by anyone who has ridden a crowded bus or elevator.

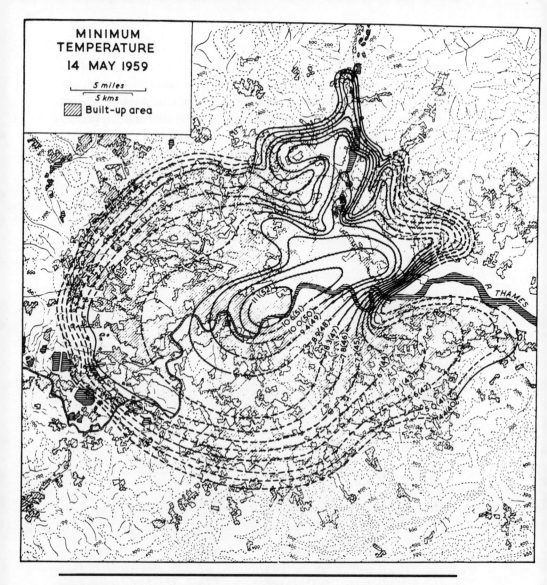

FIGURE 2.3
Temperature contours in greater London (each contour represents a temperature change of 1°F.) clearly demonstrate the origin of the term "urban heat island." The innermost circle, the center of London, is 12 degrees Fahrenheit hotter than the outermost circle at the metropolitan outskirts.

The disparity in air temperature between the city center and rural periphery is most pronounced on clear, calm nights a few hours after sunset. On such nights, the countryside loses heat rapidly to the cloudless sky. The city cools off more slowly: it has absorbed more heat, and the reradiation of that heat to the night sky is inhibited by parallel building walls. By morning, the temperature difference between city and country is minimal and may even be reversed, but by midafternoon, the city is hotter again.

The city's central business district, with its tall, densely spaced buildings on narrow streets with confined courtyards, typically forms the heat island's core. Here the thermal capacity of buildings and pavement is greatest and the air circulation poorest. Landscaped parks and river valleys, on the other hand, are relative cold spots within the heat island.

Urban form and density influence the intensity of the heat island more than does city size. Areas of similar urban development type and density in Leicester, England (population 270,000) and ninety miles away in London (population 8,250,000) have experienced the same excess of temperature over nearby rural areas on the same nights.[26] In fact, mini heat islands have even been measured in small courtyards and shopping malls (figure 2.4).[27]

FIGURE 2.4
Shopping mall heat island, generated by dense buildings and surrounding parking lot. Here, air above the center of the parking lot (innermost circle) is 4 degrees centigrade (7.2 degrees Fahrenheit) hotter than in a suburban neighborhood one block away (outermost circle).

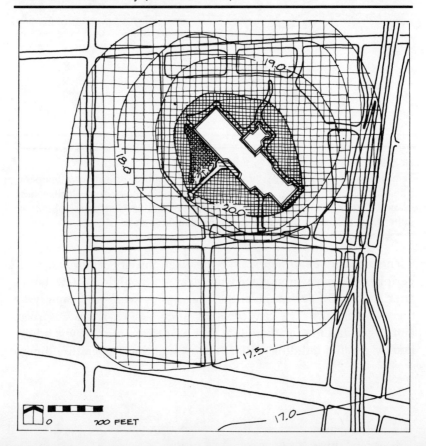

Wind speed, cloud cover, and atmospheric stability also affect the shape and intensity of the urban heat island. A breeze displaces the heat island downwind; a strong wind may disperse it entirely. The wind speed required to disperse the heat island varies with city size; London requires a wind of 12 meters (39 feet) per second whereas Reading, England, with a population of 120,000, only requires a wind of 4.7 meters (15.4 feet) per second.[28] Under cloudy conditions, less solar radiation reaches the ground, and the heat island is, therefore, less pronounced. Under inversion conditions, when the atmosphere is stable and heat is inhibited from rising, the heat island is intensified. The shape and intensity of the heat island fluctuate within a city in response to seasonal and annual changes in these variables.

The heat island may have a beneficial or a detrimental effect on energy conservation. The heat island reduces winter heating bills, but in warm climates these savings may be offset by the increased need for air conditioning in summer. Air conditioning requires more energy than heating and, furthermore, it produces heat, aggravating the heat island. A study of twelve cities in different parts of the United States indicated that heating was required on 8 percent fewer days in the city than in the outlying region, but that air conditioning was required on 12 percent more days.[29]

The urban heat island causes excess deaths in the city during heat waves. During a heat wave in the summer of 1966 the normal death rate was exceeded by 50 percent in New York City and 56 percent in St. Louis.[30] Persons over the age of 80 and those suffering from hypertension, heart and lung disease, and diabetes were the most likely to die from heat stress. Deaths were most frequent among the poor in the densest parts of the city and least frequent among the most affluent and in the suburbs. Several factors contribute to this. Air conditioning is less common among the poor, and pavement radiates as much as 50 percent more heat than does grass. People in the densest parts of the city are therefore subject not only to higher air temperatures but also to the additional heat radiated from surrounding pavement and buildings.[31]

A Mosaic of Microclimates: Street Canyons, Plazas, and Parks

Every city is composed of a mosaic of radically different microclimates, which are created by the same processes that operate at the citywide scale. The same phenomena that characterize the urban mesoclimate exist in miniature throughout the city—small heat islands, microinversions, pockets of severe air pollution, and local differences in wind behavior. Three common city microclimates demonstrate many of these variations: street canyons, paved plazas, and parks.

The street is central to the lives of urban poor and rich alike. A child in Harlem plays stickball in the street; adults congregate on the stoop. A child on Park Avenue rides his tricycle up and down the sidewalk under the doorman's watchful eye; his parents jog beside morning traffic. Lives are lived out on the street—playing, strolling, walking, driving, strutting, hustling, sitting, watching. The street is the city's life line and stage. It could be a delight. Today it is one of the unhealthiest urban environments.

Poisonous gases hang in the air above the street and toxic dust coats the roadway and sidewalk. Cars, buses, and trucks congest the streets, accelerating and braking, emitting streams of carbon monoxide, nitrogen oxides, and bits of lead and unburned fuel. The stop-and-go traffic characteristic of a busy street produces more pollutants than traffic moving smoothly at constant speed along the highway because the concentration of exhaust waste is greatest at an irregular rate of combustion. Oil droplets from the engines are turned into a fine aerosol; asbestos is rubbed from brake linings; the street pavement literally grinds the rubber from rolling tires into a fine dust.

A downtown street canyon lined by tall buildings not only generates a high level of noxious substances, but also inhibits their dispersion. The volume and speed of vehicular traffic determine to what degree the air at street level is contaminated. Distance from the road and ventilation determine the distribution of pollutants and the degree to which they concentrate in a given area. Airborne particles of lead can decrease 50 percent in the interval between the road's edge and 50 meters (164 feet) away.[32] The sidewalk and building entries in a street canyon are located within the zone of highest accumulation.

A local inversion may form at the bottom of a shady street canyon in the morning, trapping the exhaust from rush hour traffic at breathing level. Unless dissipated by winds, the inversion persists until the midday sun reaches the street and warms the surface and air at ground level. By that time, concentrations of carbon monoxide and other poisons may have reached levels sufficient to affect anyone exposed to this air for as little as an hour. Pedestrians, traffic cops, street vendors, and taxi drivers are not the only ones affected. If the intake shafts for subways or air conditioning vents for buildings are located near street level, subterranean and indoor concentrations may match those on the sidewalk.[33] A study on the first, third, and fifty-fourth floors of one Toronto office building showed that carbon monoxide concentrations were only 28 percent less on the first floor than on the sidewalk, 37 percent less on the third floor, and over 60 percent less on the fifty-fourth floor.[34] Carbon monoxide concentrations in the lower floors of buildings near congested urban streets can aggravate heart disease.[35]

The ventilation of street canyons depends upon the width of the street, the heights and shapes of surrounding buildings, the street's orientation in relation to prevailing wind directions, and the overall pattern of winds in the surrounding city (see figure 2.5). When streets are aligned parallel to the direction of the wind, wind speeds may flush out the air at street level, carrying off fumes and dust. Streets perpendicular to the prevailing winds, however, receive little or no effective ventilation. Turbulence at street corners does not disperse pollutants, but merely swirls them around in the air, and the stagnant air in midblock permits them to collect. Downdrafts at the base of tall buildings, swooping down from rooftops, bring

---

FIGURE 2.5
Pattern of air pollution in a street canyon, a function of wind direction and shape and size of the canyon. Note that smoke emitted at rooftop may be swept down to street level.

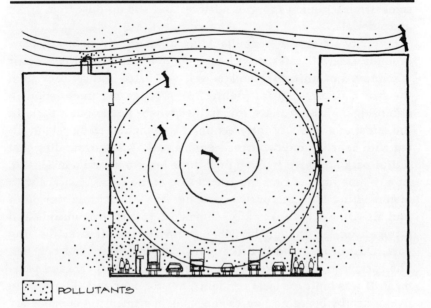

POLLUTANTS

FIGURE 2.6
A traffic island park in Cambridge, Massachusetts, enveloped in exhaust from buses, cars, and trucks. Anyone sitting there inhales a poisonous atmosphere.

smoke from chimneys to ground level and stir up dust from street and sidewalk.

Busy city streets are not suitable locations for sitting areas, playgrounds, sidewalk cafes, or vegetable gardens until the streetside air is improved or unless the area is well ventilated and set back from the street. Central Square (figure 2.6), a congested intersection in Cambridge, Massachusetts, exemplifies where not to put a park. In the midst of a five-way intersection is a triangular traffic island fitted with benches and two trees—ergo, a park. And surrounding that pitiful park are three traffic lights, three bus stops, and a taxi stand. At any time lines of cars and trucks stop at the lights, taxicabs with motors idling and a bus or two stand nearby—all emitting streams of foul air. On a windless, stuffy, summer day, carbon monoxide and nitrogen oxides, though invisible, permeate the air over the tiny park. Dust of lead and hydrocarbons coats the bricks and benches. The park is an oven, baked in heat from surrounding cars and pavement. It was built for local residents, mostly poor and elderly, who live in nearby boarding houses and small apartments. A summer day finds several stalwarts sitting in the tiny triangle, barely moving, looking slightly disoriented. Is their confusion and lethargy due to senility? Or is it carbon monoxide poisoning? Such well-meaning but misguided attempts to provide parks for people in the poorest and densest parts of the city are found in nearly every city. Central Square would be better off with a grove of trees on the triangle rather than the sham of a sitting area.

Urban plazas should be amenities; most are not. Crowds throng the most successful, filling every sittable niche at lunch hour; the failures are deserted. Success or failure has much to do with comfort; unfortunately, comfort is usually a minor concern in the design of outdoor places, if it is considered at all. A barren plaza at the foot of a tall building can be one of the most uncomfortable places in the city, and may even be dangerous.

Winds sweep down and around adjacent buildings and blast unchecked across an open plaza. The winds in plazas and in arcades beneath tall buildings may accelerate to quadruple the speed in protected streets nearby. Since wind force increases exponentially with speed, wind four times as fast hits pedestrians with sixteen times the force.[36] Two elderly women died in Britain in one year from head injuries suffered after being knocked over by winds at the base of a tall building.[37] Plazas are frequently too shady in winter and exposed to too much sun at the hottest time of day in summer.

City Hall Plaza is one of Boston's major outdoor public spaces, a grand plaza of brick surrounding a striking, modern city hall. Its monumental scale sets off the monumental building. The visual effect is enhanced by the federal government buildings that face on it—it is Boston's Government Center. But the plaza, however impressive as a setting for architecture and a center for government, is a disaster for physical comfort. In summer, it offers no shade to relieve the heat generated by the sun and augmented by hot pavement. Only when there are sea breezes from the nearby waterfront is the plaza bearable. During the long Boston winter, the plaza is a no man's land. Winds from the harbor rip across the unbroken expanse of brick. There is no protection from driving snow and rain. The plaza's size, slope, and steps defy attempts at snow removal. The walk of several hundred feet across the plaza from the Government Center subway station to City Hall or to the federal buildings is an ordeal not lightly undertaken in winter's rain and snow or spring slush. The effect of climate has negated the intended symbolic accessibility of government. Granted, there are equally important concerns for designers—both functional and aesthetic—as comfort, but if a place is sufficiently uncomfortable, that discomfort may undermine all other considerations. Boston has a long winter and a short spring and fall. The design for any public space should respond to those basic climatic facts. However beautiful and expansive, City Hall Plaza is misplaced in Boston; its form is suited to a more benign climate like that of Italy or California.

In contrast to the plaza, a shady park absorbs less heat during the day and loses it more rapidly after sunset. The microclimate of a large, tree-filled park resembles that of a woodland. It shows up as a "cold spot" on an infrared photograph taken from the air at night. Rock Creek Park in Washington, D.C. can be more than 5 degrees centigrade cooler at night than adjacent residential neighborhoods and over 9 degrees cooler than the central business district.[38] Although daytime air temperatures are similar to those above adjacent city streets, the park feels cooler because there is more shade, less glare, and less heat radiated from lawn and trees. The climatic effect of a shady park extends to adjacent streets. A tree-lined street adjacent to a park seems cooler in summer than a treeless street two blocks away. A landscaped park also has cleaner air than the surrounding city, in part because the park is not emitting air contaminants, but also because the leaves and twigs of trees and shrubs filter out dust from the air. Nineteenth-century urbanists created large landscaped parks in the inner city as "lungs for the city." Today they are disappearing or in decline, victims of slashed municipal budgets and easy prey to public building programs in search of open land. New parks, completely paved and with few, if any, plants, are replacing them. There is little to distinguish these "parks" from the city around them, either climatically or aesthetically.

Many of the social costs of continuing to discount climate and air quality in city design are already manifest: increased mortality among the elderly, the sick, and the very young; lead poisoning among children; degraded health of city residents and workers; increased energy demands; and property damage. Without intervention, these problems will intensify.

Despite cheerful predictions that air quality in most cities will meet national standards by 1987, existing programs, on which such predictions are premised, are faltering. Industry complains of the high cost of pollution control, and a society faced with unemployment and an uncertain economy weighs the cost of air quality against jobs. Oil shortages and rising prices encourage many cities and industries to substitute with coal. Control of automobile emissions alone could solve carbon monoxide and ozone problems, but these rely upon the compliance of millions of individual car owners, each of whom thinks his own role insignificant. Releasing a canister of poison gas on a sidewalk is a criminal act, yet those who destroy the emission control devices on their cars, who burn leaded gasoline, who leave their engines running when parked at the curb are engaged in activities no less irresponsible.

The lessons of history are clear. In economic crisis or fuel shortage, in the face of short-term self-interest, concern for air quality is abandoned. Attainment of better air quality must not depend on the control of emissions alone, but should be coordinated with a city design that encourages the dispersion and filtration of pollutants and improves the overall city climate. Most metropolitan plans and new building projects exacerbate air pollution and accentuate the worst problems of city climate. Industry and highways are located in basins with limited air circulation. More and more cars are funneled into narrow, downtown street canyons by new, larger expressways. Schools, playgrounds, small sitting areas, and intake vents for air conditioners are all placed along busy streets. New buildings block ventilating winds, and create stagnant air pockets and hurricane force downdrafts. Parks are built with more pavement and fewer trees, fountains, and pools; and they are located without regard for their potential to improve air quality and comfort.

Meanwhile, urban designers import Italian piazzas to Boston and Karachi; architects design the same new building forms in New York, Jeddah, Nairobi, and Hong Kong, with interior climates maintained by furnaces and air conditioners. To manipulate the city's climate for health, comfort, and energy conservation is imperative, yet the designers and planners of modern cities seldom do so. The builders of ancient cities addressed these issues with more concern and more skill.

CHAPTER 3

Improving Air Quality, Enhancing Comfort, and Conserving Energy

THE BUILDERS of ancient cities recognized the benefits of adapting urban form to climatic conditions. The Roman architect Vitruvius cautioned his contemporaries of the first century A.D. to give careful consideration to sun and winds when designing new towns in outlying provinces:

> The town being fortified, the next step is the apportionment of house lots within the walls and the layout of streets and alleys with regard to climatic conditions. They will be properly laid out if foresight is employed to exclude the winds from the alleys. Cold winds are disagreeable, hot winds enervating, moist winds unhealthy. We must, therefore, avoid mistakes in this matter and beware of the common experience of many communities. For example, Mylitene in the island of Lesbos is a town built with magnificence and good taste, but its position shows a lack of foresight. In that community when the wind is south, the people fall ill; when it is northwest, it sets them coughing; with a north wind they do indeed recover but cannot stand about in the alleys and streets, owing to the severe cold. . . . If the streets run full in the face of the winds, their constant blasts rushing in from the open country, and then confined by narrow alleys, will sweep through them with great violence. The lines of houses must therefore be directed away from the quarters from which the winds blow, so that as they come in they may strike against the angles of the blocks and their force thus be broken and dispersed.[1]

John Evelyn urged his contemporaries to improve the air quality of seventeenth-century London for the benefit of "health, profit and beauty." He understood the effect of winds, topography, and air temperature on the dispersion of pollutants. His recommendations ranged from the development of alternative fuel sources to the application of emission and land-use controls.[2]

Traditional "primitive" building forms and village plans vary from climatic zone to climatic zone, reflecting the stresses posed by each. In hot, humid climates, overhangs provide shade. Buildings are open and raised off the ground and houses are spaced widely to promote ventilation. In hot, arid climates, thick stone or earthen walls moderate daily fluctuations in temperature; small windows and doors limit the penetration of sunlight and prevent the escape of cool interior air. Buildings are huddled in each other's shade; plants are nurtured in small, enclosed courtyards.

Many solutions to air pollution, energy conservation, and comfort available today have been applied for centuries, if not millennia. Their success and similarity derive from an understanding of the processes governing sun, wind, and the production of air pollutants. Today these processes are far better understood than ever before, but that knowledge is infrequently applied. A few contemporary parks and plazas, like Paley Park at 53rd Street near Fifth Avenue in New York City, have incorporated the most basic principles of climatic comfort—a fact that contributes to their overwhelming social success. They rank with the best historic examples and are worthy of study. As of yet, only a handful of cities—Stuttgart, West Germany, and Dayton, Ohio, among them—have developed comprehensive metropolitan designs based on the more refined information that is now available. Although their specific solutions may not be transferable to another city, the basic notion will always apply: the key is an understanding of process.

Sun, Winds, and Emissions

Buildings gain and lose heat, and pollutants are concentrated or dispersed by the same mechanisms everywhere—in Tokyo or Tucson, at the scale of the city or the street corner. Factories, power plants, and incinerators; cars, trucks, and buses; and thousands of small commercial and domestic furnaces all contribute to the city's air pollution.

Understanding how pollutants are emitted is the first step toward control and dispersal. There are three types of sources—point, line, and area—each characterized by the variety and quantity of pollutants produced, and the likely pattern of their dispersion. A point source, such as a power plant or factory, can be pinpointed and monitored. One can measure the specific pollutants and their quantity, and the height, speed, and temperature of the pollutant plume. The dispersion of emissions under given meteorological conditions can be predicted, along with the size and shape of affected areas downwind. Point sources can be regulated during inversions and located in areas with good ventilation, distant from houses, schools, and parks.

A line source—a major traffic artery, for example—is less readily measured and controlled, but the types and amounts of pollutants produced on a road can be estimated, nevertheless, if daily fluctuations in traffic volume and speed are known. Dispersion from a line source is more difficult to predict than that from a point source, because line sources pass through different terrain and different types and densities of urban development. Pollutants disperse readily from an elevated highway, but accumulate when the highway is below grade or enclosed by adjacent buildings.

An area source is the sum of many small pollution sources, which remain anonymous by virtue of proximity or similarity of pollutants, an umbrella for all the small residential and industrial polluters of the city. Area sources account for a major portion of ground-level air pollution. Yet the individual sources cannot be singled out or measured. Area sources are, in consequence, extremely difficult to regulate, except by large-scale efforts such as changing the source of domestic heating for an entire area of the city. Many European cities have experimented with such "district heating," but U.S. cities have yet to apply it widely as a pollution control and energy conservation measure.

The city dissipates, deflects, intensifies, and generates air movement that can, if guided, disperse pollution. The complexities and contradictions of air flow in the city are difficult to master, but the reward is great since air movement can help dilute pollutants, enhance comfort, and conserve energy. Air movement is accelerated, slowed, or deflected as it moves over surfaces and around obstacles. The rougher the ground surface, the more the air is slowed down. An obstacle's density, the position and size of openings, its dimensions, shape, silhouette, and orientation determine at what spots winds are reduced or increased and in what direction they are de-

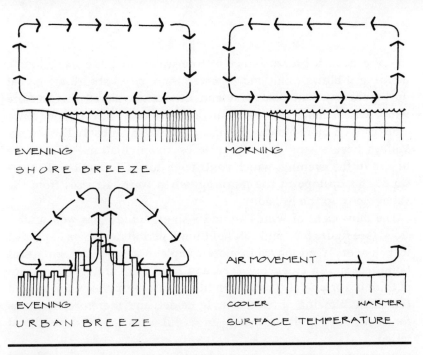

EVENING   MORNING

SHORE BREEZE

EVENING   AIR MOVEMENT

URBAN BREEZE   COOLER   WARMER

SURFACE TEMPERATURE

FIGURE 3.1
The daily cycle of thermal breezes along shorelines and in cities, both formed
by the identical principle. As warm air rises over a heated surface (e.g., along
the shoreline, the ground by day and the water by night), cooler air is sucked
in to replace it, initiating a breeze in calm weather.

flected. The same principles hold true whether the obstacle is a single building, a group of buildings, or an entire city. Ventilation
promotes air quality and summer comfort, but wind chill increases
winter discomfort, and wind infiltration increases heating bills.
When designing air movement, a balance must be struck between
ventilation and comfort, and among the needs of different seasons.

Mild thermal breezes blow when regional winds are very light,
generated by the difference in surface temperatures between the city
and adjacent countryside, water bodies, or hillsides (figure 3.1). Urbanization in itself produces one type; the city's physiographic setting produces two others—shore and valley winds. When the urban
heat island is most pronounced, it initiates a centripetal pattern of
air flow from the cooler outskirts of the city to the hotter center. Air
flows inward at a few feet per second until slowed, blocked, or heated, then rises, gradually cooling with height, and sinks back over
the countryside.

Anyone who has lived by the shore of an ocean or large lake
knows the daily pattern of onshore–offshore breezes. Land warms
faster than water during the day and cools more rapidly at night. In

the afternoon a breeze blows off the water onto the land; in the morning it blows from land to water. Since cities absorb more heat during the day than most rural land, they can accelerate this onshore wind, which may then penetrate more than a mile inland; since cities cool off more slowly, the offshore wind is probably less strong. Valleys have a similar daily cycle of air circulation—downslope breeze in the evening, which contributes to the formation of inversions, and upslope in the morning, when warm air rises from the valley floor up the hillsides.

The movement of winds around a single building is well understood (see figure 3.2), and rules of thumb permit designers to predict its behavior. Wind moves in more complex ways through groups of buildings and in cities, however, and here there are very few rules of thumb. Fortunately, actual conditions can be duplicated in a wind tunnel by blowing air over a scale model; and therefore strategies for manipulating air movement in useful ways can be devised and tested.

Four major processes of energy transfer govern how buildings and people gain or lose heat: radiation, conduction, convection, and evaporation. Radiation is the primary source of heat gain. Radiation, evaporation, and convection are the major processes by which heat is lost.

Human comfort is a function of many factors: air temperature, air motion, humidity, metabolic rate, and clothing are primary. Air movement and mean radiant temperature vary more radically

---

FIGURE 3.2
The complex pattern of winds around an isolated building creates conditions where a person may sit in comfort in one spot and be knocked over by the force of the wind in a spot only twenty feet away. Wind speeds increase with height, so that winds hit different parts of the building with varying force.

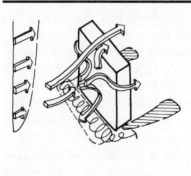

⇨ WIND DIRECTION   〰 INCREASED WIND SPEEDS

among different city environments than do air temperature and humidity, and can be more readily manipulated through urban design. The radiant temperature of surrounding pavement and walls can be decreased or increased by the promotion of shade or sun or by the selection of building materials for their thermal properties. The importance of controlling direct sunlight and wind is well recognized; the contribution of radiant heat to comfort is often overlooked. The body produces two to three times more heat walking than sitting—metabolic rate is controlled by decreasing or increasing activity. Requirements for comfort therefore vary with activities of different intensities.

What degree of air pollution or comfort is "acceptable" will depend on how many people use a place, when they use it, how long they stay there, and whether they can choose to avoid it. All the pollution problems of the city cannot be solved at once, but the most polluted and uncomfortable places, where many people spend much of their time, must be the first priority for any city.

Improving the Air along Streets and Highways

The street cannot be avoided. Most people live, work, travel, and play on or near the street. Yet, as noted earlier, it is one of the most contaminated environments in the city, where air pollutants are often the least monitored and the least regulated.

Contamination on the street is caused by one major source: transportation; and so long as private automobiles are a major mode of urban transportation, pollution of the street will continue. Even so, better air quality on the street could be readily achieved. One can predict concentrations of specific pollutants at any point, given distance from roads, the width and height of the street canyon, and wind speed and direction. The fewer the cars, and the faster and more constant their speed, the fewer pollutants are produced. The greater the distance from the road, the fewer pollutants in the air. The wider and shorter the street canyon, and the fewer eddies and calms, the more pollutants are dispersed. In addition to emission controls and traffic regulations, street design standards could also reduce the pollutants emitted on the street and prevent their concentration. Judicious location of houses, businesses, and playgrounds could limit people's exposure.

There are precedents for public regulation of traffic, for standards for street design, and for zoning of land use, because streets and highways are public spaces, built, maintained, owned, and controlled by local, state, or federal government. A few public agencies could effect an enormous improvement in air quality by the enforcement of existing regulations and standards and the creation of a few new ones.

Planners have traditionally relied upon several strategies for reducing the emissions of air pollutants and their impact upon people: designing transportation networks and land use patterns to minimize travel and encourage the use of mass transit; enhancing smooth traffic flow; and protecting residential areas. Less attention has been given to the redesigning of the street or highway right-of-way and the regulation of adjacent land uses to encourage the dispersion of pollutants and limit exposure to them.

Traffic engineers distinguish among a hierarchy of roads—local streets, collectors, arterials, and expressways—each with characteristic functions, traffic speeds and volumes, size, and patterns of daily use. But basically there are only two types of roads, one for traffic and one for people. Efficiency of movement is paramount on expressways and arterials; access and the quality of the living environment should take precedence on collectors and local streets.

The social importance of the local city street was demonstrated in a study of a neighborhood in Baltimore that showed that neighborhood residents, predominantly lower-income blacks, preferred to socialize on the street than in nearby parks and playgrounds. Parks were frequently deserted, while the street front on an adjacent block was bustling, with people sitting, playing, or talking.[3]

As the environments in which millions of families bring up their children, they might better be called "family streets." They introduce most of our children to our cities. These family streets should be sanctuaries for adults, an escape from the bustle of city life, a place for withdrawal and self restoration. But they also have a micropolitical role. They can become the stable units in a society riddled with placelessness, anonymity, alienation, and loneliness, remote from an often incomprehensible government. The street block is one focus for localism and decentralization of services. It is more compact, intense, and coherent than the neighborhood, and it has different kinds of problems. For all these reasons, its protection from intrusion and disruption becomes of value not just to local residents, but to cities and to society as a whole.[4]

Although local streets average up to 2,000 cars per day,[5] their important social functions are disrupted when there are more than 800 to 1,200 cars.[6] Many local residential streets function as collectors, carrying many more than 2,000 cars per day. The British have a

FIGURE 3.3
Dutch woonerf, a residential street with special traffic regulations where cars share the street with people and gardens.

name for such streets—"rat-runs." "Rat-runners" are drivers who weave their way across town through local streets in order to avoid traffic lights and congested streets. Reevaluating the role of the car on local streets is essential both to the improvement of health and comfort and to safety and quality of life.

The Dutch have developed a new type of street, the "woonerf," that enhances the social role of the residential street (figure 3.3). The woonerf ("residential yard" in Dutch) is a precinct with its own traffic rules: children and adults have precedence over cars and they use the entire roadway; cars must drive at a walking pace (about ten miles per hour). In the woonerf, distinctions between street and sidewalk are eliminated, and the resulting street space is shared by cars and pedestrians. The woonerf originated in Delft, where conventional streets were transformed by repaving them to eliminate curbs, by introducing obstacles like mounds, raised planters, and trees which forced drivers to wind their way around them, and by consolidating parking (see figure 3.4). The Dutch have created 800

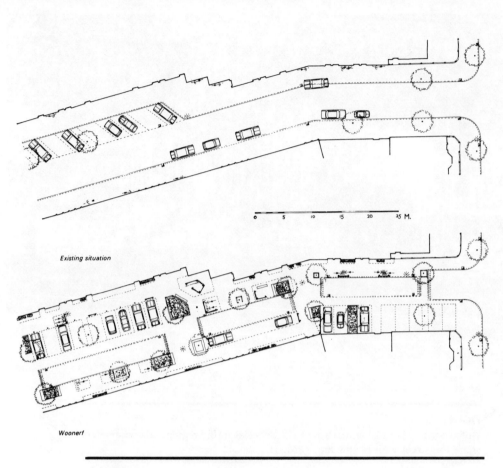

Existing situation

Woonerf

FIGURE 3.4

Plans show how existing streets are converted into woonerven. The roadway is narrowed, parking consolidated, and benches, trees, and gardens added.

---

woonerven in 200 cities and there is a long waiting list for future conversions.[7] German cities have implemented a similar concept called "Wohnbericht." Boston, an American city whose downtown streets resemble those of many European cities, has recently installed one woonerf in the South End, on Appleton Street. The conversion transformed Appleton Street from a shortcut to the Southeast Expressway into a social street for local residents. The decrease in traffic is dramatic, and the benefits to air quality on this residential street are likely to be pronounced.

Unlike local streets, expressways and arterial streets should promote the efficient movement of fast, heavy traffic, and should be designed to disperse air pollutants and limit people's exposure to them without impeding traffic movement. Arterial streets average 24,000 vehicles per day, and they generate a zone of air pollution that extends about fifty meters (164 feet) from the edge of both sides

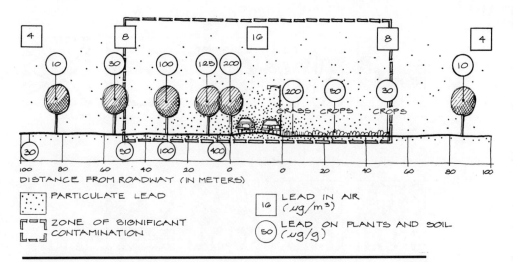

DISTANCE FROM ROADWAY (IN METERS)

FIGURE 3.5

The problem: lead is concentrated in air, soil, and plants along streets, a function of traffic speed, volume, and distance from roadway. Here, along a street averaging 24,000 vehicles per day, under calm conditions, lead in the air above the street is sixteen times the "normal" urban atmospheric lead content, falling off to eight times normal fifty meters (164 feet) away.

of the road (see figure 3.5).[8] In the area immediately adjacent to the road, the most highly polluted, the lead content of the air is sixteen times the "normal" urban atmospheric lead content. At fifty meters (164 feet), lead in the air is only eight times normal.[9] Since the concentration of pollutants falls off sharply at ten meters (33 feet) and continues to decline with increasing distance from the roadway, border areas of at least ten meters (33 feet), should separate the road edge from the sidewalk. Rows of trees, planted in the buffer zone, will enhance the setback by filtering fumes and dust and reducing street noise (see figure 3.6). Frankfurt, Germany, one of a number of

FIGURE 3.6

The solution: a multifaceted approach to limit air pollution exposure along streets: traffic regulations to reduce the production of lead and other pollutants; landscaping to capture particulates; and setbacks to minimize exposure. Traffic volume determines size of setback.

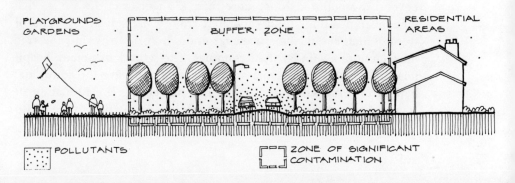

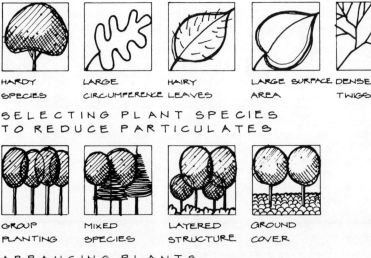

HARDY   LARGE   HAIRY   LARGE SURFACE DENSE
SPECIES   CIRCUMFERENCE   LEAVES   AREA   TWIGS

SELECTING PLANT SPECIES
TO REDUCE PARTICULATES

GROUP   MIXED   LAYERED   GROUND
PLANTING   SPECIES   STRUCTURE   COVER

ARRANGING PLANTS
TO REDUCE PARTICULATES

FIGURE 3.7
Using plants to reduce particulate air pollution. Certain types and arrangements of plants create effective air filters.

European cities that have long recognized the value of street trees for this purpose, plants four rows of trees along major boulevards. Wiesbaden recommends two rows of trees along each side of major city streets.[10]

Trees remove some of the carbon monoxide and particulates emitted by vehicular traffic, a function enhanced by several factors (see figure 3.7). Because the removal rate of gaseous pollutants is dependent upon the tree's vigor, species should be selected for their hardiness under city conditions. Trees will filter particulates most effectively if they have dense branches, rough bark and twigs, and hairy leaves with a high ratio of surface to volume.[11] Since soil is also an effective sink for pollutants, removal of pollutants is enhanced when trees are planted in soil covered with leaves and plants, rather than pavement.

Schools, houses, sitting areas, and playgrounds should be set back beyond the polluted zone, more than 150 feet from the street edge whenever possible,[12] and separated from the roadway by belts of trees, which should be spaced far enough apart to permit the free movement of air under their canopies. The setback of homes, hospitals, offices, and stores from arterial streets will have the additional benefit of enhancing ventilation and preventing the formation of stagnant air pockets. The height of buildings in relation to the width of the street should permit sunlight to reach the street by midmorning in order to dissipate local inversions at street level and to allow the penetration of ventilating breezes to disperse and dilute contaminants. Cities should study the effects of varying wind directions and speeds upon the shape and size of the polluted zones. (Wind tunnel tests are currently the most reliable way to predict air movement at this scale, but computer models that predict the diffusion of air pollution in urban street canyons may ease this task in the future.)

Although the location and width of expressways are frequently influenced by existing urban conditions, there is more flexibility for selecting a new highway's location and making improvements in an existing right-of-way than there is in enlarging existing arterials. New highways should be located in areas with favorable ventilation and separated from places where people live and play. The right-of-way should include the entire area of the polluted zone, on both sides of the road. It should be planted with trees and shrubs to filter pollutants. Bicycle and jogging trails and vegetable gardens are not suitable uses for expressway rights-of-way.

Collector streets, in contrast to both arterials and local streets, are neither entirely for traffic nor entirely for people. They distribute traffic throughout the city and are heavily traveled by cars and trucks, serving as many as 15,000 vehicles per day, yet they are also the place where many people shop and work. The polluted zone of collector streets is likely to be smaller than that of arterials, but the same design principles apply. Sidewalks should be wide and separated from the roadway by a large border area planted with trees whenever possible. Small parks and plazas located along collectors should be set back and separated from the street by rows of trees.

Not all cities, especially older ones, can comply with standards for new street design. The intricate maze of narrow medieval streets characteristic of European cities like London, Copenhagen, and Amsterdam, the street canyons hemmed in by towering buildings epitomized by New York City, and the expansive streets of midwestern cities like Dayton—each pattern engenders its own problems and requires its own solutions. Local streets may be redesigned and reconstructed with relatively little impact on the rest of the city, but strategies for improving health and comfort on major streets are often at odds with the need to promote access and efficiency of movement. The woonerf concept is appropriate only where most cars have a local destination and traffic is below 300 cars per hour.[13] Any technique that reduces traffic speed on major streets will only exacerbate air pollution.

The air pollution problems of collector and arterial streets should be considered both individually, street by street, and in relation to one another. Limiting automobile traffic or banning it entirely, especially in narrow, poorly ventilated streets, may be the only solution to an intolerable problem.

Madison Avenue, in New York City, is not narrow by standards of most cities, but the height of the buildings that line it produces a deep canyon. Madison Avenue runs north to south on Manhattan Island and the sun often does not reach street level until midday. The result is frequent morning inversions that trap the exhaust from rush hour traffic at street level (see figure 2.1). Park Avenue, a much wider street one block away, is much better ventilated. The morning sun probably prevents inversions in the many east–west streets which cross Madison Avenue. Design palliatives will make no dent in Madison Avenue's air pollution, and further construction of tall buildings will certainly aggravate it. The only alternative, in this case, is to ban or limit traffic where skyscrapers crowd the street.

In Europe there are many precedents for eliminating cars, trucks, and buses from city streets. Stockholm, Rotterdam, Bologna, and Vienna have all banned traffic from various parts of the downtown, as have some American cities. Strøjet (Danish for "stroll"), a connected system of narrow streets in central Copenhagen, has been dedicated to pedestrians since 1962. Today there are more than 2,000 stores along Strøjet, among them the city's most expensive department stores and boutiques, as well as some of its most popular restaurants and cafes. Strøjet appeals to tourists and natives alike. People—strolling, strutting, sunning, sitting, watching, and eating—have replaced the car on the street; delivery trucks have access in the early morning only or from streets at the side or the rear.

Creating More Comfortable Parks and Plazas

Public squares have always been in fashion. They were at the heart of ancient Greek and Roman cities, medieval towns, and later provincial villages, as well as the modern metropolis. They are places to see and be seen, to shop and conduct business, to promenade and politic. The best plazas are pleasant places most of the year, moderating the heat of midsummer and warming the chill of early spring and late fall. Such places are rare and prized.

Shady havens are comfortable places to sit. Paley Park in New York City (figures 3.8 and 3.9) is such a haven off busy, noisy, mid-

FIGURE 3.8
Paley Park, one of the most intensively used parks in New York City, a comfortable, shady haven.

FIGURE 3.9
Plan of Paley Park, showing the simplicity with which its climatic effect is achieved: a waterfall, vine-covered walls, and a canopy of trees.

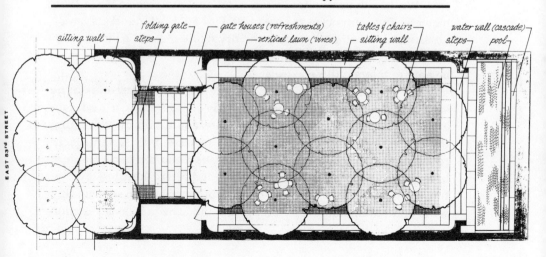

town East 53rd Street. On a hot, humid, airless summer day, this small park is refreshingly cool. At lunchtime it is crowded with shoppers and office workers. Paley Park is quite small and intimate—the size of one building lot. Adjacent buildings tower over the park, yet it does not feel cramped. A dozen honey locusts, their trunks slim columns, form a lacy roof over the park. The leaves admit a filtered, dappled sunlight. A denser tree, like the Norway maple, would have cast a dark shade and made the park an oppressive hole. A waterfall is the endwall of the park. Its soothing, rushing sound masks the street noise outside. Water splashes onto the surrounding pavement and cools the air as it evaporates. On a hot day, the seats closest to the water are claimed first. The two sidewalls are covered with ivy, which blocks both reflected sunlight from the walls and the radiant heat they might otherwise emit outward. Chairs and tables are movable, locked in at night for security. The distance between chairs can be adjusted to accommodate groups, couples, or solitary visitors. Chairs can be moved close to the waterfall or further away and in or out of the sun, depending on whether the day is hot or cool. Paley Park is often copied. It is an excellent example of how a dramatic change in urban microclimate can be accomplished in a very small space.

A sunpocket, a protected place that feels 10 degrees to 40 degrees Fahrenheit warmer than a more exposed spot nearby, can extend the use of an outdoor space by two to three months in a cool climate. It is a paved, south-facing corner, protected from the wind; its walls catch the sunlight and reflect it back into the space. Its pavement, preferably dark, absorbs and reradiates heat from the sun and heat reflected off surrounding walls. A pedestrian can sit quite comfortably in a New York City sunpocket in April or November without a coat. While a thermometer in the wind and sun reads 52°F, a thermometer in a sunpocket may read 80°F or 90°F.[14] Sunpockets have a desertlike microclimate—warm and dry while the sun is out, cold on a winter night after sunset—so plants chosen for such a place must be able to tolerate these extremes.

Shady havens, like Paley Park, and sunpockets are based upon the same principles of heat exchange. Shady havens prevent heat gain and encourage heat loss by blocking direct sunlight, by preventing the absorption of heat in surrounding surfaces and its subsequent reradiation, and by encouraging evaporation and the penetration of breezes. Sunpockets enhance heat gain and retard heat loss by capturing sunlight, by facilitating the absorption of heat in surrounding walls and pavement, and by blocking wind. The judicious selection of location, form, and building materials contributes to the success of a shady haven or sunpocket. A southwest orientation is optimal for sunpockets. Whenever possible, shady havens should be located to capture sea breezes, hillside breezes, and prevailing summer breezes. Selection of the right materials is fundamental. Shallow, porous, heterogeneous pavement (brick in sand) absorbs heat more slowly and stores less than a deep, dense, homogeneous pavement (concrete). Light, smooth pavement (concrete or marble) absorbs less and reflects more radiation than dark, rough pavement (asphalt). Wet surfaces (pavement, roofs, ponds) produce a cooling effect as water evaporates. Trees cool not by shade alone. Water, pumped from the ground, evaporates from their leaf surface so long as water in the ground is plentiful.

Ideally, shady havens and sunpockets should be located throughout the city, integrated into plazas and parks. They can be simple and inexpensive. Paley Park is between Fifth Avenue and Madison Avenue in a fashionable section of Manhattan and has a lavish maintenance budget. Many similar parks built since, such as Waterfall Garden in Seattle, Washington, and Greenacre Park in New York City, were also costly to build and maintain, but such expense is not essential. A similar microclimate effect could be achieved in a vacant lot on a much smaller budget. City "weed" trees, like ailanthus, provide shade within a few years after planting and need not be purchased. Vines on walls and low plants on the ground reduce glare and radiant heat. A simple sprinkler—a cheap alternative to pools and fountains—increases both physiological and psychological comfort, even in a humid climate.

Designing a Cleaner, More Comfortable, and Energy-Efficient City

To be most effective, the design of a single street, park, or plaza should be part of a comprehensive strategy to improve air quality, conserve energy, and improve comfort throughout the city. Problems at one street corner may find their cause elsewhere, and solutions to air quality may increase discomfort.

Take the example of downtown Dayton, Ohio, where winds are a problem on plazas and sidewalks at the base of tall buildings. A particularly nasty situation is the entry to a high-rise apartment complex for the elderly. Residents who venture out to the nearby senior citizens' center or shopping district struggle against strong gusts. Add icy sidewalks in winter and such forays become perilous.

This problem was studied by graduate students in landscape architecture at Harvard University. They had spent months studying climate and its application to urban design, and they marshaled all the new tools that they had acquired to solve this problem of a windy street corner. They proposed different configurations of trees, awnings, and walls, then tested their designs in a wind tunnel. The effect on wind speeds was insignificant. The steel wool mounted on pins used for trees on the model was destroyed by the force of the wind. The students lamented that the severe downdrafts had not been anticipated before the apartment complex was built, for then the entry and the building could have been redesigned. Beyond destroying the building and reconstructing it there seemed to be no satisfactory resolution to the problem. This conclusion is where most such studies end. Fortunately, this study was an academic exercise, and the elderly housing project but one short case study, part of an overall investigation of climate and air quality in the city as a whole. The students went on to prepare a master street-tree plan for the entire downtown and in the course of that work found an answer to the problem of the elderly housing complex.

The answer lay in looking at the city as a whole. Dayton's downtown is surrounded on three sides by open land which presents little friction to the wind. Parking lots, institutional grounds, a highway, and a river ring the city. Winter winds from the northwest sweep unbroken across an expanse of parking lot, then hit tall buildings like the elderly apartment complex with full force, sweeping down and around them. The link between windswept parking lots at the periphery of downtown and turbulence around tall buildings in the center was clearly demonstrated in wind-tunnel tests where the effect of winds of differing force and direction was simulated by blowing air over a scale model of the entire downtown (figure 3.10). When trees were added to parking lots on the northwest edge, the wind problems around the entry to the apartment complex were reduced to the point where awnings and trees around the building could solve the remaining problem. Once recognized, the solution seems simple. But the method for identifying the solution was revolutionary.

This was the first time designers had studied a scale model of an entire downtown in a wind tunnel for the sole purpose of developing a comprehensive plan that would resolve ground-level wind

FIGURE 3.10
Model of downtown Dayton in wind tunnel used to predict wind problems
and test solutions. Studies of the entire city rather than a single building reveal
that small changes can have unexpected and far-reaching consequences. Air
blowing through spires and across grid simulates wind behavior as it approaches Dayton over the surrounding suburbs.

problems. Wind tunnel studies are rarely undertaken before buildings are designed and constructed. They are most often conducted
when a disastrous wind problem becomes apparent after construction—when doors won't open, when windows pop out, or when
pedestrians are knocked to the ground. A scale model of Prudential
Center near Boston's Copley Square, as well as of places in other
parts of the country, decorate the walls of M.I.T.'s wind tunnel, un-
spoken testament to the commercial, aesthetic, or political disasters
they represent. The Dayton model was six feet across; small enough
to see the city as a whole, but large enough to depict the detail of
sidewalks and streets, parks and plazas. One inch on the model was
equivalent to fifty feet on the ground. All the buildings of Dayton's
downtown were represented in wood, and had been made by two
Dayton park department employees in the city's shop. An assistant

to Dayton's city manager transported these model buildings to Cambridge in suitcases. Students at the Harvard Graduate School of Design mounted the buildings on a round base complete with streets, highways, river, and parks, and even individual trees represented by steel wool on pins. They then used the model to study the effect of different wind conditions and solar orientations on comfort and air quality in downtown Dayton.

Like many cities, Dayton has wide streets and much open land near downtown. Since not all six lanes of downtown streets were required to accommodate traffic, students proposed that median strips and sidewalks be widened and planted with trees. The configuration of street tree planting and the species of trees recommended varied from street to street, reflecting the street's orientation to sun and wind, the width and height of the street canyon, and its importance to traffic and commerce. Students determined the location of trees by reference to maps of sun and wind problems which they had drawn up using the model.

Because parking spaces abounded, parking revenues would not be decreased by adding trees in the lots. There were four different considerations in designing the parking lot plantings: to reduce the force of the winds before they hit the city center; to be equally effective in reducing winds from different directions; to provide shade to the surface of the parking lot; and to avoid trapping pollutants from automobile emissions under the tree canopy. The resulting design was a grid of trees evenly spaced along the periphery and within the parking lot. Planting the trees in a grid rather than in parallel rows would make the trees effective in reducing winds from many directions. The trees were spaced close enough to provide shade but far enough apart to permit ventilation. The design for the parking lot for the southwest varied slightly from that for parking lots to the northwest. The prevailing winds in the summer come from the southwest, so providing shade to the parking lot surface was more important than slowing the wind. The trees in the parking lot to the northwest were spaced further apart, creating a rougher surface and thereby slowing the wind more effectively.

The students presented the results of their semester's work, a master plan for street tree planting in downtown Dayton, to the Downtown Dayton Association, a group of local merchants, businessmen, and interested citizens.[15] They estimated that the cost of installation and maintenance of the trees would be no more than what the merchants currently paid for their streetlighting, an assessment based on the length of street frontage.

The student's plan is only one part of Dayton's climate project. Through an ingenious marshaling of federal funds, grants from private foundations, the expertise of students and faculty at a number of colleges throughout the United States, and the donation of time from many individual city residents, Dayton has put together an impressive constellation of urban climate projects. In 1980 the United States Forest Service lent Dayton a climatologist who studied the city's climate and air quality and assessed its needs. When more data were needed about temperatures in the city, the city manager's office, through appeals on television, organized an army of volunteers throughout the city to record temperatures on particular days at specific times. The resulting information permitted the climatologist to draw conclusions about Dayton's temperature regime with some confidence.

In 1981 the City of Dayton constructed an experimental parking lot composed of turf blocks (a tessellated pavement of grass and concrete—see figure 3.11) rather than the conventional asphalt. The

FIGURE 3.11
Turf-block parking lot. Grass grows in the holes of precast concrete blocks, kept short by traffic. This material absorbs far less heat than asphalt.

turf-block parking lot absorbs and reradiates less heat to adjacent building walls and sidewalks; air temperatures on sunny afternoons over the turf-block parking lot are routinely 4 degrees Fahrenheit cooler than over a nearby asphalt parking lot.[16]

The city has recently embarked upon an experimental highway planting program, and is permitting natural vegetation to regenerate along selected segments of the highways which ring the city. Dayton hopes to filter pollution, reduce highway noise, reduce wind velocities before they reach the downtown, and to provide an attractive gateway into the city. It also hopes to cut maintenance costs, as mowing will not longer be necessary.

In 1980 Dayton launched a newsletter, *International Dayton Line*, to inform other cities about its urban climate project. The newsletter now reaches more than 700 readers, and it has become a clearinghouse for information about cities which are attempting to apply innovative approaches to climate, air quality, and city design. Other U.S. cities like Cincinnati, Buffalo, and Lafayette, Indiana, have been inspired by Dayton's example and have initiated similar programs.

Dayton's climate project was launched by a former city manager after he saw a film documenting the achievement of Stuttgart, West Germany, an industrial city of 630,000. Like many inland valley cities, Stuttgart is plagued by extended periods of weak winds and frequent persistent inversions (247 days per year) which result in dangerous concentrations of air pollutants.[17] For more than three decades, climatologists, city planners, landscape architects, and architects have worked together to implement a bold plan to alleviate the city's air quality problem. The planners of Stuttgart have engineered air circulation on an unprecedented scale. They have directed and diverted air flow through the city and guided the location of industries, highways, and residential districts to benefit air quality and climate. They have implemented a comprehensive plan and coordinated many smaller projects throughout the city.

Having plotted the patterns of air circulation through and around Stuttgart (see figure 3.12), climatologists continue to survey levels of air pollution and dust to pinpoint the most critical areas. Initially, they released smoke to trace the flow of air into the city. More sophisticated techniques, including the use of infrared aerial photographs, are now used to provide the same information. Studies identified undeveloped hillsides above the city as a major source of clean, cool air which flows nightly down ravines into the city. At the time their crucial role in city ventilation was discovered, the wooded hillsides were rapidly being converted to residential suburbs. Because of their importance to the whole community, the city

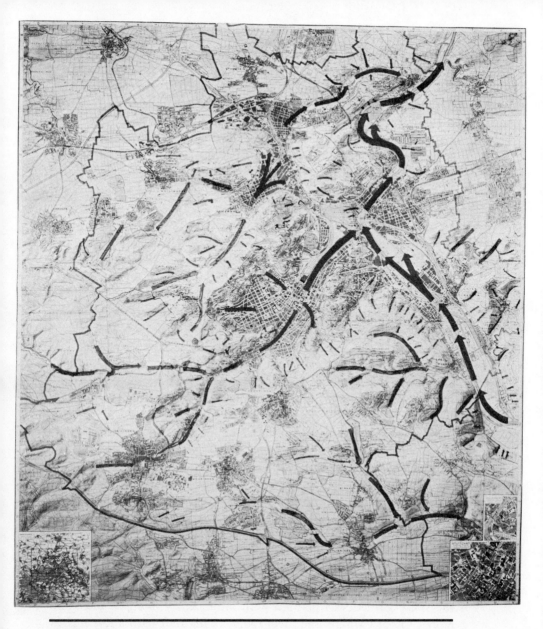

FIGURE 3.12
Air-flow patterns in Stuttgart, Germany. At night, under calm conditions, cool, clean air flows down the hillsides into the city, pushing out hot, dirty air in the downtown.

restricted the development of those hillsides and incorporated them into a radial open space system extending from the rural outskirts of the city to its center. As hot, polluted air rises over the downtown, cool, fresh air is pulled in along the open space corridors to replace it. This air movement is slow and weak, easily dammed by a wall or building and effective only when the velocity of regional winds is less than two meters per second. During the frequent, lengthy periods of low regional winds, this hill-to-valley air movement provides the only ventilation in downtown Stuttgart. It cools the city at night, a time when the city would otherwise be much warmer than the suburbs. Land use within "fresh air channels" is therefore strictly regulated by the city. One hundred meters is the preferred minimum width for these air flow channels, which are planted with grass and trees.

Emission of pollutants in Stuttgart was attacked on several fronts. Inversions normally affect a relatively shallow layer of air over the city. If the chimney stacks of industries, public incinerators, and power plants are tall enough to pierce the top of the inversion layer, their emissions will escape the volume of air trapped near the ground. Municipal incinerators and power plants were consolidated and moved downwind from the city, and tall smoke stacks, 160 to 180 meters high, were installed.[18] Many industries have since followed the city's example. Traffic was banned from poorly ventilated downtown streets. The burning of oil and coal was prohibited in sections of the city where wind velocities are insufficient to flush the air. In these areas, only natural gas is used for cooking; the city provides water warmed by municipal incinerators to heat homes. Together, these efforts have substantially decreased air pollution. Stuttgart has also taken measures to provide more comfortable outdoor spaces and to reduce summer air conditioning costs. Meteorologists and planners on the staff of the Chemical Investigations Office review plans of new buildings to determine their impact on climate and air quality at street level and recommend revisions in building design to improve ventilation and microclimate. The agency recently suggested the widening of several streets in the downtown area to improve air circulation. The Theodorheusstrasse was widened, and the space gained was planted with large, thirty-five-year-old sycamores.[19] Roof gardens and "wet roofs" (a flat roof with a few inches of ponded water) have been introduced to reduce the heat absorbed by buildings. Parking lots have been converted from asphalt to turf blocks to decrease the heat absorbed. The city built shady, landscaped parks, linked to air flow channels wherever possible, to provide pleasant oases, to cool adjacent neighborhoods, and to filter dust from the air. Such efforts have perceptibly improved the microclimate in downtown Stuttgart.

The Stuttgart solution is most applicable to cities with frequent, low winds and persistent inversions. Other cities in Germany have implemented Stuttgart's approach, and those with similar topographic and climatic features have been most successful in its application. By harnessing natural patterns of air flow to ventilate the city and by regulating polluting activities, Stuttgart has transformed itself from a city with poor air quality into a model for the world.

The city of Davis, California, has pioneered multifaceted legislation for energy conservation, including a new building code, ordinances that encourage the use of solar energy systems, and the development of alternative transport to the private automobile. The city decided to concentrate on building construction and transportation, since a survey of residents conducted in the early 1970s had demonstrated that automobiles represented 50 percent of all energy consumption, and space heating and cooling an additional 25 percent. The new building code, developed with the assistance of researchers at the University of California, Davis, regulates both the siting and design of new buildings, including solar orientation, insulation, amount of window area, exterior roof and wall colors, and overhang shading. Prior to the building code, most homes were built with air conditioning. With improved design, residents now find air conditioning unnecessary.

Davis has explored many ways of reducing automobile use. The city council decided to develop a system of bikeways in 1968, and since that time has introduced convenient, low-cost public transportation. By encouraging cottage industry, the city also hopes to reduce commuting.

The Davis experiment has proved highly successful. A small city of 33,000 people, Davis was able to explore, implement, and test techniques for energy conservation which may now be adapted to larger cities. Since energy conservation decreases both waste heat and pollutants, improved climatic comfort—a result of careful siting and housing design—and improved air quality—a result of decreased automobile traffic—are important by-products of the Davis plan.

A Plan for Every City

Both the Stuttgart plan and Paley Park affect the microclimate and air quality at street level. Stuttgart's is a grand scheme; it affects an entire city and captures the imagination. Paley Park is a modest project; it improves the microclimate of one small space, but delights those who use it. Although the impact of the grand scheme is greater, its scale is daunting and may not be replicable in another city. The modest project can be readily repeated in infinite variations, adapted to the special character of other places.

An understanding of the climatic and air pollution patterns of the city as a whole should underlie every project, whether ambitious or modest. A city's regional climate, topographic setting, pollution sources, and urban form determine its most critical problems of climate and air quality. Specific phenomena, their spatial patterns, and relative importance vary from city to city. Are long, cold winters a problem, or hot, dry summers? Too much wind or too little? Susceptibility to regional or local inversions? Large, industrial polluters upwind of the city, or the accumulation of automobile exhaust within the city? Identifying the major sources of air pollution within the city, the dispersion patterns of pollutants, and areas like valley bottoms and narrow street canyons that are prone to inversions will aid in singling out the most severely contaminated places. Plotting daily temperature variations within the city, including "hot spots" and "cool spots" will identify some of the city's most uncomfortable places and also may help to predict thermal breezes. Knowing the pattern of air movement around and within the city will permit its use as a resource to help disperse pollutants and enhance comfort and energy conservation. The daily and seasonal variation of air movement, including the direction, speed, and frequency of regional winds, as well as of valley, shore, and other thermally induced breezes, is potentially of great importance, particularly during episodes of stagnant weather.

Comprehensive strategies to improve air quality, enhance comfort, and conserve energy for heating and air conditioning through urban form should:

- address the city's most critical climatic and air pollution problems, with particular attention directed to the improvement of conditions in the most severely contaminated and the most uncomfortable areas
- investigate alternative modes of transportation and sources of energy that would curtail air pollution and explore settlement patterns that would facilitate their implementation
- encourage new industry, public utilities, and highways to locate in well-ventilated areas where they will not contaminate residential and commercial neighborhoods under prevailing wind or inversion conditions
- locate parks and other landscaped open space to preserve fresh air flow into the city, to enhance ventilation, and to dilute and remove pollutants
- exploit the potential of large-scale tree planting within the city to offset the heat island effect in summertime and to mitigate wind problems.

Every new building, street, highway, and park within the city should be designed to avoid detrimental alterations to the climate and air quality of the surrounding area and whenever possible to improve them. Every project, however modest, should:

- address the relationship of its location to the critical climate and air quality problems of the city as a whole as well to those of the site and its immediate neighborhood
- exploit those aspects of the citywide and local climate that can be used to resolve the above problems
- locate new playgrounds, bicycle paths, jogging or walking trails, and sitting areas away from arterial streets, highways, and other air pollution sources
- maintain a setback from major streets and highways based upon traffic volume and prevailing wind directions
- exploit opportunities for passive energy conservation in the design and siting of buildings and parks
- orient buildings, streets, and parks to funnel desired breezes and block unwanted winds
- utilize building and landscape materials to create a desirable microclimate—to capture or reduce heat absorption and to increase or decrease wind velocity.

Every city must weigh the consequences of ignoring climatic concerns and the potential benefits of a comfortable city with cleaner air against the costs of implementing such strategies. To change the climate or even the ventilation pattern within an entire city is an overwhelming and ambitious undertaking. It has been done, but it is likely to be attempted only in cities where air pollution is a public health problem of enormous and widely recognized significance, as in Stuttgart. The potential impact and opportunity is greatest in new or fast-growing cities with a predictable or severe air pollution problem, like Tucson, Arizona, or Denver, Colorado. Unchecked development in Tucson and Denver will have disastrous consequences for health. Sorely needed are carefully laid plans for future urban growth including the search for alternatives to the private automobile as well as the careful siting of industry and highways in relation to residential districts and to topographic features favoring pollution dispersion.

For older cities, or those with less severe problems, it is more feasible to change the city's climate piecemeal, as parts of the city are altered or rebuilt. Here, it is more practical to focus on the most critical areas in the city: the most uncomfortable and most contaminated places and the most important public spaces or those used by the most people. These can be redesigned to make them healthier, more comfortable in summer and winter, and to extend their use earlier into spring and later into fall. The knowledge and technology exist; the costs for incremental improvement, when combined with new construction, are small. The social and economic costs of disregard are great.

PART III

Earth

CHAPTER 4

Shifting Ground and Squandered Resources

CITIES are fragile creations balanced on the earth's crust, exposed to the slow but inexorable pace of erosion and sedimentation, vulnerable to every tremor of the violent forces beneath, and dependent upon dwindling mineral resources. The scope of geological time dwarfs human memory and permits the illusion that man is in control. The intermittent nature of cataclysmic events invites complacency. The results of geological processes are best appreciated by an overview spanning many human lifetimes.

The decline of many ancient cities is now credited to geological as well as social forces: to sedimentation and soil salinization; to repeated earthquakes, landslides, and subsidence; to depletion of resources. In building and maintaining cities, human beings have assumed a dominant role as geological agents. The topography of cities is constantly modified. Hills are leveled; low-lying basins are filled; waterways are dredged. Buildings create a new topography, and pavement a new ground surface. Holes drilled for wells, foundations, and tunnels make a new direct connection between ground surface and buried bedrock. Undertaken for the benefit of society, these activities may accelerate or trigger geological forces and precipitate disaster. Mexico City has sunk twenty-five feet, at times as much as two feet per year. Groundwater withdrawal is the cause. Groundwater withdrawal has also caused thirty square miles of Tokyo Bay to sink seven feet below sea level, exposing the two million people who live there to devastating floods and typhoons. Irrigation and seepage from water mains and cesspools can trigger massive landslides on unstable slopes, burying houses and snapping water, gas, and electric lines. Cities degrade or destroy the geological resources on which they depend. The city grows in response to economic and social pressures with little regard for the minerals which lie beneath it. The result is often increased costs when resources become inaccessible or depleted and must then be imported.

Although knowledge of city geology is extensive, it is customarily employed mainly to short-term advantage: to design and construct foundations for buildings and highways; to exploit those minerals which the current market values; and to patch damage from landslides, subsidence, and earthquakes after the fact. It is too seldom applied to the prevention of disaster, to the preservation of mineral resources for future generations, and to the safe disposal of urban wastes. Increased hazards, squandered resources, and increased costs to every city resident are the result.

Shifting Ground

The solidity of the earth is an illusion. At any moment, large blocks of "solid" ground may crack, heave, flow, slide, swell, or sink. It is mainly through ground movement that geological forces cause death and destruction. Geological hazards are a multibillion-dollar problem. Earthquakes, landslides, erosion, swelling soil, volcanic eruptions, and subsidence will cost $32 billion between 1970 and the year 2000 in the state of California alone.[1] The hazards increase when man is unwise enough to occupy particularly unstable land or to activate a dormant process. Cities are more vulnerable than the countryside to earthquakes, landslides, subsidence, and other hazards. When catastrophic events occur in densely settled areas, risk of personal injury and property damage is intensified.

Earthquakes topple buildings, crumple pavement, and sever gas, water, and telephone lines. Earthquakes killed 350,000 people and caused $10 million in property damage worldwide during the twenty-five-year period between 1926 and 1950.[2] Damage and deaths from earthquakes increase in cities with dense populations and buildings. The great earthquakes of the past, like the San Francisco earthquake of 1906, would be even more destructive in today's densely populated large, cities. However, the potential hazard is

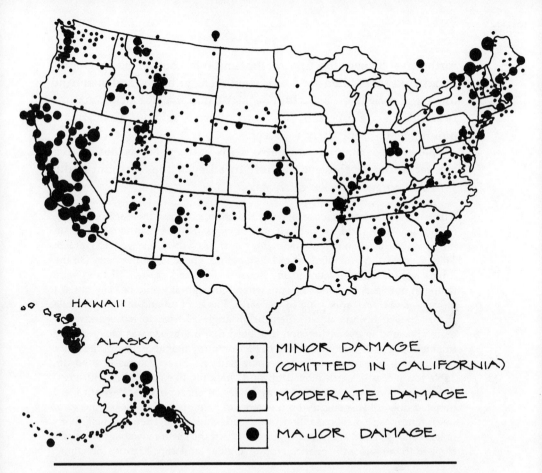

MINOR DAMAGE
(OMITTED IN CALIFORNIA)

MODERATE DAMAGE

MAJOR DAMAGE

FIGURE 4.1
Map of damaging earthquakes recorded in the United States, showing dense clusters along the Pacific coast, around Boston and in southeastern Missouri.

particularly great in cities like Boston or Charleston, South Carolina, where the risk of earthquakes is unrecognized by most residents. Although seismic activity is greater and earthquakes more frequent in Seattle, San Francisco, and Los Angeles, Boston and Charleston have also had major earthquakes and are at risk of others in the future (see figure 4.1). Some geologists feel that nineteenth-century earthquakes in Missouri were among the largest ever to occur within the United States. Three earthquakes in 1811 and 1812 changed the course of the Mississippi River: "The whole land was moved and waved like the waves of the sea with the explosions and bursting of the ground, large fissures were formed, some of which closed immediately, while others were of varying widths, as much as 30 feet," wrote a contemporary observer.[3]

Some areas within a city are at much higher risk than others. Most earthquake damage occurs on the unstable soils of steep slopes, floodplains, and filled land, on or adjacent to active faults, and in low-lying coastal areas. Building construction is also a factor: masonry buildings are especially prone to collapse, whereas wood-frame buildings are particularly resistant.

The ground shaking associated with earthquakes is destructive and terrifying, as conveyed vividly by an eyewitness account to the 1964 Anchorage, Alaska, earthquake:

I had just started to practice playing the trumpet when the earthquake occurred. In a few short moments it was obvious that this earthquake was no minor one: the chandelier, made from a ship's wheel, swayed too much. Things were falling that had never fallen before. I headed for the door. On the driveway I turned and watched my house squirm and groan. Tall trees were falling in our yard. I moved to a spot where I thought it would be safe, but as I moved I saw cracks appearing in the earth. Pieces of ground in jigsaw puzzle shapes moved up and down, tilted at all angles. I tried to move away, but more appeared in every direction. I noticed that my house was moving away from me, fast. As I started to climb the fence to my neighbor's yard, the fence disappeared. Trees were falling in crazy patterns. Deep chasms opened up. Table top pieces of earth moved upward, standing like toadstools with great overhangs. Some would turn at crazy angles. A chasm opened beneath me. I tumbled down. I was quickly on the verge of being buried. I ducked pieces of trees, fenceposts, mailboxes, and other odds and ends. Then my neighbor's house collapsed and slid into the chasm. When the earth movement stopped I climbed to the top of the chasm. I found angular landscape in every direction.[4]

The intensity of this ground shaking in the suburb of Turnagain Heights was due not only to the earthquake's magnitude and the proximity of the author to an active fault, but also to the instability of the underlying soil. The ground shakes with several times more intensity on thick deposits of saturated sediments than on bedrock. Ground shaking may also cause fine-grained soils to liquefy, and may initiate landslides on steep slopes. In the 1964 earthquake in Niigata, Japan, entire high-rise apartments built on alluvium toppled as the liquefied soil flowed out from under them. Such high-risk areas are predictable. Turnagain Heights had been identified by a report published five years prior to the earthquake as an area of great hazard, but unfortunately, the report went unread by all but geologists. Buildings on landfills over former bay and marshlands sustained the most damage in the San Francisco earthquake of 1906, while buildings on bedrock received only slight damage. The eastern parts of San Francisco, built upon reclaimed land, are still among the areas of highest future risk. The state of California estimates that ground shaking will probably cause more than $21 billion in damages between 1970 and 2000, far exceeding the losses from any other geological hazard in that state.[5]

The 1906 San Francisco earthquake displaced ground twenty feet along parts of the San Andreas Fault. Stream channels were changed, houses split, and utilities snapped. The ground along a fault line may move horizontally or vertically; it may creep gradually or move rapidly and violently. Forty-two feet is the maximum displacement recorded during a single earthquake.[6] Houses, schools, and hospitals built immediately on or adjacent to an active fault risk damage from ground displacement—even a movement of one inch can have a catastrophic effect. Many housing developments, public buildings, hospitals, and schools in California are located astride active faults. As of 1969, two hospitals and nine schools sat atop the Hayward Fault between the cities of Berkeley and Hayward, California.[7] Movement along fault lines ruptures gas, water, and sewer pipes, creating health and fire hazards after an earthquake.

Ninety percent of the deaths from the 1964 Alaska earthquake were caused by tsunamis, sea waves generated by earthquakes or volcanic eruptions. Tsunamis may reach heights of over 100 feet and, traveling at 400 to 500 miles per hour, may reach distant coastlines within hours. When tsunamis hit low-lying coastal areas, they may drive a mile or more inland and up to twenty-seven feet or more above sea level, destroying everything in their path.[8] Tsunamis may be generated by earthquakes thousands of miles away. Waves originating from the 1946 Alaskan earthquake devastated the coastal areas of Hilo, Hawaii, smashing houses facing Hilo Bay, ripping railroad tracks, burying coastal highways, and washing parts of a steel railroad bridge nearly one thousand feet inland. The catastrophe, which came without warning, cost Hawaii 159 lives and $25 million in property damage.[9]

The San Fernando earthquake of 1971 struck a heavily populated part of California, costing sixty-five lives and $500 million in property damage. Fortunately, the earthquake came in the early morning hours; a few hours later, the loss of life would have been far more devastating. Masonry buildings constructed before 1933 sustained the most damage, although newer structures designed according to more recent building codes were also damaged. Forty-four people were killed at the Sylmar Veterans' Hospital (figure 4.2) when the central structures, built in 1926 of unreinforced masonry, collapsed "like smashed orange crates."[10] The outer structures of the hospital, built in 1937 and 1947, postdated improved building codes and sustained little damage. Older school buildings were also damaged and

FIGURE 4.2
Veterans' Administration Hospital in Sylmar, California, damaged by San Fernando earthquake of 1971. The smashed central structures were built in 1926; the intact outer structures were built later, after building codes required earthquake-resistant construction. (Photo: *Los Angeles Times*)

condemned as a result, but even buildings constructed according to the most up-to-date building codes were seriously damaged. Three five-story staircases at the newly dedicated Olive View Hospital pulled away from the main building and collapsed. Freeways and overpasses throughout the San Fernando area cracked and collapsed. Water lines were broken in 1,400 places.[11] Coming after nearly forty years of improved seismic building codes, the destruction caused by the San Fernando earthquake was sobering.

Many existing buildings in earthquake-prone cities will not survive a major earthquake. Even a moderate earthquake will destroy flimsy structures. If homes, hospitals, and schools continue to be built in hazardous areas, if unsound buildings are not strengthened and architectural details like cornices and parapets not removed or supported, if brittle utility lines are not replaced with more flexible ones, and if old or unsound dams and reservoirs are not strengthened, then future earthquake damage in cities will be catastrophic.

Landslides are more widespread and more frequent than earthquakes, with damage in the United States amounting to more than $1 billion annually.[12] During the winter of 1977–78, landslides caused $50 million in damage within the city of Los Angeles alone.[13] Landslides occur on steep slopes and on gentle ones, and consist of falls, slumps, slides, and flows that can cover an entire town in minutes or take years to creep down the slope.

Sites of ancient slides thousands of years old, in precarious equilibrium, will move again if disturbed. Landslides may be triggered by natural events such as earthquakes, groundwater seepage, or abundant rainfall, but in cities they are usually caused by human activities: by steepening slopes, by overloading or undercutting unstable slopes, and by altering groundwater conditions. Fill for a backyard or a new street, lawn watering, and the infiltration of sewage effluent from septic tanks or leaky sewer mains can each convert a relatively stable slope to a slide. Ninety percent of landslides in California and in Allegheny County, Pennsylvania, for instance, have been attributed to human activity.[14]

In the 1960s a California court declared a landslide as an Act of Man rather than an Act of God, holding the Los Angeles County Highway Department responsible for reactivating an ancient landslide in Portuguese Bend and awarding damages to an association of homeowners. The residents had built houses on this old landslide in the early 1950s. Water from lawn irrigation and effluent from cesspools probably increased the instability of the slope, setting the stage for a major slide. When, in 1956, the Los Angeles County Highway Department was constructing a new highway upslope from Portuguese Bend, the entire 100-acre slope began to move. As the slope moved, water and drainage pipes broke, lubricating the slide. Eighteen years later, the slide had moved 230 feet. It continues to move downslope nearly 10 feet per year and there are now few houses left. At one time the slide could have been prevented; the cost of halting it is now estimated at $10 million.[15]

Swelling soils are the most costly and widespread of geological hazards in the United States. They crack building foundations and walls, and heave city streets and sidewalks: a 3 percent increase in soil volume damages foundations; some swelling soils expand more than 50 percent. Cost of repair to a damaged structure may equal half the initial construction cost. Damage to a twelve-year-old junior

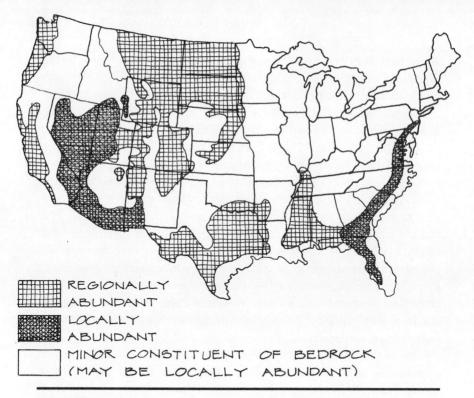

REGIONALLY ABUNDANT

LOCALLY ABUNDANT

MINOR CONSTITUENT OF BEDROCK (MAY BE LOCALLY ABUNDANT)

FIGURE 4.3
Map showing areas of the United States prone to swelling soils. Inflicting more property damage each year than any other natural hazard, swelling soils are nevertheless a frequently unrecognized problem.

high school in Denver, for example, cost taxpayers nearly half of the initial cost of $1.5 million.[16]

Each year, shrinking or swelling soils inflict at least $2.3 billion in damages to houses, buildings, roads, and pipelines—more than twice the damage from floods, hurricanes, tornadoes, and earthquakes! . . . Within the average American lifetime, 14 percent of our land will be ravaged by earthquakes, tornadoes, and floods—but over 20 percent will be affected by expansive soil movements. . . . Over 250,000 new homes are built on expansive soils each year. Sixty percent will experience only minor damage during their useful life, but 10 percent will experience significant damage—some beyond repair. . . . One person in ten is affected by floods; but one in five by expansive soils.[17]

Swelling clays underlie over 20 percent of the land in the United States (see figure 4.3), including all of Colorado's major cities. Cities like Denver with pronounced dry and wet seasons, where soil moisture fluctuates widely, have the greatest problems of swelling soil because expansive clay soils shrink and swell in response to moisture. Most city skyscrapers have well-engineered foundations, but

TOTAL SUBSIDENCE
IN FEET

FIGURE 4.4
View of Long Beach, California, showing degree of ground subsidence since 1920 caused by oil and gas extraction. Numerals indicate how many feet ground has sunk. Parts of the harbor have sunk twenty-nine feet and are now well below sea level, protected from flooding by expensive levees.

many homes, schools, and small commercial structures are built on swelling soils without proper precautions.

Over decades, the ground under an entire metropolitan region may gradually collapse. A single building or street may disappear in a sinkhole overnight. Ground subsidence is usually a direct effect of human activities—the pumping of gas, oil, and groundwater; underground mining of coal or stone; and building on unconsolidated landfill. Long Beach, California, has sunk twenty-nine feet (figure 4.4); Houston, Texas, ten feet; and Mexico City, up to twenty-five feet, occasionally at a rate of two feet per year. The extraction of underground oil, gas, and water decreases the pressure in the rocks underneath these cities, causing them to compact. In inland cities, damage is confined mainly to structural foundations and utilities. In coastal cities the results may be catastrophic. Much of Long Beach was initially only five to ten feet in elevation, so the twenty-nine-foot subsidence placed much of the area below sea level. Port facilities, streets, and industries were inundated at high tide. Pipelines buckled, and foundations sheared. The damage was remedied but at tremendous cost. Sea walls and levees were built to restrain the ocean and some structures were raised, at a total cost of more than $100 million.[18] Venice, Italy, built on sandbars only a few feet above sea level, has long been plagued by flooding. Groundwater withdrawal by industry on the nearby mainland has accelerated the subsidence of Venice during this century and has aggravated an already severe flood hazard. Portions of Venice are now submerged at high tide, and, in 1966, storm tides flooded 80 percent of the city, damaging its architecture and destroying much of its art. After the 1966 flood, groundwater pumping was halted and plans undertaken to stabilize subsidence. Thirty square miles of Tokyo along Tokyo Bay have subsided up to seven feet below sea level, also a result of ground water withdrawal. The city built dikes around the entire area and restricted groundwater pumping, but the two million people who live in East Tokyo are still threatened by the storm waves of typhoons and tsunamis and by potential failure of the dikes during an earthquake.[19]

Many cities, like Denver and Pittsburgh, grew up in mining regions and have since expanded over old mines. Unfortunately, old mine maps are often inaccurate and rarely show the actual extent of mining; many of these old mines were insufficiently shored and are now unstable. Buildings, streets, and utilities fall into holes when the ground collapses over mined-out areas beneath. In 1977, a two-car garage in Youngstown, Ohio, disappeared when the ground over a 230-foot mine shaft collapsed; twenty-three houses were damaged or destroyed in 1963 when the ground fell in over a mine in Pennsylvania.[20]

Sudden ground collapse also occurs in cities underlain by limestone. Sinkholes develop where portions of the limestone underneath are dissolved by water, frequently as a result of human activities like water withdrawal and leaky water and sewage pipes. In the state of Alabama alone, humans have induced 4,000 sinkholes since 1900.[21]

As cities grow, they expand onto land reclaimed from former marshes and swamps and old building sites and garbage dumps. In coastal cities like Boston, half the downtown may have been constructed on filled land, whose stability depends upon its content and the length of time it has been in place. Garbage, rubble, and the wood of old wharves and sunken boats decompose at different rates and may cause subsidence for many years. In the San Francisco Bay area, one-third of the original bay has been filled since 1849.[22] The original fill consisted of rubbish, old ships, and building rubble whose differential settlement soon induced cracking, tipping, and collapse of buildings. Between 1864 and 1964 the fill along Market Street in San Francisco settled almost nine feet. Whole cities or parts of cities in the Netherlands and Japan are built on land reclaimed by fill. Tilted buildings supported by buttresses, a common sight in Amsterdam, are evidence of settlement in the water-saturated fill beneath them.

Unstable ground underlies parts of all cities, but it is not evenly distributed from city to city and country to country. The type and formation of rocks beneath the city, its physiographic setting and historic growth, and the location, design, and materials of its buildings, streets, and utilities all determine the extent of the hazards to which a city's residents are exposed. Unfortunately, geological hazards rarely occur in isolation. Cities prone to earthquakes, for example, often have a constellation of other geological problems, including landslides and subsidence.

Squandered Resources

Mineral resources are nonrenewable, and high-quality deposits which may be extracted economically are limited. They are not evenly distributed across the landscape; the result of ancient geological processes, their location is highly variable, but predictable. The importance of oil, gas, coal, and metal ores is widely recognized, but it is not well known that the second largest mining business in the United States is actually the quarrying of sand and gravel. Cities use sand, gravel, and crushed stone in enormous quantities. Together, these materials comprise 95 percent of the asphalt on roads and parking lots, and 75 percent of the concrete used for foundations, buildings, and sidewalks. An ordinary house requires 50–100 tons of sand and gravel. In the United States, per capita use of sand and gravel in 1970 was five tons.[23]

Many cities are ignorant of their aggregate resources, lost unwittingly under homes and streets. Other communities are aware of their undeveloped resources, but are unwilling to permit their exploitation. Quarry operations and local communities are usually at odds; upon occasion every town in a metropolitan region passes an ordinance prohibiting new quarries. The consequences of such attitudes are borne by all, directly, through the increased cost of a new house, or indirectly, through higher taxes for road construction and maintenance.

Transportation accounts for most of the cost of sand, gravel, and crushed stone. Transporting sand or aggregates from twenty miles further away doubles the cost, and thirty-four miles is generally the maximum economically feasible distance for hauling sand and gravel.[24] Thus the most valuable deposits, those nearest the city, are also those most in conflict with urbanization. In Denver, Colorado, 58 percent of the sand and gravel resources within fifteen miles of downtown Denver are inaccessible either because they have been built upon or because they are too close to existing homes to permit mining.[25] California estimates that the loss of sand and gravel resources to urbanization will cost the state $17 billion between 1970 and the year 2000 (nearly three times the estimated losses from floods), a figure based on increased transportation costs, the cost of relocating mining operations, and the cost of additional processing necessitated by the use of lower grade deposits.[26]

Contaminated and Compacted Land

The earth is increasingly a repository of poisonous residues. Hazardous wastes and garbage are buried in the ground—invisible, but with far-reaching effects. Toxic dust and soot from city air settle on soil; heavy metals from residues of gasoline and oil, pulverized rubber from car tires, and salts from de-icing compounds poison soils near streets. Pesticides and paint residues contaminate soil around buildings and on vacant lots; toxic wastes contaminate soils of industrial sites and dumps.

The earth has always served as a receptacle for human waste, and modern cities that occupy the sites of ancient cities are built on the mounds of their predecessors' garbage. Finding an appropriate site for garbage has been a perennial problem of cities, as testified by an inscription on a wall at Aphrodiasias (ca A.D. 325): "Whoever throws rubbish here shall incur the curse of the 318 fathers," [27] but that problem is now intensified by the magnitude of urban waste and its toxicity. Three-quarters of the garbage generated daily in the United States is collected in open dumps, where it is burned or piled up.[28] Such dumps pose a health hazard not only during their operation, but for many years afterward. Water which seeps into the ground and through the dump has contaminated groundwater; methane gas, which forms when organic material decomposes, reaches dangerous concentrations when unvented and explodes, and, together with carbon dioxide, poisons plants. But it is the disposal of hazardous wastes that has become one of the most pressing issues of modern times. Countless old dump sites are buried beneath the surface of many cities, especially in older industrial areas. Where these dumps harbor toxic chemicals and radioactive materials and where homes and schools have been built upon them, there have been tragic consequences: increased miscarriages and birth defects, and progressive respiratory and nervous disorders among children and adults. Nor do the contaminants always remain localized; they are frequently transported by water and air to affect a far larger population (see chapter 12).

The toxicity of streetside soils may not be as contaminated as those of old industrial dumps, but they are far more prevalent (see table 4.1). The soil adjacent to a busy city street may contain thirty times the lead of a nonroadside soil in its upper five centimeters (two inches).[29] Distribution of lead in roadside soil is determined by the same factors that influence the concentration of lead in roadside air:

TABLE 4.1

Concentration of Elements in Urbana, Illinois,
Street Dust

Element	μg/g	Element	μg/g
Manganese	350 ± 30	Uranium	3.5 ± 0.7
Zinc	320 ± 30	Samarium	3.4 ± 0.5
Barium	310 ± 54	Calcium	2.7 ± 0.5%
Nickel	250 ± 60	Antimony	2.2 ± 0.3
Strontium	250 ± 50	Cadmium	1.6 ± 0.2
Chromium	210 ± 20	Dysprosium	1.6 ± 0.2
Zirconium	120 ± 14	Cesium	1.1 ± 0.2
Bromine	84 ± ?	Selenium	1.0 ± 0.3
Cerium	29 ± 1	Ytterbium	1.0 ± 0.2
Rubidium	29 ± 5	Potassium	0.94 ± 0.13%
Arsenic	11 ± 1	Sodium	0.53 ± 0.05%
Lanthanum	10 ± 1	Terbium	0.44 ± 0.13
Cobalt	6.8 ± 0.4	Europium	0.4 ± 0.03
Iron	6.2 ± 0.5%	Silver	0.2 ± 0.09
Hafnium	5.0 ± 0.5	Lutetium	0.16 ± 0.4
Gallium	4.9 ± 0.9	Lead	0.1 ± 0.02%
Thorium	4.3 ± 0.3	Mercury	0.09 ± 0.008
Scandium	4.2 ± 0.3		

SOURCE: Philip K. Hopke, Robert E. Lamb, and David F. S. Natusch, "Multi-elemental Characterization of Urban Roadway Dust," *Environmental Science and Technology* 14 (1980):165.

traffic volume and speed, distance from the road, and wind speed and direction. Some effect extends up to 250 meters (820 feet) from the road, but the greatest influence is within 50 meters (164 feet), and the first 10 meters (33 feet) are by far the most contaminated.[30] Salt is another common contaminant of roadside soils in cities where salt or calcareous sand is applied to icy pavement in winter. Road salt has contaminated groundwater supplies and killed street trees in many New England communities.

The contamination of soils around houses is a serious problem, especially in cities with many wooden buildings. Because urban yards are small, play areas and vegetable gardens are frequently very close to the buildings; old building sites transformed into playgrounds or urban gardens may contain toxic soils. In 1977 a survey of garden soils in Boston found lead levels of 200 to 4000 parts per million in two-thirds of the sixty-four gardens tested.[31] Samples taken from backyard gardens, neighborhood garden plots, and playgrounds averaged 800 parts of lead per million. These are frightening statistics in light of studies that have found observable increases in children's blood lead levels when they are exposed to soil or dust of more than 1,000 parts per million.[32] The Boston study identified four environments likely to contain high soil lead: areas adjacent to major streets; areas adjacent to wooden structures painted with lead paint; vacant lots on the site of old wooden structures; and garden soil amended with sewage sludge containing lead.

FIGURE 4.5
The compaction of city soils retards water infiltration and drainage, inhibits gas exchange, creates an oxygen-deficient environment, eliminates soil organisms, prevents root growth, and increases thermal conductivity.

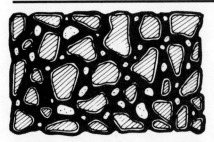
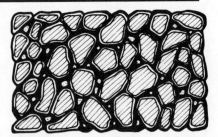

UNCOMPACTED SOIL   COMPACTED SOIL

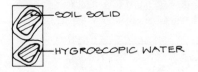 SOIL SOLID

HYGROSCOPIC WATER

 CAPILLARY WATER

 SOIL AIR (N, O, CO_2)

Not only contamination but compaction of city soils deprives the city of resources (see figure 4.5). The density of city soils is one of the primary reasons for the demise of trees in city parks and streets, and one of the least recognized. The weight of the buildings, pavement, vehicles, and people compacts the soils beneath them, affecting even the soils of city parks. Compaction increases the amount of heat that soils absorb and store, reduces the movement of air and water through the soil, inhibits the growth of plant roots, and exterminates the soil organisms which make nutrients available to plants. An ideal soil for plant growth is half soil minerals and humus and half pore space filled with water and air. Continuous large and small pores are critical for the free movement of water, air, and soil organisms through the soil. Pore space is drastically reduced in the typical, compacted urban soil, amounting to only 13 percent of the total soil volume. Thousands of tourists have trampled the upper layers of soil on the Mall in Washington, D.C., to the density of concrete.[33]

Urban soils are an ignored resource. The Soil Conservation Service has meticulously mapped and described soils throughout the United States, but these surveys typically stop at the limits of urbanization, with all urban soils designated as "urban land." The use of a single label for urban soils belies their primary characteristic: heterogeneity. Neglect of urban soils leads to expensive and embarrassing blunders (see figure 4.6).

The risk of geological hazards and the loss of geological resources are among the best documented and most widely recognized problems of the urban natural environment. Yet 90 percent of the deaths and half of the property damage from earthquakes could be prevented with current technology. Similarly, 95 to 99 percent of damages from landslides and all damages from swelling soils could be prevented with better planning and proper design and construction. Most sand and gravel resources could be saved if they were protected until they could be exploited.

Nevertheless, current policy and practice in most cities intensify hazards and accelerate losses. Hospitals, schools, and homes are built on or near active faults, high-rise apartment complexes and office buildings on unstable soils that will liquefy during earthquakes. Homes and highways are developed on ancient landslide deposits and landscaped with plants requiring irrigation. Buildings destroyed by earthquakes and landslides are reconstructed on the same spot, setting the stage for yet another disaster. Entire metropolitan regions are subsiding, exposing whole populations to flood risk and

a

FIGURE 4.6
Taken over a period of twelve years, this series of photographs demonstrates
the fate of an award-winning landscape design that failed to take account of
underlying soil and drainage conditions. Widespread disregard for urban soils
accounts for poor survival rates of urban street trees and landscaping.

b

c

d

building damage. New buildings and streets are planned on land that contains valuable sand and gravel deposits; houses surround quarries. Homes and schools are built atop old dumps containing hazardous wastes; and vegetable gardens and playgrounds are located on contaminated soils.

In the third century B.C., Hammurabi of Babylon prescribed strict punishment for builders who failed their responsibilities:

If a builder build a house for a man and do not make its construction firm, and the house which he has built collapse and cause the death of the owner of the house, that builder shall be put to death. . . . If it destroy property, he shall restore whatever it destroyed, and because he did not make the house firm and it collapsed, he shall rebuild the house which collapsed at his own expense.[34]

It is no longer always possible to trace responsibility for a disaster to a single individual. The responsibility today is a collective one. Resistance to land use regulation and stricter building codes is common; the cost is borne by all.

CHAPTER 5

Finding Firm Ground
and Exploiting Resources

THE EARTH supports homes, highways, factories, and the city's lines of communication and energy, and nurtures plants and the food that sustains the city. Every nation and thus ultimately every city depends upon geological resources for fuel, metals, precious minerals, and building materials, and exploits the ability of the earth to accommodate, and in some cases cleanse, wastes.

The builders of ancient cities often exploited the form of the land to secure their protection and to enhance their society's monuments. Their skill, exemplified in the situation of the Acropolis in Athens, is admired today. The limestone, brick, or granite particular to a given locale have a characteristic color and lend themselves to specific building forms by virtue of their strength, size, and shape. Cities built from local stone have a distinctive identity: the limestone of Jerusalem and Paris, the red brick of old Philadelphia, the granite of Edinburgh.

The information needed to protect a city from geological hazards and to conserve and restore its resources is more readily available today than ever before. The processes by which geological hazards arise and the ways in which they are intensified by human activities are well understood. The location of both geological hazards and geological resources is easily identified, their relative risk and value easily assessed. Effective means of preventing or mitigating loss, including the wise location of land uses, the careful design and construction of buildings, streets, and landscaping, have been tried and proven. The city of Los Angeles, for example, has pioneered a grading ordinance aimed at preventing landslide damage. The California State Geologist's Office has developed an Urban Geology Master Plan that is a model for other states and communities. The U.S. Geological Survey has demonstrated the application of geology to city design in many case studies throughout the country. The experience exists, it need only be tapped. All cities have the responsibility for the conservation of building materials and the restoration of derelict land; some cities must also preserve other mineral resources and protect themselves from single or multiple geological hazards.

Forces of Earth, Water, and Gravity

The shape of the land, its stability, and the nature and location of the resources it harbors are determined by both forces which erupt from within the earth and forces that operate on the earth's crust. Those within the earth are nearly always beyond human control, their mystery not wholly unraveled; in contrast, the forces of water and gravity which mold the surface are readily altered by human activities.

Huge plates consisting of entire continents ride the globe. In constant motion, they collide or split; earthquakes and volcanoes on the sea floor and at the surface are common features of the plate boundaries. The distribution of major earthquakes traces these boundaries, on the Pacific coast of North and South America and along the line of islands which border the coast of Asia, as well as in other parts of the world (figure 5.1). Areas at most risk to earthquakes and volcanic eruptions are predictable; such areas can only be avoided or their damage mitigated.

Water and gravity together wear down the earth's surface, eroding hills, transporting sediments, filling valleys, and extending shorelines. An understanding of how and where these processes occurred in the past permits geologists to predict the location of related mineral resources, like sand and gravel deposits, oil, and natural gas. Humans frequently augment the force of water and gravity, accelerating erosion and triggering landslides. Yet human effect need not be detrimental; with a little knowledge, water and gravity can be managed to human benefit. Many hillsides, clay soils, and certain terrains are in precarious equilibrium. In each case it is necessary to

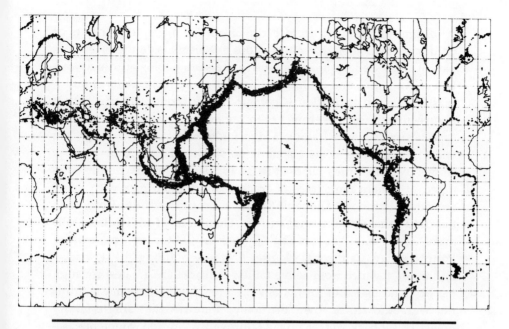

FIGURE 5.1
Principal earthquake zones of the world. Each dot on this map represents an earthquake; together they clearly delineate borders of continental plates along which earthquakes commonly occur. All of Japan and most of Central America lie within earthquake zones.

understand the factors that can maintain and enhance stability. In landslide-prone areas, for example, stability is enhanced by draining the hillside, maintaining a dense cover of plants, and by avoiding the creation of steep slopes.

The locations of geological hazards and resources are usually well known, and maps easily obtained or prepared. While many hazards can be overcome or mitigated only by expensive structural engineering, less costly measures based on an understanding of earth processes can be equally successful, especially if considered in early stages of planning and design.

Finding Firm Ground

Hazards can be prevented, mitigated, or avoided by proper siting, construction, and building design. Every city should know the hazards to which it is subject, the most hazardous places, and how many people are at risk.

To diminish the risk from earthquakes, for example, the state of California mandates that cities adopt a "seismic safety element" as part of their General Plans, requires the state geologist to map certain active faults, and prohibits construction on these faults of buildings for human habitation (Geologic Hazard Zones Act of 1972). It also requires local governments to review all developments within "special study zones" along active faults one-quarter mile or less wide.[1] Designating a fault zone is no simple matter. Faults are not single, discrete "lines" across the landscape, but are frequently composed of a main fault trace of cracked and broken rock with many secondary branches. The fault "zone" may vary in width from a few hundred to many thousands of feet. Thousands of individual faults make up the San Andreas Fault System in California. The town of Portola Valley, California, requires that new buildings be set back a minimum distance from active faults.[2] Setbacks are greatest for high density land uses and for faults whose precise location and width is not well known. A town ordinance requires that single-family homes be set back 50 feet from a fault whose location can be precisely determined and 100 feet from a fault whose location is less well known. Apartments, hospitals, and schools must be set back 125 feet from well-known faults and 175 feet from less well-known faults. Only uses which will sustain little damage and endanger few people are permitted within fault zones: plant nurseries, golf courses, parks, cemeteries, parking lots, and highways. Similar judicious siting of land uses is appropriate for other zones of high seismic risk, for example, active landslides, soils subject to liquefaction, and tsunami run-up zones. New public buildings, hospitals, schools, police and fire stations, and buildings occupied by many people, like apartment complexes and hotels, should be constructed outside these hazardous zones.

In 1974, the city of San Francisco adopted a Community Safety Plan.[3] The plan identifies those areas of San Francisco that will sustain the most damage in an earthquake from ground shaking, landsliding, liquefaction, tsunamis, and failure of reservoirs (see figure 5.2). The plan also estimates potential damage from improper building construction, as buildings built before 1948 were not subject to the current building code. Since 1969, older buildings that are reno-

FIGURE 5.2
Earthquake hazard areas as delineated by San Francisco in its Community Safety Plan. The nature and degree of risk vary widely from one part of the city to another, differences which the city's plans must take into account.

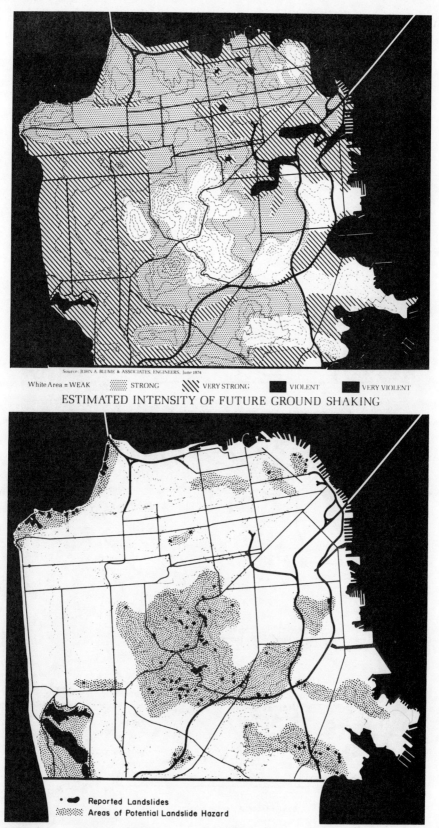

Source: JOHN A. BLUME & ASSOCIATES, ENGINEERS, June 1974

White Area = WEAK ░░░ STRONG ░░░ VERY STRONG ▓▓▓ VIOLENT ███ VERY VIOLENT

ESTIMATED INTENSITY OF FUTURE GROUND SHAKING

• ▬ Reported Landslides
░░░ Areas of Potential Landslide Hazard

POTENTIAL LANDSLIDE AREAS

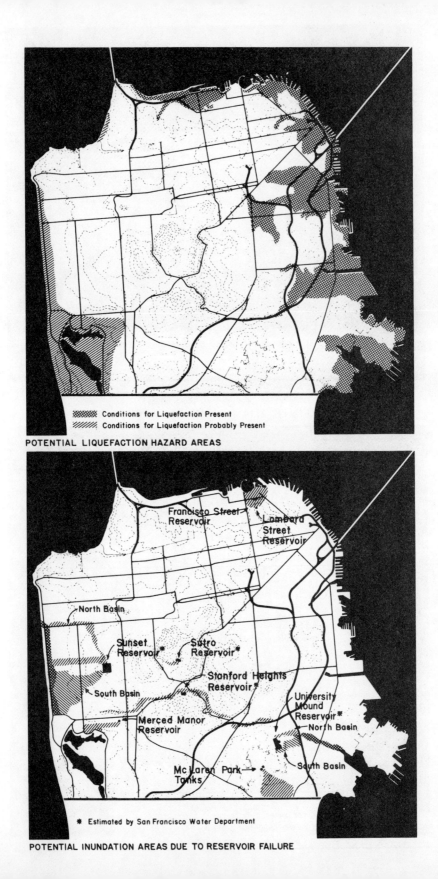

Conditions for Liquefaction Present
Conditions for Liquefaction Probably Present

POTENTIAL LIQUEFACTION HAZARD AREAS

Francisco Street Reservoir

Lombard Street Reservoir

North Basin

Sunset Reservoir*

Sutro Reservoir*

Stanford Heights Reservoir*

South Basin

University Mound Reservoir*

North Basin

Merced Manor Reservoir

Mc Laren Park Tanks

South Basin

* Estimated by San Francisco Water Department

POTENTIAL INUNDATION AREAS DUE TO RESERVOIR FAILURE

vated more than 30 percent must also meet modern seismic building code standards. San Francisco's downtown is served by an auxiliary water supply system which has its own reservoir and cisterns at key intersections. This system is designed to withstand earthquake damage and thus to enable fire fighters to put out the many fires that inevitably follow an earthquake. In 1906, much of San Francisco was destroyed by fire when the water system, broken in 23,000 places throughout the city, provided no water pressure. The Community Safety Plan urges the replacement of San Francisco's brittle water mains with more flexible pipes. In addition to outlining emergency measures to be implemented during and after an earthquake, the plan proposes how reconstruction should proceed. This is probably one of the most important parts of the plan, since immediately following the disaster there is the most support for rebuilding and "doing it right." The more time has elapsed, the more pressure grows to rebuild quickly and expediently, as illustrated by the reconstruction of both San Francisco after the 1906 earthquake and Anchorage after the 1964 earthquake, where in the absence of a plan, homes and other structures were rebuilt on hazardous locations following old, outmoded methods.

Most seismic building codes are concerned mainly with building structure, in other words, they are aimed at insuring that a building will remain standing after an earthquake. Since the damage to nonstructural parts of a building may be over half its replacement cost, and since architectural elements like parapets, facade panels, and windows may break off or shatter, posing a hazard to people within and outside the building, the American Institute of Architects recommends that designers take more than structural integrity into account.[4]

There is little excuse for landslide damage; 95 to 99 percent of such damage can be avoided by regulation of land use, design, construction, and maintenance. The basics of landslide prevention have been understood for centuries. The city of Bath, England, lies in one of the most extensively landslipped areas of Britain. Until its rapid growth in the eighteenth century, the city was confined to stable ground on the floor of the Avon Valley. When the Georgian residential terraces, squares, and crescents, for which Bath is famous, were constructed on hillslopes above the city, landsliding problems resulted. The construction of Camden Crescent in the 1790s was halted by extensive landsliding. The slope was finally stabilized in the nineteenth century by tunneling into the hillside to intercept groundwater and by developing most of the hillside as public gardens.[5]

The most hazardous slopes are best left alone, but it is not always desirable, nor is it always necessary, to avoid landslide-prone areas altogether. Some of the most valuable real estate in Los Angeles and Seattle lies on landslide-prone slopes. In many cases the problem can be overcome by controlling steepness of slopes and subsurface and surface drainage. The character of landscaping is important. Careful attention to grading in the construction of a building can be undone by installing a landscape that requires lavish irrigation. A native plant community or plants that do not require irrigation should be used on hilly, landslide-prone terrain. Such plants reduce the infiltration of surface water into a slope, dry out the surface soil, and bind it with their roots.

The city of Los Angeles has pioneered landslide reduction in the United States. The evolution of its Hillside Grading Regulations is an illustration of how effective measures may develop as a direct response to disaster (see table 5.1). Citizens of Los Angeles demanded the original version of the grading regulations in 1952 after landsliding caused $7.5 million in damage in a single season. Revisions have followed every disaster since—in 1956, 1957, and 1962—and

TABLE 5.1

Grading Regulations and Property Damage Reduction, Los Angeles, California, 1969[a]

	Sites Developed Prior to 1952	Sites Developed 1952–62	Sites Developed 1963–69
Number of sites constructed	10,000	27,000	11,000
Total damage	$3,300,000	$2,767,000	$182,400[b]
Average damage per site	$330	$100	$7[c]
Percentage of sites damaged	10.4	1.3	0.15

Source: Robert W. Fleming, David J. Barnes, and Robert L. Schuster, "Landslide Hazards and Their Reduction," *Geological Survey Yearbook* (Washington, D.C.: U.S. Geological Survey, 1978).

[a] Los Angeles had no grading code prior to 1952; the code was introduced in 1952, then revised in 1962.

[b] More than $100,000 of the $182,400 occurred to sites that were currently being graded. Even the best of grading projects are susceptible to damage during construction.

[c] If the total damage value is used, the average damage value per site is about $17. The value of $7 per site was obtained by deducting the damages to sites under construction.

have resulted in the extremely effective instrument the Hillside Grading Regulations are today.[6] All construction projects that involve grading must obtain a permit. Grading plans are reviewed before construction begins and inspected after it is completed. An "as built" grading plan and technical reports must be submitted for approval. Only if these are acceptable does the city prepare a grading certificate and release performance bonds. The success of Los Angeles' grading ordinance is a consequence of its strict enforcement and the wide availability of geological and soils information provided by federal, state, and county governments. The effectiveness of Los Angeles' Hillside Grading Regulations was demonstrated in the winter storms of 1978 when 93 percent of all landslide damages in the city involved sites graded before the current regulations were in effect. Damage was also more severe in these areas: 155 homes were destroyed or had to be vacated.[7]

Swelling soils are so widespread in some urban areas, like Denver, that avoiding them completely would be impractical. Fortunately, proper foundation and building design, drainage, and landscaping can minimize damage. Since the soils swell in contact with water, keeping water away from the foundation is fundamental. Grass and shrubs, preferably those that require little or no watering, should be kept four to five feet from the foundation and trees should be planted further than fifteen feet away.[8] Foundations should be specially designed and interior walls detached from floating floor slabs that can move with the soil.

Ground subsidence, a problem which may affect both a region and a single home, has varying solutions, depending upon its cause. Tokyo, Long Beach, Mexico City, and Venice have all halted or slowed subsidence by a combined program of reducing withdrawal of fluids from the ground and enhancing the infiltration of rainfall or treated wastewater. Huge recharge basins are now a feature of the urban landscape in cities like Los Angeles where one such 450-acre complex holds water up to four feet deep in large, flat ponds.[9] Subsidence over landfill can be controlled by selection of the materials used for fill and the method of their placement. Waiting until the inevitable subsidence occurs will minimize damage to structures: 90 percent of the settlement occurs within the first two to five years; within two years the land settles by up to 25 percent of the original thickness of the fill. Deposits of methane gas can also be tapped profitably in many landfills. If planned wisely, the reclamation of landfill sites and the utilization of mined-out areas may provide the city with a resource rather than a hazard.

Conserving and Exploiting Resources

The exploration of mineral resources need not conflict with other uses of the land, and may even enhance them. Each city should identify the significant mineral deposits within and near it and devise a plan for their protection, for the regulation of their eventual exploitation, and for the subsequent reclamation and use of the mined-out land.

A new use created by mining sometimes far exceeds the economic value of the mineral resource itself. In Duisburg, Germany, mining coal under the harbor revived that city's doomed port. Duisburg is the main inland port on the Rhine River and one of the largest inland ports in the world; it has been an important port for six centuries. Until recently, the port's future was threatened by a six-and-one-half-foot drop in water level since 1900. The harbor master devised an ingenious solution. Because of the hazard of subsidence, mining of coal deposits under the city had been prohibited for years. In a meticulously plotted and executed plan, 12 million tons of coal were mined from under the harbor to induce subsidence. When the mines collapsed, and the ground beneath the port with them, the water depth was raised nearly six feet.[10]

Kansas City, Missouri, is the underground capital of the world, with more than 44 million square feet of warehouses, factories, and offices converted from old limestone mines. The limestone was initially mined for its economic value, but now the creation of new underground space is more profitable than the stone itself.[11] Acquisition of underground space has become the primary reason for some mining, and the sale of rock is used to offset the cost of developing the space. Mining operations have been modified slightly to accommodate future use. Previously, irregularly shaped and spaced pillars of limestone were left to support the ceiling. Now twenty-foot by twenty-foot square pillars are carved out at regular intervals, spaced thirty feet apart. Brunson Instrument Company was the first to occupy underground space mined to its specifications. The company, manufacturers of surveying equipment used on the moon, was hampered by the vibrations in its original location at the surface. Precision settings could be done only between 2:00 and 4:00 A.M., when traffic vibrations were minimal. In 1960 the firm occupied its present quarters, 140,000 square feet of vibration-free space, seventy-seven feet below the ground.

The advantages of underground space in Kansas City are many. Rents and overhead are low: rents average 40 percent below those at the surface; heating and cooling are 75 to 80 percent below surface costs. The temperature is a constant 56°F; the relative humidity is steady. The mines are convenient to local markets, interstate highways, and continental railroad lines. The construction, hollowed out of solid rock, has unlimited bearing strength and is fireproof as well as noise and vibration free. Entrances are easily secured. In 1953, the first underground freezer was built in Kansas City for frozen food storage. Cheap storage, access to transportation, and a central location between the food producers of California and the Southwest and markets of the East have made Kansas City a major food-distribution center.

If the future use of the site is planned before mining, exploitation of mineral resources produces long-term benefits. The pits and mounds of a quarry can be transformed into a park; an 18-hole golf course near Los Angeles is the product of a gravel mine. In Montclair, New Jersey, where a college's plans for expansion were blocked by a large hill, 864,000 square feet of level land were created by the excavation of nearly 3 million tons of trap rock sold for a profit.[12]

The city of Phoenix, Arizona, coordinated the progressive use of a 140-acre site as a sand and gravel quarry, a sanitary landfill, and a park. All three uses progressed simultaneously on different parts of the site. First the city mined sand and gravel for use in road construction. During this process, pits and mounds were created on the once flat landscape and a flood-prone portion of the site molded to accommodate flood waters. Next the city piled garbage into rolling hills, compacted it, and covered it with layers of sandy desert soil daily. Trees and landscaping were added after the landfill operations were complete.[13]

A city should establish a mineral conservation district to protect its most valuable mineral deposits. Interim uses within the district should be those which would not preclude mining, such as temporary storage facilities, plant nurseries, parkland, livestock paddocks, and pasture and cropland. Permits for extracting minerals should be conditional upon a satisfactory plan for both operation and reclamation. Because mining operations may generate noise, dust, truck traffic, subsidence, erosion, and water pollution, cities should require potential quarry operators to demonstrate how they plan to control dust and odors, reduce erosion, reduce noise, and screen their operations from view, and should establish routes for truck traffic which will minimize disruption and road damage.

Soil is the crust of the earth in which life is rooted—a porous

FIGURE 5.3
Community gardens in Boston, converted from derelict land on vacant lots.

medium between rock and air. It is neither entirely mineral nor entirely organic; it is composed of sand, silt, clay, air, water, and the decomposed remains of plants and animals. The simple act of digging garden soil in preparation for spring planting triggers strong emotions: a sense of connection to the earth, to the regeneration of life. It is an act of nurturance and an expression of faith in renewal. Urban gardening has always been popular in Europe. Every walled medieval town had its orchards and kitchen gardens. Today, bits of leftover land along railroad tracks and streams are divided into allotment gardens, and acres of tiny plots are laid out at city outskirts. Vacant lots in the center of American cities were cultivated intensely in the late nineteenth century to provide poor families with a means of producing their own food.[14] Allotment gardens were also widespread during the two world wars, but until recently were never as popular in the United States as they have always been in Europe. In the past decade, hundreds of acres of vacant lots in U.S. cities have been transformed into vegetable and flower gardens (see figure 5.3). Some are the outgrowth of spontaneous community interest, others the direct result of community organizing by groups such as the Boston Urban Gardeners and New York City's Green Guerillas. Such places have provided a common ground for all ages, races, and ethnic groups: the old and the young, black and white, Puerto Rican and Chinese. In Boston, elderly emigrants from the rural south who possess valued knowledge about growing crops draw new respect from cocky youth. Small plots supply some urban gardeners and their families with fresh vegetables all summer and a surplus to can for the winter. Family grocery bills have been cut by as much as $600.[15]

Along with the renewed interest in urban gardening has come increasing concern for the contamination of urban soils. In Boston, collaboration between the Environmental Protection Agency, the Soil Conservation Service, the local University of Massachusetts Extension Service, and the Boston Urban Gardeners resulted in an effective lead-testing program and recommendations for how urban gardeners might best avoid lead contamination.[16] Soil tests should be conducted for all urban soils. Gardens should be located away from old painted structures and all roads. They should be more than fifty feet from a heavily traveled street.

If there is lead in the soil, chances of removing it are slim. The amount of lead a vegetable absorbs depends upon the acidity of soil and the type of vegetable. The more acid the soil, the more readily plants take up lead. If the soil is acid, lime should be added to raise the pH to 6.5 to 7.0. Leafy green vegetables such as spinach, beet tops, loose-leaf lettuce, herbs, turnip greens, and collards are the most susceptible to lead contamination. They should never be grown within fifty feet of a major street or in soils containing any amount of lead. Root crops, carrots, radishes, beets, onions, and turnips are moderately susceptible to lead contamination and should only be grown in soils with a low lead count. Fruiting crops—eggplants, tomatoes, squash, melons, cucumbers, and peppers—and tight-headed or protected crops like sunflowers, corn, and cabbage are the least likely to take up soil lead. They can be grown in soils with a moderate lead content, but should be grown in containers if the soil has a high lead content. Only flowers and ornamental plants should be grown in soil with very high lead levels. All vegetables grown in urban gardens should be washed thoroughly to remove any heavy metals that have settled in the dust from the air. Children should not be permitted to play in the soils with medium, high, or very high lead content.[17]

Urban soil represents an underutilized resource of great potential, capable of producing high yields of both food and ornamental plants and of assimilating non-toxic wastes. Managed wisely, urban soil can enhance the survival of plants in an urban landscape (see chapter 9).

Designing a Safer, More Economical City

The cities of California, their population threatened by multiple geological hazards, provide many examples of enlightened urban planning and design. In recent decades, the state of California has provided its cities with mandates, incentives, and information to facilitate that effort. In 1973, the California Department of Conservation issued the *Urban Geology Master Plan for California,* a publication intended to serve as a basis for policymaking by state and local government. It reviewed the hazards facing California cities and identified the resources endangered by urban development, defined the measures available to mitigate those problems, and estimated their cost and benefits (table 5.2). The plan estimates that the cost of deaths and damage from geological hazards and the loss of mineral resources due to urbanization will amount to more than $55 billion in California alone between 1970 and the year 2000, and reports on the relative losses attributable to ten separate problems: earthquake shaking, loss of mineral resources, landsliding, flooding, erosion, expansive soils, fault displacement, volcanic hazards, tsunami hazards, and subsidence.[18] The plan concludes that the application of current state-of-the-art mitigation techniques would save over $38 billion between 1970 and the year 2000 at a cost of little more than $6 billion.

Japan, an island country faced with rapid urban growth, a shortage of land, and multiple geological hazards—earthquakes, tsunamis, subsidence, landslides, and volcanic eruptions—has also achieved many impressive accomplishments. Beginning in 1959 with a subsoil map of Tokyo, Japanese cities have constructed an

TABLE 5.2

Projected Losses Due to Geological Problems in California and Potential Loss Reduction, for the period 1970–2000[a]

Geological Problem	Projected Total Losses, Without Improvement of Existing Policies and Practices[b]	Possible Total Loss Reduction, Applying All Feasible Measures		Estimated Total Cost of Applying All Feasible Measures, at Current State of the Art		Benefit Cost Ratio If All Feasible Measures Were Applied and All Possible Loss Reductions Were Achieved
		Percentage of Total Loss	Dollar Amount	Percentage of Total Loss	Dollar Amount	
Earthquake shaking	$21,035,000,000	50[c]	$10,517,500,000	10	$2,103,500,000	5
Loss of mineral resources	17,000,000,000	90	15,000,000,000	0.53	90,000,000	167
Landsliding	9,850,000,000	90	8,865,000,000	10.3	1,018,000,000	8.7
Flooding	6,532,000,000	52.5	3,432,000,000	41.4	2,703,000,000	1.3
Erosion activity	565,000,000	66	377,000,000	45.7	250,000,000	1.5
Expansive soils	150,000,000	99	148,500,000	5	7,500,000	20
Fault displacement	76,000,000	17	12,600,000	10	7,500,000	1.7
Volcanic hazards	49,380,000	16.5	8,135,000	3.5	1,655,000	4.9
Tsunami hazards	40,800,000	95	37,760,000	63	25,700,000	1.5
Subsidence	26,400,000	50	13,200,000	65.1	8,790,000	1.5
Total	$55,324,580,000	69	$38,411,695,000	11.2	$6,215,645,000	6.2

SOURCE: John T. Alfors, John L. Burnett, and Thomas E. Gay. "Urban Geology Master Plan for California—A Summary." In Geology in the Urban Environment, ed. R. O. Utgard, G. D. McKenzie, and D. Foley (Minneapolis: Burgess, 1978).
[a] All figures are 1970 dollars.
[b] These values are based on the assumption that no change is made in the 1970 type, effectiveness, or level of application of preventive and remedial measures. Ninety-five percent of the loss would be in urban areas.
[c] The reduction of life loss would be 90 percent.

accurate picture of the ground beneath them, an overview painstakingly constructed from a collection of all subsurface tests conducted in each city. A special committee for ground investigation in cities, appointed by the Japanese Ministry of Construction, published a set of "Instructions for Collection and Arrangement of Pre-Existing Materials" and "Standard Specifications for Ground Investigation Work in Cities" in 1960.[19] To encourage cities to assemble and map geological information, the Japanese national government also supported half the cost of these investigations, resulting in an invaluable series of urban geological records.

A Plan for Every City

It is self-evident that cities plagued with recurrent earthquakes and landslides or blessed with rich deposits of coal and oil should be concerned about the nature of the ground beneath them. But even cities without such dramatic problems must protect access to construction materials and insure the stability of buildings, streets, and utilities. Every city should assess the nature of the earth that lies beneath it.

The greatest obstacle to preparing a comprehensive plan and to designing projects that respond to the city's geology and soil is lack of detailed information. Specific geological hazards and resources, their spatial pattern, and their relative importance vary greatly from city to city depending on the nature of the ground beneath. Are earthquakes a problem, with attendant landslides or are there extensive areas of shrink–swell soils? Is regionwide subsidence a problem, or local subsidence over old mines or sinkholes? Is sand and gravel an important resource, or quarry rock, coal, or natural gas? Identifying the spatial pattern of hazards and mineral resources will help single out those places where the degree of risk is most severe and where the exploitation of mineral deposits is in conflict with urbanization.

Some issues are best addressed at the metropolitan scale. The significance of any individual mineral deposit, for example, can only be assessed in relation to the rest of the city's deposits. A comprehensive strategy to stabilize the ground and conserve mineral resources should:

- address the city's most critical geological hazards and most significant resources, with particular attention to reducing risk in the most hazardous areas and to protecting the most valuable resources
- locate new public buildings, including hospitals, schools, and public utilities, outside high-risk areas and encourage new industry and housing development to do the same
- provide a plan for relocation and reconstruction after disasters like earthquakes and tsunamis
- establish mineral conservation districts for the city's most significant mineral resources and encourage land uses which would not preclude extraction
- provide a plan for the eventual reuse of mineral conservation districts after resources have been exploited.

Every new building, street, and park within the city should be designed to prevent or mitigate hazards and to conserve and restore resources. Every project should:

- address the geological hazards and resources which exist on the site and in its immediate neighborhood
- site buildings and phase construction to exploit mineral resources on the site
- site and design buildings and landscaping to avoid or mitigate hazards
- exploit the site's distinctive geological character.

The initiative for comprehensive studies of urban geology will always be greatest in countries like Japan and in states like California prone to recurring hazards. Cities like Tokyo, San Francisco, and Los Angeles have pioneered solutions to a wide array of geological problems from which more fortunate cities with fewer or less severe hazards can learn. All cities stand to gain from an assessment of geology. Every city has some geological problems that, although inconspicuous or hidden, have a costly, cumulative effect. Cities can be designed to withstand or avert geological disasters, to promote judicious exploitation of mineral resources, and to restore ravaged urban land. Billions of dollars and millions of lives are at stake.

PART IV

Water

CHAPTER 6

Floods, Droughts, and Poisoned Water

POISONED WATER, floods and droughts plague the city. Brown rivers loaded with sewage, sediment, bits of garbage, and poisonous chemicals flow through the city, a dirty soup from which many cities draw their drinking water. In some years, floods alone account for more property damage in the United States than any other single natural hazard, yet drought is an increasingly common urban phenomenon. All cities, even those in humid climates, must soon face the loss of their most precious resource—an abundant supply of uncontaminated water.

Water is the city's life blood: it drives industries, heats and cools homes, nurtures food, quenches thirst, and carries waste. Cities import more water than all other goods and materials combined. Sufficient water is not only a prerequisite for health, it is essential for life. Despite their desperate need for water, and despite the fact they are forever short of water, cities befoul and squander it. Every rain sweeps dirt, debris, heavy metals, and animal feces from streets and parking lots into rivers and lakes. The storm sewers which drain the city's paved surface aggravate floods and prevent groundwater recharge, and the resultant lowered stream flows concentrate pollutants. Even as the city water supplies dwindle, drinking water irrigates drought-sensitive lawns and landscaping.

Taken together, urban activities, the density of urban form and the impervious materials of which it is built, the pattern of settlement and its relation to the natural drainage network, and the design of the drainage and flood control system produce a characteristic urban water regime. Abundant and rapid storm water runoff creates extremely high stream flows during and immediately after storms and lowers stream flow between them. Pavement and storm sewers reduce infiltration and lower the level of water beneath the ground. Urban activities and their location, and urban form and materials, influence the degree of flooding and where it occurs, the degree of pollution and where it is concentrated, and the amount of water consumed. The characteristics of urban water dynamics, pollution, and use are well understood, their causes and effects well known, but that knowledge is too seldom applied. The planners, designers, builders, and managers of cities all too often treat the problems of flooding and storm drainage, water pollution, water use, and water supply separately.

Increased Floods

All but the largest creeks and streams of the pre-city landscape have vanished from a modern map. Covered and forgotten, old streams still flow through the city buried beneath the ground in large pipes, primary channels of a subterranean storm system. Their muffled roar can still be heard beneath the street after a heavy rain; they are invisible, but their potential contribution to downstream floods is nevertheless unabated and magnified. Floods increase in magnitude and destructiveness with each increment of urban growth; urbanization can increase the mean annual flood by as much as six times.[1] Rapid stormwater runoff and narrower, shallower floodplains, constricted by buildings and levees and clogged with sediment, are the cause. As urban storm drainage systems drain water efficiently from roofs, streets, and sidewalks, the flood control system must be continually augmented to prevent flooding downstream.

The concrete, stone, brick, and asphalt of pavement and buildings cap the city's surface with a waterproof seal. Unable to penetrate the ground and unimpeded by the city's smooth surface, the rain which falls on roofs, plazas, streets, and parking lots runs off the surface in greater quantities, more rapidly than the same amount of rain falling on the spongy surface of a forest or field. The densest parts of the city increase storm water runoff the most; runoff decreases in the less densely populated parts of the city, and drops off sharply in wooded parkland. Gutters, curbs, and drains collect rainfall and direct it to sewers, which transport it rapidly to streams and lakes. The denser the city, the higher the proportion of pavement to plant cover, and the more efficient the storm drainage system, the greater the quantity of storm water that reaches streams and rivers in a short space of time. Storm sewers transport water from one point to another; they do not reduce or eliminate water, they merely change its location. Traditional storm drainage practice protects local streets, basements, and parking lots from flooding, while contributing to major flood damage downstream.

The torrential peak flows of urban storm water overwhelm the capacity of storm-swollen streams, their floodplains filled and constricted by buildings, roadways, levees, and floodwalls. The resulting floods are higher, flow more rapidly, and are more destructive than floods from comparable storms before urbanization. The 1973 flood of the Mississippi River at St. Louis was similar in magnitude to the flood of 1908; yet the flood waters were more than eight feet higher in 1973. The 1973 flood was the highest in the 189 years that records had been kept, even though experts estimate that it had a recurrence interval of only thirty years.[2] It was not the magnitude of the flood itself, but rather the confinement of the river by levees and the deposition of sediment in the river channel that contributed to the height of the 1973 flood. As urban floodplains and river channels are confined to control floods and enhance navigation, they are also made shallower, as a by-product of other human activities. Construction and demolition expose soil to erosion, and storm water carries sediment into streams. A construction site produces ten to one hundred times the amount of eroded sediment that is produced by farms and forests.[3] More than 4,500 tons of soil was eroded during a five-year period from a single twenty-acre construction site in Montgomery County, Maryland.[4] The cumulative impact on urban water bodies is substantial. Eroded sediments silt stream channels and harbors, decreasing their flood capacity.

The river and its floodplain are a unit. The floodplain is the relatively flat area within which the river moves and upon which it regularly overflows. Unobstructed, the dynamic flow of water constantly erodes one bank and deposits sediments on the opposite bank. River channels do not remain forever at the same location; unless confined, the channel, over the course of time, eventually occupies every location within the floodplain. The shape and size of a natural river channel reflects the size and frequency of floods to

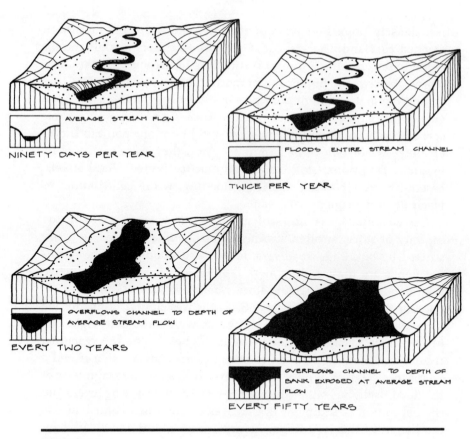

AVERAGE STREAM FLOW

NINETY DAYS PER YEAR

FLOODS ENTIRE STREAM CHANNEL

TWICE PER YEAR

OVERFLOWS CHANNEL TO DEPTH OF
AVERAGE STREAM FLOW

EVERY TWO YEARS

OVERFLOWS CHANNEL TO DEPTH OF
BANK EXPOSED AT AVERAGE STREAM
FLOW

EVERY FIFTY YEARS

FIGURE 6.1
Floodplain dynamics. Rivers overflow onto their floodplains with predictable
frequency, and structures built within the floodplain area risk destruction.

which it is subjected, and two times every year, the river fills its
channel, brimming to the banks; about once every two years, the
river overflows onto the floodplain to the depth of the average flow
in the channel (see figure 6.1).[5] When homes and businesses occupy
the floodplain, they not only risk destruction, but also cripple the
ability of the floodplain to contain flood waters. In some cities,
buildings, parking lots, and other urban development occupy much
of the floodplain: 89.2 percent of the floodplain in Phoenix, Arizona;
83.5 percent in Harrisburg, Pennsylvania; 62.2 percent in Denver;
and 53.3 percent in Charleston, South Carolina.[6]

When the storm drainage system increases peak stream flows, and
homes and businesses occupy the floodplain, flood control structures are usually built to protect them. The reliance upon massive
engineering works, like dams and levees, minimizes the damage

from frequent floods, but may contribute to deaths and greater destruction from less frequent major floods.[7] Extensive flood protection works inspire an illusion of safety that may promote dense occupation of flood-prone areas. The stage is then set for enormous loss of life and property when these flood protection works fail or are overtopped or inundated by extremely heavy rains. A 1972 flood in Rapid City, South Dakota, killed 237 people and injured 3,057 when flood waters overflowed the storage reservoir and breached the dam upstream of the city. Many residents, confident of the dam's ability to protect them, stayed in their homes despite warnings to evacuate. The river rose fourteen feet in four hours and as much as 3.5 feet during a single fifteen minute period.[8] The flood devastated 1,335 homes and demolished 5,000 automobiles. Of the estimated $160 million in property damage, less than $300,000 was insured.[9]

Cities are not at equal risk to floods. A city's regional climate and seasonal pattern of rainfall, the amount of floodplain within the city, and the extent to which the floodplain is developed all contribute to the relative degree of flood hazard. Coastal cities in the eastern United States lie in the path of hurricanes and are prone to flooding from a combination of heavy rainfall and surging flood tides. Flood hazards on the West Coast of the United States are increased by the added threat of earthquake-generated tsunamis. Cities in semiarid and arid climates may also have flood hazards; their shallow, wide floodplains, relatively dry much of the year, may be deceptive. James Michener described the South Platte River that flows through Denver as a "sad, bewildered nothing of a river . . . a sand bottom, a wandering afterthought, a useless irritation, a frustration, and when you've said all that, it suddenly rises up, spreads out to a mile wide, engulfs your crops and lays waste your farms."[10] Most of the year, the South Platte consists of a shallow trickle engulfed in a wide, flat, sandy floodplain, but heavy seasonal rains convert the river into a raging torrent. In June 1965, fourteen inches of rain fell over parts of Denver within a few hours. Flood waters rose quickly, overflowed the banks and slammed debris against bridges, forming dams so that the flood surged around them into the adjacent city. When the storm had passed, most of Denver's bridges were destroyed, and highways and buildings buried in tons of silt. The flood was the worst disaster in Denver's history, taking twelve lives and costing $300 million in damages.[11]

The extent to which the floodplain is constricted and built upon can aggravate the city's natural flood hazard. The amount of floodplain a city contains and the proportion of that area that is developed varies from city to city. Eighty-one percent of Monroe, Louisiana, and 40 percent of Charleston, South Carolina, lie within the floodplain, while floodplain comprises only 2.4 percent of Spokane, Washington.[12] The design of a city's storm drainage system can also aggravate or alleviate flood hazard. The faster stormwater reaches streams and rivers, the more floods increase; the more stormwater is retarded, the more floods are reduced.

The effect of a storm drainage system is not limited to flood hazard; it can also increase water pollution and water use. Typically, the storm drainage system aggravates pollution by delivering slugs of sewage and runoff after storms and by decreasing stream flow between storms so that discharges from industry and treatment plants are undiluted. Cities that draw their water supply from urban rivers must then contend with vacillating flows and increased contamination. When sewage and stormwater systems are combined, as they are in many older cities, the surge of stormwater following a rain frequently overwhelms the capacity of sewage treatment plants, so that both rainwater and untreated sewage dump directly into water bodies. Since the ground, sealed by pavement and drained by pipes, absorbs little water, the amount of water stored in the ground, from which plants obtain their supply, is reduced. The lowered groundwater is insufficient to maintain stream levels between storms and sustain plants during dry spells.

Poisoned Water

The disgusting odor and appearance of water in the wells and rivers of dense cities has been a source of concern for centuries. Although, in the fourth century B.C., Hippocrates had warned that polluted water posed a serious health hazard, it was not until 1854, when John Snow, a London physician, traced the source of a cholera outbreak to polluted water from a single well, that the link between water and disease was definitively established. In thirteenth-century London, both the Crown and the City attempted repeatedly and ineffectively to halt pollution of the Thames, but the river continued to be an open sewer (figure 6.2).[13] The Thames was a grossly polluted river in 1855, when Michael Faraday complained in a letter to the *Times* that "the whole of the river was an opaque pale brown fluid . . . near the bridges the feculence rolled up in clouds so dense that they

FIGURE 6.2

"Monster Soup commonly called Thames water. Being a correct representation of that precious stuff doled out to us. Microcosm dedicated to the London Water Company." A cartoon by Paul Pry, 1829.

were visible at the surface."[14] The following year, 1856, was the "Year of the Stink," and sheets soaked with disinfectant were hung in Parliament to combat the stench of the river.[15] A century later, in the 1950s, the Thames was still so polluted that it was virtually fishless for a forty-three mile stretch in the proximity of London.[16]

Recurrent epidemics swept nineteenth-century European and North American cities with terrifying frequency. Cholera epidemics hit London in successive outbreaks: in 1832, 1848, 1849, 1853, and 1854. Cholera killed 3,500 New Yorkers between June and October of 1832; during the height of the epidemic, 100,000 people, approximately half the population, fled New York.[17] Pathogenic organisms—bacteria, protozoa, worms, viruses, and fungi—are responsible for outbreaks of waterborne diseases. The diseases they cause range from potentially deadly bacterial infections, like cholera and typhoid fever, to intestinal parasites and skin rashes. Most pathogens enter surface water via human and animal feces. Inadequately treated sanitary sewage and urban runoff account for nearly all water contamination by pathogens. As municipal sewage treatment improves, the pathogens present in urban runoff assume a new, until recently unrecognized, importance. Urban runoff has the bacterial contamination of dilute sewage and often exceeds concentrations considered safe for water sports by two to four orders of magnitude.[18] The city's dog population contributes an enormous load of untreated sewage to urban runoff. The water near storm and sanitary sewer outfalls exhibits the highest concentration of pathogens, and is most contaminated immediately after a storm.

The specter of waterborne epidemic disease which haunted cities of the past has been laid to rest in the twentieth century by sewage treatment and the chlorination of public water supplies, but new poisons now threaten drinking water. The impact of cholera and typhoid fever was felt overnight, and their cause, once recognized, was swiftly eradicated. In contrast, the effects of the new poisons are gradual and cumulative. The diseases they generate and the genetic change they precipitate will not become fully evident for years, at which point they may not be readily removable from the environment. To complicate matters further, many of these pollutants have synergistic effects which increase their toxicity; some combine with chlorine to produce new, toxic compounds.[19]

The Environmental Protection Agency has identified 129 "priority toxic pollutants," including heavy metals, pesticides, and organic toxicants. Many are poisonous even in extremely small concentrations, and in low doses over a long period of time can cause neurological damage, cancer, miscarriages, and birth defects. Extremely low, but harmful, concentrations of heavy metals, pesticides, and organic chemicals are often difficult to detect and to remove from water.[20] The existence of so many toxicants also complicates both their measurement and impact. Toxic chemicals are a by-product of modern industrial processes, agricultural practices, and fuel consumption. Toxic pollutants enter streams, rivers, and lakes in industrial discharges, in urban stormwater runoff, and in the fallout of urban dust; they leach into groundwater from sanitary landfills, toxic waste disposal sites, and chemical spills. A 1977 study of surface water quality by the U.S. Environmental Protection Agency demonstrated that heavy metals and synthetic organic pollutants are a significant and widespread problem in water near industrial areas.[21] As industry processes waste more effectively, urban runoff is emerging as a major source of toxic pollutants. Every heavy rainfall sweeps the dirt and debris of the city streets into storm sewers, and with it heavy metals and other toxic materials, oil, and grease.

Turbidity and warmer temperatures, the increase of nutrient salts, and the loss of dissolved oxygen degrade the water quality in urban rivers, streams, and lakes. These factors have less dramatic effects on human health than do pathogens and toxicants, but drastically affect aquatic life and may produce smelly, dirty water with a strange taste. Urban rivers are turbid; the suspended sediment in urban runoff is the major cause of turbidity, but solids from domestic sewage and industrial discharges are also factors. When nutrients like nitrogen and phosphorus reach rivers and lakes in large quantities, they trigger a prolific bloom of algae that chokes waterways with living and decaying plants. As plants decay, they consume dissolved oxygen and produce an unpleasant smell. Fish and many aquatic plants require oxygen, and the most sensitive species die as dissolved oxygen decreases. Lack of oxygen was the major cause of the lack of life in the Thames River in the 1950s. Nutrients enter surface water in sewage and urban runoff containing animal feces and fertilizers.

The character and severity of the water pollution problem varies from city to city. A city's major industries, the degree and type of air pollution, the nature of its sewage treatment and storm drainage systems, and the existence of industry, agriculture, or other cities upstream all determine which water pollutants are a problem. The most unfortunate cities are those, like New Orleans, which are located near the mouths of major rivers, downstream of millions of pollutant sources. The fate of New Orleans' water supply is beyond the city's control.

In 1977, the Council on Environmental Quality studied EPA records of water quality in 159 cities. The average concentration of bacteria exceeded levels considered safe for drinking water in one-quarter of the samples.[22] In Philadelphia, Charlotte, Roanoke, Omaha, and Denver, bacteria exceeded safe levels over 90 percent of the time.[23] Cities which draw their water from lakes and rivers polluted with such high levels of bacteria are caught in an increasingly difficult dilemma. On the one hand, water must be treated with chlorine to prevent the spread of epidemic disease; on the other hand, chlorine combines with some organic pollutants to produce new carcinogenic compounds. Mercury is a problem in all of the twelve major United States river basins sampled by the Environmental Protection Agency in 1977; concentrations exceeded water quality criteria in more than three-fourths of the sample stations, with median values ranging from eight to forty times the standards set by the EPA for the protection of aquatic life.[24] Concentrations of cadmium and selenium also exceeded the proposed EPA criteria for water quality in at least 10 percent of all the samples.[25]

A city's regional climate and precipitation patterns, its underlying geological conditions, the character of water circulations in its rivers, streams, lakes, ponds, and marshes, the types of land uses occupying flood-prone areas, the pattern of its sewage system, and its urban form—all these factors influence where, when, and how water pollutants are concentrated or diluted. Lakes may be more susceptible to pollution than rivers. Water in a river moves steadily toward the mouth; water circulation in lakes is more complex. Circulation time, the time it takes the water in a lake to be completely replaced, varies with the size of the lake's drainage basin, the amount of rainfall it receives, and the depth and surface area of the lake. Circulation time determines how susceptible the lake or pond is to pollution. The longer the circulation time, the more sensitive the lake to contamination, and the more difficult its recovery. Urban harbors and marinas, whether on lakes or rivers, are protected from currents and wave action and have reduced water circulation; therefore, like small lakes and ponds, they are highly sensitive to pollution. Trash and other pollutants accumulate in slips and canals that receive little flushing.

Although lakes and rivers are generally more contaminated than groundwater, they exhibit pollution more quickly and respond to improvement more rapidly. The quality of groundwater is less easily monitored than surface water. Pollution may go undetected until it reaches a well, at which point the source of contamination may be difficult to locate. Water moves very slowly through the ground, and abandonment may be the only alternative when a well becomes contaminated. Leaks from sewers, disposal of toxic industrial wastes, leaching from sanitary landfills, salt from highway de-icing, fertilizers and pesticides, leaks from chemical storage tanks, and the intrusion of sea water or saline groundwater are increasingly polluting groundwater. The pollution of groundwater by hazardous waste now threatens the public water supplies of Tampa, Florida, and Atlantic City, New Jersey, a reservoir in King of Prussia, Pennsylvania, which supplies drinking water to 800,000 people, and the water supplies of countless other communities, many of them as yet undocumented.[26]

Dwindling Water Supplies

Without water, a city cannot survive. Disputes over water rights were among the most bitter and violent struggles in the history of the American West. Today, cities separated by a third of a continent,

Denver and Los Angeles, dispute the use of the same Rocky Mountain water. Within the next decade, many cities will face a major water crisis.

The combination of contamination and lowered groundwater has always threatened city water supplies. Privies and graveyards befouled wells, and garbage and sewage polluted rivers and lakes. Until the twentieth century, Chicago dumped its sewage into and drew its water from Lake Michigan. In 1891, typhoid fever took 2,000 lives, a death rate of 173 out of every 100,000 citizens. Chicago cut this death rate by almost 90 percent by diverting its sewage away from Lake Michigan.[27] The construction of the Chicago Drainage Canal in 1900 reversed the flow of the Chicago River, so that sewage flowed to the Mississippi River. This proved a fine solution for Chicago, but created new problems for other cities downstream on the Des Plaines, Illinois, and Mississippi rivers. Other cities, like Boston and New York, had earlier opted to abandon local wells and to import water from distant reservoirs.

The alteration of the city's hydrology by pavement and sewers and their effect on both water availability and water quality had been recognized well before the twentieth century. Benjamin Franklin left a legacy to the city of Philadelphia, recommending that it be used to secure a public water supply. His will, read in Philadelphia in 1790, stated:

And having considered that the covering of the ground-plot of the city with buildings and pavements, which carry off most of the rain, and prevents its soaking into the Earth and renewing and purifying the Springs, whence the water of wells must gradually grow worse, and in turn be unfit for use, as I find has happened in all old cities, I recommend that at the end of the first hundred years, if not done before, the corporation of the city Employ a part of the hundred thousand pounds in bringing by pipes, the water of the Wissahickon Creek into town, so as to supply the inhabitants . . . [28]

Franklin's prophecy regarding the pollution of urban wells was borne out in Brooklyn, New York. From its initial settlement until 1947, Brooklyn depended on well water. To avoid contamination by surface cesspools, wells were drilled to ever-increasing depths. By 1936, following the installation of sewers and pavement of streets, accompanied by increased pumping, the water table dropped more than thirty-five feet below sea level.[29] The saltwater contamination that resulted led to the abandonment of virtually all the wells by 1947. With pumping halted, the water table gradually rose again, flooding basements and subway tunnels constructed when the water table was lower and causing hundreds of thousands of dollars in damage. Brooklyn, like many suburban communities whose wells have become contaminated, tied into the larger metropolitan water supply system, further increasing the demand for distant water sources. The problem repeats itself in the remainder of modern Long Island, completely dependent upon groundwater, whose wells are continually threatened by contamination and salt-water intrusion.

Approximately three-quarters of all American cities obtain their water supplies from groundwater and three of the thirty-five largest rely on local groundwater alone—Miami, San Antonio, and Memphis. Of the remaining thirty-two, fifteen tap either the Great Lakes or water from major rivers, and twelve garner water from a combination of sources, often importing water from great distances.[30] Each city not only competes with other cities for water but also with local industries that obtain their own water. Supply has never kept pace with demand. Cities must constantly search further and further afield to appropriate water. Only cities which draw from a vast, uncontaminated reservoir of groundwater or from a large, freshwater lake or river are exceptions. Much of New York City's water comes from the Catskill Mountains over one hundred miles away; Boston's water from the Quabbin Valley in central Massachusetts sixty-five miles away; and Los Angeles diverts some of its water from the Colorado River, with its source on the west slope of the Rocky Mountains over six hundred miles away. As growing, dispersed suburban and rural settlements obscure the boundaries between cities, and as the central city loses political power, cities find it more difficult to appropriate distant water supplies.

At the same time urban water supplies are threatened by contamination and depletion, water is squandered. Americans have long used more water per capita than Europeans. The average per capita use in London, Berlin, and seven other European cities was only 39 gallons per day before World War II. During that same period, the average daily consumption in ten American cities was 155 gallons, or nearly four times that amount.[31] By 1975, per capita water use in the United States had reached 168 gallons per day.[32] The average American uses 20 to 80 gallons per day at home. It takes approximately 6 gallons to flush an average toilet, 20 to 40 gallons for a bath, and 20 to 30 gallons to run a washing machine. A leaky faucet dripping one drip per second wastes 4 gallons per day. Watering a garden of 8,000 square feet requires 80 gallons a day in a humid climate and 500 gallons per day in an arid climate.[33]

Uncontaminated fresh water is a diminishing resource. Using drinking water to flush toilets and water lawns is a scandalous waste. Increased industrial demand for water, the invention of domestic appliances like washing machines, and the popularity of a pastoral landscape which requires extensive irrigation, have all contributed to spiraling water use. On the average, domestic use of water accounts for approximately one-third of the water withdrawn from municipal water supplies. Industry utilizes water mainly for cooling and accounts for over a third of the water demand, on the average, but may represent a much greater proportion in some cities. Commercial and public use of water and water lost through leaks in underground pipes account for the remainder. The amount of water lost through leaks is probably equal to the sum of all public water use: for fire fighting, street cleaning, park irrigation, and water for public buildings, swimming pools, and fountains.[34]

Together, dwindling, poisoned water supplies and flooding represent the most significant threats to health and safety of city residents. Water comprises approximately three-quarters of our body. No other resource affects the health of every citizen so intimately and thoroughly, yet cities continue to operate, as they have throughout history, with marginal water systems. Cities respond to each water crisis with narrow solutions which address immediate needs at minimum cost, but ignore the need to promote water conservation and to overhaul overtaxed and outdated collection, storage, and distribution systems. Even as the city thirsts, rainfall is not permitted to enter the ground, but is quickly diverted by the storm drainage system. Parks are built with more pavement and fewer trees, permitting less water to infiltrate the ground. Storm sewers drain the rainfall from parks, and water sprinklers irrigate plants. A water-demanding aesthetic of trees and lawns proliferates in the parks of cities in semiarid and arid climates, further straining the paltry water supply and polluting it with fertilizers, pesticides, and herbicides.

Toxic heavy metals and organic chemicals represent the greatest waterborne threat to health since the epidemics of infectious disease in the eighteenth and nineteenth centuries. Industry and waste disposal sites are located on aquifer recharge areas, and contaminants seep into groundwater. Storm sewers deliver their complement of toxicants to surface water.

As new development locates in headwaters, and houses and businesses crowd and constrict the floodplain, the magnitude of flooding and the damages it inflicts increase. Cities must manage their water resources more wisely. At stake is survival itself.

CHAPTER 7

Controlling and

Restoring the Waters

WATER is a source of life, power, comfort, and delight, a universal symbol of purification and renewal. Like a primordial magnet, water pulls at a primitive and deeply rooted part of human nature. More than any other single element besides trees and gardens, water has the greatest potential to forge an emotional link between man and nature in the city. Water is an element of wondrous qualities. It is a liquid, a gas, or a solid. It absorbs energy and transforms it. It transports other elements in suspension and solution, shaping the landscape and nurturing life. It permeates the terrestrial environment—air, earth, and all living organisms. Pure, in the right place, and at the right time, water is an essential resource; impure, and at the wrong place and time, water is a life-threatening hazard.

An abundance of potable water is a crucial concern of all cities. To this concern, we owe some of the greatest architectural monuments of human history and some of the most impressive engineering works: the aqueducts of Rome and Nîmes and the qanāts of Persia. Eleven aqueducts, bringing water from ten to fifty-nine miles away, supplied Imperial Rome with approximately 35 million gallons of water per day.[1] The aqueducts delivered water to reservoirs from which it was distributed to all parts of the city. Pliny described this feat as one of the greatest achievements of Roman civilization: "But if anyone will note the abundance of water skillfully brought into the city, for public uses, for baths, for public basins, for houses, runnels, suburban gardens and villas; if you will note the high aqueducts required for maintaining proper elevation; the mountains which had to be pierced for the same reason, and the valleys it was necessary to fill up; you will conclude that the whole terrestrial orb offers nothing more marvelous."[2]

Water availability not only determined the site of ancient cities, but also the arrangement of buildings within them. More than 3,000 years ago, the Persians first built qanāts—tunnels many miles long and up to three hundred feet deep—to carry water from mountain slopes to cities at the desert's edge. The hydraulic gradient was a measure of status. The houses and fields of the wealthy were uphill and received the water first. They used the water and passed it on. The poor, whose homes and fields were at the lowest elevations, received the water last. Stone-lined conduits, similar in design to their ancient predecessors, provide many Iranian towns with water today. The wealthy residential districts are still elevated, the poor districts depressed.

Aristotle recognized that an ample water supply was essential to both military security and health: "There should be a natural abundance of springs and fountains in the town, or, if there is a deficiency of them, great reservoirs may be established for the collection of rain water, such as will not fail when the inhabitants are cut off from the country by a war . . . for the elements which we use most and oftenest for support of the body contribute most to health, and among those are water and air."[3]

Urban civilizations have long grappled with the problems of water supply and use, sewage disposal, storm drainage, and flood prevention. Together, these have probably received more sustained attention throughout history than any other single urban problem. There is no lack of models for successful resolution to these problems. Urban cultures that arose in the arid and semiarid climates of Persia and the Mediterranean have developed a landscape art that both conserves and displays water. Cities like Denver, Colorado, that have reclaimed their rivers for recreation, while implementing flood prevention and water quality measures, illustrate the many social and economic benefits such projects generate. Cities that have exploited the flood storage and water treatment potential of wetlands demonstrate how parks and urban wilds can serve many uses. Most of these models, however, consist of solutions to a single aspect of the water problem: either storm drainage and flood control, sewage treatment, or water supply and conservation. The comprehensive, natural drainage system of

Woodlands, Texas, a new town thirty miles north of Houston, exemplifies the advantages of considering storm drainage, flood control, water quality, and water conservation in a single scheme. Whatever the scale—from the design of a drain or a fountain to a plan for an entire metropolitan region—the key to devising efficient, effective, and economical solutions is an understanding of the many ways water moves through the city.

Water in Motion

"All the rivers run into the sea, yet the sea is never full; unto the place from whence the rivers come thither they return again."[4] The hydrologic cycle is a grand process by which rain falls on the land, is absorbed by the earth and the plants that grow in it and runs into streams and oceans, then evaporates, returning once more to the air. The power of the sun and the force of gravity drive the hydrologic cycle. The way water moves through the hydrologic cycle determines the distribution of water supplies, the occurrence of floods, and the fate of contaminants disposed of to the air, water, or land.

Only a fraction of the rain that falls on rural woods and fields runs rapidly into streams, rivers, and lakes. Leaves intercept some rain, and soil soaks up much of the remainder. Of the water that soaks into the soil, some is sucked up by plants and later returned to the atmosphere via evapo-transpiration, some evaporates directly from the soil's surface, and the remainder moves slowly through the soil as groundwater. Groundwater may eventually intersect the land's surface at stream beds and springs or may remain deep beneath the surface in vast underground reservoirs or aquifers (see figure 7.10). Only on steep slopes, on bare rock or ice, or when the soil is saturated, does water run off the ground's surface. The great capacity of soil and the organisms within it to absorb water and to filter and use the elements suspended or dissolved within it prevents floods, protects water quality, and conserves and restores water supplies.

Traditional urban storm drainage systems short-circuit this portion of the hydrologic cycle, with disastrous results. Some cities have attempted to reestablish that link in the cycle by retaining stormwater and permitting it to infiltrate the soil; others have merely detained stormwater until the flood hazard has passed and water can be treated or safely released.

Some of the sources of water pollution—factories, sewage treatment plants, erosion from construction sites, urban runoff from storm sewers, and the fallout of dust from the air—can be pinpointed to the discharge from a specific pipe or ditch; others are more diffuse. "Point" sources are readily monitored and regulated. One can identify and measure the specific pollutants discharged, plot the precise location where they enter the water, and, given the depth and size of the water body and the circulation pattern of the water within it, predict the likely pattern of their distribution. New "point" sources, like factories or treatment plants, can be located in areas with adequate water circulation, distant from swimming beaches.

As more and more industries and municipalities conform to federal water standards, "nonpoint" sources, like air pollution and urban runoff, will become more critical water pollution problems. Nonpoint sources are extremely difficult to regulate except by collecting and treating all stormwater. Flood prevention strategies that involve the retention or detention of stormwater promise to benefit water quality, since most of the suspended solids settle out in standing water and many of the nutrients, oil, and grease are filtered out as water moves through the soil.

Storing Floodwaters

The past decade has seen a profusion of outstanding, innovative approaches to flood control by American cities. Rooftops, plazas, parking lots, and parks have been designed to store stormwater, and woods and wetlands in the headwaters preserved for their natural storage capacity, thereby reducing floods and the cost of storm drainage systems and, in some cases, permitting the treatment of urban runoff. This has generally been accomplished with little or no extra construction cost, with minimal inconvenience, and has resulted in the acquisition of new recreation land. The key to preventing floods and minimizing the destruction they wreak lies in a dual strategy of storing stormwater until flooding peaks and eliminating obstacles to floodwaters within the floodplain. These principles apply whether designing a rooftop to pond and detain rain water or designating undeveloped urban wetlands as parkland to soak up and hold water in soil and plants; whether designing a pedestrian bridge so as not to block debris in floodwaters or establishing land use and building regulations in floodplains.

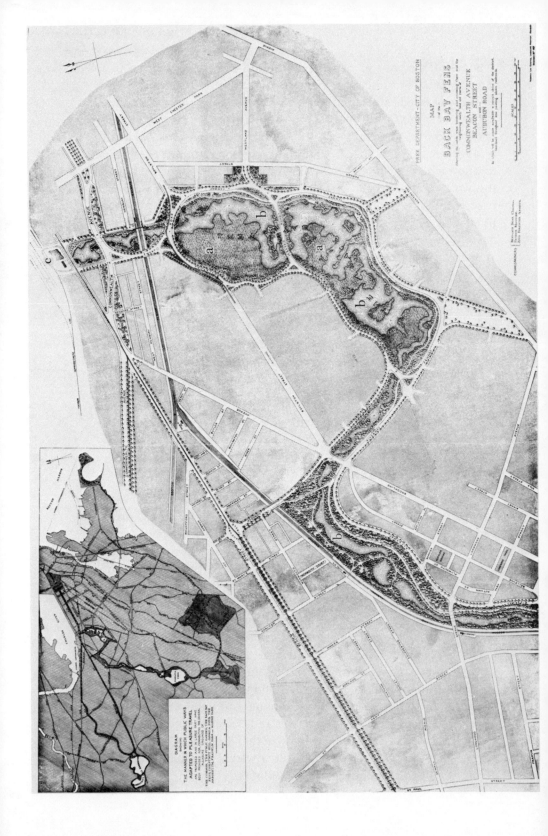

Floodwater storage and recreation are compatible in large urban parks. Parks that exploit the natural flood storage capacity of floodplains capture the water's edge for the public landscape. The recent profusion of urban parks that serve multiple purposes of flood control, water quality improvement, and recreation do not reflect a new idea, but rather the rediscovery of old solutions. Many nineteenth-century and early-twentieth-century parks, now valued for their access to urban rivers and lakefronts, were originally designed as flood control and water quality projects.

Landscape architects and urban historians regard Boston's "Emerald Necklace" park system as a landmark in American park planning, but few appreciate that a third of the system was designed as a flood control and water quality project and not primarily for recreation. The designer, Frederick Law Olmsted, created the Fens and the Riverway to combat the flooding and pollution problems of Boston's Back Bay tidal flats; public recreation was an incidental benefit and Olmsted himself objected to the use of the word "park" for the Fens, since he did not consider it an appropriate spot for any recreation beyond a stroll or drive along the border of the marsh. The statement printed on Olmsted's 1881 map, "General Plan for the Sanitary Improvement of the Muddy River," declares this intent:

The primary design of the scheme here shown is to abate existing nuisances, avoid threatened dangers and provide for the permanent, wholesome and seemly disposition of the drainage of Muddy River Valley. This is proposed to be accomplished chiefly by embanking, contracting and deepening the existing creek and ponds and excluding sewage and tides. The secondary design is to make use of the embankments required for the above purpose to complete the promenade here shown, of which the Common, Public Garden and Commonwealth Avenue would form about one-third already prepared and in use, and the Back Bay, now half-formed, and in progress, another third . . . [5]

Until recently, historians have admired Olmsted's Boston park system chiefly for its connection of the central city with outlying suburbs, in a series of parks and connecting parkways, forgetting the flood control and water quality purpose that portions of it originally served. Olmsted designed the Fens as an irregularly shaped depression scooped out of the tidal flats (see figure 7.1). The configuration

FIGURE 7.1
Plan for the Fens, Boston, 1887, showing retention basins (a) and dredged river channels (b) designed to prevent flooding in adjacent areas, and a tidal gate (c) to prevent water stagnation. Modern, "innovative" projects in Chicago and Denver are based on some of the same principles.

and size of the thirty-acre basin permitted the amount of water to double without raising the water level more than a few feet; during floods, twenty additional acres could be covered with water. Gently sloping banks and an irregularly shaped edge reduced waves. A tidal gate at the entry to the Charles River regulated the flow of the tides to prevent flooding and to enhance flushing of the basin. Part of Olmsted's plan was the restoration of the former salt marsh; he planted the banks of the basin with plants that could tolerate both salt and brackish water and withstand changing water levels. Olmsted felt that the juxtaposition of salt marsh and city

would be novel, certainly, in labored urban grounds, and there may be a momentary question of its dignity and appropriateness . . . but [it] is a direct development of the original conditions of the locality in adaptation to the needs of a dense community. So regarded, it will be found to be, in the artistic sense of the word, natural, and possibly to suggest a modest poetic sentiment more grateful to townweary minds than an elaborate and elegant gardenlike work would have yielded.[6]

Portions of the Fens were planted by 1884 and within ten years had the look of a landscape that had always been there. The rapid success was largely due to the sheer quantity and diversity of vegetation planted: more than 100,000 shrubs, vines, and flowers in one area of two-and-a-half acres.[7]

The Muddy River flows into the Fens, its current alignment and shape the nineteenth century's artificial creation. The banks of the Muddy River were regraded, lined with walkways, crossed by bridges for pedestrians and vehicles, and planted with grasses, shrubs, and trees to form the "Riverway" (figure 7.2). Like the Fens, within a few decades of construction, the Riverway had the appearance of a natural floodplain penetrating the city (figure 7.3). Depressed below street level, with steep, wooded banks between the roadway above and the path below, it is still a retreat in the middle of modern Boston. The Muddy River survives more intact than the Fens. After the Charles River Dam was constructed in the early twentieth century, the salt marsh declined, the Fens lost the aid of the tides in enhancing water circulation, and ultimately became a dumping ground for fill from the subway and other projects.

Chicago, built on a flat plain only slightly higher than Lake Michigan, has been plagued by drainage and flooding problems throughout its history and has responded with ingenious solutions. In the mid 1800s Chicago raised its street level twelve feet, jacked up and elevated existing buildings, and installed a new storm sewer system. After 12 percent of the city's population died in 1885 from cholera,

FIGURE 7.2
The Riverway, Boston, ca 1892, showing graded embankments ready for planting. To the right, a mound separates the park from a recently installed trolley line.

FIGURE 7.3
The Riverway approximately thirty years after construction, having achieved a wholly "natural" appearance, the adjacent trolley line now hidden behind mound and plants.

typhoid, and dysentery contracted from a polluted water supply, Chicago established an autonomous regional agency, the Metropolitan Sanitary District of greater Chicago. For nearly a century, this organization has coordinated Chicago's flood control, storm drainage, and sewage treatment. Chicago has a combined sanitary and storm sewer system and now uses stormwater detention basins located throughout the city in floodplains to detain stormwater before it reaches storm sewers, along with an extensive system of deep, underground tunnels to store the overflow from the sewer system until it can be treated. The Melvina Ditch Detention Reservoir is one of the many large detention basins operated by the Metropolitan Sanitary District and used for both flood control and recreation. Steps lead down the basin's side slope to playfields and volleyball and basketball courts in the bottom of the basin. Children ski and toboggan down the slopes of a large earthen mound at the corner of the basin and skate on an ice rink created by flooding a large, paved area near the basin's inlet. When flooded, the reservoir holds 165 acre-feet of water.[8]

Parking lots, which account for much of the open, paved land in American cities, can also be designed to detain or even retain stormwater, as one was at the First National Bank in Boulder, Colorado, where a section of the lot can hold up to two feet of water. Consolidated Freightways in St. Louis, Missouri, constructed its parking lot to detain storm flows and netted a $35,000 savings in the cost of the storm drainage system.[9] Outside the downtown, in less dense parts of the city, it may be preferable to retain water long enough for it to infiltrate the soil. Porous pavement—porous asphalt, modular paving, and gravel—over well-drained soils or in combination with dry wells will permit more rainfall to soak into the ground rather than run off into storm sewers. A pavement of lattice concrete blocks, with soil and grass in the interstices, is widely used in European cities, and has been employed in parts of some American cities such as Los Angeles and Dayton (see figure 3.11).

Restoring and Conserving Water

The restoration of water is also an essential function. A sewage treatment facility can be attractive and, in certain phases of its operation, compatible with recreation. In 1967, after the state of Michigan threatened to cite the city of Mt. Clemens for pollution of the Clinton River, the city combined a new sewage treatment system with a park.[10] Combined storm and sanitary sewers comprised 90 percent of the Mt. Clemens sewer system, and sewer overflows during rainstorms had been responsible, in part, for pollution of the river. After several years' study, the city determined that collecting, storing, and treating the combined overflow was more feasible, more efficient, and less costly than separating the storm and sanitary sewer systems, and that it also offered an opportunity to create new parkland. The city constructed its new sewer overflow treatment facility with three small lakes and a park on a former sanitary landfill site. Sewer overflows remain in the first lake for anywhere from one to four days, until they can be treated in the processing building, then the water is released for aeration to the second lake for an additional seven days. By the time the treated effluent reaches the third lake, 2.3 acres and 9 feet deep, it is appropriate for boating and fishing and for irrigating the park's landscape. In winter, when the third lake freezes, it is used for skating and ice hockey. The city plans to stock it with fish and construct a dock for summer recreation.

Arcata, California, exploits the properties of plants and soil to assimilate wastes, by using a wetland as part of its wastewater treatment process. Arcata renovated and reconstructed a degraded, existing wetland adjacent to its sewage treatment plant to enhance the quality of its water after treatment.[11] The reconstructed wetland serves other functions including wildlife habitat and recreation (see chapter 13). Other cities, including Austin, Texas, have experimented with natural or constructed wetlands to treat sewage effluents. Because wetland or aquatic plant systems to treat wastewater require more land area than conventional treatment methods, they are likely to be most appropriate for small-to-moderate-sized cities. The danger of introducing concentrated heavy metals and toxicants into the food chain rules out the use of such systems when effluent is heavily contaminated by these pollutants. Wetland treatment systems will be most useful in providing advanced treatment where traditional chemical methods are too costly, and they are likely to become more common as current successes become better known.[12]

Sewage treatment can both conserve water and create an aesthetic resource. Five miles out of Santa Fe, New Mexico, a resort named The Bishop's Lodge has built a package sewage treatment facility to provide irrigation water for the resort's pasture and garden (figure 7.4). It forms an unusual amenity in this water-poor landscape. Treated wastewater tumbles down waterfalls and cascades through

FIGURE 7.4
FIGURE 7.4
A rocky cascade at Bishop's Lodge, New Mexico, part of a man-made system
of waterfalls and sculpted channels designed to treat sewage effluent.

sculpted channels and streams from high ground into a large pool.
These "seven magic pools" provide tertiary treatment to the wastewater by aerating it and exposing it to sunlight.[13] The water cascades
a hundred feet to the resort's entrance; landscaping and earth
mounds screen the treatment plant from view. Water conservation is
an important benefit. Formerly, The Bishop's Lodge used 10,000 gallons of well water per day to irrigate its lawns, nearly one-third of
the total daily consumption. Irrigation water now consists entirely
of treated sewage effluent, an example to inspire cities to explore
waste treatment that is beautiful as well as economical.

Irrigation is used routinely to maintain lawns and trees in the city,
but as water shortages increase, the city must explore a more water-
conserving and drought-tolerant landscape. The landscape tradition
that arose in the urban civilizations of the arid and semiarid regions
surrounding the Mediterranean offers many models for the modern
city, for example, the protected courtyard garden or patio. The courtyards nurture lush vegetation with minimal irrigation by protecting

plants from dehydrating winds and radiated heat; the barren streets of the city heighten the aesthetic relief of the courtyards. The garden art of the Mediterranean and the Middle East also exploits the many physical properties and aesthetic qualities of water with great economy. A Persian garden accomplishes a great emotional and aesthetic effect with only a trickle of water. The subtle, refined, and profound treatment of water in the Hispano-Islamic garden makes a 100-foot jet of water elsewhere seem a vulgar display of power. An art that developed over the course of thousands of years and spread with the Moslem religion west across North Africa to Spain and east to Pakistan and India, the Islamic garden takes many forms. Each form, however, reflects the inspired manipulation of water, employing the sight and sound of water to engender a cool atmosphere of serenity and retreat. Water cascades down sculpted channels or through plain runnels into brimming basins. Slight variations in the shape of the channel produce wave patterns that catch the light in diverse ways. Water may appear precious, like a gem, as it flows over blue tiles. Water may bubble up from below the surface, or trace a graceful arc, or flow as a sheet over a molded edge. Water-poor cities should conserve their water by reserving irrigation for special or symbolic places or protected spaces where plants require minimal water. The importance of these places will thereby be heightened. Paley Park owes much of its success as an urban retreat to the contrast between its environment and the noisy, hot, dry city surrounding it.

The design for Foothill College, in the semiarid climate of Los Altos, California, as originally conceived, created an oasis garden to exploit the aesthetic impact of the contrast between irrigated and nonirrigated landscape. The architects designed the college as a compound of buildings, surrounding a central courtyard, on a hilltop, with parking below. The courtyard was designed as an oasis garden with lush vegetation sustained by irrigation; the hillside was seeded with drought-tolerant grasses. The contrast between the dry, brown hillside and the green, protected courtyard lent to the interior an atmosphere of comfort, retreat, and renewal. Since the college began to irrigate the hillside also, however, this atmosphere has been largely lost. It may be recaptured when water shortages in Northern California force the college to reduce irrigation.

In cities of a temperate, humid climate, enough rain falls to support a diverse community of plants without irrigation, so long as that water is permitted to infiltrate the soil and plants are protected from winds and radiant heat. Chestnut Park in downtown Philadelphia is paved and landscaped with plants native to that region. Rain falling within the park seeps between cracks in the pavement to the soil below. A deep layer of gravel beneath the topsoil serves both as a drainage device and as a reservoir, storing the water until plant roots can absorb it and preventing roots from becoming water-logged. The plants have flourished and require no irrigation. Meanwhile, the park contributes no stormwater runoff to the city's sewers.

Designing the City to Conserve and Restore Water and to Prevent Floods

The prevention of floods and the conservation and restoration of water will only be accomplished by the cumulative effect of many individual actions throughout the city. But the impact of each will be insignificant, and might even be counterproductive, if not part of a comprehensive plan that takes into account the hydrologic system of the entire city and its region. Water pollution or flooding problems at one place may be generated somewhere else, and a solution to the water supply problem may, in the end, aggravate water pollution. The most effective, efficient, and economical solutions to urban water problems are frequently found upstream of where the problem is felt most forcefully.

The Charles River watershed is the most densely populated river basin in New England. Its headwaters are sparsely developed, but the cities of Boston and Cambridge crowd the banks of its lower basin. The U.S. Army Corps of Engineers, in a 1965 flood control study of the Charles River watershed, concluded that a new dam must be built across the mouth of the Charles River to control flooding from urban runoff in the lower basin and that over the next thirty to forty years flood-control measures upstream must be taken to prevent flooding in the lower basin. They estimated that upstream flood-control structures would cost $100 million and, instead, recommended an action requiring one-tenth the cost:

The flood control management plan recommended by this Corps' study calls for federal acquisition and perpetual protection of seventeen crucial natural valley storage areas totalling some 8,500 acres. The logic of the scheme is compelling. Nature has already provided the least cost solution to future flooding in the form of extensive wetlands which moderate extreme highs and lows in stream flow. Rather than attempt to improve on this natural protection mechanism, it is both prudent and economical to leave the hydrologic regime established over the millenia undisturbed. In the opinion of the study team, construction of any of the most likely alternatives, a 55,000 acre/foot reservoir, or extensive walls or dikes, can add nothing.[14]

The effective role of the wetlands in flood prevention was demonstrated while the Corps of Engineers was engaged in its study. In 1968 a large storm hit Boston, and urban runoff in the lower basin crested at the old Charles River Dam within hours. The upstream peak took four days to reach the dam. The wetlands in the headwaters filled with water, gradually releasing it over the course of a month. One stretch of the river widened from fifty feet to nearly a mile.[15] Boston's second circumferential interstate highway was under construction at the time, and because rapid urbanization threatened the wetlands, the Corps decided that acquisition of the wetlands was the most effective method of preserving their flood storage capacity. They selected seventeen natural storage areas,

FIGURE 7.5
Natural Valley Storage Areas, Boston: wetlands purchased as part of a flood control program to store floodwaters until peak flows subside downstream. The 8,500 acres of wetlands cost one-tenth the price of dams and levees a more traditional approach would have entailed.

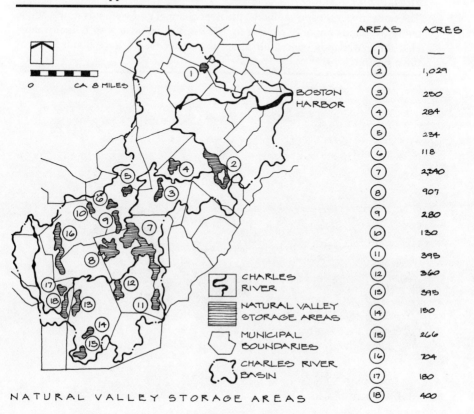

AREAS	ACRES
1	—
2	1,029
3	250
4	284
5	234
6	118
7	2,340
8	907
9	280
10	130
11	395
12	360
13	395
14	180
15	266
16	704
17	180
18	400

CHARLES RIVER

NATURAL VALLEY STORAGE AREAS

MUNICIPAL BOUNDARIES

CHARLES RIVER BASIN

NATURAL VALLEY STORAGE AREAS

FIGURE 7.6(a)
Natural valley storage area in summer, with both the Charles River and adjacent wetlands clearly visible.

FIGURE 7.6(b)
The same area after spring floods, the river channel and wetlands now a single entity. Wetlands not only provide overflow space, but also absorb floodwaters. Had these wetlands been built upon, this water would have flooded downtown Boston.

ranging in size from 118 to 2,340 acres, from among 20,000 acres of wetlands in the middle and upper reaches of the Charles River (see figures 7.5 and 7.6). In 1974, Congress approved and appropriated $10 million to buy the wetlands for nonstructural flood control. The Corps of Engineers made the first purchase in 1977. It will retain ownership of the land, and the Massachusetts Fisheries and Wildlife Division will manage the areas as wildlife refuges.[16]

Denver, Colorado, is an outstanding example of a city that has implemented a comprehensive, coordinated set of strategies for managing its water. The devastating property losses caused by the 1965 flood provided the incentive for the formation of the Urban Drainage and Flood Control District in 1969. Earlier, each of the region's thirty-four independent local governments had employed different methods for calculating flood risks and for designing the capacity of their storm drainage systems. Some had designed storm drainage systems to accommodate a fifty-year storm; others had provided for floods from a two-year storm.[17] The Urban Drainage and Flood Control District now works with local governments to insure the adoption and implementation of adequate and consistent floodplain regulations and to undertake master plans for individual watersheds. The *Urban Storm Drainage Criteria Manual*, published in 1969, guides the work in the district and insures consistent, state-of-the-art drainage and flood control across the entire metropolitan region. The manual covers issues of policy, law, and planning related to flood control and storm drainage, the calculation of stormwater runoff, the design of the storm drainage system, and the mitigation of flood damage.

Each year Denver's Urban Drainage and Flood Control District compiles a list for master planning of between five and ten projects for which district aid has been requested by local governments. The project must be multijurisdictional, and local governments must agree to pay half of the cost of the study and half the cost of construction, and to assume ownership after completion.[18] The district maps the one hundred-year floodplain, prepares an outline of the work to be done, and coordinates consulting engineers on behalf of the local governments. The studies cover an entire drainage basin, rather than piecemeal projects. The master plan spells out where flood problems exist and recommends remedial measures. Its recommendations will include the adoption of floodplain regulations and the implementation of such projects as stormwater detention, channel improvements, and check dams along streams to create ponds and slow stream flow. The city and county of Denver now require property owners to pay a storm drainage service charge to help finance the construction and maintenance of the stormwater system. The amount of building and paved surface on the property determines the rate billed. In 1981, when the service charge was enacted, the city estimated that annual revenues would amount to $4.7 million.[19]

Citizens of Denver have transformed a ten-mile stretch of the South Platte River, which flows through downtown Denver, from a rubble-strewn, filthy, open sewer, lined by garbage and derelict land, into a landscaped park for water sports, public gatherings, bicycling and hiking, and nature study. Like the Urban Drainage and Flood Control District, the development of Denver's South Platte "Greenway" has its roots in the disastrous flood of 1965. A flurry of investigations and reports followed the 1965 flood, but little was done about the South Platte itself until a flood in 1973, an election year, brought the issue of the river and flood hazard under the public eye again. A nine-member task force, the Platte River Development Committee, appointed by Denver's mayor and backed by over $2 million in seed money from the city, proceeded to lay plans for the river, raise additional money from public and private sources, and implement park projects.[20]

The Platte River "Greenway" (figure 7.7) now links eighteen parks with fifteen miles of interconnected trails; with 450 acres, it is Denver's largest single park. When complete, the "Greenway" will extend twenty-five miles upstream to the foot of the Rocky Mountains and twenty miles downstream to a state recreation area on the Colorado plains. Proponents hope that suburban communities will develop trails along the Platte's tributaries, so that eventually 120 miles of continuous river trails would lace the metropolitan region. The entire ten-mile Platte River "Greenway" is now a regional center for boating, lined by bicycle and hiking trails, and punctuated by parks. Check dams in the South Platte were designed to create white water "staircases" for canoes, kayaks, and rafts. Competitions are now held along the man-made "Challenge Run" and slalom kayak course. At one spot, where an eight-foot dam needed to retain water for a power plant made the river impassable by boat, a boat chute was created to permit boats and rafts to negotiate the dam without portage and to serve simultaneously as a flood control device. Care-

---

FIGURE 7.7
The Platte River Greenway. Designed to accommodate both floodwaters and recreation, the Greenway is now Denver's largest single park with 450 acres and fifteen miles of interconnected trails.

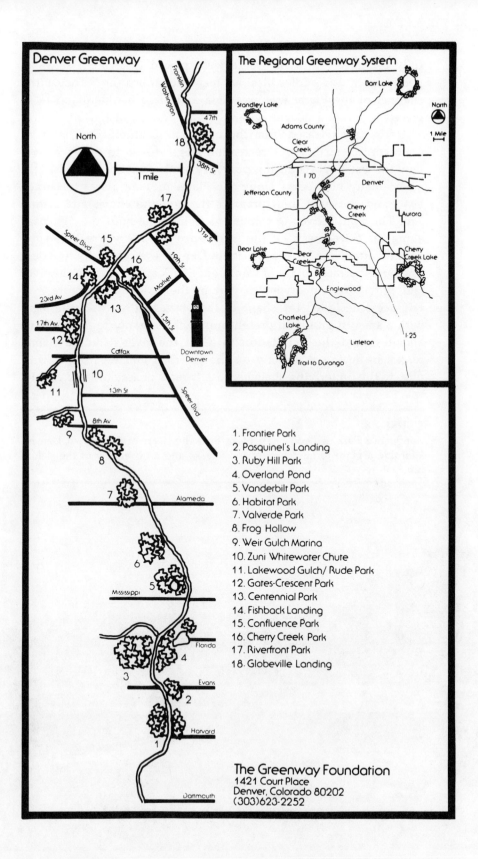

Denver Greenway

North

1 mile

Franklin
Washington
47th
38th St
31st St
18
17
Speer Blvd
15
16
19th St
Market
14
23rd Av
13
17th Av
15th St
12
Colfax
Downtown
Denver
10
11
13th St
8th Av
Speer Blvd
9
8
7
Alameda
6
5
Mississippi
Florida
4
3
Evans
2
Harvard
1
Dartmouth

The Regional Greenway System

North

1 Mile

Barr Lake
Standley Lake
Adams County
Clear Creek
I 70
Denver
Jefferson County
Cherry Creek
Aurora
Bear Lake
Bear Creek
Cherry Creek Lake
Englewood
Chatfield Lake
Littleton
I-25
Trail to Durango

1. Frontier Park
2. Pasquinel's Landing
3. Ruby Hill Park
4. Overland Pond
5. Vanderbilt Park
6. Habitat Park
7. Valverde Park
8. Frog Hollow
9. Weir Gulch Marina
10. Zuni Whitewater Chute
11. Lakewood Gulch/ Rude Park
12. Gates-Crescent Park
13. Centennial Park
14. Fishback Landing
15. Confluence Park
16. Cherry Creek Park
17. Riverfront Park
18. Globeville Landing

The Greenway Foundation
1421 Court Place
Denver, Colorado 80202
(303)623-2252

fully arranged weirs and rocks were placed to create a series of pools, riffles, and eddies ideal for recreational boating.[21] The central channel of the Platte was excavated and large boulders and rocks placed to create a deeper stream during periods of low river flow. Water is now released from the upstream Chatfield Dam, a major flood control facility, in "recreation slugs" timed to enhance river flow for water sports during peak weekend recreation periods.

The many new parks along the Platte provide places to launch boats and to watch their progress through the chutes and slalom run. The Platte River Development Committee built the first park along the "Greenway" at the confluence of Cherry Creek and the South Platte River, where the city of Denver was originally founded. The large, terraced plaza of Confluence Park steps down to the river and provides an overview of part of the slalom run (figure 7.8). Engineers designed the shape of the plaza and the opposite bank with a smooth profile to present minimal resistance to floodwaters, and designed the foundation to resist the river's hydrodynamic forces, by laying it directly on the riverbed and securing it with piles to the underlying shale bedrock.[22] Years of accumulated rubble,

FIGURE 7.8
Confluence Park, a flood-proof plaza near the heart of downtown Denver, affording a place to launch rafts and kayaks and an overview of the slalom run.

which had blocked floodwaters and increased flood depth, were used in the construction of paths, boat chutes, and bank improvements. An amphitheater across the river from Confluence Park was created with fill from river debris and the ruins of a bridge demolished by the 1973 flood. Pedestrian bridges, which link Confluence Park with the amphitheater and opposite banks in other parts of the "Greenway," are designed to pose no obstruction to floodwaters, since a major cause of past flood damage was the piling-up of debris at bridges in dams which diverted floodwaters into adjacent parts of the city. The wooden pedestrian bridges are designed to come loose from their concrete piers when floodwaters reach the bridge deck. Cables attached to the bridge will hold it against the downstream bank until flooding subsides.[23] All of the parks along the floodway are designed not only to resist flood damage, but also to provide flood storage. The grading for a new bicycle path at Centennial Park, for example, was based on flood hydraulics.

With increased use of the river for walking, bicycling, and boating has come a heightened awareness of the river's water quality and a strong constituency for improving and maintaining that quality. Many sources of water pollution have been removed from the river banks as a consequence: a dump has been converted to a nature preserve; a highway maintenance yard piled with salt and sand has become Frog Hollow Park. Pressure has been brought upon the city to cease dumping street sweepings and salt-laden snow in the river. The residential neighborhoods bordering the South Platte, several of them Denver's poorest, have gained new parks and a river environment free from former nuisances and hazards.

The Platte River "Greenway" was accomplished through the coordinated efforts of public and private organizations and individual citizens. The Platte River Greenway Foundation, established as a nonprofit, tax-exempt institution, ultimately collected over $6 million from federal, state, and local governments, from private foundations, and from individuals. The foundation, though private, cooperated closely with the city from its inception; funded and coordinated the implementation of projects on behalf of the city; and then turned over the responsibility of maintenance to the city's parks department.[24]

Rooftops, plazas, and parking lots often provide the only space to detain stormwater in densely built downtown areas, and Denver is no exception. The city of Denver requires new and renovated buildings in the Skyline Urban Renewal District to detain stormwater on site. The alternative, upgrading the existing storm sewer system to

FIGURE 7.9
Skyline Plaza in downtown Denver ponds up to several inches of stormwater, releasing it gradually. There is space to detain stormwater even in the most congested parts of cities.

accommodate the increased runoff, would have been prohibitively expensive and would have increased flooding in the nearby South Platte River. Developers have used a combination of rooftops, plazas, and parking lots to detain stormwater. Roofs in the Denver area are designed to support a snow load equivalent to approximately six inches of water. Engineers designed a "detention ring" to fit around the drain of a flat roof, which ponds up to three inches of water, then releases it at the rate of one-half inch per hour. A safety feature permits a severe storm to overflow the ring. Denver-area plazas and parking lots have been designed to store stormwater runoff with minimal inconvenience to pedestrians (figure 7.9). One depressed, downtown Denver plaza, constructed above three floors of underground parking, accommodates runoff from the ten-year storm; stormwater drains directly to the sewer at the rate of one inch per hour. Ponding does not disrupt use of the plaza, since elevated portions of the plaza permit pedestrians to walk across it when lower portions are flooded.

Existing building codes in most American cities require that roofs be designed to withstand the equivalent of six inches of water over a short period (usually twenty-four hours), and a few cities have incorporated rooftop detention of stormwater into building codes. European cities like Stuttgart have applied the use of "wet roofs" to reduce the building's heat load as well, and thus decrease energy consumption for air conditioning. If incorporated into roof garden design, stormwater detention can also become an aesthetic amenity.

In little more than one decade, Denver has achieved considerable success in reclaiming its waters. Consider how much might be accomplished in the construction of a new city unhampered by existing buildings, streets, and drainage systems. Such a case is the new town of Woodlands, Texas, with a projected ultimate population of 150,000. When developer George Mitchell first decided to build a new town on 20,000 acres of pine–oak woodland north of Houston, he envisioned a city that would spring up in the midst of the woods, in harmony with the forces of nature. He formed the Mitchell Energy and Development Corporation and hired an interdisciplinary team of planners, engineers, scientists, and market specialists. Initially this team consisted of four firms. Over the following decade the team was expanded to include a well-staffed corporation with dozens of consultants. By 1971, when the preliminary ecological planning study and parallel market research were complete and a general plan for the new town was underway, water had emerged as the critical factor. The Woodlands' "natural drainage system" exploits the capacity of natural, wooded floodplains to accommodate stormwater runoff and of well-drained soils to soak up and store rainfall. It reduces the combination of increased flooding and lower stream flows normally associated with urbanization, it maintains water quality, and recharges the aquifer that underlies neighboring Houston (figure 7.10). The wooded floodplain, drainage channels, and recharge soils form a townwide open-space system, a natural drainage system that represents a substantial savings over the cost of constructing a conventional storm sewer system. When it was originally proposed, engineers compared the cost of the natural drainage system to that for a conventional storm system and estimated that the natural drainage system would save the developer over $14 million.[25]

Much of the Woodlands site is very flat, with extensive areas of poorly drained soils. The construction of a traditional storm drainage system would have entailed clearance of extensive woodlands, and lowered water tables with loss of trees. It would also have in-

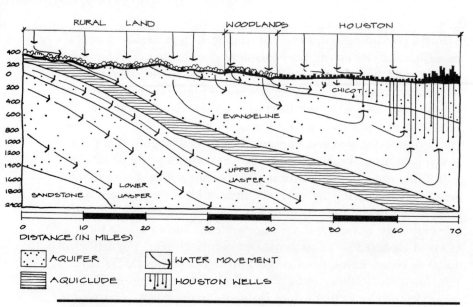

FIGURE 7.10
Aquifers underlying Houston and Woodlands, Texas. The new town of Wood-lands was designed so that rain would continue to soak into the ground to replenish the Chicot and Evangeline aquifers, from which nearby Houston draws its water supply.

creased flooding and degraded water quality downstream and, com-bined with an estimated 15 million gallons per day withdrawal from underlying aquifers, might have contributed to further ground sub-sidence under the city of Houston (see chapter 4). The firm of Wal-lace McHarg Roberts and Todd, landscape architects and ecological planners, conceived a natural drainage system to resolve these prob-lems and enable the developer to retain his vision of the future city.[26]

The natural drainage system is composed of two subsystems: one stores and absorbs rainfall from frequent storms; the other drains floodwater from major storms (see figure 7.11). The general plan responded to the major drainage system by locating large roads and dense development on ridge lines and higher elevations, while pre-serving the floodplains in parks and open land, and allocating low-density housing to the intermediate area. Use of the floodplains and drainage channels as open space works well from both ecological and social standpoints. Most of the spectacular trees on the site occur within the floodplains of two major creeks—large, evergreen mag-nolias, water and willow oaks, and towering pines. These same floodplains also harbor a diverse, abundant native wildlife, includ-ing white-tailed deer, opossum, armadillos, bobcats, and many birds,

164

and provide the corridors along which they move. The wooded easements required for drainage and flood control purposes are in most
cases sufficient to insure that all but the most sensitive wildlife species may remain. A continuous system of hiking, equestrian, and
bicycle trails runs along the drainage network, linking all parts of
the new town.

Although this larger floodplain network drains runoff from major
storms, well-drained soils and ponds absorb or store rain close to
where it falls, either in private yards or in nearby parks. This local
drainage system responds to subtle changes in topography and soils.
Roads, golf courses, and parks are designed to impound stormwater
and enhance its absorption by well-drained soils. Maintaining the
structure of these soils, so essential to their ability to absorb water,
required strict regulation of construction activities. Areas designated
as "recharge soils" were left wooded. In some cases, building construction proceeded within a fenced-off zone that extended only a
few feet on all sides from the building foundation. This practice has

FIGURE 7.11
The "natural drainage system" at Woodlands, Texas, exploits well-drained
soils to absorb rainfall and wooded swales and stream valleys to carry off the
stormwaters, thereby preventing floods downstream. Using existing, wooded
floodplains for the storm drainage system secured a linked system of parks
and trails throughout the town and saved millions of dollars.

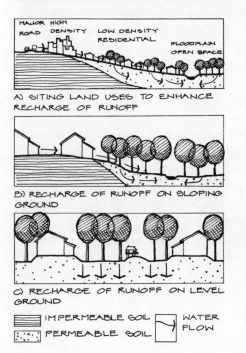

A) SITING LAND USES TO ENHANCE RECHARGE OF RUNOFF

B) RECHARGE OF RUNOFF ON SLOPING GROUND

C) RECHARGE OF RUNOFF ON LEVEL GROUND

IMPERMEABLE SOIL

PERMEABLE SOIL

WATER FLOW

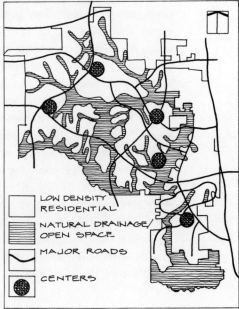

LOW DENSITY RESIDENTIAL

NATURAL DRAINAGE/ OPEN SPACE

MAJOR ROADS

CENTERS

D) PLAN OF WOODLANDS, TEXAS

produced a new town with the appearance of having literally sprung up within the woods.

Models estimating the increase in peak flows generated by development at the Woodlands revealed that they will increase by only 55 percent, as compared to the 180 percent increase resulting from current "normal" development in Houston.[27] Studies indicate that the water quality of urban runoff in the phase one portion of the new town is much better than that of other Houston residential areas. The final test of the natural drainage system occurred when a record storm hit the area in April 1979. Nine inches of rain fell within five hours, and no house within the Woodlands flooded although adjacent subdivisions were awash.[28]

The economic benefits of a natural drainage system may not elsewhere be as dramatic as in Woodlands with its extensive flat areas and poorly drained soils, but they will accrue nonetheless. The Woodlands is and will continue to be a showpiece of drainage design, from the most mundane details of pavement and channel design to the coordination of soils, ponds, swales, and floodplains into a comprehensive drainage system.

A Plan for Every City

The successful management of water in the city will require comprehensive efforts, many individual actions, and the perception that storm drainage, flood control, water supply, water conservation, waste disposal, and sewage treatment are all facets of a much broader system. Every city should construct a framework within which both the consequences of major metropolitan efforts and the cumulative effect of individual actions can be appreciated.

The flow of water into and through the city—including where it comes from, how and where it is used, treated, and released, and the seasonal variation of this pattern—varies from city to city, depending on regional climate, topographic setting, pollution sources, and urban form. Do floods threaten a major portion of the city; and is development upstream the greater problem or constriction of the floodplain within the city? Is the city's water supply threatened by pollution of groundwater or surface water, or by competing demands with other towns and cities in the region? Are large, industrial pollutors the problem, or combined sanitary and storm sewage overflows? Are extremes of high flows and low flows a problem, or limited water circulation? Identifying the areas at most risk to flood hazard and those that currently provide flood storage will help in devising a comprehensive flood control strategy. Identifying the major sources of water pollution within the city, the dispersion patterns of pollutants within surface and groundwater, and water bodies with poor circulation will aid in singling out the most severely contaminated places. Knowing the most significant water resources, those that currently provide the city with water or have the potential to do so in the future, and the areas that are most sensitive to water pollution, like aquifer recharge areas, headwater streams, lakes, and ponds, will help to preserve those resources.

A comprehensive plan to prevent floods and conserve and restore the city's water should:

- address the city's most critical problems of flooding, water pollution, and water supply, with particular attention to reducing risk in the most flood-prone or contaminated areas
- protect the city's most important water resources, both those currently used for water supply and those with potential to satisfy increasing demand
- locate new parks and other landscaped open space to preserve flood storage in the headwaters and the floodplain downstream, and to enhance recharge of groundwater
- encourage new industry, waste disposal sites, and other polluting land uses to locate outside floodplains and groundwater recharge areas that are highly vulnerable to water pollution
- locate new public buildings outside flood-prone areas and encourage new residential and commercial development to do the same
- provide a plan for relocation and reconstruction after a major flood
- explore settlement patterns that would facilitate the reuse of wastewater after treatment
- exploit the flood protection and water-restoring abilities of existing wetlands
- increase the visibility of water in the city as well as public access to it.

Every new building, street, parking lot, and park within the city should be designed to prevent or mitigate flooding and to conserve and restore water resources. Every project should:

- address the relationship between the project's site and the city's critical flooding, water pollution, and water supply problems, as well as specific hazards and resources that exist on the site and in its immediate neighborhood
- site and design buildings and landscaping to avoid flood damage
- exploit the ability of rooftops, plazas, parking lots, and the earth to detain or retain stormwater runoff

167

- design parks in floodplains to store floodwater and withstand flood damage
- design the size, depth, shape, and shoreline of urban water bodies to enhance water circulation and store stormwater
- select hardy plants that require little, if any, irrigation, fertilizers, or pesticides, and protect plants from desiccating winds
- utilize stormwater, if sufficiently uncontaminated by salts and pollutants, or treated wastewater to meet plant water needs
- exploit the aesthetic properties of water without wasting it.

Water problems and their severity vary from city to city, but every city must manage its own water resources. Cities of the past and present plagued by water problems have pioneered solutions to flood control, water conservation, and water restoration. Many of these models are applicable to every city, not just those with semi-arid climates or with intensely developed floodplains. Opportunities for preventing floods, for preserving water quality, and for conserving water exist in the design of every new building and park as well as every metropolitan plan, at the center of downtown and at the urbanizing metropolitan fringe. When the urban water crisis comes, it will probably hit fast-growing cities in arid regions first, but it will extend inevitably to cities in humid regions as well. Eventually, every city will have to design a comprehensive plan for water management, including the regulation of urban form and density in headwaters and floodplains, the regulation of water use, with attendant implications for landscape design, and the careful siting of waste disposal sites and industrial and sewage outfalls.

The knowledge for such a plan exists today; the underevaluation of water is the major obstacle to its implementation. Once the water crisis forces cities to charge full value for water, the support for water conservation will follow. When cheap water is a thing of the past, rainfall will be cherished, runoff utilized, and flooding reduced. Cities will protect their water from contamination and reuse it after treatment. City parks and private grounds will acquire a drought-tolerant landscape. The use of water in public spaces will be restrained, but the impact will be powerful.

In the next decade, the dilapidated, outmoded water supply, wastewater treatment, and storm drainage systems in many older American cities will have to be overhauled. This will entail the expenditure of billions of dollars and considerable upheaval in dense urban centers. Short-term expediency must not prevail; the opportunity for redesign must be seized.

PART V

Life

CHAPTER 8

Urban Plants:
Struggle for Survival

T HE STREET TREE is an endangered species. A large, landscaped midcity park is a white elephant, easy prey to municipal building schemes. In 1970, Detroit, Philadelphia, and Dayton cut down more trees than they planted. Detroit removed 10,623 trees in that year and planted only 2,457.[1] Many mourn the fall of a row of elms, but few appreciate how commonplace the event of loss or how massive the citywide impact. Although the gradual decline and disappearance of trees from city streets and city parks is going virtually unnoticed, cities will soon be hotter, dirtier, less attractive, with more devastating floods, more erosion, and poorer water quality, as a direct consequence.

It takes more than forty years for most trees to mature; yet in the city the average lifetime of a street tree planted today may be only ten years.[2] Mature trees arching out over the street is an image to which urban designers and residents alike cling, but the days of such trees in the center of American cities are numbered. The benefits are most evident after they are gone. All who have experienced the disappearance of mature trees from the street can testify to the result. The street, sidewalk, and adjacent buildings feel much hotter, the air grittier. Street noise echoing off building walls and unmasked by the rustle of leaves seems much louder. Seasons pass unheralded; property values of adjacent residences decline. Newly planted street trees do little or nothing to mitigate the damage. One can only pray for their survival and wait another thirty years.

Today the great nineteenth-century parks, havens of city trees, are in decay. Trees set apart on a mown lawn cannot regenerate themselves; yet they are not being replaced by planted saplings. Many of the parks built in the previous century are no longer "lungs for the city," but merely sites of twentieth-century buildings and parking lots for park administration, horticultural societies, museums, zoos, ice-skating rinks, swimming pools, stadia, and schools. The splashes of green on any city's land-use map are misleading; many are barren of plants. Trees play only a minor, decorative role in most recent downtown parks.

City plants are a natural resource, but human function and fashion are often more influential than natural processes in determining the location and arrangement of plants. Activities, urban forms and materials, and the infrastructure of central cities create new habitats for plants, many of them hostile. The failure to perceive the city forest as a whole, with each part fitted to its location, is at the root of the city plant's struggle for life, and has led to gross mismanagement of an important resource. Skimpy park maintenance budgets, combined with negligence, hamper or forestall essential maintenance of existing parks. Yet little attempt is made to redesign those parks to require less maintenance, and, to compound the problem, new parks require equally high maintenance. City officials shave pennies in the installation of new trees, but burn dollars removing those trees after they die. A squandered legacy, hostile habitats, an expensive aesthetic, and neglected resources may eventually lead to barren cities.

A Vanishing Legacy

In 1890, a Bostonian could walk down from the State House through the Common and the Public Garden, up Commonwealth Avenue Mall, around the Fens and along the Riverway, past Leverett and Jamaica Ponds, through rows of trees along the Arborway, to the Arnold Arboretum and Franklin Park. The designer, Frederick Law Olmsted, considered this linked system of parks and parkways, called the "Emerald Necklace," among his finest work. At the turn of the century it was unrivaled anywhere in the United States.

The Emerald Necklace was a hard-won prize, achieved by repeated lobbying and negotiations to overcome financial, political, and environmental difficulties. In 1870, the potential of the Fens and Muddy River for a park was not self-evident, nor was the need for a huge, landscaped park at the city's outskirts. Olmsted and the Boston park commissioners, who were won over by his persuasive arguments, foresaw the future growth of the metropolis. They designed and built the Emerald Necklace not just for the pleasure, but also for the health and welfare, of contemporary and future residents of Boston.

Today the Emerald Necklace is fragmented and tarnished, its parkways sliced by expressway ramps, its bridle paths and promenades converted to car lanes, its parks in decay. The Emerald Necklace represents the vision of the nineteenth century and the negligence of the twentieth. The Emerald Necklace was systematically degraded in the twentieth century, sometimes wittingly, sometimes through ignorance. The parkways were among the first victims. The separate lanes for pleasure vehicles, horses, pedestrians, and for access to adjacent houses, were widened and converted to car lanes in response to the demand for more highways linking downtown to the suburbs. Pedestrians must dash across rushing traffic to reach the remaining, narrow islands with trees. The earlier link between Commonwealth Avenue and the Back Bay Fens is now an expressway ramp. The city has nibbled steadily at open land in the parks as well, permitting Sears & Roebuck to build a parking lot in the Fens and the Metropolitan District Commission to construct an indoor skating rink next to Leverett Pond. In 1975, new paths, granite curbing, and sewers were installed in the Boston Common; the construction killed more trees in that one year than Dutch elm disease had in three years. The newly installed sewers carried off water so efficiently that the trees had to be watered with trucks and hoses the following year.[3]

Beloved elm trees on Commonwealth Avenue Mall were nearly killed by too much attention rather than too little. The city built an expensive irrigation system for the trees at a cost of approximately $100,000 per block. Construction of the system caused much root damage. Once installed, automatic timers switched on the sprinklers every night. The abundant irrigation, added to the fact that the Mall was only a few feet above sea level, insured that the soil was always saturated. After a few years the trees declined, their roots rotted.[4]

The tragic case of the Emerald Necklace reads like a comedy of errors. It is difficult to imagine that such mismanagement could be widespread, but Boston is the rule, not the exception. Those responsible for the maintenance of parks and street trees often do not value them or know how to care for them. In some cities, responsibility resides in the Department of Public Works, whose major commitment is to street construction and the maintenance of utilities like sewers. Public parkland is frequently prey to highway departments and public institutions which need expansion room. Olmsted foresaw the use of parkland for buildings and poor maintenance as the greatest threats to inner-city parks, and lived to see his fears justified. If every project proposed for Central Park in New York City had been built, the park would now consist of little but buildings surrounded by landscaped bits. Proposals for churches alone would have nearly obliterated the park by 1918, had their construction been permitted. Other proposals have included graveyards, speedways, exhibition halls, and even an opera house. Only the Metropolitan Museum of Art was actually constructed.[5]

Some cities employ a forester or arborist to manage the urban forest but even this does not guarantee successful management. Undermined by political considerations, by more popular interests, and by a miniscule budget, the forester's efforts may be nullified. In Dayton, Ohio, private citizens blocked the city forester's plan to manage city trees as a renewable resource. The forester planned to harvest ailing street and park trees while they were still marketable, thereby paying both for the cost of removal and the replacement by new trees, while still garnering a surplus profit to augment the park department's dwindling maintenance budget. The plan was an application of "selective cutting," a standard method of timber management, to the urban forest. Under this plan, only diseased and dying trees with dead branches in approximately one-half or more of the crown would be harvested. The forester selected 133 walnut and oak trees for cutting, and the city invited bids from private lumber companies. The highest bid was over $127,000, of which the park department planned to spend $17,000 for replanting 150 new trees, 10–14 feet high, thus netting $110,000. But public outcry was immediate and vociferous. In the ensuing controversy, private citizens, members of the local Sierra Club and Audubon Society chapters, brought suit against the city. Two experts from the Ohio Natural Resources Department were asked to review the city's decision. One, a forester, favored the plan to manage the city's trees. The other, a naturalist, opposed the plan and favored "letting nature take her course." The court ruled against the city, and an imaginative plan to sustain city vegetation was halted before it began. The issue of preservation versus management divides the ranks of environmentalists.[6] It must be addressed and resolved. Letting nature take her course is a difficult stance to defend in the city, where most ornamental vegetation is cultivated and survives by virtue of human attention and where intensive use places great stress on natural ecosystems. The cost of that attention is a function of both natural and human factors: habitat and aesthetics.

Hostile Habitats

City plants must contend with tremendous biological, physical, and chemical stresses: too much water or too little; temperatures too cold or too hot; polluted air, water, and soil; pests and diseases. Many plants cannot survive at all; others survive in a dwarfed, distressed condition. The city contains a remarkable variety of habitats within a stone mosaic of buildings and pavement. Some habitats are extremely stressful, and the range of plants that can survive within them quite narrow; others are less so and support a wider range of plant life. Unfortunately, the city's most valued public spaces are among the most stressful; streets, plazas, and parks can aggravate the worst problems of the urban environment.

The life expectancy of the street tree, as noted, may be no more than ten years. The demise of the average street tree is due to a daily struggle for survival in which the tree weakens progressively year by year and finally succumbs to a blight or drought a healthy tree could easily survive. A city street does not provide the space, nutrients, or water that a tree needs in order to grow. It is an environment hostile to life (see figure 8.1).

Street trees, therefore, eke out a marginal existence, their roots cramped between building and street foundations, threaded among water, gas, electric, and telephone lines, and encased in soil as dense and infertile as concrete. Their trunks are gouged by car fenders, bicycle chains, and even the stakes installed to protect them. Their branches are pruned by passing buses. Leaves and bark are baked in the reflected heat from pavement and walls or condemned to perpetual shade cast by adjacent buildings. Roots are parched or drowned by a lack of water or an overabundance; in either case, their ability to deliver essential nutrients to the tree is drastically reduced.

The precarious balance between survival and extinction is easily upset. Incremental insult can spell the difference between life and death. Gusty winds on a street corner or at the base of a tall building

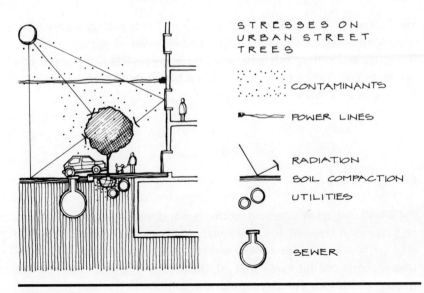

FIGURE 8.1

Urban street trees contend with great stress: intense heat or dense shade, air pollution, damage from automobiles and vandalism, paved ground surface and compacted, infertile soil, contaminated runoff, and limited soil space. No wonder the average life span of an urban street tree may be as low as ten years.

increase the loss of precious water by evaporation. Salts from de-icing compounds and dog urine alter the osmotic pressure of water in the surrounding soil, so that moisture is sucked out of the tree roots. Leaks from gas mains poison the roots, while air fouled by automobile exhaust and industrial emissions and heavily laden with dust can poison and suffocate the leaves of sensitive species. It is more surprising that street trees survive at all than that their life span is so short.

Slight differences in the street's physical environment make an enormous difference to the survival rate. Streets could be designed to provide tree roots with the space, air, and water they require. Instead, current practice aggravates already hostile conditions. Downtown streets are entirely paved from building wall to building wall. Trees are planted in tiny pits. Pavement waterproofs the ground surface and permits neither air nor water to reach tree roots below. The form of street trees reflects the water stress to which they are exposed. A parched street tree assumes the growth habit of the desert, a form adapted to conserve moisture: stunted growth, small leaves, thick bark, and stubby stems. Small leaves have a smaller surface area from which to lose water by evaporation. Thick bark forms a protective layer around the moist, vital core.

Long, leggy branches on a young tree reflect fast growth nurtured by an ideal combination of water, sun, and nutrients, a distinctive form typical of the newly planted, nursery-bred specimen. Under normal conditions, the tree fills out within a few years of transplanting, but street trees are often frozen in this juvenile form. At first glance, they appear to be newly planted. On closer examination, one sees densely spaced parallel ridges that mark each twig's tiny annual growth, scars left by each year's terminal bud. The Norway maples on Charles Street in Boston's Beacon Hill, normally very large forest trees, are more than ten years old, despite their small size and open form. Telltale lines on their twigs show only a one-quarter inch growth increment per year, hardly enough to fill in the shape of a mature tree. In a benign environment these trees can pump and transpire almost ninety gallons of water per day. Only a fraction of that amount reaches the roots of the Charles Street trees, and one-quarter inch annual growth is the limit this harsh environment will support. Forest trees like the Norway maple evolved in and are accustomed to the humid, temperate climate of the forest where each tree is surrounded by other trees, protected from sun and wind. The surface of the forest's soil is soft and spongy, accumulated from years of decomposed leaves. Tiny rootlets pack the upper few inches of soil, the major feeding zone of the forest tree. In a hostile environment like Charles Street these trees persist as dwarves until they die, when they are replaced like the petunias set out each spring in flower pots hanging from nearby lampposts.

The Norway maples on Mount Vernon Street, one block up from the totally paved environment of Charles Street, fare much better. Superficially, the two environments look identical; at that location, both streets are narrow, with brick sidewalks and no adjacent yards. The important difference is that on Charles Street the sidewalks rest on a waterproof concrete base, while on Mount Vernon Street they lie on a bed of sand that permits air and water to flow through cracks to the tree roots beneath. But bricks in sand is a pavement of the past. Bricks are regarded as potential missiles and are now almost invariably laid on concrete, cemented together like the ones on Charles Street.

As on Commonwealth Avenue, street trees frequently die from too much water rather than too little. The soil around tree roots can become waterlogged, a paradox caused by compacted subsoil and modern methods of tree planting. When street trees are planted in small pits dug in the compacted urban soil, the tree's roots and the topsoil placed around them are imprisoned as surely as if they had been put in a concrete pot. The result is the "teacup syndrome": any water which finds its way into the tree pit cannot drain out through the compacted soil beneath. Heavy rainstorms or a leaky sewer will flood the roots and prevent air from reaching them. The roots become waterlogged rather than dehydrated (see figure 9.3).

Trees on a plaza may face even worse conditions than those on streets. Most plazas are not built over soil, but are actually the roofs of basements or subways, and plaza trees are therefore usually planted in pots, either sunken or raised. Soil depth and weight are limited by the strength and size of the structure underneath. Rarely is sufficient soil provided to sustain large trees over a long lifetime. A raised planter, just large enough for a single tree, is one of the city's worst environments, a fact attested to by the many empty concrete planters filled with trash, which litter plazas. When the sides of planters are exposed to air, the soil in a pot freezes and heats up rapidly, and tender roots are alternately burned and frozen in climates with pronounced seasonal changes. Plazas are also often located at the foot of tall buildings, where gusty winds dehydrate both tree and soil.

Large city parks, one would think, provide an optimal habitat for trees. But one glance at trees in a well-loved and well-used downtown park reveals many of the same stresses observed in street and plaza trees. They are dwarfed, their age belied by their height but given away by their girth. Densely packed soil—compacted by feet, tractor-pulled lawn mowers, and maintenance trucks—is the primary cause of their diminished size. The upper layer of soil on the Mall in Washington, D.C., between the Capitol and the Washington Monument, is as dense as concrete. The elms that line the Mall are less than thirty feet high, although they were planted more than fifty years ago. One would normally expect an elm of that age to be considerably larger.

People represent the greatest threat to trees and grass in parks, both through unwitting overuse and by outright acts of destruction. Vandalism of city trees is probably as old as the first public park. Vandalism has plagued Boston Common (which Bridenbaugh says is the first public park in the United States) ever since it was set aside as a common field in 1640. Town meetings of the seventeenth and eighteenth centuries record both the incidence of vandalism and the steps taken by the town to prevent and punish such acts. In 1764 the selectmen levied fines for breaking down the posts between the

Common and adjacent Tremont Street and proceeded against citizens who persisted in driving their carriages and horses on the Common. To prevent further incursions, the town meeting in 1771 ordered that the Common be enclosed by a fence. In that same year a private citizen offered a reward for the identification of the person who "hacked" down a tree bordering the Common, and two years later two vandals went to jail for destroying trees on the Common.[7]

Few, if any, cultivated "ornamental" plants grow on the disturbed soil of abandoned land, one of the most characteristic habitats of North American cities. A newly cleared vacant lot is a harsh environment. The nature of the "soil" depends upon what was previously on the lot. The "soil" of a demolished building site consists of rubble and fill: chunks of brick or stone and bits of mortar, wood, glass, metal, and dirt. It is desiccated, highly compacted, contaminated with insecticides and pesticides, and contains little organic material. Its surface is hard and cracked, uninsulated in summer or winter and therefore either very hot or very cold. Only a few plants can colonize vacant lots, hardy breeds capable of surviving the stresses of bare, disturbed soil. They are mainly annual and biennial plants, xerophytic, light- and heat-demanding, frost-hardy, deep-rooted, and fast-growing.

It is ironic that although these plants flourish in the most hostile of urban environments while cultivated plants languish in less stressful habitats, they are despised as weeds. Although it is generally true that the more hostile the environment, the greater the cost of maintaining plants, the weedy flowers, shrubs, and trees on abandoned urban land disprove the rule. Landscape aesthetics has economic implications.

An Expensive Aesthetic

Trees arching out over streets and green lawns with shade trees are a popular landscape aesthetic. To most people, nature in the city *is* trees, shrubs, and grass in streets, parks, and private yards, but these are actually the least "natural" of urban plant communities. The composition and arrangement of these plants are functions of land use and fashion rather than natural processes. On streets, trees of a single species are planted equidistant in rows to achieve a uniform visual effect. They survive only with careful maintenance and decline with neglect. The combination of the hostile city environment and restricted municipal budgets has disastrous consequences for this high-maintenance landscape.

In the United States, street tree species must usually be selected from a short list, often comprised of no more than eight or ten species of "suitable" trees, which survive city conditions reasonably well without much care. Thornless, fruitless, tidy, shapely trees are preferred. Species go in and out of fashion. Fads lead to massive plantings of a single species, not only in streets, but throughout the city in parks and private yards. This produces a precarious situation, for entire streets may be quickly stripped of trees by a single blight, and an entire city may lose most of its trees within a decade.

In the past thirty years, Dutch elm disease has precipitated just such a situation in many North American cities. Before 1950, the American elm was among the most commonly planted trees in northeastern and midwestern cities. Cities like Minneapolis, planted almost entirely with elms, lost most of their trees over a brief period. In a single decade, between 1955 and 1966, over 90 percent of the elms in Illinois towns with no disease control programs died.[8] Even municipalities with expensive, comprehensive, disease control programs still lost 3 to 24 percent of their original elms during that same decade, and 10 to 46 percent after an additional five years.[9] The cost of removing so many dead elms strained municipal budgets. It was estimated that Chicago lost 295,000 elms over twenty inches in diameter between 1968 and 1978, and that removal costs amounted to approximately $24 million.[10] These losses have had dramatic consequences for the landscape of many American cities.

Cities have not learned from history; the London plane tree, the Norway maple, and, recently, the honey locust have enjoyed similar fads. Heavy investment in a few species has fueled the active research in plant diseases of the overplanted street trees, and heroic efforts are made to find new antidotes or to develop new, disease-resistant breeds of trees. But cities continue to plant only a few species and to line boulevards with the same tree from end to end, setting up a legacy of potential devastation for the next generation.

To most North Americans, a manicured lawn with mature shade trees is the ideal park. This pastoral landscape, reminiscent of English country estates, has its origins in the cool, humid climate of Britain, but has been replicated throughout the United States and throughout the world without regard to climate. It has the look of domesticated land, of a grazed, wooded pasture, rather than a forest. It is a highly artificial plant community, whose persistence depends

FIGURE 8.2
Sheep grazing the lawn of Franklin Park in Boston, ca 1916, now replaced by lawn mowers. Sheep still graze the lawns of many English estates.

upon intensive, expensive maintenance. The lawn is at odds with the trees and the environment they create. Although grass needs less water than trees, it may not be able to compete with tree roots for water and nutrients. Turf thrives on open sun and a chemically neutral soil. Maintaining a healthy lawn under shade trees requires constant battle. The forest trees planted in most parks, like the Norway maple and horse chestnut, cast shade too dense for grass to flourish beneath them. Leaves must be raked, lime added to the soil, and the seedlings clipped. This is not a self-regenerating landscape. As mature trees decline, the landscape must be perpetuated by planting new trees.

The antecedents of the pastoral urban park are the English country estate and royal hunting preserves. The word "park," in its original sense, referred to an enclosed tract of land held by royal grant for keeping beasts of the chase. It was later extended to represent the ornamental woodland and pasture around the country house used for recreation and for keeping deer. Maintenance cost was never an issue in the formulation of the aesthetic. An army of gardeners and grazing sheep and deer cropped the lawn and kept the woodland in check. When Frederick Law Olmsted designed Prospect Park in Brooklyn and Franklin Park in Boston, it was accepted that sheep would graze the large meadows in both parks (see figure 8.2). Today the task requires a fleet of lawnmowers powered by gas and oil. Sheep can easily nibble the grass at the base of trees, but large lawnmowers find it much more difficult to negotiate tree trunks. When cherry trees were planted in the lawn along the shoreline at Hain's Point in Washington, D.C., the cost of maintenance reportedly increased tenfold. A job that had formerly been done by one person in a week now took ten people more than a week, since twenty- to thirty-inch walk-behind mowers replaced a fifteen-foot-wide tractor-pulled mower. The cost of maintaining such parkland is even greater in semiarid climates, like that of Denver, which do not naturally support forests. In such regions, trees and lawn must be sustained by irrigation, straining scarce municipal water supplies. Today large urban parks are in decay in both humid and semiarid climates in Chicago, Boston, and Denver. The enormous budgets required to maintain them exceed the resources of these cities. Vast areas of parkland are no longer seen by the city as an asset, but a liability.

Not all urban plants require cultivation. While trees in city streets and parks languish, others flourish in sidewalk cracks and vacant lots. *Ailanthus altissima*, also known as the tree-of-heaven and the "tree that grows in Brooklyn," is the queen of city trees. Originally imported from China in the eighteenth century as an ornamental plant, ailanthus now prospers in vacant lots, city dumps, backyards, and sidewalk cracks. It can grow several feet a year under the most adverse conditions. Unfortunately, ailanthus gives up in strength, longevity, and elegance what it gains in fast growth and hardiness. It is a messy tree with a coarse silhouette and vile-smelling male flowers. These characteristics do not endear ailanthus to foresters, landscape architects, and public works departments. Nevertheless, in some parts of the city, the tree-of-heaven may cast the only shade apart from buildings. It is a democratic tree, making no distinction between the wealthiest neighborhoods and the poorest; it grows in all parts of the city. Residents of Roxbury, one of Boston's inner-city neighborhoods, call it "ghetto palm." Sumacs and sunflowers grow in railroad yards, rubble heaps, and other neglected lands within the city. Europeans prize the sumacs' lush, dense foliage and their brilliant crimson fall color and cultivate them as ornamentals. Ailanthus, sumac, sunflowers, and other weedy wildflowers colonize the wastelands and forgotten corners of the city and provide, at no cost, many of the same services that the cultivated plant communities do. In urban wastelands, they decorate what would otherwise be a desolate environment. But most city dwellers are blinded to their beauty by a more domesticated aesthetic. An unappreciated and neglected resource, their energy goes unharnessed.

The cost of continuing to neglect plants in the inner-city landscape is tangible and far-reaching: the intensification of the worst aspects of city climate; increased energy demands; reduced absorption of air pollutants; increased flooding; degraded water quality; and, in residential areas, depressed property values.

At a time when their value is clearly established, most plants, through negligence, ignorance, and folly, are being eradicated from all but a few public spaces. City parkland is appropriated for expressways, parking lots, and new buildings. Proposals to cut trees provoke public outcry, but appeals to increase park department budgets are refused again and again. Despite dwindling budgets, parks requiring a high degree of maintenance continue to be designed routinely or, in the name of economy, parks are built with no plants at all. Street trees of a few limited species are planted in tiny holes, their roots encased by concrete pots or dense subsoil. Most trees will survive the contractor's one-year guarantee but few will live beyond ten years, and the city will be left with a lost investment, unrealized benefits, and the added sting of removal costs.

CHAPTER 9

Nurturing the Urban Biome

GARDENING is among the oldest of human arts, and trees have been venerated by many human cultures. The cult of trees was part of ancient Persian and Assyrian religions, for which a tree with a stream at its roots was a symbol of eternal life, and tree planting a sacred occupation. The Persians taught boys the art of planting trees as part of their education. Trees have been a pleasure to city dwellers since Sennacherib laid out a public park 2,500 years ago for the citizens of Nineveh in Mesopotamia: "I made gardens in the upper and in the lower town," he said, "with the earth's produce from the mountains and the countries round about, all the spices from the land of the Hittites, mer, vines from the hills, fruits from every country; spices and sirdu-trees have I planted for my subjects."[1] Given this ancient practice of building urban parks and the venerable professions of horticulture and forestry, it is astonishing that modern methods of cultivation and management of urban vegetation are so crude. The solutions needed for increasing the survival rate of urban plants and managing the urban landscape more economically are relatively simple. Plants are not inert sculpture, and they have a few basic requirements for survival: they respond to their environment in predictable ways and, if left alone, arrange themselves in space and time according to well-understood principles. The alteration of that natural arrangement by human intervention requires an expenditure of energy.

Nurturing the urban biome will require a thoroughgoing overhaul in current approaches to selection and design of urban open space and the planting and management of urban vegetation. Fortunately, there are many role models available for cities wishing to insure the survival of the urban vegetation they plant, to enhance its beauty, and to reduce the cost of maintaining it. The National Park Service in Washington, D.C., has investigated new methods of planting street trees and renovating damaged parkland. The city of Boston has identified "urban wilds" throughout the city as a natural resource. West Berlin is considering transforming an urban "wilderness" into a nature park. Zurich manages its extensive city forest as a revenue-producing resource. An understanding of individual plants and their needs, and of the dynamics of their relationships with each other and their environment, underlie all these solutions.

The Necessities of Life

Cities throughout the world create similar habitats (see table 9.1): streets and highways, squares and plazas, parks and sports fields, the grounds surrounding institutions like hospitals and universities, private yards and gardens, leftover land on swamps and steep slopes, and derelict land in vacant lots, garbage dumps, abandoned quarries, and industrial sites. The specific plant species in each habitat vary from city to city with climate and culture, but plants in all cities are governed by the same processes and respond to the same environmental variables. The urban forest can be maintained and managed economically once it is designed to harness these processes.

Because plants are living organisms, a few necessities are essential for survival. The absence or insufficiency of a single limiting factor, be it water, air, light, or nutrients, will result first in reduced growth, then in decline and death. The survival rate and life span of urban plants can therefore often be enhanced dramatically by a slight improvement of a single factor in their habitat. Left to themselves, plants grow in "communities," groups of plants adapted to similar environmental factors. A plant community and its environment are inseparable; equivalent environments, undisturbed by man, support a similar assembly of plants (see figure 9.1). This principle is equally valid at global, continental, regional, and local scales, and can be applied to great advantage in the selection of plants for the urban landscape.

TABLE 9.1
Urban Vegetation Habitat Types

Habitat Type	Plant Community Characteristics

Deliberately introduced and cultivated:
  Roadsides
    Street medians and sidewalks
    Highways
  Urban squares and plazas
  Parks
  Sports fields
  Institutional grounds
  Private yards
	Plant community is a function of fashion and land use
	
	Succession is arrested
	
	Zonation is primarily a response to human activities

Uncultivated:
  Remnants of native vegetation
    Hydric (floodplains, swamps, marshes)
    Mesic or xeric (steep slopes, ravines,
      rocky outcrops)
  Walls
  Pavement
  Transportation corridors
    Roadsides
    Railroad rights-of-way
    Canals
  Abandoned land
    Vacant lots (former building sites)
    Derelict industrial land
    Old quarries
  Landfill, garbage dumps, and sewage
    treatment sites
	Plant community is a function of environmental factors and land use
	
	Different successional stages are present
	
	Zonation is primarily a response to environmental factors

Since plants vary in their tolerance to environmental conditions, hardy species will survive where more sensitive species would succumb. Transplant a species of forest tree to the city street, for example, and it must contend with an environment different in every respect from the forest in which it evolved and to which it is adapted: individual trees, spaced far apart, with bark and the underside of leaves exposed to sun and reflected heat; pavement and dense, infertile, oxygen-deficient soil; and erratic water availability. A wiser course is to select trees whose native environment is similar to the city street. Floodplain trees, for instance, contend with repeated floods, which prevent the accumulation of leaf mold and topsoil and saturate the earth, rendering it just as deficient in oxygen as compacted urban soils. It is therefore not surprising that floodplain trees like red maple, the London plane tree, and ailanthus flourish in the city. Matching urban habitats with analogues in "wilder" settings,

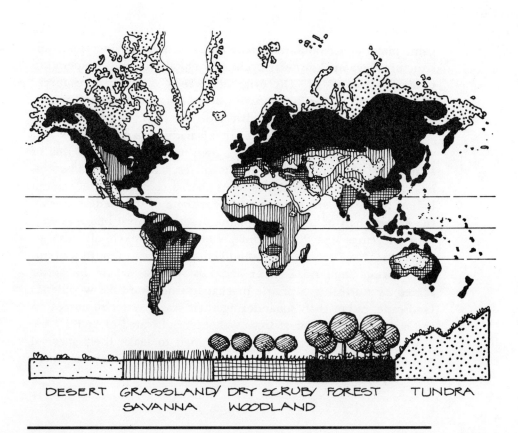

FIGURE 9.1
Distribution of major plant formations, primarily a response to rainfall and temperature patterns. Both the structure of the formation and form of individual species are adapted to those factors.

DESERT   GRASSLAND/   DRY SCRUB/   FOREST   TUNDRA
          SAVANNA   WOODLAND

and identifying the plant community within each, yields a palette of plants which are likely to survive with minimal coddling.

Urban vacant lots have an analogue in land cleared for farming and lumbering or by fire and landslides. Similar types of plants colonize abandoned fields in the countryside and vacant lots in the city. They are temporary plant communities, the initial pioneers that colonize and heal barren and disturbed habitats. Weeds in a vacant lot gradually build soil from unsorted sediments. They retain moisture, protect the soil from evaporation, fertilize it annually with dead weeds and roots, hasten the decomposition of mortar and rubble, and create an environment favorable to microorganisms and other plants. If undisturbed, perennials crowd out the pioneer annual and biennial plants within a few years, and are, in forested regions, eventually overtopped in turn by trees. As succession proceeds, organic material accumulates, shade and soil moisture increases, soil structure develops, mineral cycling is enhanced, and temperature variations moderated. The original "weeds" are urban resources which require no fertilization and no soil amendments and whose energy may be harnessed and directed.

Cultivating an urban landscape that is native to a city's region will yield an image based on that city's own natural legacy, not that of some other place and time. The city of Jerusalem straddles two biomes, a fact which contributes to its special character. The western half of the city is one with the dry woodland of the Mediterranean; the eastern half of the city is of the desert. A forest image is well suited to cities like Philadelphia, Vienna, and Tokyo; all three of these cities have a temperate, humid climate which supports a deciduous forest. Semiarid Denver and Los Angeles would be better served by nurturing a prairie or chaparral (orchardlike woodland) landscape, rather than squandering their scarce water resources on the maintenance of forest trees. Whether cultivated or "wild," the city's plant communities can be designed to make their survival more secure, their appearance more lush, and their management more economical.

Nurturing City Plants

The corridors formed by streets, highways, and railroad tracks are among the most significant and extensive of urban open spaces. As channels through which people enter and leave the city and move around within it, they influence how the city is first perceived by a visitor, how it is remembered, and how it is viewed day to day by the people who live within it. Trees on streets represent most cities' greatest investment in plants. They influence the climate, air quality, and appearance of the places where people live and work. The promenade has long been a favored urban recreation, and tree-lined streets have served this purpose for at least four hundred years, if not longer.

The story of the urban street tree provides an insight into the evolution of the city and highlights cultural differences among countries. The appearance and proliferation of the street tree from the end of the sixteenth century through the course of the seventeenth marks a period of rapid change in European urban society. The origin and precise form which street trees took varies from country to country within Western Europe, in response to varying needs for military defense, rapidity of urban growth, different patterns of land ownership, the relative importance of different economic classes, and the relative strength of the royalty. These multiple origins and forms are embodied in the words used to describe important city streets—*boulevard, avenue,* and *allée. Boulevard,* in French, originally meant bulwark or bastion, and "boulevards" were part of the defensive system of ramparts and outworks that surrounded the city. The primary purpose of the city wall was military defense, but after the invention of gunpowder necessitated replacement of the old, narrow, masonry city walls (see figure 1.7) with large, earthen walls, the wall became a popular place for public promenades. In time, cities in Holland, Germany, and France planted trees atop these wide earthen walls. When the walls were destroyed in later centuries, they were replaced by broad tree-lined streets, which retained the name *boulevard.* When Baron Haussman sliced new, broad, tree-lined streets through the middle of old Paris and dubbed them boulevards, the military allusion would not have been lost on contemporary Parisians. Thus the Boulevard Montmartre is on the site of the old city wall which ringed Paris and was part of the promenade dedicated to the citizens of Paris by Louis XIV, whereas the Boulevard de Sébastopol, which cuts through the center of Paris, aided in the defense of the city from its populace, rather than from foreign invaders.

The word *avenue* is derived from the Latin word meaning "to approach." In seventeenth-century France it was employed to denote the entry road to an important palace. Louis XIV lined the three avenues approaching Versailles with multiple rows of trees. He did the same with the avenue approaching the Tuileries, later renamed the Avenue des Champs-Élysées. *Allée* is derived from the French word *aller,* meaning "to go out," originally used in seventeenth-century France to designate a tree-lined garden path going out from a palace. Unter den Linden, a fashionable Berlin promenade since the late seventeenth century, was originally named the Linden Allée and was laid out on the former path between the duke's palace and his hunting ground, the Tiergarten. Thus, all three words once had specific associations—*boulevard* with military defense and *avenue* and *allée* with the aristocracy—but are now used in French, as well as in many other languages, to denote any broad, tree-lined street.

The popularity of the street tree increased with rapid urban growth. As cities became denser and were severed from their countryside by suburbs and extensive fortifications, street trees became more and more common. By the mid-seventeenth century, the highways approaching major Dutch cities were lined with single or double rows of trees, and as the cities expanded, the streets and canals facing the homes of wealthy burghers sported newly planted trees. Seventeenth-century Dutch paintings show wooden tree guards to protect tree trunks from damage. The urban environment was less hostile to trees than now, but it was never ideal, and maintaining street trees always required effort. For centuries, that effort has been considered worthwhile.

The current, dismal survival rate of urban street trees can be improved, but not without cost. Success is assured only if trees are selected from among appropriate species, planted adequately, and soundly maintained, a rare combination in modern cities. Street tree survival need not, however, be a game of chance. The Ohio Shade Tree Project, after more than ten years of evaluating the ability of various tree species to survive urban stresses, has published a list of shade trees that will survive and even thrive on city streets.[2] The list is much more extensive than those used by many North American cities. Planting a tree well—to promote drainage and aeration, to provide irrigation and fertilization, to minimize soil compaction, and to avoid the accumulation of salts—is not cheap, but it is wise to remember the old nurserymen's maxim: "Plant a one dollar tree in a ten dollar hole." This advice was not lost on many nineteenth- and early-twentieth-century landscape architects, like the Olmsteds, who frequently planted street trees in pits two to three times the size of standard modern pits.

Alarmed by the mortality rate of modern street trees, some cities, on symbolic or major streets where the survival and growth of street trees is deemed important, are now spending close to ten times the value of the tree in preparation of the hole and pavement around it. A new homogenous soil was created on Pennsylvania Avenue in Washington, D.C., prior to the planting of new willow oaks. The new soil mixture replaced existing soils to a depth of thirty-two inches and extends to a minimum of sixteen feet in diameter around each tree. A fourteen-foot–diameter irrigation ring under the concrete sidewalks promotes irrigation, fertilization, and aeration, while an underground drain carries away excess water, and a tree grate around the base of each trunk inhibits soil compaction. The cost of the new pavement, soil, and drain around each tree exceeds $5,000.[3] Despite this elaborate system, trees in the sidewalk have not fared as well as trees planted in the adjacent lawn (figure 9.2).

Street trees in the new Denver Transitway Mall were equally costly,

FIGURE 9.2
Two rows of street trees on Pennsylvania Avenue in Washington, D.C., showing response to different soil conditions. The same size when planted four years earlier, sidewalk trees are now noticeably smaller than those in open soil, despite the elaborate system constructed to support them.

but were planted according to a slightly different system. The Denver trees were placed in precast concrete vaults with removable concrete lids. The vaults permit compaction of the surrounding soil to prevent future settlement without affecting the soil immediately around the tree roots. Perforations in the lid and an air space between lid and soil permit air circulation. The cast-iron grate around each tree trunk has removable rings to accommodate tree growth. Openings in the side of the vault admit irrigation and drainage pipes and may even allow roots to grow out into the surrounding soil. The tree pits can be flushed with water once a year to remove de-icing salts that have accumulated during the winter. Each entire system, including the tree, costs approximately $5,500.[4]

A city can afford such expensive solutions only in a few streets. There are other, less expensive alternatives. The contrast between the compacted subsoil and the planting soil of the tree pit, the primary cause of the "teacup effect," can also be mitigated (see figures

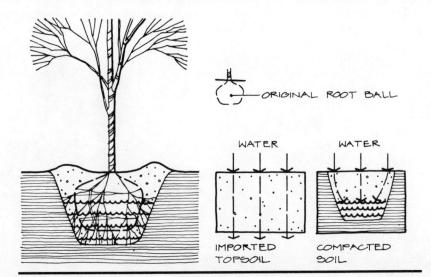

—ORIGINAL ROOT BALL

WATER

WATER

IMPORTED TOPSOIL

COMPACTED SOIL

FIGURE 9.3
The problem: the "teacup" syndrome, common cause of death in newly planted urban trees. In wet seasons, accumulated water sits in tree pits, unable to drain, and tree roots rot; in drought, roots cannot penetrate compacted subsoil to reach ground water.

FIGURE 9.4
The solution: planting techniques that permit air and water to move through the soil and provide room for roots to grow will increase both life span and size of urban trees.

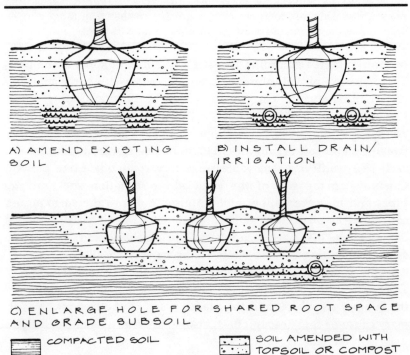

A) AMEND EXISTING SOIL

B) INSTALL DRAIN/ IRRIGATION

C) ENLARGE HOLE FOR SHARED ROOT SPACE AND GRADE SUBSOIL

COMPACTED SOIL

SOIL AMENDED WITH TOPSOIL OR COMPOST

9.3 and 9.4). Instead of replacing the excavated urban soil with top-soil, some agronomists recommend amendment of the urban soil with organic matter and a coarse material like cinders or expanded shale. Amending the existing soil, rather than replacing it, reduces the contrast between the soil of the tree pit and the adjacent soil, enhancing drainage and root growth. The University of Pennsylvania has replaced a narrow strip of concrete sidewalk between street trees with porous stone dust, a by-product of the stone-crushing process. The hope is that this porous strip will permit the access of air and water to tree roots.

A four- to six-foot square planting hole will support a mature tree of only twenty to twenty-five feet in height.[5] To accommodate larger growth, additional space must be provided, and in some urban neighborhoods, private yards provide the necessary open soil for root growth. Where there are no private front yards, healthy, mature growth can be achieved if trees are planted in clusters, rather than spaced out along the sidewalk. Bloomsbury and Russell squares in London and Louisburg Square in Boston are excellent examples of how many buildings can take advantage of a single cluster of trees. If sufficient space cannot be found on the street, it is wiser to forgo the trees completely.

Highway and railroad rights-of-way are much less exacting environments than the street. They are buffers between traffic and adjacent property, are generally not subject to being walked or driven on, and can serve an aesthetic, as well as a safety, function. Wissahickon and East and West River drives comprise a major traffic link between northern suburbs of Philadelphia and the downtown area. The river drives, on the east and west banks of the Schuylkill River, are among the most beautiful approaches to a city anywhere. They create a distinctly different image of the city than does the highway to the airport, the route traveled by visitors who arrive and leave by plane. From the airport route, which runs past automobile graveyards and enormous storage tanks, the city appears dirty, dreary, seedy, and decayed.

Most visitors are introduced to a city via highways; the first impression of most cities is more like Philadelphia's airport route than its West River Drive. For several years, city planners in Dayton, Ohio, have promoted the idea of reforesting expressway rights-of-way and have coined a new name, "River Dell," for the freeway ramps that lead to the central business district. They envision visitors of the future approaching Dayton through a forest, with occasional glimpses of the skyline through the trees. In 1978, Dayton planted the first trees in River Dell and, in 1982, it began an experimental program to permit the natural progression of plant succession along certain stretches of highway.[6] The hope is not only to create a more beautiful city image, but also to reduce maintenance costs by eliminating the need to mow most of the area, and to reduce noise and air pollution in adjacent neighborhoods. (See the discussion of the Dayton Climate Project in chapter 3.)

In a busy plaza, plants should be well positioned to produce shade and reduce glare. To achieve the benefits of a comfortable microclimate the plants themselves must survive in the plaza, one of the most hostile of urban habitats. It is not sufficient to merely select hardy species. Plazas filled with ailing honey locusts and English ivy abound.

A small plaza in Philadelphia, dedicated to architect Louis Kahn, demonstrates both a sensible and an unsuitable approach to planting trees in a plaza. Known to local residents as "Kahn-crete Park," the park is composed mainly of concrete with some brick paving. Half of the plaza is at street level, with trees planted in tiny holes within the pavement. The other half consists of an enormous raised concrete planter filled with trees, surrounding a small, elevated seating area. Within a few years of installation the trees planted in pavement were dead or dying, while trees planted at the same time in the open soil of the large planter were thriving. A group of trees protects individuals from extremes of sun and wind. Planters that are sufficiently large to accommodate many trees do not have the severe problems of temperature fluctuation and desiccation that plague small planters designed for single trees.

A midcity plaza is frequently a roof garden, built over subways or underground office space and parking garages. Roof gardens are among the most expensive urban spaces to build and maintain. Structural considerations restrict soil depth and weight, factors that may severely retard plant growth by limiting water, nutrients, and root support. These conditions are further exacerbated by the gusty winds common on both street-level plazas and rooftops. The University of California has developed a light-weight soil mixture specifically for rooftop gardens, but a combination of pipelines and drains are necessary to provide the frequent watering and fertilization essential to plant growth and survival. Even with the most tender care, many plants cannot exist more than ten years in such conditions. Success requires selection of plants from a small list of hardy species, attention to soil mixture and drainage, and careful maintenance. Although the costs of installing and maintaining rooftop gardens are high, their combined aesthetic, climatic, and hydrologic benefits can repay the investment. Successful public plazas are among the most intensely used urban open space resources. A garden in the sky is a rare and delightful place, as witnessed by the accounts of the hanging gardens of Babylon, one of the seven wonders of the ancient world.

All parks in the city are not used equally intensely, nor must they be maintained equally. Some parks are more important than others, more symbolic, more central. Downtown parks are likely to be smaller and more formal than parks at the city's outskirts. Generally, the more people use the park, the more maintenance it requires, but maintenance can be reduced and survival enhanced by the wise selection and arrangement of plants. The landscaping around the Verex Corporation in downtown Madison, Wisconsin, is composed of plants native to the prairie–woodland edge. The formality of the landscaping complements the building: trees, shrubs, and ground cover are planted in massive, slightly raised, molded concrete containers that set the landscaping off from the adjacent sidewalks and entrance. The textures of the sumacs, cedars, and birches are luxuriant, their colors rich and diverse, and their silhouettes framed by the dark tinted windows behind them. Adapted to the harsh conditions of an old field, they thrive in the urban environment and require far less attention than the conventional lawn, trees, and flower beds surrounding another corporation down the street.

Exploiting Urban Wilds

The use of successional plant communities represents both an aesthetic alternative to a formal and pastoral parkland and an opportunity to provide more parks on reduced maintenance budgets. Such landscapes are becoming increasingly popular, particularly in Dutch cities. Holland is a densely settled country which survives by virtue of intensive management of the landscape. New land is constantly reclaimed from the sea to provide space for more homes and more agricultural fields to feed the growing population. The price exacted from this intensive use of the land has been a more uniform and monotonous landscape. Many native plants are now extinct; 56 percent of the entire Dutch flora are rare and only 20 percent are common.[7] In response to this disappearance of their native landscape, the Dutch have applied their skill at land management to the creation of meadows and forests within their cities. To the Dutch, successional meadows and woodlands are pockets of wilderness, a symbol of the forces of nature, rather than human abandonment. At first, as noted by their early proponent Jacques Thijsse, these "wild" urban parks were intended as instructive gardens: "I dream of a garden where the public, young and old, ignorant and informed can witness and experience the whole season of our native plants, from the first of January to the thirty-first of December. A garden where the town dweller can surrender himself to the flora and fauna."[8] Over the past forty years, this Dutch landscape design tradition has evolved, still retaining a didactic emphasis, but also emphasizing creation of an environment where children can give their fantasy free reign and adults share in the responsibility for its shape and cultivation.

An early experiment was the creation of the Bos Park, or "Forest Park," near Amsterdam in 1929. The builders of the Bos Park created one thousand acres of woods on a new polder, land recently reclaimed from water. The massive tree planting not only provided shelter from the wind, but also dried out the poorly drained polder. Initially, fast-growing pioneer species like the poplar and willow were planted in large quantities throughout the park, and forest species, like oak, beech, ash, birch, and maple, were planted in smaller groves. The poplar and willow were then thinned out and, after the first fifteen years, gradually replaced by the forest species.

In the 1960s, the Dutch took the forest and meadow aesthetic originally developed in the Bos and other urban parks and extended it into the heart of the city, in apartment complexes and along roadsides. The city of Delft created an experimental park on an eleven-acre site within a new apartment complex called the Buitenhof, or "country garden." Instead of regrading the site and landscaping it with new trees and shrubs, the city left the vegetation which had established itself during construction and permitted natural succession to take its course, with some help. A few native trees and shrubs were planted in order to hasten this process, and a mixture of barley, oats, rye, wheat, white and red clover, flax, poppies, and phacelia was sown on disturbed ground in order to establish a pleasant, wildflower meadow quickly.[9] Rather than laying out an extensive network of paths, the city established a few paths and encouraged residents to trample others where needed. The city built a small playground within the park, but for the most part, children preferred to play in the unstructured wild garden. Children made their own paths and small open places, unhampered by any rules or signs admonishing them to "keep off the grass," "keep on the path," or "don't pick the flowers." Both city park managers and the residents of the adjacent apartment buildings cooperated in the Delft experiment. The Netherlands Institute for Preventative Medicine investigated how residents used the park and how they felt about it. The study concluded that children, in particular, found it more attractive than conventional playgrounds, and that it represented a more efficient use of space.[10] The study's conclusions underscore the role that waste and abandoned land can play in child development, not as a substitute for playgrounds and more formal parks, but as a complementary type of play space.

The cities of Utrecht, Amsterdam, Haarlem, and The Hague now all have such parks. Improved methods of establishment and maintenance have evolved with increasing experience. The Dutch have found that a more diverse plant community with fewer undesirable plant species develops more readily on infertile soil. This irony decreases the cost of park construction, since the importation of topsoil and the application of fertilizer are not only unnecessary, but undesirable. The planting of massive quantities of very young tree saplings, or "whips," and relatively few of the more expensive larger trees, keeps construction costs down. Implementation of these "wild" parks is not accomplished overnight, but may extend up to a decade, during which time densely planted trees are thinned and unwanted weed species removed by hand. For this initial period, the park is a high-maintenance, high-cost landscape that requires knowledgeable management. Eventually, it will be virtually self-maintaining, so that in the long run it would be less expensive to maintain than the pastoral park. The Dutch have found that local residents are a potential source of maintenance manpower during the crucial period of landscape establishment. Many residents have, in turn, found gratification in shaping the urban landscape around them.[11]

The Dutch have also converted many highway medians and roadsides to wildflower meadows. Most are mown only once a year, at the end of May or the beginning of June, when seeds have been produced and the grass is still short enough to be left on the ground after mowing. One highway right-of-way, the Beneluxlaan, in Amstelveen near Amsterdam, has not been cut since 1975 and still remains an attractive meadow.[12] In the United States, as in Holland, seedlings and shrubs are cropping up along many expressways, as highway departments cut back their mowing schedules. Unfortunately, this is only a response to restricted budgets, not part of an overall scheme to manage the city's vegetation. Multiple advantages—both economic and aesthetic—could be garnered, however, if highway maintenance programs were designed to do so. Adjacent to the roadway, where trees would pose obstacles, a shrub cover or meadow could be managed to inhibit tree growth. The Dutch experience is one model, a management program for power line easements developed at Connecticut College Arboretum is another. The Arboretum's plan calls for the establishment of dense shrubbery which crowds out tree seedlings. It requires an initial period of management, after which it is virtually maintenance free.[13]

To date, the wild urban garden has not met with the same success in the United States as it has in Europe. The successional meadow or woodland is untidy compared to manicured parks and yards. To many Americans it is a sign of neglected and abandoned land. The aesthetic of successional vegetation is subtle, and how it is perceived depends on context. In a wooded area or along a stream at the city's edge, a field of wildflowers appears "natural"; transported downtown and surrounded by streets and buildings, the same meadow looks "abandoned." "Natural area" parks are therefore most widely appreciated when they are on the outskirts of the city and on the edges of inner-city neighborhoods on tracts of more than one acre. The introduction of a "natural," successional plant community into a downtown American park is difficult and risky. There have been many failures and few successes. If the meadow aesthetic is to be appreciated in an urban setting, care must be taken to select attractive plants, to design the edge between the park and adjacent streets and buildings with great care, to devise a simple maintenance program, and to solicit the participation of people who live and work nearby. "Time Landscape" near Washington Square in New York City was intended as a relic of the Manhattan environment prior to its settlement by humans. The artist conceived of it as a living, evolving sculpture, which would progress from successional meadow to forest, and consulted geologists and biologists to gain an understanding of the pre-city landscape. He obtained the use of a small plot of land, molded the topography in imitation of glacial land forms, and planted native vegetation. Non-native urban weeds, like ailanthus, and the seedlings from nearby street trees have joined the original native plants, and now a broken umbrella, apple cores, and trash litter the tiny, fenced landscape. It looks little different from thousands of vacant lots in New York City, except that a plaque explains its foiled intent.

Larger sites in British, Dutch, and German cities—many of them abandoned construction sites, derelict industrial land, or bombed ruins—on which plant succession has been permitted to take its course, are now being incorporated into established urban park systems. For example, in West Berlin, the old Anhalter and Potsdam railroad station, which was the largest passenger station in Europe before it was destroyed by bombs in World War II, is now a tangled wilderness in the middle of the city. Sixty percent of the 150-acre site has remained in rubble, and over the course of thirty-five years, a remarkably diverse vegetation developed. One-third of all flora found in Berlin grows in this area—106 tree species and 307 species of grasses, herbs, mosses, and ferns, including 17 endangered species of ferns and flowering plants, as well as 20 other plants considered rare, and one species that had earlier disappeared from the city.[14] Only a few of the trees on the railroad triangle site are actually native to the Berlin region (for example, willows: *Salix alba, S. caprea, S. purpurea;* buckthorns: *Rhamnus frangula* and *R. catharticus*). The remaining tree species are non-native fruit trees, ornamental trees, and street trees which have run wild, as well as the ubiquitous urban weed trees like *Ailanthus altissima.*[15] Dense wooded thickets, wildflower meadows, and pockets of cattails and phragmites, laced with ruined walls, old bridges, and overgrown railroad tracks, create an eerie and exciting landscape. The Berlin Technical University has proposed a design for the site which would set aside half as a nature park and develop the remainder as garden plots, intensive recreation areas, sports fields, and playgrounds. The management of the nature park portion, as proposed, would be minimal and inexpensive, consisting mainly of rubbish removal and infrequent mowing.

Similar "found" urban wilds exist in the cities of North America where bits of untended nature linger in forgotten corners in vacant lots, abandoned quarries, wet lowlands, and steep slopes. Some of these urban wilds represent the cosmopolitan mixture of plants typical of land that has been used and abandoned, others the remnants of native plant communities which persist in places uninviting to development. The cosmopolitan, successional plant communities are typical of abandoned land in the inner city: vacant lots, old quarries, and abandoned industrial sites are common near the center of most North American cities. Remnants of native plant communities are usually on the urban fringe, but can occur quite near downtown, especially in cities with varied topography or in coastal cities with wetlands—in the Los Angeles canyons, the Toronto ravines, and New York's Jamaica Bay. These tracts generally increase in size and number with distance from the city center, and are composed of native plants and possibly a few, naturalized, alien species. These native plant communities, if sufficient in size and left to themselves, are self-regenerating and require minimal, if any, maintenance. They have evolved over many years in response to the climate of the region and the specific character of the site. Compared to cultivated and other untended urban plant communities, they are less likely to contain the same plant species when they occur in cities in different geographic and climatic regions. They place the city in its regional context and differentiate it from other cities, rather than setting it apart from the surrounding landscape. Within these remnant plant communities—be they forest, desert, or grassland—different groups of plants grow on uplands and lowlands, on northern and southern hillsides, and in shallow, rocky soils and deep soils. Both the remnants of native plant communities and the urban successional plant communities represent unexploited resources in most cities, natural areas which are frequently more expressive of the special character of a particular city—its geological origins, topographic setting, indigenous vegetation, and history—than are its manicured parks.

Wildflower meadows and salt marshes, glacial ponds, rocky outcrops, and upland woods ranging in size from one acre to hundreds of acres are found within the city limits of Boston (see, for example, figure 9.5). In 1974, the Boston Redevelopment Authority initiated a two-year study to inventory the city's remaining natural areas and to classify them according to their significance, vulnerability to development, and value as a recreation resource for local neighborhoods. The 1970 census had identified 4,560 acres—or 14 percent—of Boston's land area as "extractive" or "vacant land and agriculture."[16] The Boston Redevelopment Authority examined all land in these categories and determined that 2,000 acres, in 143 different sites, were natural areas worthy of conservation. All city neighborhoods, with exception of those immediately adjacent to the downtown, contain urban wilds. The most significant sites are large tracts of land, ranging from 25 to 100 acres, with a scenic, rural appearance and a diversity of natural features and vegetation. Many of the sites are clustered together:

Along the Neponset River in Dorchester and Mattapan, several outstanding natural areas remain. Behind the mill buildings at Dorchester Lower Mills, the walls of a rock gorge composed of Roxbury pudding stone rise seventy feet above the river. The gorge is heavily wooded by red maple trees and an unusual ground cover of evergreen ferns can be seen. Further up behind Bel Mel Street in Mattapan, a two acre meadow with several specimen willow trees gently slopes toward the river. At the northern edge of the meadow, a massive rock outcrop rising twenty feet provides the focal point for the area.[17]

FIGURE 9.5
Meadow and woods at Brook Farm, site of an experimental nineteenth-century community, one of many "urban wilds" throughout Boston within minutes of densely populated areas. Frequently, urban wilds have historic, ecological, or aesthetic significance.

Some sites on cliffs and hilltops afford sweeping views of the city skyline. Others, in tidal coves and saltwater marshes, offer views out across Boston harbor to the Boston Harbor islands and the Atlantic Ocean. Some of these natural areas are owned by government agencies, but most are privately owned.

Private citizens and city officials, who deemed the most significant natural areas too important to be left unprotected, have sought a means of acquiring these areas for the city. In 1977, the Boston Natural Areas Fund—a private, nonprofit corporation—was founded to acquire the land identified by the urban wilds inventory and to transfer ownership to the city. In the first three years, the Boston Natural Areas Fund raised $331,000, of which $84,000 was used to purchase five properties, a total of thirty acres, consisting of the most interesting urban wilds sites available for sale. The land was subsequently conveyed to the city of Boston and triggered $700,000 in matching funds from state and federal government.

Designing the Urban "Forest"

Many European cities have long managed their forests as a renewable resource. Public forests cover nearly one-quarter of Zurich and constitute most of that city's open space. The forests protect steep mountain slopes from erosion and the city's water supply from degradation, and provide more tangible financial benefits as well. They are managed to produce a sustained yield; the profits from timber production pay for forest maintenance, administrative costs, and forestry research.[18] Zurich's forestry program in not exceptional in Europe. Public forests in Paris, Frankfurt, and Oslo are managed by professional foresters for wood production, as well as for recreation and conservation of water resources.

Similar programs in the United States have been disappointing. Some, like Dayton's, were defeated before they began. Others, like the Chicago Forestry Scheme, achieved an initial success that has not been sustained. In the early 1970s, Chicago was faced with hundreds of thousands of dead or dying elm trees, anti-air-pollution legislation that banned burning of tree litter within city limits, and an increasing scarcity of landfill sites. In 1972, the Bureau of Forestry purchased a machine to cut harvested trees into wood chips. Approximately 15 to 20 percent of the dead trees removed in 1972 were converted to wood chips and sold for a profit exceeding $22,000.[19] This sum represented only a small protion of the bureau's annual budget, but the city hoped to expand the operation. Plans were made for a more ambitious program to exploit new markets for wood products, but these never materialized. To date, techniques of forest management have not been fully applied in North American cities. A program to manage the city's forest for sustained yield and to exploit new markets for city wood products holds much promise.

Washington, D.C., is one of the most intensively maintained urban landscapes in the world, a landscape that survives by virtue of careful management of plants and soil. The National Capital Region of the National Park Service is responsible for the planning, design, and maintenance of Washington's national parks. Faced with the annual hordes of tourists and recurrent festivals and mass demonstrations that trample the soil of the Mall and monument grounds to the density of concrete, the National Park Service has generated most of the research conducted on urban soils and plant stress in the United States. The Ecological Services Laboratory, an interdisciplinary, applied research organization which is part of the National Capital Region, is a center for research on urban tree survival and urban soils. Its ongoing research program has provided many of the solutions now being implemented in Washington and in other cities, and promises to uncover further solutions as current research matures. Experiments in soil restoration follow every Fourth of July celebration and every festival and mass demonstration.

One site on the Mall, the area adjacent to the Reflecting Pool, has had a particularly long history of soil abuse and has consequently required much attention to maintain an attractive landscape. During the Second World War "temporary" office buildings were installed, and these were not demolished until the 1960s. In 1968, the area was the site of Resurrection City, and between 1973 and 1976 it was the site of the American Folklife Festival. Officials estimate that up to 4 million visitors attended the American Folklife Festival during the summer of 1976 alone. Anticipating the compacting effect of 30,000 to 60,000 people per day, the National Park Service spread one to three inches of wood chips over the entire twenty-five acre site as a cushion.[20] Faced with a field of dense mud at the end of the summer, the Park Service weighed the options of reseeding versus resodding. Resodding is expensive, but yields a predictable, immediate result. The decision was to reseed instead, and to renovate the soil using an experimental compost composed of wood chips and sewage sludge. This experiment was successful. The Washington, D.C., Sewage Treatment Plant got rid of its sewage sludge, and the Park Service saved $160,000 over the cost of resodding. The compost, known as "Com-Pro," is now available to gardeners in the Washington area.

The National Park Service employs one full-time agronomist to supervise the management of lawns in the National Capital's parks. It is his job to reestablish a green lawn after each Fourth of July celebration has reduced the grass around the Washington Monument to churned mud so dense that it can scarcely be plowed by the sharp disks designed for that purpose. He works with research agronomists at the Ecological Services Laboratory to develop and test innovative approaches to park design and maintenance. In the summer of 1982, the National Park Service investigated eighty-four different varieties of bluegrass for their ability to withstand heavy trampling and still maintain a good visual appearance. Plots for each of the different varieties were staked out and planted on the grounds of the Washington Monument. A few months after installation, a large group of demonstrators established their headquarters on top of the test plots. Researchers, thinking that none of the turf could possibly survive, were dismayed. Most of the turf did in fact succumb, but several varieties survived, and these are now the subject of more intensive investigation. Not far from the bluebrass plots, the National Park Service conducted another turf experiment. A single type of grass, fescue, was subjected to twenty different establishment and maintenance treatments: five different techniques of soil preparation and turf establishment; four different levels of fertilizer application; and the use of herbicides versus no herbicides. The least expensive combinations of establishment and maintenance which still resulted in an attractive turf were singled out for further study. Most research on turf varieties used in urban parks is conducted on the back lots of state universities and U.S. government agricultural experiment stations, an environment which bears little resemblance to stressful urban conditions. The Washington, D.C., experiment will give a far better picture of which grasses are able to withstand urban stress with minimal maintenance.

The Ecological Services Laboratory is also searching for ways to increase the survival rate and life-span of urban street trees. When recently planted street trees fail, research agronomists visit the site, attempt to assess the cause, and suggest revised planting techniques before the trees are replaced. As a result of these observations, they frequently recommend provisions for drainage of the soil around the tree's roots and, to avoid the "teacup syndrome" described earlier, they suggest that the trees not be planted in imported topsoil, but rather in the soil dug from the pit itself, amended with a compost of wood chips, leaf mold, and sewage sludge. Few cities can afford the intensive management the Washington landscape receives, but all will benefit from the research required to sustain it.

A Plan for Every City

The preceding chapters have documented the many ways in which plants contribute to a safer, healthier, cleaner, more energy efficient, and more beautiful urban environment. If those benefits are to be realized, city plants must survive. The survival of plants in the city is an issue that must be addressed at all levels: through a broad overview of city plant communities as well as through attention to the mundane, technical details of planting and maintenance.

Each city must define the most critical problems of its plant communities and establish priorities for their resolution. This is equally important whether a city contemplates formulating a comprehensive plan to manage its vegetation or merely wishes to insure that the design for a single park or plaza will result in a resource rather than a burden. Critical problems of urban vegetation vary from city to city according to climate, history, and landscape tradition. Are trees and lawns which require irrigation in a water-poor climate a problem, or trees that are languishing in poorly drained soil? Is the city relatively barren of vegetation, or saddled with streets and parks filled with aged, declining trees which must all soon be removed? The city's most significant vegetation resources should be identified and their condition assessed. Such resources include remaining "urban wilds" in both public and private ownership, as well as the city's most symbolic, most intensively used, and otherwise important landscaped places. It is especially important to consider the age of plant communities and whether they are self-renewing or must be replaced. The full range of both existing and potential plant communities should be identified, including the pattern of their distribution and their relative significance. Many cities now employ a computer inventory system to facilitate the management of urban street trees.

A comprehensive strategy to increase the survival rate, augment the diversity, enhance the appearance, and moderate the cost of maintaining urban plant communities should:

- address the most critical problems of the city's plant communities, both untended and cultivated
- address the evolution of those plant communities over time, including a strategy for the regeneration of plant communities that are not self-sustaining
- explore the feasibility of designing and managing trees on streets and in public reservations as a renewable resource and a source of revenue
- investigate a graduated maintenance plan for municipal parks according to intensity of use, and explore landscape designs that would facilitate its implementation
- explore varied landscape palettes suited to the city's diverse parks and preserves which, given the city's climate and habitats, will not tax the municipal water supply or maintenance budget
- locate new parks and other open space to preserve the city's most beautiful or most significant plant communities, to enhance its appearance and distinctive identity
- exploit the potential of vegetation to improve climate and air quality, slope stability, and water quality, to prevent flooding, to increase the diversity of breeding wildlife, and to enhance the city's appearance.

Every new street, plaza, and park should be designed to promote the survival of the plants within it, with a maintenance program appropriate to its function, context, and available resources. The design for every project should:

- address the relationship between the site and citywide patterns of vegetation, as well as the problems and potential posed by the plant communities of the surrounding neighborhood
- exploit the specific habitat afforded by the site to increase the diversity of plant communities
- respond to how intensely the project will be used, the resources available for maintenance, and maintenance practices
- exploit hardy indigenous and naturalized plants which will survive urban stresses
- utilize plants to create a desirable microclimate, filter air pollutants, stabilize slopes and erodable soils, absorb stormwater runoff, filter water pollutants, and provide shelter and food for wildlife.

The economic and aesthetic impact of the Dutch elm disease took many cities by surprise. The current gradual, but inexorable, decline of urban trees is taking place over a longer period of time, but will eventually yield the same result. The final disappearance of mature trees from parks, plazas, and streets may not engender surprise, for by that time we may have ceased to expect trees to survive in the city. Every city must weigh the benefits that trees yield to comfort, health, protection of air and water quality, prevention of erosion and land slipping, moderation of flooding, aesthetic enhancement, and energy conservation against the costs of maintaining urban vegetation. Those cities whose mature plant communities are in greatest jeopardy should plot a comprehensive strategy immediately. Other cities, with less severe problems, may choose to focus on each new park as it is built or upon a few older parks in need of renovation.

The application of forest management techniques offers the possible generation of revenue to offset the costs of building and maintaining municipal parks. The integration of urban wilds into city parkland offers an aesthetic counterpoint to the rest of the urban landscape. The use of hardier turf and trees in city parks, the substitution of thriving "weeds" for more sensitive plants, the transformation of portions of existing parkland into a lower maintenance landscape, and harnessing the energy of natural processes of plant succession all promise to enhance the survival rate of urban vegetation while simultaneously lowering the cost of maintenance.

CHAPTER 10

Pets and Pests

S CATTERED, fragmented remnants of woodland, meadow, and marsh embedded within the urban fabric are islands surrounded by a sea of buildings and pavement. Most native wildlife cannot survive in the harsh, impoverished habitats of the city. Those that do thrive in the city are opportunists who adjust their behavior to human activities and structures: by using food stores and garbage for food, and buildings, gardens, and small woodlots as habitat; or by attracting human companionship. Pigeons, starlings, and house sparrows replace songbirds; hosts of rats infest buildings and sewers. Feral cats and packs of stray dogs scrounge in garbage, and their pampered counterparts are fed and sheltered.

Cities transform woods, fields, marshes, and streams into buildings and pavement, formal parks and gardens, filled land, and concrete drainage channels. Remnants of native vegetation which might otherwise support breeding species of native wildlife are either too small or too scattered. Most of the wildlife that does survive are not natives, but immigrants like rats, roaches, and scavenging birds, who adapted long ago to a landscape dominated by humans. These become pests when the city's rich food source—created by careless food storage and garbage disposal—supports a burgeoning population which is unchecked by predators.

The displacement of native wildlife by pests and pets would probably go relatively unnoticed were it not for the attendant public health problem, property damage, and nuisance that the pests create. Man has regarded rats with dread and loathing since the Middle Ages. The city's rat population probably exceeds its human population. Each year, rats inflict property damage, and each year cities spend millions of dollars on rat control. In 1971 alone, the city of Baltimore spent over $1 million for rat control.[1] The cumulative droppings of large flocks of starlings and pigeons befoul and deface buildings and sidewalks where they roost and may even constitute a health hazard. Less recognized is the nuisance posed by domestic and stray dogs whose feces litter the grass of urban parks and are flushed from streets to rivers and streams after every rain.

The conflicting values that humans hold toward urban wildlife present the greatest obstacle to managing them and resolving the problems they pose. While some people view pigeons, starlings and squirrels as a nuisance, others nurture them with crusts of bread. While some people cherish the opportunity to watch migrating water fowl or listen to a diverse repertoire of bird songs, others are blind and deaf to the spectacle. Nor do people share the same attitudes toward pets. Dog owners and other park users often compete with violent passion over a rare expanse of lawn. In the city, humans subsist in an uneasy cohabitation with other animals.

Impoverished and Fragmented Habitats

Urban wildlife must contend with great stress: polluted air, water, and plants; sparse, scattered plant cover; pavement and compacted soil; and a dense population of humans and their pets.[2] Whether herbivores, carnivores, or omnivores, animals are ultimately dependent on plants for food. Since cities introduce an entirely new set of plant communities, only those animals able to exploit new food sources and shelter can survive. Even when cities incorporate remnants of native vegetation, these are rarely of sufficient size to support breeding species of native wildlife that depend, either directly or indirectly, on that vegetation for food. Air and water pollution markedly reduce the species diversity of the urban insect population, and the population of insectivores is correspondingly small. For those species able to take advantage of them, the city provides a surprisingly large number of new habitats, including buildings, parks, yards, sewers, transportation corridors, and dumps.

The interior and exterior of buildings and other structures provide an array of habitats. The ordinary home may harbor rats and house mice, cockroaches and ants, spiders, flies, clothes moths, and other bugs. House sparrows build nests under eaves and in vents. Buildings with parapets and ledges provide roosts for pigeons and starlings. The pigeon's rock dove ancestors live on cliffs and feed on adjacent farm lands. Starlings, which since the late nineteenth century have adopted the center of cities as their primary roosting place, first roosted in the trees of urban parks and then moved to the sills and ledges of adjacent buildings. The roofs and parapets of tall buildings afford nesting sites for many cliff-dwelling birds, including kestrels in London and peregrine falcons in Montreal, Chicago, New York, Boston, and Philadelphia. Many birds, including pigeons and house sparrows, use metal girders on bridges and railway stations as if they were tree branches. Bats and gray squirrels sometimes inhabit attics, especially if buildings are dilapidated. When buildings provide both shelter and abundant food supply, they may support a large animal population. Food warehouses are a favorite habitat of rats, mice, and house sparrows.

Along with the wildlife that enters buildings uninvited are the animals that humans have domesticated and keep for pleasure, sport, or food. Cats and dogs are among the most abundant city pets. There may be as many as one dog for every seven people in the United States. Although the ratio is likely higher in rural areas than in cities, nevertheless, some studies have estimated that more than one-half of the nation's dogs live in cities.[3] Door-to-door interviews in the city of Baltimore revealed that 37 to 51 percent of all families in urban neighborhoods owned a dog.[4]

Small urban parks with formal gardens and large urban parks with clipped lawns and scattered trees offer little security from predators and a narrow range of plants as a food source. The number of species they harbor is correspondingly small—mainly squirrels, house sparrows, starlings, and pigeons. Although private yards and gardens in older suburbs afford a wider choice of cover and plant food, few species can survive when restricted to the domestic garden; most need access to large open spaces. Thus the potential species which an individual homeowner can attract to a backyard garden depends as much upon the proximity of a large, preferably wooded, area as it does upon the arrangement and selection of plants within the yard. A small, downtown residential garden, surrounded by buildings and pavement, will still attract mainly squirrels, starlings, and house sparrows, even if stocked with plants attractive to other wildlife. Garbage dumps attract many urban wildlife species and their predators. Gulls, crows, house sparrows, starlings, pigeons, kestrels, and pied wagtail are the principal bird species of rubbish dumps in London. The kestrels prey on rodents, and the other birds scavenge bits of food from the garbage. Flocks of gulls in the city at times exceed 4,000.

Transportation corridors, like highways, canals, and railroad rights-of-way, are potential channels of movement for urban wildlife, but the rights-of-way of clipped grass with few shrubs and trees are unlikely to serve this purpose. Rats and raccoons use storm and sanitary sewers for movement and shelter. The combination of a ready food supply from garbage cans and the protection afforded by storm sewers can yield raccoon populations considerably higher than those in more rural areas. The population density of raccoons in a suburb near downtown Cincinnati can reach one raccoon per 1.4 acres; the density commonly found in wildlife refuges and rural areas is one raccoon per twelve to forty-five acres.[5] When their population density is high, raccoons become a nuisance to the human population, rather than an amenity.

The pollution of water and the sediments in urban streams, rivers, and lakes eliminate many aquatic species.[6] The loss of dissolved oxygen triggered by the release of excessive organic nutrients in urban stormwater and sanitary sewage produces fishkills if it occurs precipitously and a shift in fish species if it occurs over a longer period of time. As dissolved oxygen decreases, bass, perch, and pike replace trout, chub, and whitefish, and are replaced in turn by carp and sunfish. The large quantities of suspended sediments in urban water bodies decrease the penetration of light and thus the aquatic plants that are able to grow and the fish and other organisms that depend on the plants for food and shelter. Heavy metals, pesticide residues, and other toxic chemicals also accumulate in aquatic organisms until they reach fatal concentrations. In the 1950s, the Thames River in London had little or no oxygen and, apart from eels, was virtually fishless for a stretch of over forty miles.

Despite the fact that the city creates many new habitats and despite an abundant food source in human waste and garbage, the number of wildlife species surviving in a downtown urban environment is small and restricted primarily to alien species that adapted long ago to the urban environment. Tiny patches and strips of habitat attractive to native wildlife are fragmented islands embedded in a matrix of structures and pavement. This fragmentation of habitat eliminates most wildlife that travel on or under the ground. Although birds can fly from patch to patch, they rarely do unless the islands of attractive habitat are large and connected. The number of species of breeding birds declines drastically from the rural fringes of a city to its downtown area. More than ninety bird species breed within a 24-kilometer (14.9 miles) radius of Manchester, England, yet only six bird species breed in the city center, and the number increases very gradually with distance from downtown: eleven species at 1.2 kilometers (.7 miles); twenty-two species at 3.6 kilometers (2.2 miles); forty-five species at 7.25 kilometers (4.5 miles); sixty-eight species at 13.7 kilometers (8.5 miles); and eighty-one species at 19.3 (12 miles) kilometers.[7] The form of the city limits both the abundance and diversity of those wildlife that would be an amenity. At the same time, most wildlife that do thrive in the city become pests.

Wildlife as a Nuisance

Some of the most common urban wildlife are potential carriers of diseases transmissible to humans. A fungus in starling droppings has been linked to cases of histoplasmosis, a pulmonary disease,[8] and a fungus in pigeon droppings to cryptococcosis, a disease that can affect the lungs and central nervous system.[9] Warm-blooded animals are potential transmitters of rabies. Of 4,427 cases of rabies reported in the United States in 1972, 78 percent were transmitted by wild animals: 60 percent by skunks; 19 percent by foxes; 15 percent by bats; and 5 percent by raccoons.[10]

Domestic pets like dogs represent a greater threat to public health than most city residents realize. Dog bites are the most commonly perceived problem; in 1970, there were 6,809 reported bites in the city of Baltimore alone. With an urban population one-seventh the human population, dogs impose more wastes on the city's environment than can be readily assimilated. New York's Environmental Protection Agency has attempted to measure the magnitude of this impact and estimated that New York City's dog population deposits somewhere between 5,000 and 20,000 tons of feces annually.[11] Urban parks with lawns, surrounded by dense residential districts, are little more than dog toilets. In parks like Philadelphia's Rittenhouse Square, it is difficult to find a feces-free space on the grass to sit on. Soil in playgrounds and parks contaminated by dog feces, if injested by small children, may be a source of worms.[12] Dog feces contribute to the bacterial contamination of urban runoff, which is equal to dilute sanitary sewage.[13]

Free-ranging dogs, whether pets or strays, are a greater nuisance

211

than leashed dogs. Free-ranging dogs inflict most of the reported dog bites, and they often complicate rat control. They rummage in garbage, making it accessible to rats, and they slow down rat control crews. People often avoid using rat poison for fear that it would poison the dogs. Rats, moreover, feed on dog feces.[14]

Domestic animals have always been an urban nuisance. In colonial North America, free-ranging hogs and dogs were a menace to pedestrians and property.[15] Most cities solved the hog problem by the mid eighteenth century, but not without considerable uproar. When New York banned swine from the city in 1744, a widow asked "if hogs must go, why not also banish cats and dogs?" In colonial cities, as today, it was free-ranging dogs that created the principal dog problems. The city of Philadelphia permitted citizens to kill strays and levied enormous fines for owners who let their dogs run loose. In 1722, Philadelphians could "kill on sight authors of any canine disturbances," and by 1727 all owners of dogs were ordered to keep them chained up on penalty of a large fine. Packs of stray dogs are still a problem in cities throughout the world, as documented in Britain, the United States, and Japan.[16] As in the past, the problem is caused mainly by people. Some stray dogs may be the offspring of other strays, but most are escaped or abandoned pets, and some are dogs whose owners allow them to run free.

In 1960, a flock of starlings flew up in front of a climbing airplane shortly after its takeoff from Logan Airport in Boston. The result was a crash with sixty people dead.[17] In many cases, collisions between birds and aircraft involve gulls, because airports are frequently located at the outskirts of cities, on marginal lands—on filled marshland, along lakes or oceans, in close proximity to municipal dumps.[18] Many of these sites were bird habitats before they were airports, and the addition of standing water, buildings on which to perch, and the elimination of many predators, often make airports attractive habitats for birds.

Where pigeons and starlings use buildings for nesting and roosting, their excreta may build up on walls and on the pavement beneath, defacing the property. Rats and birds that get into food storage areas can cause considerable property loss. Mammals, like squirrels, often destroy plants in gardens and parks. Between early spring and late summer of 1977, gray squirrels destroyed 2,000 geraniums and damaged newly planted trees worth approximately $4,500 in Washington, D.C.'s, Lafayette Park.[19]

At the root of all or most urban wildlife problems lie the actions of people who fail to perceive the consequences and who often have conflicting attitudes toward sharing their habitat with other animals. Careless disposal of food and garbage supports the population of many urban pests. It is people who maintain pets and permit them to befoul the urban environment. When people feed migrating birds, encouraging them to become year-round residents, they often transform them into pests who befoul water and the parks where they nest. In the 1970s, a few Canada geese began to winter over in Toronto and Philadelphia. They chose parkland along the shore of the Toronto Islands in Toronto and along the Schuylkill River in Philadelphia for their home. Citizens, delighted at the spectacle, fed the geese. The hand-outs continued, and each year the number of geese that remained grew. Finally, because of their sheer numbers, the geese polluted the waters of the Toronto lagoons and the Schuylkill River with their excreta.

The case of Lafayette Park illustrates the complexity of the problem and the conflicting values involved. After squirrels damaged landscaping in Lafayette Park, which is across Pennsylvania Avenue from the White House, a dispute arose between park staff concerned with protecting the park's landscaping and park visitors concerned with the welfare of the squirrels. After extensive damage to the park's trees and flowers in 1977, National Park Service staff began to relocate the squirrels to areas outside the city. Complaints from local residents and subsequent news media coverage halted the relocation program. In an attempt to resolve this conflict, the National Park Service undertook a study of the situation. The study revealed several interesting and previously unrecognized facts: that the density of squirrels in Lafayette Park was higher than the highest densities previously recorded, much higher than in suburban woodlots; that this density was due to the surplus food fed to the squirrels by park visitors; that the squirrels were eating only part of the food left for them, with the remainder being eaten by rats and birds; and that the removal program, rather than relieving the park damage, probably aggravated it. The squirrels were indeed damaging the park. Investigators observed them "stripping, gnawing, peeling, and ingesting bark," and constantly pruning trees to maintain their leaf nests, of which there were a particularly large number. In March, Lafayette Park supported 9.1 squirrels per acre, but after the breeding season in spring and summer, the population rose to 20.6 squirrels in November. The relocation program was doomed from the start, notwithstanding public outcry. It seems that the food supply in the park was so abundant that squirrels immigrated from the surrounding neighborhood to replace those that had been removed. Tension between the immigrant squirrels and established residents manifested itself, ironically, in increased plant damage.

At the heart of the squirrel density problem were a few people who supplied the squirrels with enormous quantities of food. Supplementary food, above and beyond what the squirrels foraged for themselves, represented 37 percent of their diet in April and May and 75 percent of their diet in October. Peanuts comprised 35 percent of all the food eaten by the squirrels. Six dedicated souls provided 90 percent of this supplementary food. Two of these "zoo keepers," as they were dubbed by the investigators, visited the park six days a week during the winter and five days a week during the summer. These two "zoo keepers" brought eight pounds of raw peanuts each visit during the summer and sixteen pounds of raw peanuts each visit during the winter, or over 3,000 pounds per year, at a cost to them of over $800. Other visitors to the park also stopped to watch the squirrels and fed them food, but did so infrequently and in small amounts. Squirrels ate only 27 percent of the food left by the "zoo keepers" and buried an additional 34 percent. The remaining 39 percent was eaten by other inhabitants of the park—mainly rats, starlings, pigeons, and house sparrows. As long as the "zoo keepers" continue to provide such an abundant surplus of food, the park will support its dense population of squirrels, and its trees will continue to be stripped.

The United States has spent over $200 million annually on the management of game species. Yet it has largely ignored the wildlife with which people come in contact every day, unless they become a nuisance.[20] Meanwhile, more and more habitat is created that is attractive to the common urban pest, and less and less habitat remains to support more desirable species. A few simple alterations, accomplished at little, if any, additional cost could remedy this situation.

CHAPTER 11

Designing Wildlife Habitats

MAN has always derived sustenance, sport, companionship, comfort, and delight from animals. An abundant source of fish or animals enabled some early human societies to establish stable settlements, but hunting and fishing were pursued as sport even after they were no longer required for survival. Many early Persian gardens were hunting grounds and, as already noted, many parks in European cities are former royal hunting grounds, including Regent's Park and Hyde Park in London and the Tiergarten in Berlin. It is entirely appropriate that these still support a diverse population of urban wildlife.

The dog, originally domesticated as hunter and shepherd, maintained a privileged position as human companion long after its economic importance disappeared. In Medieval Christian symbology, the dog represented fidelity. Songbirds, like the nightingale and the mockingbird, have long figured in folklore. Interest in birds has continued to the present. Bird feed has become a big business in the United States; in 1974, the sale of birdseed amounted to $170 million. Researchers estimate that approximately 20 percent of American households buy an average of sixty pounds of birdseed each year.[1]

It is unfortunate that much of the human contact with wildlife in cities is negative. With proper planning and management, urban pests could be controlled, the negative effects of urban pets mitigated, and the diversity of birds and other wildlife fostered. Although pest control and pet management mainly entail regulating human activities, rather than manipulating urban form, the introduction and encouragement of "desirable" wildlife is largely dependent upon the preservation and creation of habitat. Residents in several American cities have demonstrated their interest in urban wildlife. In 1976, Missouri voters approved an amendment to their state constitution to add one-eighth cent to the state sales tax to provide funding for the Design for Conservation Program. The amendment received most of its support from city residents of St. Louis, Kansas City, and Springfield.[2]

There are many successful models for attracting a diverse and abundant urban wildlife. Regent's Park and Hyde Park in London, Rock Creek Park in Washington, D.C., and Mt. Auburn Cemetery in Boston are all noted for the number of bird species they support and are well frequented by bird watchers. Stream valleys and railroad rights-of-way in London and ravines in Los Angeles link the city with its rural outskirts and permit the penetration of wildlife into the city. The new towns of Columbia, Maryland, and Woodlands, Texas, have retained wooded stream valleys which accomplish the same purpose.

Food, Water, Cover, and Territory

A few basic principles should guide urban wildlife management, whether the goal is to increase diversity and abundance of desired species or to control the numbers and spread of pests. Wildlife are linked to each other and to plants by the sum of the relationships between the eater and the eaten, known as the food web. Every species has particular requirements for its habitat, without which it cannot survive.

Herbivores eat plants, carnivores eat other animals, and omnivores eat both, following a sequence known as the food chain, which passes energy and materials from one organism to another. The food web for a given ecosystem is the sum of all the food chains within it. Urbanization disrupts the food web, and the elimination of a single species or group of species provokes a chain reaction. Many insects, for example, cannot survive in cities, and insectivores are therefore less common. The removal of a predator may result in the creation of a pest. Rats, starlings, and pigeons have few predators in the city. Apart from domestic and feral dogs and cats, urban carnivores are scarce. The most successful urban wildlife, including most urban pests, are omnivores, because they are less dependent upon a single type of food source.

Every animal has specific requirements for food, water, cover, and territory, without which it cannot survive. Food preferences and cover requirements for many wildlife are well known.[3] When these are provided in combination with adequate water, sufficient space for ranging, and protection from predators like dogs and cats, there is a good possibility that, if a given species is native to the region, it can be supported. The size, shape, and location of the habitat are important (see figure 11.1), as is its physical connection to large patches of habitat in or outside the city (see figures 11.2 and 11.3). Habitat size is frequently the most important limiting factor in cities, where patches and strips of suitable habitat are isolated in a matrix of buildings, pavement, and lawn. The goal of urban wildlife management should be to create habitats within which animal communities can be self-renewing.

Densely built downtowns offer a very narrow range of habitat. The species that survive, and often become pests, are largely dependent upon human food sources and an ability to find suitable habitat in and on human structures. Starlings and house sparrows build nests in unblocked eaves, and pigeons nest and roost in exposed high beams. Pigeons and starlings both roost on buildings with ample ledges. Architectural design that eliminates nooks, crannies, holes, and protected ledges will substantially reduce the attractiveness of buildings as habitat.[4]

Effective pest control must combine restriction of food sources and of accessibility or availability of cover. Some animals become pests only when they occupy habitat that conflicts with human activities. In such cases, especially where the presence of animals poses a nuisance or safety hazard, habitat management is often the most effective means of control. Thus, airports should be managed as unattractive bird habitats: food sources, like fruit trees and shrubs, should be eliminated; grass should be kept no higher than five to eight inches. Airport buildings should be designed so as not to provide attractive shelter, and to prevent ponding of water on rooftops. Water impoundments should be avoided. Dumps and fish-processing plants, which attract large flocks of birds, should not be located near airports.

Pets become pests only through human neglect or ignorance. More strict regulation of urban dogs, requiring owners to leash dogs and to dispose of their wastes, would eliminate most of the health nuisances they pose. Some cities now provide "dog toilets" in parks.

Ample opportunity exists within the city to increase the diversity and abundance of urban wildlife. Increasing the diversity of "desirable" species will not solve the pest problem, but it may mitigate it by providing more competition for pest species. By designing and managing the urban landscape with an appreciation for the habitat needs of different species, an abundant and diverse wildlife can be encouraged where they will provide an amenity and excluded where they might pose a nuisance. The goal should be to create wildlife habitats within the city that will support breeding populations and permit migration between the city and the countryside.

Creating Viable Habitats

Although the number of breeding bird species normally decreases with proximity to the city's center, large parks that afford sufficient cover and food, as well as diversity of habitat and corridors linking the downtown to the countryside, can overturn this rule. Many London parks are dramatic testimony to this fact. Of the approximately eighty to one hundred breeding species of birds found in any one area of the British Isles, about seventy to eighty are the maximum possible in the cities.[5] The actual maximum recorded is fifty to sixty breeding species when suburbs and city are taken together, and twenty-five to thirty breeding species in large urban centers. A large British park, with diverse vegetation, may support more than twenty-five breeding species of birds, regardless of how close it is to the city center; a small or poorly vegetated city park or housing area may support no more than fifteen breeding species. London is particularly fortunate in the number and size of its urban parks. Regent's Park and Hyde Park are both near the center of downtown London, yet Regent's Park harbors approximately thirty-four species of breeding birds and Hyde Park twenty-nine. Wandsworth Common, seven miles further from downtown London, supports only eighteen species. It is a much smaller park isolated within a densely populated area.[6]

Size, shape, and continuity of suitable habitat are critical to maximizing the diversity and abundance of species. One large and continuous habitat will support more species and individuals than an equal area divided into smaller, isolated patches. Take, for example, a woods surrounded by homes. A few birds will live largely within the area of domestic gardens, while others will live within the wooded edge. Other species will live neither near the edge of the woods nor in gardens, but make their home in the center of a forest-

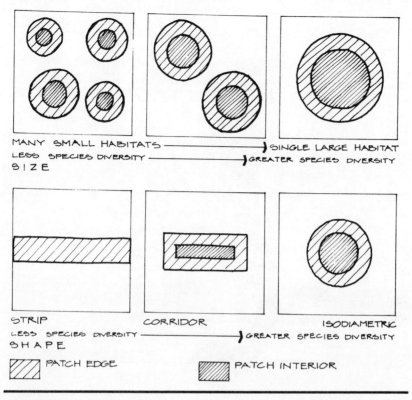

MANY SMALL HABITATS ─────────────→ SINGLE LARGE HABITAT
LESS SPECIES DIVERSITY ──────────→ GREATER SPECIES DIVERSITY
SIZE

STRIP   CORRIDOR   ISODIAMETRIC
LESS SPECIES DIVERSITY ──────────→ GREATER SPECIES DIVERSITY
SHAPE

▨ PATCH EDGE   ▨ PATCH INTERIOR

FIGURE 11.1

Principles of biogeography applied to the design of wildlife habitat. To increase species diversity, larger areas are preferable to smaller, and wider dimensions preferable to narrower.

---

ed region. If the woodlot is too small, it will consist entirely of edge species; if sufficiently large to comprise much interior woods, it will also support those species and thus a greater diversity (figure 11.1).[7]

Wildlife do not recognize property boundaries, and private grounds within the city, both institutional and domestic, can augment the size of urban open spaces and the links between them. Cemeteries, for example, represent approximately 35 percent of the open space in the city of Boston and its suburbs, and ninety-five bird species have been identified in Boston's cemeteries, among them the great blue heron, sharp skinned hawk, sparrow hawk, bobwhite, ring-necked pheasant, black-billed cuckoo, belted kingfisher, rufussided towhee, and Wilson's warbler.[8] Many of the birds were nesting, not only the common species like robins and blue jays, but also yellow-shafted flickers, song sparrows, catbirds, ring-necked pheasants, and mockingbirds. The cemeteries also harbor numerous amphibians and reptiles: common garter snakes; stinkpots; snapping, box, and painted turtles; newts and dusky salamanders; common

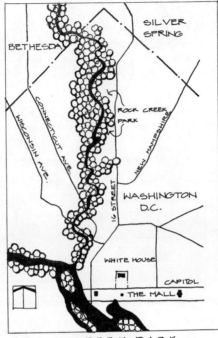

A) ROCK CREEK PARK

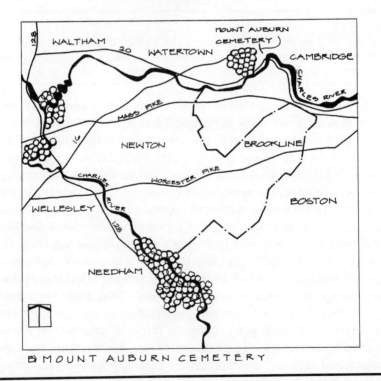

B) MOUNT AUBURN CEMETERY

FIGURE 11.2
Rock Creek Park and Mount Auburn Cemetery, two large urban parks that owe the diversity and abundance of wildlife to their location along river corridors linking city and countryside.

toads; bullfrogs; and green, leopard, and pickerel frogs.[9] The number of birds in each cemetery correlated directly with its size and diversity and with the quantity of the vegetation it contained.

Mt. Auburn Cemetery is an urban mecca for Boston bird watchers. The first "garden" cemetery in the United States, it was laid out in the 1830s with ample woods and multiple ponds, a landscape tradition sustained throughout its history. The current administration considers wildlife when it designs new plantings. The success of Mt. Auburn Cemetery as a wildlife sanctuary is due not only to its size and landscaping, but also to the fact that it abuts the Charles River and is therefore not an island surrounded by city, but a peninsula jutting out from the river corridor (see figure 11.2).

Some of the wildlife population supported by large urban parks will extend into adjacent residential areas, but only when landscaping provides that opportunity. Rock Creek Park in Washington, D.C., is in a broad stream valley between downtown Washington and suburban Maryland, sufficiently large and continuous to harbor a diversity of bird species (figure 11.2). Two very different neighborhoods abut the park on east and west. To the west are tree-lined streets with single-family homes and landscaped yards, as well as some row houses and apartments. To the east is a much denser neighborhood, with few trees and little landscaping. The diversity of birds and the ratio of urban pest birds to songbirds varies dramatically from east to west (figure 11.3). In the east one finds house sparrows, pigeons, and starlings in abundance and extremely few songbirds. The numbers of starlings and house sparrows increase with distance from the park. In the landscaped yards to the west, one finds half as many sparrows, fewer starlings, and one-fiftieth the pigeons that one finds to the east, but many more robins, mockingbirds, cardinals, catbirds, blue jays, song sparrows, and wood thrushes.[10] Thus, given an environment attractive to the more aesthetically desirable bird species, the typical urban bird pests are reduced in numbers.

Size and continuity alone are insufficient to guarantee a diverse, abundant wildlife. The species of plants, their age and condition, and the complexity of their spatial arrangement are all important in determining whether the environment provides the opportunity for food and nesting needed by a given species to carry out its life cycle. Some birds rely on certain plants for feeding and use others for nests. Some plants are used by many birds, others by few. The common apple tree provides a preferred nesting site for many birds, including the robin, the great crested flycatcher, and the red-eyed

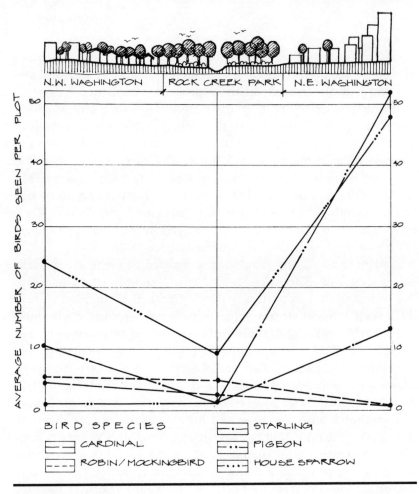

FIGURE 11.3
Correlation between bird diversity and abundance and urban landscape in Rock Creek Park and adjacent Washington, D.C., neighborhoods. Songbirds, common within the park and landscaped neighborhood to the west, are rare in the barren, densely settled neighborhoods to the east. Pest species are far more prominent on the east.

vireo. Forty-three bird species eat its fruit, which is the preferred food of sixteen species, including the ring-necked pheasant, the downy woodpecker, and the blue jay. The yellow-bellied sapsucker eats both its sap and its fruit, the cedar waxwing its flowers, and grosbeaks its buds.[11] The crab apple, among the most commonly planted urban ornamentals, also provides food and cover for many species. Other common ornamental plants, such as forsythias and hydrangeas, are rarely used by birds.

Parks and private grounds composed of diverse topography, diverse types and arrangements of plants, will support a greater number of bird species. Topographic variation should be exploited to create many microenvironments. Adjacent patches of meadow, shrubby edge, and woodland with abundant understory will support a more diverse wildlife community than a single meadow or woodlot. Existing remnants of urban forest or meadow can be managed so as to enhance their value as wildlife habitat, and new habitat can be created by the establishment of new plant communities on derelict land such as landfill sites or abandoned quarries. The creation of new habitat should be undertaken with caution and guided by an understanding of the regional ecology and the development of small-scale experiments. Establishing natural areas to support breeding species of desired wildlife is a complex task. The absence of a single, critical organism can make it impossible for a plant or animal community to perpetuate itself, and can thus undermine the entire endeavor. It is always essential to know which wildlife species one is designing for, so that the habitat includes the appropriate organisms and spatial requirements.

Transportation corridors, especially if located along stream valleys, have great potential for increasing the abundance and diversity of wildlife in the city when they permit wildlife movement from countryside to downtown and between otherwise isolated islands of habitat. Railroad rights-of-way in London follow a radial pattern and, together with stream valleys, form routes along which wildlife from the suburbs and metropolitan outskirts may move into what would otherwise be isolated habitats within the city. Some corridors not only provide for dispersal, but are also themselves permanent habitat. Where the railroad cuts through chalk deposits, and a diverse plant community covers embankments, there are likely to be a number of animals living within the corridor. If the soil is sandy, the corridor may even support rabbit warrens and fox dens.[12] The wider the corridors, whether railroads, canals, stream valleys, or highways, and the denser and more diverse the plant cover they support, the greater the number of animal species which will use them to migrate in and out of the city.

Designing the Metropolis for Wildlife

The ecology of the metropolitan region, its climate, topography, and native plant and animal communities, as well as the existence of large, undisturbed habitat near the city, determines the ultimate range in species that might be accommodated in a particular city.

Only by looking at the city as a whole with its many types and sizes of open spaces can this potential diversity be realized. Possible wildlife habitat consists of virtually all unpaved, unbuilt-upon land in the city, including the private grounds of colleges and universities, schools, hospitals, prisons, corporations, zoos, cemeteries, churchyards, sand and gravel quarries, canals and reservoirs, golf courses, sewage treatment facilities, industrial parks, gardens, parks, and urban wilds. In some instances, a greater abundance of species may be supported by merely providing a link between one small island of habitat and another.

The new towns of Columbia, Maryland, and Woodlands, Texas, have each managed to incorporate wildlife by clustering residences to secure a large, linked, open-space system. The U.S. Bureau of Sport Fisheries and Wildlife worked with planners at Columbia to retain wildlife habitat.[13] Not only were existing forests, meadows, bushy hedgerows, and stream valleys retained, but their ecological diversity was increased. One-quarter to one-half acre clearings were created in the woodlands, and the debris, ground vegetation, and leaf litter were left undisturbed. A four-year rotation for mowing the grasslands was proposed. The invasion of urban pest species like house sparrows, pigeons, and starlings has been minimal, and much of the native wildlife has remained.

Several states have initiated programs to promote urban wildlife. In 1973, the New York Department of Environmental Conservation inaugurated one of the first such programs, its goals to "increase the abundance, variety, and visibility of desirable wildlife and their habitats in urban and suburban areas; to increase urban and suburban residents' contacts with wildlife and encourage the understanding of ecological principles and concern for environmental conservation; and to preserve and enhance the long term variety and biological productivity of urban and suburban areas of wildlife habitats."[14] Several projects were underway in 1979: an inventory of existing and potential wildlife habitat in urban areas; an urban wildlife park concept with an initial pilot program in Albany; the sale to urban landowners of shrubs that attract songbirds; an educational program for schoolteachers; and the provision of information to urban planners.[15]

The state of Missouri launched an urban wildlife program with revenues from the state sales tax. The program supports two urban biologists for St. Louis and Kansas City who provide private citizens, land developers, and government agencies with information about urban wildlife. In 1978, it began an urban fishing program in Kansas City and hired two management biologists to oversee that activity and to give technical advice on fisheries in other cities. A habitat inventory was conducted for Kansas City, identifying where opportunities remain for wildlife management in parks, cemeteries, along streams, greenbelts, boulevards, and parkways. An Urban Wilds Acres program was instituted to acquire natural areas near cities. The state is conducting an experimental program to release wild turkeys in Kansas City, has distributed educational packets on conservation to schoolteachers, and has instituted a backyard wildlife program.[16]

A Plan for Every City

A plan to enhance wildlife habitat may not only increase the abundance and diversity of desirable wildlife species in the city and thus the aesthetic pleasure they provide, but may also decrease the prevalence of some pest species. By controlling the location of wildlife habitat, conflicts between wildlife and human activities can be minimized.

Every plan or design for wildlife in the city should be based upon a firm understanding of the region's ecology, including not only the species that currently live within the city, but also those species that potentially could be supported. It is important to understand the requirements of each species for food, cover, water, and territory, as well as the interactions among species with which they interact. Every city should identify those areas that are currently reservoirs of breeding wildlife, as well as additional areas that might be modified to support diverse wildlife, and should determine whether it is on a major flyway for migratory birds and, if so, which areas birds currently use as resting spots. Critical wildlife problems vary from city to city. Are rats a problem, or packs of stray dogs? Are flocks of starlings, pigeons, or migrating birds which now winter-over a problem, or pets exceeding the ability of the environment to assimilate their wastes? Wildlife problems will likely be most critical in specific areas within the city. Knowing the features of the physical environment that perpetuate a problem will aid in its resolution.

A comprehensive strategy to decrease pest problems and enhance wildlife diversity should:

- address the city's most critical pest problems, with particular attention directed to the improvement of conditions in those areas with the most severe problems

- increase the diversity of wildlife in areas where wildlife would not conflict with human activities
- develop new wildlife habitats to increase the diversity of habitats within the city by acquiring urban wilds and reclaiming derelict land and by exploiting both public and private open land to augment potential wildlife habitat
- locate parks and other open space and exploit public and private corridors (including railroad and highway rights-of-way, utility easements, stream valleys and canals) to link existing or potential wildlife habitat to other habitats within the city and to open land at the city's outskirts.

New buildings, highways, and parks within the city should be designed to encourage the diversity and abundance of desirable wildlife species and to be unattractive habitats for pests. Every such project should:

- address the relationship between its location and the critical pest problems of the city, the needs of the city's other wildlife, and the most critical pest problems and wildlife resources on the site and in its immediate neighborhood
- exploit the proximity to existing wildlife habitat or citywide corridors to promote the abundance and diversity of wildlife
- provide suitable habitat for desired species by selecting appropriate plants as food sources, arranging plants so as to provide cover for nesting, feeding, and protection from predators, and coordinate landscape maintenance with wildlife needs like mating and nesting.

Increasing the abundance and diversity of desirable wildlife in the city need not be expensive and need not be undertaken for the sole benefit of wildlife. The design and use of an area for wildlife habitat is compatible with many other urban functions like flood control and sewage treatment, climate modification and air quality management, erosion prevention, forestry, and recreation. There is much more opportunity for developing wildlife habitat in the city than is commonly recognized. Most work on "urban" wildlife management, what little has been done, concentrates on the urbanizing region at the city's edge, not on the more densely settled areas where most people live. Rats, squirrels, starlings, pigeons, and house sparrows will probably always reside in the city, but a more diverse and abundant urban wildlife with the aesthetic and educational benefits it entails can be achieved with management. It will not be a great source of revenue to most cities, but neither will it be a great expense. To many, observing the activities of wildlife, their foraging and eating, their mating and nest building, is an entree to the mysteries of the natural world. As such, that door must not be closed.

PART VI

The Urban Ecosystem

CHAPTER 12

The City as
an Infernal Machine

T HE MODERN CITY is an infernal machine that consumes and squanders enormous quantities of energy and materials, produces mountains of garbage, and puffs and spews out poisons. The machine evolves constantly, as a host of institutions and countless individuals simultaneously build and disassemble it, forge links and disrupt them, solve single problems and generate a multitude of new ones. The city's air, earth, water, and living organisms absorb this chaotic activity with manifest perturbation in structure, population, and the flow of resources and energy.

Any single change to the urban ecosystem produces dozens of repercussions, most of them unforeseen and unrecognized. The complexity of the urban ecosystem defies understanding, but the dangers of not comprehending are frightening. Many of these hazards are already evident: the concentration of poisons which threatens health and reproduction; the magnification of hazards and increased vulnerability to their ravages; vanishing resources; and rising costs. The faith that the natural environment possesses an unlimited capacity to furnish resources and to assimilate wastes is misguided. The trust that the resilience of the natural environment is boundless and that radical change will be manifest before it is irreversible is unfounded.[1]

Unperceived, but ever present, is the specter of irreversible change which might ultimately not only degrade the quality of life, but also threaten human survival. Contaminated air, water, and earth cause increased cancer and respiratory disease, and will ultimately have much more far-reaching effects. As the urban ecosystem accumulates and assimilates toxic wastes like heavy metals, nondegradable pesticides, and radioactive materials, neurological damage and genetic change will become more common. These are not exclusively urban problems, but they are often more obvious in the city where population and wastes are concentrated.

The problems of growing wastes and depleted resources are linked. Wastes are the residual by-products of resource utilization. The more inefficiently resources are used, the more waste is generated. The profligate use of resources exacts multiple social costs: more resources must be consumed at higher cost and remaining resources depleted; added wastes take a toll on health, and their disposal is a financial burden. The underevaluation of the residual energy and material in waste products exacerbates the massive disposal problem.

Urban form can aggravate or alleviate the city's energy and waste problems. When work and residence are widely separated, commuters consume more energy and produce more wastes. The decision of one individual to live in the suburbs and commute to work in the center-city by car has negligible impact on resource consumption and waste production. Multiply the single individual by millions and you have the air pollution problems of New York City and Los Angeles. The design of a single park or a private garden has little impact in itself, but when a high-energy landscape is replicated widely, the impact is colossal. The near universality of the lawn in park and garden is a prime example. The lawn must be mowed, irrigated, raked, and treated with fertilizers and pesticides. A single lawn seems insignificant, but multiplied by thousands of acres in a single city, the cost becomes substantial: depleted energy and water supplies, and polluted water.

Perception of isolated natural features, like rivers or street trees, as things in themselves rather than as part of ongoing processes to which they owe their form and continuing evolution, leads to expensive stopgap measures to mitigate a hazard or protect a resource, rather than to solutions that strike at the heart of the problem, and often precipitates new, unforeseen problems. Such solutions may decrease the occurrence of minor natural hazards while they increase the magnitude of major catastrophes. The cumulative effect of many single changes is often more than their sum. Building a single house in the headwaters of a stream has a negligible contribution to flooding. Construction of many houses, however, may cause higher, more frequent floods downstream. The loss of trees in streets and plazas has far-reaching consequences not only for pleasure, but also for air quality, outdoor comfort, indoor energy consumption, water quality, and property value. Costs and benefits calculated without an appreciation for the whole system and the processes that drive it invariably underestimate the value of nature in the city.

The builders of cities rarely appreciate the cumulative impact of their incremental actions. Design and planning professionals normally concern themselves with a single scale, that of an individual building project or that of planning for metropolitan-wide services. Landscape architects, engineers, or architects usually have no concept of how their projects will affect the environment of the city as a whole or how the problems with which they are grappling could be more efficiently resolved by off-site intervention. Planners often work within a single dimension—transportation, sewage treatment, water supply—with only a hazy notion of how their actions relate to other spheres. Energy consumption, resource depletion, air pollution, water pollution, flooding, and soil contamination are all treated as separate problems, each with a set of specialists and institutions charged with a narrow mandate. Uncoordinated attempts to solve narrowly defined problems are wasteful in the most costly and hazardous sense.

The Costs of Waste

The squandering of resources and the contamination of air, earth, water, and life are the two faces of urban waste. Cities are forever short of energy and raw materials and struggle unceasingly to rid themselves of their wastes. Waste disposal has been a perennial problem of cities; but the problem is more severe today than ever before.

The production of wastes correlates directly with resource consumption; energy-inefficient buildings and transportation systems and wasteful water practices lead to contamination of the environment and to more costly waste disposal. In 1965, the average city dweller used, directly or indirectly, approximately 150 gallons (1,250 pounds) of water, 4 pounds of food, and 19 pounds of fossil fuel per day. Abel Wolman writes that "This is converted into roughly 120 gallons of sewage (which assumes 80 percent of the water input), four pounds of refuse (which includes food containers and miscellaneous rubbage), and 1.5 pounds of air pollutants, of which automobiles, buses, and trucks account for more than half."[2] Based on these

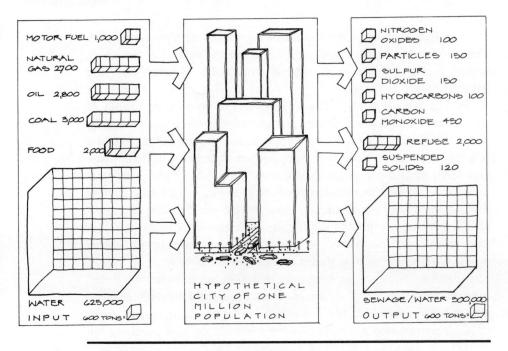

FIGURE 12.1
Every resource imported into the city, when consumed, produces waste in the form of sewage, garbage, or air pollutants.

daily requirements, Wolman sketched the inflow of water and materials and the outflow of wastes in a hypothetical American city of one million population (see figure 12.1). His hypothetical city thus imports 625,000 tons (150 million gallons) of water per day, 2,000 tons of food, and 9,500 tons of fuel (coal, oil, natural gas, and motor fuel), which is converted to 500,000 tons of sewage (of which 120 tons consists of suspended solids), 2,000 tons of garbage, and 950 tons of air pollutants (of which 150 tons consists of particulates, 150 of sulfur dioxide, 100 of nitrogen oxides, 100 of hydrocarbons, and 450 of carbon monoxide).[3]

Garbage is one manifestation of the waste problem. Americans generated 1,400 pounds of trash per person in 1978; an amount that has been slowly, but steadily increasing every year.[4] American cities dispose of a total of approximately 140,000,000 tons of garbage annually.[5] New York City alone produces enough garbage to cover all 840 acres of Central Park to a depth of twelve feet.[6] The sheer magnitude of garbage taxes the ability of a city to find the necessary space and money to get rid of it. Meanwhile, the wealth of potential resources represented by garbage is squandered. Paper, aluminum cans, glass bottles, and rubber tires could all be reused. The aluminum industry estimates that recycling aluminum cans would save 95 percent of the energy costs of transforming ore into metal.[7] Food wastes contain nutrients that could be used as compost. Instead, these aggravate the waste disposal problem. Nor is the problem limited to economics. Garbage, improperly disposed of, leads to groundwater pollution by toxic chemicals, to fire hazards, methane gas formation, and air pollution. Of 16,000 land disposal sites studied by the Environmental Protection Agency in 1976, only 5,800 were in compliance with state regulations.[8]

Reclamation or disposal of hazardous wastes is one of the most serious problems facing society today. Toxic chemicals, pesticides, acids, caustics, flammable, explosive, and radioactive materials all pose severe disposal problems. The story of Love Canal in the city of Niagara Falls, New York, where homes and a school were built on a sixteen-acre landfill formerly used to dump toxic chemicals, is but one example.[9] The tragedy at Love Canal built slowly. In the late 1950s, a few years after the first houses were constructed, chemicals oozed into creeks, and pools of brown-black liquid appeared in a local playground and in backyards of low-lying homes. Children playing near the water received burns. By the early 1970s, the dark liquid flooded basements after heavy rainfalls and corroded sump pumps. Finally, in the late 1970s, it became clear that local residents were suffering an unusual number of illnesses, miscarriages, and birth defects, and that these were worst in "wet areas," over old stream beds and marshes. One survey revealed that nine out of sixteen children born to "wet area" parents between 1973 and 1978 had birth defects. In 1980 the Environmental Protection Agency announced the results of a preliminary study of Love Canal residents: eleven out of thirty-six examined had suffered chromosome change. The validity of that study and the actual health effects of the chemicals were debated hotly by panels of experts convened by various public agencies and interest groups, but residents were finally evacuated nevertheless. Studies aside, the facts remain: of the last eighteen pregnancies among Love Canal residents, two resulted in normal births, nine in babies with birth defects, three in stillbirths, and four in miscarriages.

The tragedy of Love Canal did not end with the evacuation of those families; the threat has extended to the entire population of Niagara Falls, whose drinking water is at risk of contamination. Another dump, located on highly porous land within 200 yards of the city's largest drinking water plant, was used to dispose of 148 million pounds of chemical wastes between 1947 and 1975. An additional 47 million pounds of toxic wastes were dumped on a site adjacent to the Niagara River above the intake for one of the city's drinking water treatment plants. The expense of better initial waste treatment now pales against the costs of cleaning up soil and water, the loss of drinking water resources, and health costs. Love Canal is not an isolated case. The Environmental Protection Agency has identified 115 sites "potentially" worse than Love Canal, the price of ignorance, greed, negligence, and apathy.[10] In 1977, the Environment Protection Agency studied 50 industrial waste disposal sites and found that 43 were leaking heavy metals and organic chemicals into the local groundwater. The water at 26 of the sites was contaminated beyond the safe limit for drinking water.[11]

Nor is the problem only one of land disposal and subsequent seepage. Employees at a Louisville, Kentucky, sewage treatment plant grew ill after 25,000 tons of sludge became contaminated by residues of pesticides which had been dumped into the city's sewer system.[12] The city shut down the treatment plant, and millions of gallons of raw sewage poured into the Ohio River—water supply for many cities downstream—until the plant reopened. Since the cost of disposal is not calculated into the cost of manufacturing products and consuming them, waste disposal becomes a burden that virtually everyone shirks. The result is improper or faulty municipal sewage treatment and garbage disposal, and careless industrial disposal practices, including the growing, but unknown, number of "midnight dumpers" who dispose of toxic wastes in sewers and on streets and vacant lots. Hazardous wastes, once they find their way into groundwater or surface water, are not removed by current methods of water treatment. Not only do they remain in drinking water supplies, but some also combine with chlorine, which is used to kill pathogenic organisms in drinking water, to form new carcinogenic compounds. The potential impact is massive. Sixty percent of all Americans served by public water supplies are drinking water from sources that have already been used for domestic sewage and industrial waste disposal.[13]

In the past, health effects of contamination were felt swiftly. Waterborne epidemics of cholera and yellow fever swept cities throughout the world. From June to October in 1832, a cholera epidemic took 3,500 lives in a city whose population was just over 200,000. The entire city appreciated the hazard; in August alone, 100,000 people reportedly fled.[14] The dramatic mortality rates sparked enormous change in nineteenth-century cities. It was during this period that the massive infrastructure of the modern city was laid: public water supplies, storm sewers, and sewage treatment systems. Current apathy concerning environmental pollution is partially derived from this experience of the past, from the belief that health effects will be evidenced rapidly and that the system will respond equally rapidly to treatment.

The plight of modern cities is far more serious. Deadly chemicals pervade the air, water, and earth, but their effects are gradual and may not be fully appreciated for decades. Long-term exposure to certain toxic wastes may initiate genetic abnormalities whose full impact will not be felt until the irreversible effects on hundreds of thousands of individuals are evident. The specter of increasing cancer rates from environmental causes seems mild in comparison. In nineteenth-century cities, the public official who did not act to improve the pollution of air and water risked death in an epidemic. Today, the price of inaction will be borne not by current decision makers, but by their children and grandchildren.

Unforeseen Consequences

Many of the city's most serious problems are the unforeseen consequences of other, seemingly unrelated activities. As noted, cities are intricate systems that confound attempts to solve one problem in isolation. Every action in one part of the system produces perturbations in many others, which trigger new changes in turn, making a fragmented view of this system dangerous and expensive.

Neglecting to consider the many links between air, land, water, and life confounds attempts to control pollution. Separate disciplines address air pollution, water pollution, and soil pollution. One person's "source" is another's "sink." The air pollution literature abounds with articles advocating the use of soil or trees as a sink for air pollution, without considering what becomes of the contaminants after they are no longer suspended in the air. Pollutants flow throughout the entire system, from air to land and water and living organisms; from water into soil and organisms and back to air; from land to food and water (see, for example, figure 12.2). Thus, most of the major pollutants—especially heavy metals and toxic chemicals—flow through the biophysical environment along the pathways of the hydrologic cycle, nutrient cycles, and energy flows. Fragmentary approaches lead to solutions that would be comical if they were not tragic: city streets are swept and the sweepings are dumped in rivers;

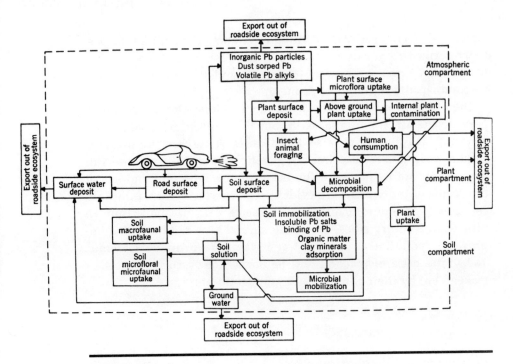

FIGURE 12.2
The spread of lead from automobile exhaust through air, water, earth, and organisms of the roadside ecosystem, along pathways of air, water, and nutrient cycles.

sewage is treated, its wastes concentrated, and the residual sludge is dumped in the ocean or on poorly controlled landfill sites.

A single-minded pursuit of flood prevention can lead to drought and water pollution and, if combined with massive extraction of groundwater, oil, and gas, can contribute to the subsidence of an entire metropolitan region. A city's storm drainage system typically whisks away stormwater before it can infiltrate the ground. The resulting decreased groundwater levels produce lower stream flows between storms, and thus a higher concentration of pollutants. When a city's storm and sanitary sewage systems are combined, as in many older cities, stormwater frequently overwhelms the capacity of sewage treatment plants, leading to dumping of raw sewage into streams and lakes. Mexico City sits in a self-contained mountain valley, obtaining its water supply by pumping groundwater from underground wells and, until recently, exporting its sewage and stormwater out of the watershed. The combination of these seemingly unrelated activities has led to a subsidence of twenty-five feet in parts of downtown Mexico City.

Some of the most tragic unforeseen consequences have arisen when technology developed in one part of the world has been transferred to another without adequate understanding of the local environment. The examples are legion, but among the most notorious is the Aswan Dam fiasco. The Aswan Dam was constructed on the upper Nile in Egypt to provide hydroelectric power and a reservoir of water in time of drought. The reservoir, planned to reach capacity by 1970, in 1980 was only half full, much of the water having evaporated or soaked into the porous sandstone that lines the reservoir.[15] The evaporation rate is 50 percent greater than estimated, due to high winds which sweep across the reservoir's surface.[16] The dam has been a hydrological and ecological disaster. The Nile delta, deprived of sediment now trapped behind the dam, has halted its outbuilding and is now being eroded by the Mediterranean Sea, up to six-and-one-half feet per year in some sections.[17]

Another result of the dam has been the spread of the disease schistosomiasis, also known as bilharziasis, a debilitating and occasionally fatal disease. Previously, the snails that harbor the schistosome larvae were swept away by the waters of the Nile; now the increase in canals with limited water circulation has precipitated a proliferation of the snails. When the water becomes contaminated with the urine and feces of humans or animals infected with schistosomiasis and abundant snail hosts are available, the disease spreads rapidly, as it has in Egypt. The disease is transmitted through water contact. Schistosomiasis is not limited to Egypt or even Africa, but also occurs in South America and the Caribbean, the Middle East, and parts of Asia. It has spread dramatically in cities and new towns when the mechanism of its transmission has been ignored or misunderstood by city planners and urban designers, who either directly increased snail habitat or failed to consider schistosomiasis in wastewater treatment. Almost every man-made lake and irrigation system in African cities has led to an increase in the prevalence of schistosomiasis.[18] In some cases, disease has been spread by well-meaning attempts to incorporate indigenous design. Tree plantings in Tehran have traditionally been planted in jubes, open sewers along the gutters on streets. Such unlined gutters and ditches are ideal habitat for the snail which harbors schistosomes. Not all wastewater treatment systems, including two very common types that have been constructed in infested areas of Africa and the Middle East, kill schistosomes and their eggs. In these days of international urban design and city planning practice, the potential for such blunders is great. Technologies developed in one environment are not always appropriate to another, nor are indigenous design traditions always advisable.

Unforeseen and ill-fated consequences are not only a product of inappropriate technology transfer; they can also be a product of the most mundane activities. The private automobile, for example, exacts an enormous and hidden price from society. Not only the individual car owner, but every member of society pays the price in terms of air, water, and soil pollution, with attendant increases in cancer, respiratory disease, and in lead poisoning among children, through the cost of constructing and maintaining roads, and through the perpetuation of a settlement pattern that drains the nation's resources. The failure to compute the whole cost of the automobile has contributed to the proliferation of a dispersed settlement pattern dependent upon private transportation, an urban form requiring the burning of more fuel with the attendant production of more wastes. It is a settlement pattern difficult to serve by public transportation, and therefore perpetuates private transportation modes. If owners were required to pay the full social cost of their automobiles there would be greater incentive for the exploration of alternative power sources or transportation types, which would in turn produce different patterns of land use than we see today, perhaps an older, vital urban core surrounded by a constellation of densely settled smaller centers, all connected by an efficient system of rail or bus.

Viewed against the impacts of the private automobile, the social cost of the lawn in civic and private landscape seems insignificant, but its cost to society in energy depletion, water consumption, and the pollution of air, water, and soil is real. Power lawn mowers consume oil and produce air contaminants. The popular turf mixtures require irrigation, even in humid climates, and sap dwindling urban water supplies. The fertilizers, herbicides, and pesticides necessary to nurture a lush, green lawn require energy to produce and transport, and when washed off in stormwater, contribute to water pollution. Add trees to the lawn, and the costs become even greater. Leaves must be raked and then disposed of, creating an air pollution problem when they are burned and a transportation and solid waste disposal problem when they are not. Leaves act as efficient air filters for the city's particulate air pollutants and are therefore likely to be loaded with contaminants, a fact which complicates their use as compost. If owners were required to pay the full social cost of their lawns—depletion of oil and water resources, health effects of water and air pollution, and the cost of solid waste disposal—lawns would be much more limited in extent and hardier turf mixes would be developed which required less fertilization and irrigation. In arid and semiarid climates, lawns would be precious.

The many links between air, land, water, and life are difficult to comprehend, even in an undisturbed ecosystem. The complexity of the urban ecosystem is bewildering, and parallel to the natural ecosystem is a social system driven by cultural, political, and economic processes. This social system exhibits the same interrelatedness that characterizes the natural system. It is not sufficient to understand either the processes of the social system or the processes of the natural system alone. Both mold the city's physical environment, which forms the common ground between them.

The dangers of persisting in a fragmented view of the city and its environment are more evident every day: the increasing frequency of miscarriages, birth defects, and neurological damage caused by environmental contamination; the increased mortality of the elderly, the sick, and the very young; permanent brain damage among children; overall degraded health of city residents and workers; increased magnitude of natural hazards; increased energy demands; depletion of high-grade mineral resources; dwindling water supplies; and the inefficient use of space and resources. The fact that environmental thresholds are poorly understood, that every action produces a complex response in the environment, with many unforeseen consequences, and the fact that severe effects are already manifest would recommend caution and immediate attention. Yet we proceed with heedless abandon to squander ever larger quantities of energy and to carelessly dispose of wastes.

The environmental quality programs initiated during the 1970s are faltering, undermined by public and private interests which favor the pursuit of individual wealth over sustaining the health and security of all. Powerful vested interests mitigate against the city and its region being managed as a system. Industry clings to the tradition of cheap, inadequate waste disposal. Municipalities, hard pressed to provide adequate services within their shrinking budgets, balk at investing in new, improved waste treatment. Government bureaucrats defend their power within single-purpose agencies. The single-purpose solutions advocated by such agencies are inefficient and costly. They insure that only the most pressing problems will be addressed, while less urgent but important problems are ignored under budgetary pressures. Disciplinary and professional boundaries also splinter potential multipurpose solutions. Governments, private institutions, and corporations are staffed with specialists trained in separate disciplines, who speak with each other infrequently, if ever, and who each approach a problem from a specific point of view: economists, lawyers, air quality specialists and water quality specialists, ecologists, civil engineers and planners, landscape architects and architects. Even the academic disciplines concerned solely with the natural environment rarely communicate: climatologists and geologists, hydrologists and soil scientists, botanists, zoologists, and ecologists.

The city resembles an infernal machine, built by simultaneous decisions at many scales: the decision to build a single building or to move from city to suburb, the plan for a new highway or a new industrial plant. Who is coordinating this construction? The professionals responsible for molding the actual form of the city, its buildings and spaces—landscape architects, architects, and engineers—seldom work at more than one scale. All too often, they either design specific buildings and parks without perceiving the cumulative effect upon the city and the region as a whole or, on the other hand, they lay plans for the future of entire neighborhoods and regions without grounding those plans in the nature of specific buildings, parks, and streets which will, together, either support or undermine those plans. Buildings and parks are thus designed with little attention to energy conservation, resulting in the consumption of ever more energy and the generation of ever more waste. Parks are designed so as to require irrigation, draining the city's dwindling water supply. Gushing fountains are installed in arid climates and, even if recirculating, lose much water to evaporation. Urbanization within the city and at its fringes covers mineral deposits, further depleting the supply of limited resources nearby and necessitating their transport from more distant sources. New residential districts are built far from commercial and industrial centers, with a pattern predicated on the use of private transportation, a form which will prove inflexible to future needs for a more efficient transportation system. Design and technology developed for cities in temperate climates are transported to desert and humid tropical climates, where they fail to fulfill their purpose and may create new problems as well.

New information that would permit better design and management of the urban ecosystem is not being generated as rapidly now as it was during the past decade. Government support for such research has dissolved. The barriers that separate academic disciplines are stronger than the links, a fact that mitigates against an understanding of the urban ecosystem. Much more is known about botany, geology, sociology, and economics than about the links between them. The rewards for remaining within an academic discipline, and the penalties for working outside the mainstream of that discipline, far outweigh any advantages and guarantee that interdisciplinary work will be the exception rather than the norm for some time to come.

Abandoning the city for outlying suburbs and rural areas, without questioning the attitudes that spawned the city's problems, guarantees that a retreat to the countryside will provide only temporary respite from those problems. If a dispersed settlement pattern becomes the norm, more energy will be required to sustain it, and thus more wastes produced. The isolation of the city and the refusal to grapple with its environmental problems will only hasten the deterioration of the countryside. It is in the common interest of the city and the countryside surrounding it to manage the region as an interlocking, interdependent system. It is in the interest of remote areas that cities provide a healthier and more attractive environment, just as it is in the interest of urban areas that resources in remote areas be exploited judiciously.

CHAPTER 13

Designing the
Urban Ecosystem

THE HEALTH AND WELFARE of city residents depend upon the efficient provision of sufficient energy, water, food, and other resources, and on the safe disposal of wastes. Until the seventeenth and eighteenth centuries, most cities were closely tied to the countryside, and the city and its surroundings were therefore more easily and informally managed as a system. Urban manure was carted out to the neighboring farmland to fertilize the fruit and vegetables which nurtured the city. As cities grew larger, the task of managing city and surrounding region as a system became more difficult, yet more imperative. Late-nineteenth-century sanitarians, landscape architects, and engineers viewed the city as a unified system, "a vast, integrated unit with the efficient functioning of one part dependent upon the efficient functioning of all the parts."[1] A new professional corps of sanitary engineers, in response to the enormous public health problems of large cities, designed and constructed water supply systems, sewer systems, and garbage collection and disposal systems in city after city. They exacted new political powers for municipal institutions and the authority to exert those powers beyond city boundaries when necessary. They urged regional cooperation in providing water and sewers, and gained state approval for the creation of new, regional authorities like Boston's Metropolitan Sewage Commission, founded in 1889. George Waring, appointed commissioner of the department of street cleaning in New York City in 1895, urged a new attitude toward the city's garbage:

The "out-of-sight, out-of-mind" principle is an easy one to follow, but it is not an economical one, nor a decent one, nor a safe one. For other and more important reasons than the hope of getting money out of our wastes, should we pursue the study of the treatment of these wastes, and try to devise a less shiftless and uncivilized method than that which we now use.[2]

Waring advocated that each householder separate garbage, so that it could be more efficiently reclaimed and disposed of. Landscape architect Frederick Law Olmsted advocated the economical use of urban open space, not only to provide recreation opportunities for the city's growing population, but also to preserve natural resources, to provide for flood control, to protect streams, rivers, and lakes from pollution, and to provide a pleasant setting for travel and residence.

The ambitious municipal undertakings of the late nineteenth and early twentieth centuries brought a dramatic increase in health to city residents. Urban mortality rates plummeted; deaths from typhoid fell an average of 65 percent in many major cities.[3] Today the tools at society's disposal are far more potent than those available to the urban reformers of the nineteenth century, and the possibilities for change far more sweeping. Current knowledge of urban nature permits more comprehensive solutions. Previously, data was gathered and catalogued laboriously and updated with Herculean difficulty. Today, satellites collect information automatically from their remote vantage point high in the atmosphere and relay it to computers on the earth. This information is available to anyone who requests and is able to read it. The collection, assimilation, manipulation, and display of information, once such a monumental task, is now accomplished nearly effortlessly. Contemporary systems-modeling techniques and information-handling methods facilitate comprehensive, multipurpose solutions. They need only be exploited.

An ecosystem, as we have reiterated, is more than the sum of its parts. Energy and materials flow in cycles through the urban ecosystem, linking air, land, water, and living organisms in a vast network. Identifying the links in the network and their relative importance yields new insights and inspires more efficient deployment of activities, resources, and space. With such knowledge, cities can conserve resources and minimize wastes; they can dispose of and reclaim wastes economically, safely, and aesthetically; they can design individual parts of the system to serve more than one purpose, and assess costs realistically. A few cities have applied this knowledge.

Some, like Philadelphia, have utilized sewage to reclaim derelict land. Others, like Woodlands, Texas, have demonstrated how a city's open space can fulfill many functions simultaneously. Toronto and Dallas have both assembled and assimilated the information necessary to begin to make informed decisions regarding the urban ecosystem, knowledge that is as valuable to the design of a single park or highway as it is to a plan for the city as a whole.

Pathways of Energy and Pollution

The ecosystem concept provides a powerful tool for understanding the urban environment: it furnishes a framework for perceiving the effect of human activities and their interrelationships; it facilitates weighing the relative costs and benefits of alternative actions; it encompasses all urban organisms, the city's physical structure, and the processes which flow within it; and it is appropriate in examining all levels of life, from an urban pond to megalopolis. Regarding the city as an ecosystem permits every individual to perceive his cumulative impact on the city, and the designer of every building and park to perceive its place within the whole. It also permits the planner of a transportation network or regional park system to trace the effect of comprehensive change on smaller pieces of the system. A knowledge of the system's dynamics yields a different appreciation for boundaries in space and time than is normally permitted in day-to-day pursuits and highlights the shortcomings of designing solely within political boundaries and time spans of less than several human generations.

The flow and transformation of energy and materials forges the links between the air, land, and water of the urban ecosystem and the organisms that live within it. By plotting the pathways along which energy and materials flow through the urban ecosystem, one also traces the routes along which pollutants disseminate and where energy is expended and stored. Most of the processes governing the movement of energy and materials through the urban ecosystem have already been noted: processes of heat gain and heat loss, erosion, the hydrologic cycle, photosynthesis, respiration, and the food web. Like the hydrologic cycle, the nutrient cycles of carbon, nitrogen, and phosphorous also link living organisms to air, earth, and water.

The physical structure of the urban ecosystem comprises land, water, and plants, as well as human artifacts built within it, and their configuration, density, differentiation, and connectivity. The urban ecosystem is dependent upon the importation of energy and materials which are transformed into products and consumed, and the by-products—thermal, material, and chemical wastes—released. Compared to less disturbed and more "closed" ecosystems, it is an "open" system, whose continued survival depends upon the continued import of energy and materials. The urban ecosystem contains many smaller systems: parks, ponds, woodlots; some could be managed as more "closed" systems, requiring fewer inputs of energy and producing fewer wastes. The substitution of a managed urban forest ecosystem for cultivated lawns is a good example. When individual parts of the urban ecosystem are designed to fulfill more than one function, energy may be conserved. Designing a park to funnel cool air into the city, detain stormwater from surrounding streets, and buffer a residential neighborhood from the noise and air pollution of nearby highways may be more energy efficient than designing separate solutions to each problem.

Ecosystems differ in their ability to withstand disturbance and assimilate waste. Resilience is a measure of the system's capacity to absorb change, and some ecosystems are more resilient than others. Every ecosystem has a characteristic domain of stability in which the flux of energy and materials ebbs and flows and organisms grow, reproduce, and adapt to change. An ecological community can withstand considerable perturbations, so long as these do not exceed the capacity of the system to respond. Knowledge of the bounds within which a given system can respond permits its use for processing human wastes while protecting its integrity. The boundary conditions of most ecosystems are not well understood, but represent one of the greatest potential contributions by ecologists to urban design and planning.[4] Warm, humid environments can assimilate a greater quantity of organic wastes than cold, dry environments. Stream, salt marsh, and soil ecosystems are well equipped to process particulate organic materials, like pieces of decaying plants and the nutrients in sewage, but have little ability to assimilate inorganic materials.[5] Marshes and soil can therefore be utilized to treat sewage, so long as their processing capabilities are not exceeded. Several cities are now managing natural or artificially created marshes as part of their sewage treatment plant, as well as for wildlife habitat and recreation.

The dynamics of the urban ecosystem are poorly understood, but even a crude knowledge facilitates an identification of the existing and potential links between all parts of the system, and a more efficient management of urban resources and wastes. Since ecosystem concepts can be applied to systems as small as a pond or as large as an urban region, even the design for a single park should be approached with an appreciation for both the smaller and the larger system of which it is part, and the requisite inputs of energy, water, and materials and generation of wastes entailed by alternative designs. Plans to manage the urban ecosystem as a whole should be undertaken with caution. It is important to remember that the effects of actions taken within the complex urban ecosystem are often counterintuitive. Not only are many consequences unforeseen, but actions may at times produce the opposite of the intended effect. As the component parts and the links between them become better understood, models for the urban ecosystem will become more refined and the consequences of actions more predictable.

Using Energy Efficiently

Every building and group of buildings, with its surrounding plazas and landscape, every park, and every street and highway should be designed both as a system in itself, as part of a larger district which is a subsystem of the city, and as a tiny piece of the overall metropolitan ecosystem. Each park should be designed to fulfill not just one function, but many functions. The form of individual buildings, plazas, parks, streets and highways, and the larger residential and commercial, open space, and transportation systems to which they belong, can be manipulated to improve air and water quality, to prevent or mitigate natural hazards, to reclaim derelict land, to conserve energy and resources, and to enhance the city's beauty.

Buildings are mini ecosystems. Pipes and wires link every building to the city's water supply, utilities, and sewage system. Water and energy flow in, sewage flows out, and waste heat radiates to the surrounding environment. The building interacts not only with the urban infrastructure, but also with the surrounding air, land, and water. The building absorbs heat and light from the sun and reemits and reflects them; it intercepts rainwater and concentrates it in drain pipes. The building imports and burns fuel and emits gases and particles; it deflects winds, both slowing and accelerating them. The building's size, shape and orientation influence not only the amount of energy required to heat and cool its interior, but also the comfort and air quality of the spaces around it. The flexibility of its design determines the amount of energy required in the future to adapt it to new uses.

Every building contributes to the character of a local system and is influenced by that system in turn. The density of buildings in relation to the space surrounding them determines the magnitude of the heat island effect; the denser the buildings, the higher the temperature and the more air conditioning is required in summer. But the character of the surrounding spaces can also increase or decrease the building's heat load. Pavement absorbs heat and reradiates it to the building; trees and vines shade the building and surrounding surfaces. Densely built urban form generates more waste and stormwater runoff than a less dense settlement pattern, but it can also be more efficiently provided with energy, water, and other resources and with waste collection and treatment. When wastes are concentrated, the resources within them may be reclaimed more economically. The configuration of buildings and the spaces between them determine how air moves through the city and whether it is well ventilated. A cluster of towers surrounded by open land or water produces a different wind pattern than a city composed of many smaller buildings all the same size. Winds accelerate over open water or expanses of pavement and if blocked by towers create severe wind problems at street level. Dayton's example is a case in point. Wind problems in the downtown are not solely a function of either tall buildings or extensive open land—parking lots, expressways, and river—on the city's perimeter, but of their combined effect. In Dayton's case, wind problems on a specific street corner are most effectively solved, not at the spot where the problem is evidenced, but by increasing the friction of the surface over which the wind moves at the outskirts of downtown.

The locations of the places where people live and work influence how far they must travel to work, shop, and play. In the old city centers, residence, industry, and commerce were mixed; the modern trend is toward large districts with predominantly one use, be it residential, commercial, or industrial. The resulting increased distances between home and work, shopping and recreation, entail both a greater consumption of energy and a greater generation of wastes.

Streets and highways, along with other transportation routes like railroad rights-of-way and canals, comprise the corridors along which people move from place to place within the city. The shape of that transportation network and the distribution of arteries and minor routes determines how efficiently people, goods, and materials flow through the city and how wastes are dispersed or concentrated. Movement requires energy, and every transportation mode has characteristic requirements for energy and patterns of wastes. Nineteenth-century streets were littered with horse manure, and twentieth-century streets are contaminated with the heavy metals and poisonous gases produced by the automobile. The amount of traffic on a street, its volume and speed, determines how much poison is produced; the street's size, degree of enclosure, and orientation in relation to wind direction influence the location, shape, and extent of the polluted area around it. Streets and highways should be located and designed to buffer adjacent homes and places of work from the noise and air pollution they generate. As the city's circulation system, the transportation network exerts a powerful influence on the growth and fate of the city and its many constituent parts. The impacts generated by the construction of a single highway play themselves out over centuries. New transportation routes should be planned with great caution.

A park is more amenable to management as a "closed" system, requiring minimal inputs of energy and exporting few wastes, than any other component of the urban ecosystem (see figures 13.1 and 13.2). Viewed in the broadest sense, parks range from the most intensively used plazas and playgrounds to large tracts of "wild" areas that receive little use. Generally, the more intensively used a park,

---

FIGURE 13.1
The problem: parks requiring major inputs of energy and producing polluting wastes.

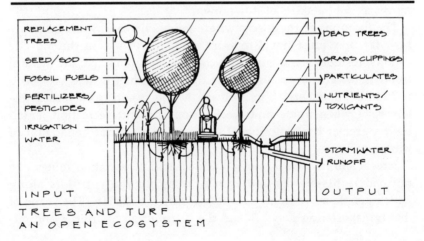

TREES AND TURF
AN OPEN ECOSYSTEM

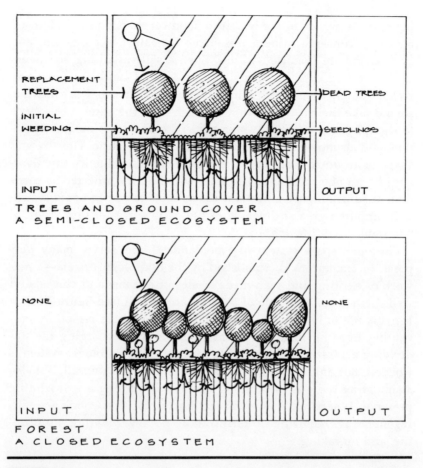

REPLACEMENT TREES

INITIAL WEEDING

DEAD TREES

SEEDLINGS

INPUT

OUTPUT

TREES AND GROUND COVER
A SEMI-CLOSED ECOSYSTEM

NONE

NONE

INPUT

OUTPUT

FOREST
A CLOSED ECOSYSTEM

FIGURE 13.2
The solution: parks designed and managed as "closed" systems, consuming fewer resources and producing fewer wastes.

the more energy required to sustain it. Plazas, playgrounds, and downtown parks provide a delight to many and are well worth the investment they require. They can, however, serve other purposes besides play. Trees and plants can absorb air pollution, reduce the heat load on adjacent buildings, and, in abundance, even reduce the heat island effect in an entire downtown. Downtown parks and plazas should also be designed to reduce flooding, by detaining storm-water temporarily.

The more a park resembles a natural ecosystem, the more easily it can be managed as a relatively closed system. Parts of large parks, leftover land on steep slopes or along floodplains, and even weedy vacant lots, can all be designed as self-maintaining, self-regenerating systems, which not only absorb floodwaters, but also hold unstable land, conserve mineral resources for future exploitation, and even assimilate imported wastes. Such a self-sustaining ecosystem can be created even on a small vacant lot and can be employed to reclaim derelict land with minimal expense. Parks and urban wilds should take their configuration as much from the pattern of a city's topography and geology, water bodies, remnants of native vegetation, and air movement as from the built urban fabric. The size and shape of an uncultivated plant community will influence the diversity of both plant and animal species within it. If connected by corridors of sufficient size and plant cover, the city's open space system will support a greater diversity of life, with a greater proportion of "desirable" wildlife species.

The open space system of Woodlands, Texas, serves many purposes. Its framework is established by the hydrologic system—a network of existing and man-made swales of streams and creeks, and well-drained soils capable of soaking up rainfall (see figure 7.11). It benefits not only the new town, but also the whole region by preventing flooding in downstream Houston and recharging the underlying aquifer (see figure 7.10). Most of this hydrologic system is wooded, not only serving to soak up and carry off rainfall, but also assimilating the wastes in urban runoff and offering a vast wildlife preserve. Where understory is left uncleared, the woods are self-regenerating, requiring no fertilization, no new planting, no pruning, and no raking.

Exploiting Urban Wastes

The very nature of the city is to import resources and consume energy and material in massive quantities. No matter how much the city reduces its consumption, no matter how efficient its buildings and transportation system or how many parks are managed as closed systems, the safe disposal of wastes will always be an important issue. Comprehensive plans to manage the city's wastes must include provisions for reclaiming and reusing the resources in wastes, for assimilating nontoxic wastes, and for finding safe storage space for toxic wastes until technology exists to reclaim the resources they contain or to render them harmless.

The reclamation of resources in wastes is an old idea. In 1870,

Frederick Law Olmsted urged cities to exploit the opportunities inherent in their dense settlement pattern: "Experiments indicate that it is feasible to send heated air through a town in pipes like water, and that it may be drawn upon. . . . Thus may come a great saving of fuel and trouble in a very difficult department of domestic energy. No one will think of applying such a system to farm-houses."[6] More than a century later that possibility is still promising.

The community of Tapiola, Finland, has harnessed its waste heat since 1953.[7] Stuttgart developed a district heating system as part of its overall program to conserve energy and reduce air pollution, by using the waste heat from electrical power generation and municipal incinerators to heat water, which is then piped throughout the city to heat homes and stores. A municipal incinerator in Chicago captures 70 percent of the recoverable heat and converts it to steam. Approximately one-half of the steam produced is used to power in-plant equipment, and the remaining half is sold to nearby industries.[8] To date, however, European cities have led in utilization of thermal waste.

Spurred by the more stringent water quality standards required by the Clean Water Act of 1977, and by the financial incentives for applying innovative or alternative wastewater treatment technology, many American cities have developed and implemented non-traditional methods of waste disposal: applying effluent to constructed and managed wetlands; using sewage sludge to reclaim strip mines and other derelict land; and recycling sewage sludge for compost. The reuse of residual wastes has cut the cost of better water quality and has even resulted in the addition of new parkland. Some waste management plans are most appropriate to small cities with few toxic wastes and with open land available nearby; other strategies are most cost effective in large cities with huge quantities of concentrated wastes.

The city of Arcata, California, exploits the properties of plants and soil to assimilate wastes by incorporating a wetland as part of its sewage treatment process.[9] Arcata renovated a degraded marshland and old solid waste landfill site adjacent to the sewage treatment plant. The wetland system was constructed by dredging and grading to create different water levels and enhance water circulation. Secondary effluent from the treatment plant is discharged into the wetland for further treatment. The reconstructed wetland was also designed to function as a wildlife habitat and a recreation area; islands in the center of the marsh provide protected feeding and nesting areas for mating birds. The vegetation planted in and around the marsh was selected both for its value as a food source and for shelter. Peregrin falcons are regular visitors to the sanctuary, and migrating ducks, gulls, terns, and phalaropes stop briefly on migratory flights along the Pacific flyway. Bird watchers view wildlife unobtrusively from behind camouflaged observation posts. The city is also experimenting with a related aquaculture project. Salmon are raised in water fertilized by treated effluent from the sewage treatment plant. By 1985, Arcata hopes to establish the full salmon cycle—raising the fish, permitting them to migrate to the ocean and to return two years later to lay their eggs. Faculty from nearby Humboldt State University, who are directing the pilot study and cooperating with the city on the aquaculture project, hope to demonstrate that the use of a constructed marsh is an effective and economical alternative to conventional methods of tertiary sewage treatment. It should not be attempted, however, where effluent is contaminated by heavy metals and other toxic wastes.

The city of Philadelphia generated 190 dry tons of sewage sludge per day in 1981, an amount projected to increase to 305 tons per day by 1985.[10] Sludge, a by-product of sewage treatment, contains the solids filtered from wastewater. Sewage sludge is rich in organic nutrients like phosphorus and nitrogen and it is sometimes contaminated with heavy metals and toxic chemicals; it therefore poses a major solid waste disposal problem in all large cities. Prior to such legislation as the 1971 Marine Protection, Research, and Sanctuary Act, many coastal cities dumped sewage sludge in oceans and lakes. When the Environmental Protection Agency required Philadelphia to halt ocean dumping, the city was forced to examine alternatives for sludge disposal. Initially disputed in a series of lawsuits, the proscription of ocean dumping spawned a multifaceted program to convert sewage sludge into marketable resources. "Philorganic," "Minemix," "Gardenlife," and "Ecorock" are all products derived from sewage sludge since 1980—sold, given away, and used by the city of Philadelphia in municipal parks and construction projects. Liquid "Philorganic" is sludge containing up to 50 percent organic matter with 3 to 4 percent nitrogen.[11] It is sprayed on grain or sod farms as fertilizer, but is not recommended for use on vegetables. The city has also applied "Philorganic" as fertilizer on municipal parks, ballfields, and golf courses, and has used it to reclaim vacant lots and old landfill sites. The use of sludge as compost demanded a product free of toxic contaminants. Philadelphia now requires industries that contribute effluent to municipal treatment plants to meet minimum standards for toxic wastes. As a result, Philadelphia sludge now contains only small quantities of heavy metals and inorganic toxicants.

The use of sewage sludge to reclaim strip mines has proved to be the most economical method of sludge disposal. Starting with a pilot project in 1977, the city was by 1981 using 60 to 70 percent of its sludge to produce "Minemix" for strip mine reclamation. So far, the cost of disposal has been approximately $200 per dry ton.[12] The cost of transportation is minimal, since the same trucks that deliver coal to Philadelphia haul sludge back to the mines in southwestern Pennsylvania. Abandoned strip mines are regraded, sludge and lime are mixed into the soil, and the land is seeded with a mixture of grass and legumes. Ultimately the reclaimed land will be used for grazing, after sites have been monitored to insure that no adverse environmental effects ensue. In 1981, the city planned to reclaim approximately 1,100 acres with 140,000 tons of sludge. Mine reclamation will provide an opportunity for sludge disposal for many years to come. In Pennsylvania alone, there are more than 250,000 acres of abandoned strip-mined land.[13] Chicago has used sewage sludge in a similar reclamation plan, and Baltimore also plans to implement such a program.[14]

Philadelphia also combines dry sludge with wood chips to create a soil conditioner sold under the name "Garden Life," a product packaged in forty-pound bags or sold in bulk. The mix is similar to that which the National Park Service has used to renovate compacted soil in Washington D.C.'s parkland (see chapter 9).

The cost of crushed rock rises as cities grow and quarry operations are pushed further and further from the urban center. Philadelphia's "Ecorock" is being developed as a substitute for crushed rock. It is produced by combining sewage sludge with residue from municipal garbage incinerators and heating the two materials until molten. Once cooled, they form a hard rock.

Several cities in Ohio now supply sewage sludge to farms, in a program under the direction of the Ohio Farm Bureau. The program has been limited, as studies monitor both the effectiveness of the sludge as organic fertilizers and the potential health effects. Currently, Washington, D.C., Chicago, Denver, San Diego, and Seattle are disposing of all or part of their sewage sludge in reclamation or recycling projects.[15]

Perceiving the Whole

Information of the right kind, in sufficient detail, and up-to-date, is essential to perceiving the city as a whole. The generation, collection, assimilation, and dissemination of information—information about the natural environment of a specific city, research on the urban natural environment and the investigation of potential applications of that research, and reports of successful case studies—are major but essential tasks. Without this information, any plan to design the city with nature in mind is handicapped; with this information, new insights and new solutions are possible. Knowing what information to gather and how to collect and store it, and deciding who will be responsible for its management, are crucial for success. If the wrong information is collected, it may be worthless; collecting the right information but failing to provide ready access to it is equally useless. Much valuable information already exists in pieces scattered in the files and archives of government agencies, in university research reports, in private construction documents, in government publications, and in the experience of local special interest organizations. Each separate piece of information is not terribly useful in itself, but gathered, integrated, and interpreted, the whole forms an invaluable resource.

Every city should establish a data bank to coordinate information collected by federal, state, and county agencies, by municipal departments and private institutions. City government, local organizations, and universities should cooperate in the collection and interpretation of data about the city's natural environment. The most pressing local problems should be identified and the necessary data for addressing those problems collected. Taken as a whole, this information will provide a framework within which the consequences of major metropolitan efforts as well as the cumulative effect of individual actions can be appreciated. Only then can opportunities be fully exploited, costs of alternative actions realistically assessed, disastrous consequences to health and safety forestalled, and potential multipurpose solutions fully realized.

In 1975, the city of Toronto launched a comprehensive inventory of the natural environment of its downtown waterfront—a busy port, an industrial and commercial center, with a small airport and a large park on harbor islands. The goal of the project was to add a knowledge of urban nature and the opportunities and constraints it posed to the social, economic, and political concerns which had traditionally guided development of the waterfront. Staff of the Toronto Planning Board collected data from federal, provincial, and municipal agencies, from universities and private research institutes, and from local interest groups. The amassed information was published in separate reports on climate, air quality, noise, physical geography, water, vegetation, and wildlife—reports intended as companion volumes to similar ones on housing, industry, recreation, and transportation in the waterfront. With the help of consultants, the planning staff assimilated this information and interpreted its implications for waterfront policy and plans. A pioneering study, the Toronto Waterfront Project, demonstrated the surprising wealth of existing information about a city's natural environment and about how urban nature is linked to the health, safety, and welfare of the city's citizens.[16]

In contrast to the Toronto study, which encompassed only a small portion of its downtown, the city of Dallas has conducted an ecological study of its entire metropolitan region. In 1973, faced with rapid population growth, Dallas decided to assess the relative significance of the city's natural environment and its tolerance to urbanization. The city, aided by consultants and local experts in government agencies and public institutions, collected information on the earth, water, and life systems of the metropolitan region, mapped the important features of these systems, and stored this information in a computerized data base. Computer models were then designed to measure the relative tolerance of these systems to urbanization. A major benefit of the study has been the identification of the region's significant resources and hazards: headwater streams and aquifer recharge areas that are sensitive to pollution, floodplains, and the White Rock Escarpment—an area of unstable slopes and swelling soils, diverse wildlife habitat and great scenic beauty (see figure 13.3).[17]

Since that original study, the city has adopted a natural open-space plan for the entire region as well as regulations governing development of the escarpment. The natural open-space plan identifies areas that should be acquired by the city and recommends guidelines for their management. The regulations governing development on the escarpment are based upon an understanding of earth, water, and life systems, and the interrelationships among them as well as the inferred effects of urbanization. The original ecological study merely flagged the location of areas that required special attention. These subsequent regulations have addressed each feature in greater detail, stressing how problems may be avoided. They are a model of sound regulations derived from an understanding of ecosystem processes.[18]

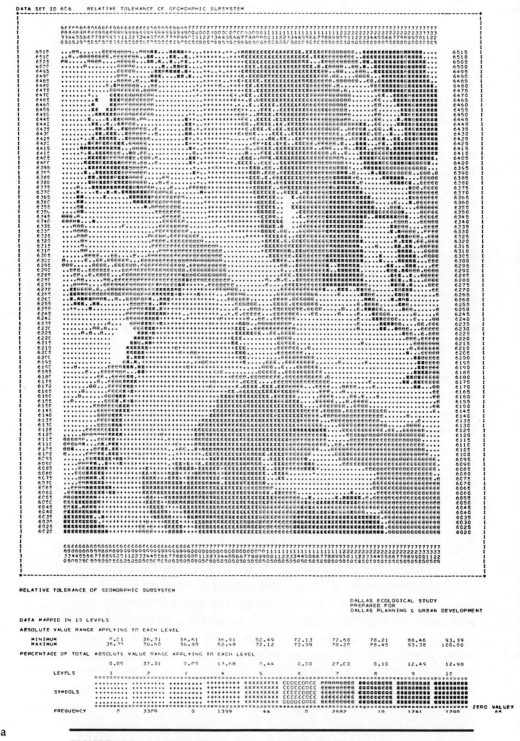

RELATIVE TOLERANCE OF GEOMORPHIC SUBSYSTEM

DALLAS ECOLOGICAL STUDY
PREPARED FOR
DALLAS PLANNING & URBAN DEVELOPMENT

DATA MAPPED IN 10 LEVELS

ABSOLUTE VALUE RANGE APPLYING TO EACH LEVEL

MINIMUM	0.01	36.31	36.61	36.91	52.49	72.13	72.60	78.21	88.46	93.39
MAXIMUM	36.30	36.60	36.90	52.48	72.12	72.59	78.20	88.45	93.38	100.00

PERCENTAGE OF TOTAL ABSOLUTE VALUE RANGE APPLYING TO EACH LEVEL

	0.00	33.31	0.00	13.68	0.44	0.00	27.00	0.10	12.49	12.98
LEVELS	1	2	3	4	5	6	7	8	9	10
SYMBOLS										
FREQUENCY	0	3309	0	1359	44	0	2682	10	1241	1290

ZERO VALUES

a

FIGURE 13.3

The Dallas Ecological Study identified the White Rock Escarpment as an important environmental resource and hazard. Here, in the lower left corner on two computer-drawn maps of the Dallas region, it appears as an area extremely

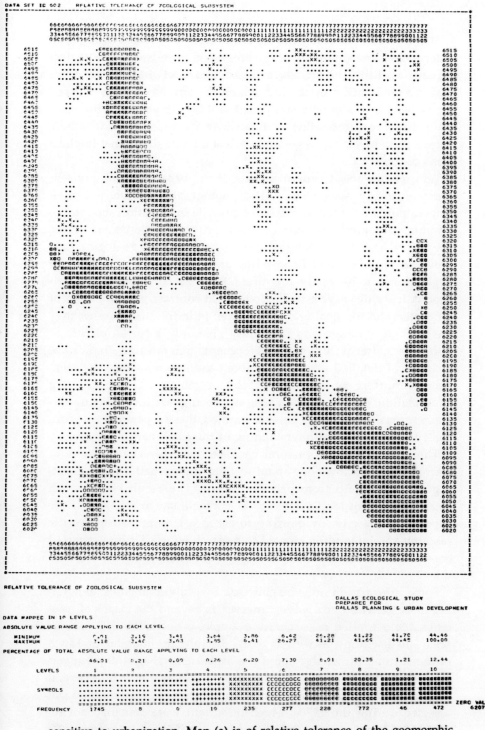

RELATIVE TOLERANCE OF ZOOLOGICAL SUBSYSTEM

DALLAS ECOLOGICAL STUDY
PREPARED FOR
DALLAS PLANNING & URBAN DEVELOPMENT

DATA MAPPED IN 10 LEVELS

ABSOLUTE VALUE RANGE APPLYING TO EACH LEVEL

MINIMUM	0.01	3.15	3.41	3.64	3.86	6.42	26.28	41.22	41.70	44.46
MAXIMUM	3.18	3.40	3.63	3.95	6.41	26.27	41.21	41.69	44.45	100.00

PERCENTAGE OF TOTAL ABSOLUTE VALUE RANGE APPLYING TO EACH LEVEL

	46.01	0.21	0.00	0.26	6.20	7.30	8.01	20.35	1.21	12.44
LEVELS	1	2	3	4	5	6	7	8	9	10
SYMBOLS										
FREQUENCY	1745	8	0	10	235	277	228	772	46	472

ZERO VALUES
6207

sensitive to urbanization. Map (a) is of relative tolerance of the geomorphic subsystem and map (b) of the zoological subsystem. Darkest tones represent the most sensitive areas, lightest tones the most tolerant.

b

Dallas' ecological study has shortcomings—the coarse detail of its information, the simplicity of the ecosystem models, and the neglect of nature within the already urbanized parts of the city. Yet it remains a landmark project, from which the city has already derived many benefits. Especially significant is its employment of the computer to store information and facilitate its updating, to combine information in various ways, and to demonstrate the spatial implications of social values.

Information about certain aspects of the urban natural environment is readily assembled. Aerial photographs and images taken from satellites exist for all cities, and provide information about topographic, geological, and surface characteristics. In the United States, the federal and state geological surveys have mapped geological hazards and resources and flood-prone areas in many cities. Types of vegetation can be easily identified from aerial photography, although few cities have actually done so. In contrast, measurements of air, water, and soil quality must be taken in individual samples; they are difficult to obtain and frequently give only a partial picture of pollution patterns. Private development generates an impressive quantity of detailed information about the ground. Since unanticipated subsurface conditions can double or treble costs of constructing a foundation, preconstruction tests and borings are invariably undertaken for major buildings. Once assembled, these separate studies can contribute to a better understanding of the earth beneath a city.

The assembly of information need not be expensive. The city of Dayton refined knowledge about its temperature patterns by soliciting volunteer help from private citizens. The result was a much clearer picture of local variations in microclimate at relatively little expense to the city. By offering to act as a laboratory for climatic research and by lending city aid to research efforts, Dayton attracted considerable scientific and planning know-how at minimal cost to the city.

Some information must be collected by individual cities; generating more general knowledge, however, is beyond the means of most cities. More applied research, for example, is needed within specific scientific discipline, as well as across disciplinary boundaries. Much of the current knowledge about the urban natural environment was generated within the past two decades. Fueled by public interest and generous federal grants, much new knowledge was accumulated and assessed during the 1970s. Much important work remains, but research funds are no longer forthcoming in sufficient quantities. At a time when major breakthroughs in an understanding of urban climate and air quality, urban geology and soils, urban hydrology and water quality, and urban plants and wildlife seemed imminent, political interests have shifted to other areas and public support has waned. This trend must be reversed. Major support should be committed to research on the interaction between the natural environment and human activities and urban settlement.

It is important that case studies of successful solutions to problems of the urban natural environment be collected and made readily accessible. The many examples are little known even to most urban planners and designers, let alone government officials in national, state, and local governments. When examples are known, they are known in anecdotal form, and technical details that would facilitate their application elsewhere are difficult to come by. There are lessons to be learned from these examples: the motivations that lay behind them; the institutional framework within which they evolved; the implementation strategies employed; and the essential information that forms their foundation.

The motivations that lie behind these solutions have been both pragmatic and idealistic. A catastrophic flood prompted the formulation of Denver's urban storm drainage strategy. The extensive damage wreaked by the 1964 Denver flood made a new regional agency—the Denver Urban Storm Drainage and Flood Control District— more palatable to the area's myriad local governments than it otherwise would have been. The realization that effective flood control was beyond both the boundaries and the means of each local government makes this regional agency effective. Litigation forced Philadelphia to develop its program for recycling the resources in sewage sludge. The vision of a single individual inspired the initiation of the Dayton Climate Project, the Boston Urban Wilds Program, and the Woodlands New Town.

Whether inspired by the vision of a better city or by fear of destruction or litigation, most of these achievements were not accomplished within a single city agency or by a single person, but as a result of cooperation between local and federal governments, universities, corporations, specialists from many disciplines, and individual citizens. Although the original incentive for Boston's Urban Wilds and Denver's South Platte Greenway came from city government, in both cases the most substantial progress in implementation was made by separate, quasi-public organizations that were formed later: the Boston Natural Areas Fund and the Platte River Development Committee and Greenway Foundation. Each is composed of both public officials and private citizens representing different interests and disciplines; and each has been supported by both public funds and private contributions.

To insure the transmission of such lessons as those described here, there should be regionwide, nationwide, and worldwide clearinghouses to which cities, researchers, and professionals might apply for description of both the technical and institutional details of successful case studies. Modern communications and information technology makes possible the storage and swift transmission of knowledge. A city in Saudi Arabia with a specific problem, for instance, could receive a list instantly, upon request, of all those cities in desert regions which had solved similar problems successfully, if only that information were collected and entered into a computerized data bank but once.

A Plan for Every City

Solutions to the problems of the city and its region must not be isolated, but rather coordinated and undertaken with as much understanding of the urban ecosystem as current knowledge permits. To facilitate a comprehensive plan for the management of the urban ecosystem and to establish a frame within which individual components can be designed, every city should identify its most critical problems and most significant resources, explore the potential links among them, and establish priorities for their resolution and protection. Although all cities share some problems, each has others that are special to its own situation. The relative severity of problems and their spatial patterns will also vary. Is air pollution the most important problem, or a dwindling, contaminated water supply? Is the city subject to devastating earthquakes, or do floods threaten a major portion of the city? Is air pollution a seasonal problem, and is it a problem of the dense central core or one that affects the entire city? It is especially important to identify those human activities and environmental conditions that aggravate or trigger a hazard. Plotting the flow of energy and materials through the urban ecosystem, with their daily and seasonal variation, will aid in devising strategies for resource consesrvation and safe waste disposal, as well as in predicting areas most susceptible to contamination. Of particular concern is the identification of specific toxic wastes produced in the city and of their disposal sites. Each city should identify the local areas within it and its region most prone or most sensitive to contamination, most at risk from natural hazards, and with the most valuable mineral and biological resources. All this information should be assembled as a computerized data base available to every citizen.

A comprehensive plan to manage the urban ecosystem should:

- address the city-region's most critical environmental problems exploiting opportunities to resolve more than one problem with a single solution, and to improve conditions in the most severely contaminated or most hazardous areas of the city
- investigate energy and resource conservation measures and the feasibility of reclaiming energy and mineral resources from wastes, and explore settlement patterns, transportation networks, and water and sewer systems which would facilitate implementation of such measures
- encourage industry to devise plans for the safe storage of toxic wastes until they can be economically recycled or safely assimilated
- link natural processes and features to health, safety, and welfare, so that social costs and benefits related to the natural environment may be weighed against other social, economic, and political concerns.

Every new building and park should be designed to require the minimum input of energy and materials, to generate minimal wastes, and, whenever possible, to serve more than one purpose. Every such project should:

- address the place of the site within the urban ecosystem as a whole, including its relationship to the city's most critical problems
- respond to the problems and the opportunities posed by the site and its immediate neighborhood
- design buildings and the landscape to conserve energy and reduce waste
- exploit the site's distinctive microclimatic, geological, hydrologic, and biological character.

Cities must resist the habit of fragmenting nature, a habit reinforced by the organization of government bureaucracies and the boundaries of professions and academic disciplines. While some specialization is necessary, the absence of a single coordinating agency prevents the effective management of resources and hazards and discourages the resolution of multiple problems with one solution. Only by viewing the entire urban natural environment as one interacting system can the value of nature in the city be fully appreciated. Only when the social values of natural processes are recognized can priorities be set, and conflicting and complementary values be resolved or married. Only then can urban form fully reflect the values inherent in nature as well as other social values.

An understanding of the urban natural environment should underlie all aspects of the physical design of the city: the location of specific land uses; the shape, size, and landscaping of urban parks and plazas; the alignment and width of streets and highways; and the overall pattern of the city's transportation network and places of work, residence, and play. In particular, the integration of all urban, open land into a unified plan promises to extend the traditionally accepted aesthetic and recreational value of open space to a crucial role in health, safety, and welfare. Parks and plazas, water bodies and streams, floodplains and marshy lowlands, steep hillsides and rocky outcrops, and even parking lots and highway corridors could be included in a cohesive open space system to improve air quality and climate, to reduce flooding and improve water quality, to limit the impact of geological hazards, such as earthquakes, subsidence, and landslides, to provide a diverse community of plants and animals within the city, to conserve energy, water, and mineral resources, and to enhance the safe assimilation of the city's wastes.

The components of such a system have been implemented, piecemeal, in many different cities in Europe, Asia, and North America, but no city has yet implemented a plan that addresses all factors of the urban natural environment in such a grand strategy. The many successes, both large and small, documented in the previous pages are inspiring, but most are limited to a single dimension: air quality and climate, urban geology, flood control, or urban forestry.

Neither new policies and regulations nor alterations in the city's physical form are sufficient in themselves to improve the environmental quality of our cities. Substantial improvement will occur only through the coordinated efforts of policymakers in public agencies and private corporations and institutions, planning and design professionals, natural and social scientists, humanists, and citizens. In the nineteenth century, cities formed new institutions to address municipal problems, institutions whose mandate often superseded private interest and whose powers extended beyond local political boundaries. The nineteenth-century achievement in sanitary reform was awesome and inspiring, but fell short in the twentieth century. Today's problems require a new effort. Modern technology is equal to the task; most existing institutions are not, though effective models do exist. Each city should consider which existing institutions or what new ones could coordinate the assembly and dissemination of information. First and foremost, each city must appreciate the social values inherent in natural processes and understand that urban form and human purpose can evolve in concert with nature.

Epilogue

Visions of the Future

The inferno of the living is not something that will be; if there is one it is already here, the inferno where we live everyday, that we form by being together. There are two ways to escape suffering from it. The first is easy for many: accept the inferno and become part of it that you can no longer see it. The second is risky and demands constant vigilance and apprehension: seek and learn to recognize who and what in the midst of the inferno, are not inferno, then make them endure, give them space.

ITALO CALVINO, Invisible Cities

THE CITY— contaminated and uncomfortable; plagued by shortages of energy, resources, and water, and by wastes and pests; vulnerable to catastrophic floods and geological disasters—is increasingly costly to maintain. This need not be. The climate projects of Stuttgart and Dayton, the flood control projects of Denver and Boston, the forestry program of Zurich, and the urban wilds program of Boston all permit a vision of what the city could be: clean and comfortable; efficient in its exploitation and use of mineral resources, energy, and water, and its reclamation of resources in residual wastes; secure from natural disasters; beautiful and memorable.

The barrier to building a better city is not lack of knowledge, but refusal to apply that knowledge. Many of the models are ancient. The germ of Stuttgart lay in ancient Greek city planning and the first-century recommendations of Vitruvius. Olmsted's design for the Fenway in 1879 preceded other, similar projects by a century. If these earlier models had become part of an abiding urban tradition, rather than sporadic incidents—discovered, forgotten, and rediscovered—the modern city would be a different place. But the preference for short-term payoffs over long-term benefits has characterized human actions throughout history. Action is taken only when disaster seems imminent. The "crisis response" has a long and ignoble tradition.

In a bounded system one must live with the consequences of one's actions. We live on a finite world, a sphere of limited dimensions, sheathed in a shallow layer of air. There is no escape, finally. The "elsewhere" to which we once transported our wastes is now or soon will be inhabited by somebody else. Escape to the suburbs or countryside is illusory. The same attitudes toward nature responsible for degrading the city are now poisoning the countryside, and the urban problems of yesterday have become the suburban and rural problems of today: air and soil pollution and contaminated water supplies. Acid rain formed from coal burned hundreds of miles away is killing fish and plants in rural lakes and forests. Clandestine disposal of toxic wastes threatens water in suburban and rural wells.

Environmental problems are not unique to the city, but simply more visible, their effects more concentrated. In the end, this may be an advantage, for problems once recognized can be solved. A centralized water supply and sewage treatment system can be monitored and regulated. The concentration of wastes in cities may make their safe disposal, treatment, and eventual reclamation more feasible. Wastes in outlying suburbs and rural settlements are dispersed. Small, local governments on the metropolitan fringe lack the administrative capacity to monitor the contamination of air and soil, and of the water in scattered, private wells. The future of the city and the country around it are bound together, and neither should be neglected for the other.

In the present lies not only the nightmare of what the city will become if current trends continue, but also the dream of what the city could be.

The Infernal City

The city's decline was gradual. It is impossible to pinpoint at what instant environmental degradation became irreversible. The effects that are now widespread in outlying suburbs and many rural settlements were first manifest in the city proper: increases in miscarriages, bizarre birth defects, and mysterious degenerative diseases, greater incidence of cancer and respiratory and heart disease. At that time, they were considered primarily urban problems from which one could escape by fleeing the city. It was only later, when more recently settled areas became haunted by those identical "urban problems," that they were recognized as problems of society rather than of the city.

The realization came too late for the city, whose more affluent population had already moved to suburbs and rapidly growing rural settlements. Motley bands of the diseased and desperately poor are now the only remaining residents. These folk live a marginal existence supplementing their crops by bartering scavenged metal, books, and other urban artifacts in nearby settlements. Jealous of this prerogative, they frequently attack the mining teams sent in to extract mineral and chemical resources from ruins and former dumps. The forests has reclaimed cities in humid regions. Although buildings of metal and glass have long since been mined, the crumbling remains of stone skyscrapers rise above the forest like rocky cliffs. Beneath the forest canopy, tree roots and vines have slowly disintegrated the pavement. In many respects, this eerie, lush wasteland is more beautiful than the late-twentieth-century city. Photographs taken decades earlier, after the Urban Water Riots, show a barren, dusty landscape. Nature has been less resilient in abandoned cities of desert and prairie; the invading brush and grass do not hide the hulk of deserted cities.

There has been much debate over when decisive action might still have averted the disasters which befell the city and which are now being felt everywhere. Some scholars maintain that it is irrelevant to identify the point of no return, since the influential and the well-to-do had abandoned the city by then, and those remaining had neither the power, the knowledge, nor the means to alter the course of events. Instead, they prefer to trace the decisive events that led to the political and social jettison of the city. Those events most commonly singled out are the Urban Birth Riots, the Urban Water Riots, and the Spring Water Scandals.

The Urban Birth Riots, prompted by the widespread miscarriages and birth defects visited upon city residents, were of unprecedented violence. These were people who had nothing to lose; they were denied not just sufficient food, water, or work, but the ability to reproduce. But by the time the urban masses realized that they had been poisoned, it was already too late. The major effect of the Urban Birth Riots was that what little commerce and industry remained abandoned the city permanently, for no one would work there. Those who could afford to had already moved to suburbs and rapidly growing rural settlements. After the Birth Riots, the last remaining skilled workers who had stayed to supervise the operations of municipal power, water treatment, and sewage treatment plants and transportation systems deserted. All now agree that these riots were not a primary cause in themselves, but merely marked the city's final collapse.

Some scholars cite the Urban Water Riots as decisive. These occurred in different cities over a period of two decades. Cities in arid regions felt the water shortage earliest, but eventually even cities in humid regions found it impossible to secure an adequate supply of uncontaminated water. Desperate attempts to annex water supplies from outlying regions were thwarted again and again, for by this time political power had shifted from the city to surrounding regions. The water shortages marked the beginning of the end. In a few cities, populations declined gradually, until a catastrophic flood, earthquake, or landslide destroyed much of the city. After the Great Earthquake, San Francisco was never rebuilt; after the Great Flood, New Orleans was abandoned.

It had already become difficult before the Water Riots to attract workers to the city. The cost of living was high and the benefits few. The city was hotter than the surrounding countryside. When energy shortages forced widespread elimination of air conditioning, most office buildings and apartments became unbearably uncomfortable, even in regions with a temperate climate. Older buildings in which the windows could be opened for ventilation commanded the highest rents. Newer buildings, even when remodeled so that some windows could be opened, were too hot for midday occupancy or comfortable sleeping at night. Many stood vacant. Trees had long since disappeared from the civic landscape, and public fountains no longer functioned. Streets offered no relief from summer heat and dusty winds. By the time the federal government relocated from Washington, D.C., to a new town in the Midwest, regional offices of federal agencies had long since moved from the center of large cities to the metropolitan outskirts.

Year after year the contamination of urban water grew worse. Under pressure from the industrial lobby and from municipal governments beleaguered by increasing costs of water purification and sewage treatment, the Environmental Protection Agency progressively lowered water quality standards and suppressed statistics on water contamination. Meanwhile, the cost of "pure," bottled water rose steadily. It was against this backdrop that the Spring Water Scandals were exposed. By the time the cost of bottled water exceeded the price of some French wines, there was a flourishing black market. When the Spring Water Scandals were uncovered in city after city, billions of gallons of contaminated water had already been bottled, marketed, and consumed as "pure." By the end of this period, even the most loyal of the cosmopolitan elite fled the city. There was little to hold them there anymore, and the last urban amenities disappeared. Museums closed and distributed their collections to many smaller branches built in suburban shopping malls. Symphony orchestras broke up into smaller ensembles and relocated to new towns and television studios. There is now substantial agreement that water contamination was the most significant factor in the city's demise and that other problems—like air pollution and the corresponding increase in respiratory and heart disease, the ravages of natural hazards like floods and earthquakes, and the rise in cost of resources—were merely secondary.

"City" problems began to be perceptible elsewhere—first in the older suburbs, then in the new towns. Both had been built no differently from the old metropolis, except that they were less dense and thus more dependent on individual transport and more expensive to serve with water, energy, and waste disposal. The older suburbs were built for a wealthier population than the poor who now inhabit them. Old single-family homes are now occupied by several families. Many attempt to eke a subsistence from home-grown crops, but most lots are too small. All parks, roadsides, and other public lands have been converted to allotment gardens. The older cities, their cores virtually deserted, are surrounded by rings of suburbs, now inhabited by those who left the city last. There is nowhere else for them to go, for the surrounding countryside is occupied. Yet they maintain a constant, outward pressure and fill every vacuum as it is deserted by the more fortunate. Many work in the new mini-cities which have sprung up around shopping malls.

During the long exodus from the city, the alternatives were neither coordinated nor well considered. The development of new towns and mini-cities paralleled the early growth of older cities; and they are now paying the same price in environmental degradation and its pervasive impact on health and safety. Meanwhile, even the remote countryside has filled in with scattered human settlements of urban émigrés. There is nowhere left to go.

Each generation as it reaches the age of reproduction now comes to regard preceding generations with bitterness. Pregnant women await the birth of their children with dread. More and more young people choose to have no children. The elderly are not respected, they are abused. Even those with strong cultural traditions of ancestor worship curse the preceding generations, who, through their scramble to accumulate individual power and wealth, created the world in which the younger generation and its children must live. The past few generations have sought desperately to recreate healthy, safe settlements. Unfortunately, there is no longer anywhere else to go. Earlier attempts to dilute and disperse wastes have led to widespread contamination in which the component minerals and chemicals cannot be reclaimed. A few scientists now say that it may be best to resettle the old cities, where deposits of heavy metals and inorganic chemicals are concentrated and reclaimable.

The Celestial City

To many, the city offers an optimal compromise between the amenities of society and those of nature. Historically, many lived in the city not by choice, but because of opportunities for work. With modern communications and information technology, it is now possible for a large segment of the working population to work at home and thus to live anywhere. Ironically, an increasing proportion of those whose work is not tied to a specific place choose to live in the city. Modern cities offer the stimulation, diversity, and cultural resources of their predecessors, as well as a closeness to nature and to the dynamics of natural processes. Fresh air and clean water, comfortable outdoor spaces, and the economical use of resources and energy are prized features of city life. The benefits are so obvious to all that it is unimaginable that things were once different. Yet every schoolchild knows that behind the achievements of modern cities lie the catastrophes and tragedies of the past. It was death, disease, and deformity from widespread water contamination and a dilapidated water supply and sewage treatment system that prompted Boston and Buffalo to pioneer techniques of water conservation and reuse that are now standard. It was the great earthquake that leveled San Francisco and the subsequent reconstruction which transformed that city into the marvel that it is today. When pollution of air and water in the late twentieth century set city against city and nation against nation, efforts to prove blame and assess damages led to the sophisticated models of air and water movement that make management of air and water in today's cities possible.

The city's transformation spanned many years, inspired by diverse motives, provoked by varied incidents. In some cities, change proceeded incrementally, at a snail's pace; other cities went through a rapid metamorphosis. The gardens and parks, the water in fountains, pools, and rivers, and the distinctive identity cultivated by every city today would be striking to a twentieth-century observer, but these are merely superficial signs of a more pervasive renewal, a partnership between nature and humankind. To the twentieth century, nature was an adversary, at times mysterious and threatening, but more often mundane and forgotten.

Nature is everywhere evident and cultivated in the city. Every residence, and nearly every place of work, has a garden, whether on rooftop, balcony, or on the ground. Every citizen has a private garden, no matter how tiny. The forms buildings take vary; each reflects not only the way it is used, its time and culture, and the skill of its architect, but also the climate of its region. Buildings in hot, humid climates funnel breezes into shaded plazas; buildings in arid regions deflect winds from protected courtyards. The tall skyscrapers that created windy, dark streets in former cities have now almost disappeared. Many cities have retained a few as historic monuments. Most large buildings have rooftop gardens, cultivated by residents or maintained by corporations for their workers, gardens that are also designed to hold rainfall in shallow pools. These gardens in the sky are best appreciated from the air on a sunny day after a rain when the sunlight sparkles across the city catching every rooftop pool. The gardens are remarkably productive and as diverse as their cultivators. Some people grow roses and others wildflowers; some prune topiary into exotic shapes and others encourage a wild, profuse growth; some people enjoy a permanent arrangement of shrubs and trees and others reap an abundant annual harvest of fruits and vegetables.

The landscape within cities is varied, suited to the specific activities and special character of different districts. Cultivated formal gardens are treasured in some districts, and urban wilds in others. Most cities with a humid climate have at least one large, pastoral park. Since these are expensive to maintain, their extent and number are an indication of a city's importance and wealth. They are especially valued as places for spectacles and civic events where all the city's residents mingle, and for large picnics of friends or extended families.

The city is filled with delightful outdoor places, lively centers where one can sit in the shade on a hot summer day or bask in the early spring or late fall sun while watching the surrounding bustle. There is almost invariably water in these places. Carefully conserved, the water is treated in marvelous variety. The sounds of gushing, falling, spraying, and dripping water are exploited. Fountains provide cool relief to summer heat, and ice sculptures form an ever-changing display as they alternately freeze and thaw throughout the winter. The manipulation of water in fountains, runnels, basins, ponds, and streams is a highly developed art. Landscape artists who specialize in water design are esteemed and in great demand. Especially respected are those artists who understand how to purify water as well as to display it. Most small cities with ample land celebrate the recycling of wastewater in a treatment park, consisting of multiple ponds, basins, fountains, flowering lagoons, and even marshes. Most citizens conserve water wisely, although some still maintain irrigated lawns and gardens as a symbol of their wealth.

Every city has a transportation system suited to its own climate, physiography, size, and settlement pattern. Types of transport are therefore as characteristic of a city as its topographic setting and the form of its buildings. Boats, bicycles, trains, air cars, and automobiles appear in many forms and combinations in different cities. Many dense cities, both old and new, have banned private automobiles entirely and instead employ an efficient fleet of vehicles, large and small, which shuttle about the city. The streets, now narrowed and planted with trees, vineyards, and vegetable plots, form green strips that run throughout the city. Other, more dispersed cities have elected to retain the private automobile, exploring new types of fuel and altering the pattern of work and residence to reduce travel.

The paths on which people move into and through the city are designed with care. Every street and highway, and every other transportation corridor, is designed for efficient movement, for pleasure, and as an asset to the neighborhood through which it moves. Small residential streets are places where living takes precedence over movement. Here, traffic shares the street with domestic activities. Major routes are designed as processionals, scaled to speed of movement. Most cities design transportation routes linking city to region and city-region to other city-regions as a symbolic statement of the underlying unity of the city-region. Highway corridors have long been converted to native forest, prairie, or desert plants. As one drives across the prairie to Aridatha, the city rises over waving grasses and wildflowers, a memorable and much photographed image.

The city of Cyrilla has designed the highways approaching its downtown as processionals where the roadside landscape becomes progressively more formal as it approaches the center. Cyrilla is famous for its magnificent rows of cedars which line the northern approach to the city. Forest encloses the major highways surrounding downtown Xylonia. A strip of wildflowers, mowed once a year, lines the median and both sides of the road. Workers who enter the city by this route learn to mark the passage of seasons by subtle changes in color: by the shifts in flower color—from yellow to red to orange to purple—that mark the fading of one plant's bloom and the blossoming of another's; and by the change from the reds, browns, and straw colors of winter grasses, to the delicate greens and pastel pinks and yellows of early spring, to the dark green spectrum of summer and the brilliant colors of autumn. Xylonia originally designed its forested highways to break the force of winds before they hit downtown towers, to protect adjacent neighborhoods from air pollution and highway noise, and to reduce the high maintenance costs that had been entailed by a mowed landscape. The forested highways are now famous chiefly as an aesthetic resource, though every city resident knows and appreciates their effect on downtown climate and air quality.

All the trees of Xylonia are managed as a great urban forest. While trees in the few remaining pastoral parks are permitted to age into picturesque senescence and some woodplots are left to pursue their own processes of self-replacement, most of the city's trees along streets and parks are intentionally planted and harvested. Depending upon the species, Xylonia manages these plantations in twenty-year, fifty-year, or hundred-year rotations. No street or park is planted of wholly even-aged trees; younger replacement trees are set out years before older trees are harvested. When planted in rows, these plantations form a magnificent grid. In contrast to its gridded forests and pastoral parks, Xylonia has converted one large, old park into a celebration of renewal. Every year one acre of the 200-acre park is left unmowed, and a stone set in the middle of the plot to mark the year. The first plot was set aside forty years ago and now consists of a mixed woodland of slim red maples, dogwoods, poplars, and Norway maples. A path connects each adjacent plot, charting a path through time. It is an annual custom for local residents to visit the plot released from lawn in the year of their birth.

Each city values nurturing the health and safety of every resident over protecting the privileges of a few. Clean air and water and security from natural hazards are deemed basic rights of every citizen. Every city therefore attends efficiently to issues of health and safety. These are regarded not as problems, but rather as an opportunity to secure additional benefits which might not otherwise be economically feasible. Thus, solutions to the city's problems—obtaining and conserving resources, disposing of and recycling wastes, insuring clean air, and supplying water—yield many other benefits: the enhancement of each city's special character and the acquisition of an extensive system of parks and urban wilds, of comfortable downtown plazas, and rooftop gardens. As every citizen knows, rooftops, plazas, and parks are all part of the city's storm drainage and flood control system, linking the land's surface with underground sewers, with treatment parks and reclamation plants, and with rivers and lakes.

Every building, every park, and every highway is designed with more than one end in mind. Each is regarded first as a unit with specific primary uses, then as an element in a small, local system of other buildings, parks, and streets, and finally as a part of a larger, regional system of land uses and environments. Thus, not only is every building constructed to conserve energy, but also to create a comfortable environment in surrounding streets, plazas, and structures. Every building and the land surrounding it is constructed not only to prevent floods in the basement, but also to avoid flooding in other parts of the city downstream. Few parks serve only as places for play. Every city is intensively cultivated and managed, and space is extremely valuable. Parks must therefore serve many purposes: for the reclamation of urban wastes, for the preservation of mineral resources, for flood storage, for the stabilization of hazardous slopes, and as managed forests. All the open spaces in the city—rooftops, plazas, parking lots, streets, highways, parks, and urban wilds—are part of an interlocking, multifaceted system.

The utilitarian attitude toward open space heightens the importance attached to a few special places within each city that serve no purpose except to contribute to the city's distinctive identity. The character of these special places varies from city to city: beautiful rock formations; a venerable stand of old trees; an overlook or vantage point from which the city can be perceived as a whole. These special places are popular not only with tourists, but also with city residents. Every city also maintains some urban wilds, whose character depends upon the city's physiography and climate. They are uncultivated places whose life force is permitted to express itself: in dense forest growth or a carpet of colorful blooms after a desert rain. Although it is inconceivable that any part of the city could remain uninfluenced by human activity, nevertheless in these places that intervention is less visible. In former times they were regarded as wastelands.

Every city is proud of its distinctive character and fosters that character by responding to its natural setting, its history, and its cultural and economic traditions. The city of Della lies in a basin formed by a major river and the confluence with its tributaries. The open space system of Della forms a radial pattern, following the stream channels and river valleys along which both water and cool air flow into the city. Stormwater detention ponds within the floodplain parks prevent flooding after the heavy summer storms and cool the air as it flows over them. Landforms molded to absorb and deflect powerful floodwaters form sensuous curves across the landscape; a line of square marble pavers set flush in the grass along the limit reached by the twenty-five-year flood charts a path through the park. Destruction from earthquakes and landslides is the major concern of the citizens of Pyrene. The city is bisected by a major fault which forms a linear spine of parks, allotment gardens, orchards, cropland, and nurseries—the city's major agricultural belt and playground. The most unstable slopes have long been converted into terraced gardens; some of these are public promenades with an overview of the city, others are privately owned and cultivated. On a major fault trace near downtown, the city erected two tall granite columns. Installed side by side twenty years ago and now six inches apart, the columns are slowly sliding past each other, riding the earth, marking its movement. In both Della and Pyrene homes have been removed from the hazardous areas: from the floodplain in Della and from the active faults, unstable ground, and landslide zones in Pyrene. This has happened gradually. After each disaster, a relocation agency helps the victims to find new homes outside the hazardous zone. The construction of new homes in these areas is not permitted. Floods and earthquakes are no longer the fearful events they once were.

Although some are more adept than others, every citizen is well versed in reading the urban ecosystem. Small children are taught to read the history of a tree's growth in its branching pattern and twigs and to diagnose a tree's health from its appearance. Every schoolchild knows the natural and social history of his or her city-region, its economic base, and the evolution of its physical form. One of the most popular games among high school students is a simulation in which they can manipulate urban form to avert environmental disaster to a city-region.

Every city and its region is managed as an integrated ecosystem and is tied into a network of other city-region systems, which in turn span provinces and nations. City-regions take many forms. Some retain the single center surrounded by subcenters and outlying countryside, so typical of early cities. Most, however, are composed of constellations of smaller city centers with overlapping areas of influence. Some centers are new towns and others are historic centers. The newer towns attract a different population than the old centers. They have provided industry with an opportunity to build new, modern installations, in a situation where many of the mistakes of the old metropolis can be avoided. An urban fields type of city-region is frequently composed of both new towns and old centers. The modern city-region did not appear overnight, but evolved gradually. When management of the urban ecosystem became regarded as essential to health, safety, and welfare, the city-region assimilated more and more of the planning, management, and regulatory functions of the old states, counties, and municipalities. State and local loyalties died hard, but the common interests of the city-region eroded the old ties over time. Old animosities within states split cleanly along city-region boundaries. Thus the widely scattered, small centers of the city-region Anona, with their agricultural base and shared watershed, formerly divided by a state boundary, have much more in common with each other than they do with the industrial city-regions in what were formerly their respective states. As new institutions reinforced these common interests, loyalties were realigned.

Each city-region monitors its environment regularly. It assimilates information from many sources, ranging from the latest federal survey to the mapping conducted for individual construction projects within the city, and converts this diverse data into a uniform format. Although each city-region strives to be distinctive, all recognize that they share many of the same basic problems. A network of information is therefore maintained within each of the physiographic regions of a country, as well as on a nationwide and worldwide basis.

Any city facing a specific constellation of problems can apply to a regional data bank, since these solutions may be most appropriate, or can request a search through national or worldwide data banks for solutions which might fit their particular situation.

What will be and what could be. In the present city lie many potential cities: the infernal city, the celestial city, and many cities in between. Current trends point to a gloomy future. Yet, nearly every element of the celestial city exists somewhere in some form, however er skeletal. We are not now and have never been on some inexorable path to doom.

The celestial city is no utopian fantasy. It is an achievable reality. It is necessary merely to recognize what is good in the present and to nurture it, to adapt successful models already forged by cities of the past and present, and to develop new ones. Recognition of the city as part of nature should inspire new policies and give life to old ones, should prompt the formation of new institutions and fuel new research, all of which should be reflected in the city's physical form. This will occur only through the coordinated efforts of all who study and shape the city: public officials and policymakers, private institutions and corporations, planning and design professionals, natural and social scientists, and all the city's individual citizens. Some cities might start with their most urgent problems—be they climate and air quality or floods and water quality, earthquakes and landslides or mining and subsidence—for which public support can be galvanized and financial support accumulated, and then find ways to include other concerns. Somewhere a visionary may persuade his or her city to take on the challenge of managing the entire urban natural environment. The reasons are compelling. At issue is not just the creation of a more secure, more beautiful, more efficient and cost-effective city, but survival itself. It is not just the city at stake, but other forms of human settlement as well. It is time to employ one of the greatest human talents, the ability to manipulate the environment, to transform an environment that has become hostile to life itself into a humane habitat which sustains life and nurtures growth, both personal and collective.

Notes
Bibliography
List of Illustrations
Index

NOTES

Chapter 1. City and Nature

1. C. F. Withington, "Geology: Its Role in the Development and Planning of Metropolitan Washington," in *Geology in the Urban Environment*, ed. R. O. Utgard, G. D. McKenzie, and D. Foley (Minneapolis: Burgess, 1978).

2. Walter Muir Whitehill, *Boston: A Topographical History*, 2 ed. (Cambridge, Mass.: The Belknap Press, Harvard University Press, 1968), p. 1.

3. Carl Bridenbaugh, *Cities in the Wilderness: The First Century of Urban Life in America, 1625–1742* (London: Oxford University Press, 1966), p. 6. Bridenbaugh notes further that in 1680 there were only four cities in England whose population exceeded 10,000.

4. Whitehill, *Boston*, p. 11.

5. Ibid., pp. 73–74.

6. Ibid., p. 62.

7. Ibid., pp. 81–84.

8. Ibid., p. 109.

9. Museum of Fine Arts, *Back Bay Boston: The City as a Work of Art* (Boston: Museum of Fine Arts, 1969), p. 38.

10. Gary B. Griggs and John A. Gilchrist, *Geologic Hazards, Resources, and Environmental Planning* (Belmont, Calif.: Wadsworth, 1983), p. 225.

11. Bridenbaugh, *Cities in Wilderness*, p. 159.

12. Whitehill, *Boston*, p. 92.

13. Ibid., p. 90.

14. Ibid., p. 150.

15. Ibid., p. 180.

16. Thomas Pemberton, 1794, quoted in Whitehill, *Boston*, p. 47.

17. Nelson, M. Blake, *Water for the Cities: A History of the Urban Water Supply Problem in the United States* (Syracuse, N.Y.: Syracuse University Press, 1956), p. 178.

18. Ibid., p. 215.

19. Bridenbaugh, *Cities in Wilderness*, p. 12.

20. Ibid.

21. Nathaniel B. Shurtleff, *A Topographical and Historical Description of Boston* (Boston: Rockwell and Churchill, City Printers, 1890), p. 320.

22. Edgar Anderson, *Plants, Man and Life* (Berkeley and Los Angeles: University of California Press, 1969), p. 12.

23. Ibid., pp. 3–5.

24. Compare the plant list in Herbert Sukopp, Hans-Peter Blume and Wolfram Kunick, "The Soil, Flora, and Vegetation of Berlin's Wastelands," in *Nature in Cities*, edited by Ian C. Laurie (Chichester, England: Wiley, 1979), pp. 125–27, with that of an abandoned quarry in Boston in Nancy M. Page and Richard E. Weaver, Jr., *Wild Plants in the City* (New York: Quadrangle/The New York Times Book Co., 1975), p. 9.

25. Bridenbaugh, *Cities in Wilderness*, p. 19.

26. Henri Frankfort, "Town Planning in Ancient Mesopotamia," *The Town Planning Review* 21 (July 1950), p. 102.

27. Georg Braun and Franz Hogenberg, *Old European Cities*, ed. Arthur Hibbert and Ruthardt Oehme (London: Thames and Hudson, n.d.), p. 57.

28. Patrick Geddes, *Cities in Evolution* (London: Williams and Norgate, 1915), p. 87.

29. Ebenezer Howard, *Garden Cities for To-morrow*, (1902; reprint, Cambridge, Mass.: MIT Press, 1965).

30. Lewis Mumford, *The City in History* (New York: Harcourt Brace Jovanovich, 1961), p. 487.

Chapter 2. Dirt and Discomfort

1. U.S. Council on Environmental Quality, *Environmental Quality—The Tenth Annual Report of the Council on Environmental Quality* (Washington, D.C.: U.S. Government Printing Office, 1979), pp. 24, 28.

2. Ibid.

3. Seneca, A.D. 61, quoted in K. C. Heidorn, "A Chronology of Events in the History of Air Pollution Meteorology to 1970," *Bulletin of the American Meteorological Society* 59 (1978):1589.

4. Ibid.

5. Ibid.

6. John Evelyn, *Fumifugium, Or the Inconvenience of the Aer and Smoake of London Dissipated*, in *The Smoake of London*, ed. James P. Lodge, Jr. (1661; reprint, Elmsford, N.Y.: Maxwell Reprint, 1969), p. 16.

7. Heidorn, "History of Air Pollution," p. 1591.

8. Ibid., p. 1593.

9. Evelyn, *Fumifugium*, p. 16.

10. U.S. Council on Environmental Quality, *Environmental Quality—The Eighth Annual Report of the Council on Environmental Quality* (Washington, D.C.: U.S. Government Printing Office, 1977), p. 153.

11. G. Godin, G. Wright, and R. J. Shepard, "Urban Exposure to Carbon Monoxide," *Archives of Environmental Health* 25 (1972):313.

12. Ibid.; A. J. Haagen-Smit, "Carbon Monoxide Levels in City Driving," *Archives of Environmental Health* 12 (1966):550.

13. Haagen-Smit, "Carbon Monoxide in City Driving," p. 550.

14. Ibid.

15. U.S. Council on Environmental Quality, *Eighth Annual Report*, pp. 168–69.

16. M. Neiburger, "Diffusion Models of Urban Air Pollution," in *Urban Climates*, World Meteorological Organization, Technical Note 108 (Brussels, 1968), p. 253.

17. Haagen-Smit, "Carbon Monoxide in City Driving," p. 550. "Serious" levels are as defined by the Health Department of the state of California.

18. Paul F. Fennelly, "The Origin and Influence of Airborne Particulates," *American Scientist* 64 (January–February 1976):53–54.

19. The source for this and the following characterizations of air quality problems in specific cities is the U.S. Council on Environmental Quality, *Environmental Quality: Tenth Annual Report*, pp. 18–32.

20. Heidorn, "History of Air Pollution," p. 1590.

21. Helmut E. Landsberg, "Microclimatology," *Architectural Forum* (March 1947): 113–19.

22. U. Hoffman, "Problems of the City Climate of Stuttgart," in *City Climate: Data and Aspects for City Planning*. FBW—A publication of Research, Building, and Living, ed. Erhard Franke. Translated for EPA by Literature Research Company, TR-70-0795 (Stuttgart, West Germany: Karl Kramer, 1976), p. 64.

23. Walsh McDermott, "Air Pollution and Public Health," in *Cities: Their Origin, Growth, and Human Impact* (San Francisco: W. H. Freeman, 1973), p. 137.

24. Helmut E. Landsberg, "Climates and Urban Planning," in *Urban Climates*, World Meteorological Organization, Technical Note 108 (Brussels, 1968), p. 367.

25. T. J. Chandler, *Urban Climatology and Its Relevance to Urban Design*, World Meteorological Organization, Technical Note 149 (Geneva, 1976), p. 26.

26. Ibid., p. 32.

27. Helmut E. Landsberg, *The Urban Climate* (New York: Academic Press, 1981), p. 120.

28. Measurements are given in metric when the original source is in metric and rounding off might distort the data.

29. Landsberg, *Urban Climate*, p. 120.

30. Ibid., 243–44.

31. Ibid., p. 246.

32. William H. Smith, "Lead Contamination of the Roadside Ecosystem," *Journal of the Air Pollution Control Association* 26 (1976):763.

33. Godin, Wright, and Shepard, "Urban Exposure to Carbon Monoxide," p. 310.

34. Ibid.

35. Ibid.

36. A. D. Penwarden and A. F. E. Wise, *Wind Environment around Buildings* (London: Her Majesty's Stationery Office, 1975), p. 3.

37. Ibid., p. vii.

38. Landsberg, *Urban Climate*, p. 233.

Chapter 3. Improving Air Quality, Enhancing Comfort, and Conserving Energy

1. Vitruvius, *The Ten Books on Architecture*, trans. Morris H. Morgan (New York: Dover, 1960), pp. 24–25, 27.

2. John Evelyn, *Fumifugium, Or the Inconvenience of the Aer and Smoake of London Dissipated* (1661; reprint, Elmsford, N.Y.: Maxwell Reprint, 1969).

3. Sidney Brower, "Street Front and Sidewalk," *Landscape Architecture* 63 (1973): 366.

4. Donald Appleyard, *Livable Streets* (Berkeley and Los Angeles: University of California Press, 1981), p. 278.

5. William R. Reilly, James H. Kell, and Iris J. Fullerton, *Design of Urban Streets*, Technology Sharing Report 80–204 (Washington, D.C.: Federal Highway Administration, U.S. Department of Transportation, 1980), p. 3.2.

6. Donald Appleyard, personal communication; Salem Spitz, "How Much Is Too Much (Traffic)," *Institute of Traffic Engineers Journal* (May 1982):44.

7. Appleyard, *Livable Streets*, p. 250.

8. William H. Smith, "Lead Contamination of the Roadside Ecosystem," *Journal of the Air Pollution Control Association* 26 (1976):763. (Measurements are given in metric when the original source is in metric and rounding off might distort the data.)

9. Ibid.

10. Mollie Hughes, personal communication.

11. William H. Smith, "Urban Vegetation and Air Quality," in *Proceedings of the National Urban Forestry Conference*, ed. George Hopkins (Syracuse: State University of New York, College of Environmental Science and Forestry, 1980), pp. 284–305.

12. This distance is based upon the polluted zone for a road averaging 24,000 vehicles per day, as described in Smith, "Lead Contamination of the Roadside Ecosystem."

13. Appleyard, *Livable Streets*, p. 249.

14. Wolfgang Langewiesche, "How to Fix Your Private Climate," *House Beautiful*, October 1949, pp. 151–53.

15. To date, this plan has not been implemented; parts of it, however, have been incorporated into smaller projects. The following graduate students worked on this project: Dana Brown, David Johnson, Peter Lukacic, and Rod Shaw.

16. David R. Smith and David A. Sholtis, "Green Parking Lot, Dayton, Ohio: An Experimental Installation of Grass Pavement. II. Performance Evaluation." (Dayton: The Heritage Conservation and Recreation Service, Lake Central Region, 1981), p. 3.

17. G. Arno Loessner, "An Air Quality Program with Visible Results," *Practicing Planner* 9 (1978):35–37. The description given here is based on this source as well as on U. Hoffman, "City Climate of Stuttgart," in *City Climate: Data and Aspects for City Planning*. FBW-A publication of Research, Building, and Living, ed. Erhard Franke. Translated for EPA by Literature Research Company, TR-70-0795 (Stuttgart, West Germany: Karl Kramer, 1976), p. 64.

18. Such solutions improve local air quality, but are likely to increase air pollution elsewhere.

19. Mollie Hughes, personal communication.

Chapter 4. Shifting Ground and Squandered Resources

1. John T. Alfors, John L. Burnett, and Thomas E. Gay, Jr., "Urban Geology Master Plan for California—A Summary," in *Geology in the Urban Environment*, ed. R. O. Utgard, G. D. McKenzie, and D. Foley (Minneapolis: Burgess, 1978), p. 326.

2. David Leveson, *Geology and the Urban Environment* (New York: Oxford University Press, 1980), p. 131.

3. Gary B. Griggs and John A. Gilchrist, *Geologic Hazards, Resources, and Environmental Planning* (Belmont, Calif.: Wadsworth, 1983), p. 19.

4. Robert B. Atwood, editor of the *Anchorage Daily Times*, quoted in D. A. Bolt, W. L. Horn, G. A. MacDonald, and R. F. Scott, *Geologic Hazards* (New York: Springer-Verlag, 1975), p. 1.

5. Alfors, Burnett, and Gay, "Urban Geology Master Plan," p. 326.

6. D. R. Nichols and J. M. Buchanan-Banks, "Seismic Hazards and Land-Use Planning," in *Geology in Urban Environment*, ed. Utgard, McKenzie, and Foley, p. 89.

7. Griggs and Gilchrist, *Geologic Hazards*, p. 40.

8. Ibid., p. 42

9. Ibid., p. 268.

10. Robert Iacopi, *Earthquake Country* (Menlo Park, Calif.: Lane Books, 1973), p. 37.

11. Griggs and Gilchrist, *Geologic Hazards*, p. 45.

12. Robert W. Fleming, David J. Varnes, and Robert L. Schuster, "Landslide Hazards and Their Reduction," in *Geological Survey Yearbook* (Washington, D.C.: U.S. Geological Survey, 1978), p. 14.

13. Griggs and Gilchrist, *Geologic Hazards*, p. 153.

14. Ibid., p. 183.

15. Bolt et al., *Geological Hazards*, p. 196.

16. Stephen S. Hart, "Potentially Swelling Soil and Rock in the Front Range Urban Corridor," in *Geology in Urban Environment*, ed. Utgard, McKenzie, and Foley, p. 113.

17. D. E. Jones, Jr., and W. G. Holtz, "Expansive Soils—The Hidden Disaster," *Civil Engineering* 43 (1973):49.

18. J. F. Poland and G. H. Davis, "Land Subsidence Due to Withdrawal of Fluids," in *Reviews in Engineering Geology* 2 (1969):210.

19. Leveson, *Geology and Urban Environment*, p. 255.

20. Griggs and Gilchrist, *Geologic Hazards*, pp. 219–20.

21. Ibid., p. 216.

22. Ibid., p. 225.

23. Leveson, *Geology and Urban Environment*, p. 105.

24. Griggs and Gilchrist, *Geologic Hazards*, p. 380.

25. Ibid.

26. Alfors, Burnett, and Gay, "Urban Geology Master Plan," p. 326.

27. Elizabeth Shreeve, personal communication.

28. Griggs and Gilchrist, *Geologic Hazards*, p. 360.

29. William H. Smith, "Lead Contamination of the Roadside Ecosystem," *Journal of the Air Pollution Control Association* 26 (1976):763. (Measurements are given in metric when the original source is in metric and rounding off might distort the data.)

30. Ibid.

31. Thomas M. Spittler and William A. Feder, "A Study of Soil Contamination and Plant Uptake of Lead in Boston's Urban Gardens," mimeographed, n.d., p. 24.

32. Ibid., p. 21.

33. James C. Patterson, "Soil Compaction and Its Effect upon Urban Vegetation," in *Better Trees for Metropolitan Landscapes Symposium Proceedings*, U.S. Forest Service General Technical Report NE-22 (Upper Darby, Pa.: Northeastern Forest Experiment Station, 1976), p. 97.

34. Robert Francis Harper, trans., *The Code of Hammurabi* (Chicago: University of Chicago Press and Callaghan & Company, 1904), p. 81.

Chapter 5. Finding Firm Ground and Exploiting Resources

1. Gary B. Griggs and John A. Gilchrist, *Geologic Hazards, Resources, and Environment Planning* (Belmont, Calif.: Wadsworth, 1983), p. 63.
2. D. R. Nichols and J. M. Buchanan-Banks, "Seismic Hazards and Land-Use Planning," in *Geology in the Urban Environment*, ed. R. O. Utgard, G. D. McKenzie, and D. Foley (Minneapolis: Burgess, 1978), p. 91.
3. The description given is based upon City and County of San Francisco, *San Francisco Community Safety Plan*, and David Leveson, *Geology and the Urban Environment* (New York: Oxford University Press, 1980), pp. 155–58.
4. Elmer E. Botsai, Alfred Goldberg, John L. Fisher, Henry J. Lagario, and Thomas D. Wosser, *Architects and Earthquakes* (Washington, D.C.: U.S. Government Printing Office, 1975), p. 69.
5. G. A. Kellaway and J. H. Taylor, "The Influence of Land Slipping on the Development of the City of Bath, England," *Twenty-Third Geologic Congress* (1968), p. 73.
6. The description given is based on Robert W. Fleming, David J. Barnes, and Robert L. Schuster, "Landslide Hazards and Their Reduction," in *Geological Survey Yearbook* (Washington, D.C.: U.S. Geological Survey, 1978), p. 19.
7. Griggs and Gilchrist, *Geologic Hazards*, p. 187.
8. Stephen S. Hart, "Potentially Swelling Soil and Rock in the Front Range Urban Corridor," in *Geology in Urban Environment*, ed. Utgard, McKenzie, and Foley, p. 120.
9. Griggs and Gilchrist, *Geologic Hazards*, p. 327.
10. Robert F. Legget, *Cities and Geology* (New York: McGraw-Hill, 1973), p. 391.
11. The description of underground space in Kansas City is based on Truman P. Stauffer, "Kansas City: A Center for Secondary Use of Mined Out Space," in *Geology in Urban Environment*, ed. Utgard, McKenzie, and Foley, pp. 176–86.
12. Robert L. Bates, "Mineral Resources for a New Town," in *Geology in Urban Environment*, ed. Utgard, McKenzie, and Foley, p. 173.
13. Richard N. Taylor, "Gravel Pit to Landfill to Park with Rolling Hills," *Public Works* 97 (1966):105–6.
14. See Thomas J. Bassett, "Reaping on the Margins: A Century of Community Gardening in America," *Landscape* 25, no. 2 (1981):1–8, for a summary of the history of allotment gardens in American cities.
15. Charlotte Kahn, personal communication.
16. Thomas N. Spittler and William A. Feder, "A Study of Soil Contamination and Plant Uptake of Lead in Boston Urban Gardens," mimeographed, n.d. The collaboration of the Suffolk County Extension Service, the University of Massachusetts, and the United States Department of Agriculture with Boston Urban Gardeners resulted in a handbook entitled *Lead in the Soil: A Gardener's Handbook*, Boston: Suffolk County Extension Service, 1979, which advises urban gardeners on the dangers of lead contamination, how to identify it, and how to mitigate it. The recommendations given in the text are taken from these publications.
17. The categories "Low," "Medium," "High," and "Possibly Dangerous" were set by the Suffolk County Extension Service to help the public understand the measure of lead parts per million (ppm). Low: 0–500 ppm; Medium: 500–1,000 ppm; High: 1,000–3,000 ppm; Possibly Dangerous: 3,000+ ppm.
18. John T. Alfors, John L. Burnett, and Thomas E. Gay, "Urban Geology Master Plan for California—A Summary," in *Geology in Urban Environment*, ed. Utgard, McKenzie, and Foley, p. 327.
19. Legget, *Cities and Geology*, p. 520.

Chapter 6. Floods, Droughts, and Poisoned Water

1. Luna B. Leopold, "Hydrology for Urban Land Planning—A Guidebook on the Hydrologic Effects of Urban Land Use," *U.S. Geological Survey Circular 554* (Washington, D.C.: U.S. Geological Survey, 1968), p. 5.
2. Thomas Dunne and Luna B. Leopold, *Water in Environmental Planning* (San Francisco: W. H. Freeman, 1978), p. 402.

3. Ibid., p. 684.

4. Harold E. Thomas and William J. Schneider, "Water as an Urban Resource and Nuisance," *Geological Survey Circular 601-D* (Washington, D.C.: U.S. Geological Survey, 1970), p. 4.

5. Luna B. Leopold, *Water: A Primer* (San Francisco: W. H. Freeman, 1974), pp. 90–91.

6. William J. Schneider and James E. Goddard, "Extent and Development of Urban Floodplains," *U.S. Geological Survey Circular 601-J* (Washington, D.C.: U.S. Geological Survey, 1973), p. 12.

7. Ian Burton, Robert W. Kates, and Gilbert S. White, *The Environment as Hazard* (New York: Oxford University Press, 1978), pp. 13–14.

8. Dunne and Leopold, *Water in Environmental Planning*, p. 393.

9. Ibid.

10. James Michener, *Centennial* (New York: Fawcett, 1978), p. 65.

11. Robert M. Searns, "Denver Tames the Unruly Platte: A Ten-Mile River Greenway," *Landscape Architecture* 70 (1980):82.

12. Schneider and Goddard, "Urban Floodplains," p. 5.

13. John Doxat, *The Living Thames: The Restoration of a Great Tidal River* (London: Hutchinson Benham, 1977), p. 32.

14. Ibid., p. 36.

15. Ibid., p. 35.

16. Alwyne Wheeler, "Fish in an Urban Environment," in *Nature in Cities*, ed. Ian C. Laurie (Chichester, England: Wiley, 1979), p. 163.

17. Nelson M. Blake, *Water for the Cities: A History of the Urban Water Supply Problem in the United States* (Syracuse, N.Y.: Syracuse University Press, 1956), p. 132.

18. Richard Field and John A. Lager, *Countermeasures for Pollution from Overflows: The State-of-the-Art* (Cincinnati: U.S. Environmental Protection Agency, 1974), p. 3.

19. U.S. Council on Environmental Quality, *Environmental Quality—The Ninth Annual Report of the Council on Environmental Quality* (Washington, D.C.: U.S. Government Printing Office, 1978), p. 139.

20. Ibid., p. 131.

21. Ibid., p. 134.

22. U.S. Council on Environmental Quality, *Environmental Quality—The Eighth Annual Report of the Council on Environmental Quality* (Washington, D.C.: U.S. Government Printing Office, 1977), p. 255.

23. U.S. Council on Environmental Quality, *Environmental Quality—The Tenth Annual Report of the Council on Environmental Quality* (Washington, D.C.: U.S. Government Printing Office, 1979), pp. 90–91.

24. U.S. Council on Environmental Quality, *Ninth Annual Report*, p. 134.

25. Ibid., p. 135.

26. Samuel S. Epstein, Lester O. Brown, and Carl Pope, *Hazardous Waste in America* (San Francisco: Sierra Club Books, 1982), pp. 441–45.

27. Blake, *Water for Cities*, p. 262.

28. Cited in Ibid., p. 4.

29. David Leveson, *Geology and the Urban Environment* (New York: Oxford University Press, 1980), p. 65.

30. Ibid., p. 44.

31. Blake, *Water for Cities*, pp. 271–72.

32. Leveson, *Geology and Urban Environment*, p. 43.

33. Ibid.

34. Ibid., p. 44.

Chapter 7. Controlling and Restoring the Waters

1. Alexander Purves Gest, *Engineering* (New York: Longmans, Green and Co., 1930), p. 100.

2. Pliny the Elder, *Natural History*, XXXVI, 15, 24, 123.

3. Aristotle, *Politics*, Book 7, Chapter 11.

4. Ecclesiastes 1:7.

5. Frederick Law Olmsted, "General Plan for the Sanitary Improvement of the Muddy River," 1881.

6. Frederick Law Olmsted, quoted in Cynthia Zaitzevsky, *Frederick Law Olmsted and the Boston Park System* (Cambridge, Mass.: Harvard University Press, Belknap Press, 1982), p. 57.

7. Ibid., p. 188.

8. John A. Lager, William G. Smith, William G. Lynard, Robert M. Finn, and E. John Finnemore, *Urban Stormwater Management and Technology: Update and Users Guide* (Cincinnati: U.S. Environmental Protection Agency, 1977), p. 141.

9. Ibid., p. 158.

10. Vijaysinh U. Mahida and Frank J. DeDecker, *Multi-Purpose Combined Sewer Overflow Treatment Facility, Mount Clemens, Michigan* (Cincinnati: U.S. Environmental Protection Agency, 1975). The description here is based both on this report and on personal communication with Mr. Mahida. The park has been less of a success than it might have been due to funding problems.

11. This description is based on an article by Robert Weireter, "Waste Not Wastewater: West: The Arcata Experiment," *American Forests* 88 (June 1982):38–53.

12. Such systems have been reviewed in recent issues of *Civil Engineering*, for example, in articles by Robert K. Bastian, "Natural Treatment Systems in Wastewater Treatment and Sludge Management," *Civil Engineering*, May 1982, pp. 62–67, and Sherwood Reed, Robert K. Bastian, and William J. Jewell, "Engineers Assess Aquaculture Systems for Wastewater Treatment," *Civil Engineering*, July 1981, pp. 64–67.

13. John Burgh, "Saving Water Scenically," *Water Engineering and Management* 129 (March 1982):46.

14. U.S. Army Corps of Engineers, *Natural Valley Storage: A Partnership with Nature* (Waltham, Mass.: Public Information Fact Sheet, Spring 1976).

15. Frank Notardonato and Arthur F. Doyle, "Corps Takes New Approach to Flood Control," *Civil Engineering*, June 1979, p. 66.

16. Ibid.

17. Elmer L. Claycomb, "Urban Storm Drainage Criteria Manual From Denver," *Civil Engineering*, July 1970, p. 39.

18. Ibid., p. 42.

19. Herbert G. Poertner, "Better Ways to Finance Stormwater Management," *Civil Engineering*, April 1981, p. 68.

20. There have been numerous works describing the Platte River Greenway, including a book by the chairman of the Platte River Development Committee: Joe Shoemaker and Leonard Stevens, *Returning the Platte to the People* (Denver: Greenway Foundation, 1981), and articles by landscape architecture and engineering consultants: Robert M. Searns, "Denver Tames the Unruly Platte: A Ten-Mile River Greenway," *Landscape Architecture* 70 (1980):382–86, and Kenneth Wright and William C. Taggart, "The Recycling of a River," *Civil Engineering*, November 1976, pp. 42–46.

21. Wright and Taggart, "Recycling a River," p. 46.

22. Ibid., p. 45.

23. Ibid., p. 46.

24. Searns, "Denver Tames the Platte," p. 386.

25. Narendra Juneja and James Veltman, "Natural Drainage in the Woodlands," in *Stormwater Management Alternatives*, ed. J. Toby Tourbier and Richard Westmacott (Newark: Water Resources Center, University of Delaware, 1980), p. 156.

26. The results of these studies are described in a series of four reports published by the firm of Wallace McHarg Roberts and Todd: *Woodlands New Community: An Ecological Inventory* (Philadelphia: WMRT, 1974); *Woodlands New Community: An Ecological Plan* (Philadelphia: WMRT, 1974); *Woodlands New Community: Phase One Land Planning and Design Principles* (Philadelphia: WMRT, 1974); and *Woodlands New Community: Guidelines for Site Planning* (Philadelphia: WMRT, 1973).

27. Juneja and Veltman, "Natural Drainage in Woodlands," p. 156.

28. Ibid., p. 157.

Chapter 8. Urban Plants: Struggle for Survival

1. Gene W. Grey and Frederick J. Deneke, *Urban Forestry* (New York: Wiley, 1978), p. 159.
2. Ruth S. Foster, "Roots: Caring for City Trees," *Technology Review* 79 (July/August 1977):33.
3. Ruth S. Foster, "Bio-Engineering for the Urban Ecosystem," in *Metropolitan Tree Improvement Alliance Proceedings* (1978):15.
4. Foster, "Roots," p. 31.
5. New York Times Magazine, March 31, 1918.
6. This controversy is not new. See Keith Thomas, *Man and the Natural World: A History of the Modern Sensibility* (New York: Pantheon, 1983), for a study of its origins and evolution.
7. Carl Bridenbaugh, *Cities in the Wilderness: The First Century of Urban Life in America 1625-1742* (London: Oxford University Press, 1966), p. 244.
8. James A. Schmid, *Urban Vegetation*, Department of Geography Research Paper, no. 161 (Chicago: University of Chicago, 1975), p. 72.
9. Ibid., p. 74.
10. Grey and Deneke, *Urban Forestry*, p. 148.

Chapter 9. Nurturing the Urban Biome

1. Marie Luise Gothein, *A History of Garden Art*, ed. Walter T. Wright (New York: Dutton, 1928), p. 32.
2. T. C. Kozel, M. J. Jansen, and G. T. Hettel, "Which Trees Do Best in the City," *Ohio Report* 63 (January/February 1978):6–9.
3. Linda Jewell, "Planting Trees in City Soils," *Landscape Architecture* 71 (1981):388.
4. Ibid.
5. Kozel, Jansen, and Hettel, "Which Trees Do Best," p. 7.
6. Fred Bartenstein, personal communication.
7. Allan R. Ruff, *Holland and the Ecological Landscape* (Stockport, England: Deanwater Press, 1979), p. 5.
8. Ibid., p. 8.
9. H. J. Bos and J. L. Mol, "The Dutch Example: Native Planting in Holland," in *Nature in Cities*, ed. Ian C. Laurie (Chichester, England: Wiley, 1979), p. 404.
10. Ibid., p. 406.
11. Ruff, *Holland and the Ecological Landscape*, pp. 92–93.
12. Ibid., p. 64.
13. William A. Niering and Richard H. Goodwin, "Creation of Relatively Stable Shrublands with Herbicides: Arresting 'Succession' on Rights-of-Way and Pasture Land," *Ecology* 55 (1974):784–95.
14. Hermann Seiberth, "The 'Railway Track Triangle' Natural Park: When Will They Ever Learn . . . ?" *Anthos* 21 (January 1982).
15. Ibid.
16. Boston Redevelopment Authority, *Boston Urban Wilds*, September 1976, p. 18.
17. Ibid., p. 29.
18. Clark E. Holscher, "City Forests of Europe," *Natural History*, November 1973, p. 53.
19. Frederick Hartmann, "The Chicago Forestry Scheme," *Natural History*, November 1973, p. 72.
20. Robert Cook and James Patterson, "Compost Saves Money in Parkland Restoration," *Compost Science/Land Utilization: Journal of Waste Recycling* 20 (March–April 1979):43–44.

Chapter 10. Pets and Pests

1. A. M. Beck, *The Ecology of Stray Dogs* (Baltimore: York Press, 1973), p. 53.
2. Except where noted, the description of urban habitat characteristics is drawn large-ly from Don Gill and Penelope Bonnett, *Nature in the Urban Landscape: A Study of Urban Ecosystems* (Baltimore: York Press, 1973). This slim volume remains one of the best descriptions of urban animal communities and strategies for their management.
3. Beck, *Stray Dogs*, p. 9.
4. Ibid.
5. James R. Schinner and Darrell L. Gauley, "The Ecology of Urban Raccoons in Cincinnati, Ohio," in *A Symposium on Wildlife in an Urbanizing Environment*, ed. John H. Noyes and Donald R. Porgulske (Amherst: University of Massachusetts Cooperative Extension Service, 1974), p. 129.
6. The description of aquatic habitats and their effect upon fish populations is drawn from Alwyne Wheeler, "Fish in an Urban Environment," in *Nature in Cities*, ed. Ian C. Laurie (Chichester, England: Wiley, 1979).
7. Michael Hounsome, "Bird Life in the City," in Ibid., p. 190.
8. R. J. P. Thearle, "Urban Bird Problems," in *The Problems of Birds and Pests*, Sympo-sia of the Institute of Biology, no. 17, ed. K. K. Murton and U. N. Wright (London: Academic Press, 1966), p. 182.
9. Ibid., p. 183; and Gill and Bonnett, *Nature in Urban Landscape*, p. 11.
10. Louis N. Locke, "Diseases and Parasites in Urban Wildlife," in *Wildlife in Urbaniz-ing Environment*, ed. Noyes and Porgulske, p. 111.
11. Beck, *Stray Dogs*, p. 54. This was prior to New York City's "scoop" law, requiring owners to clean up their pets' feces.
12. Ibid.
13. Richard Field and John A. Lager, *Countermeasures for Pollution from Overflows: The State-of-the-Art* (Cincinnati: U.S. Environmental Protection Agency, 1974), p. 4.
14. Beck, *Stray Dogs*, pp. 51–52.
15. Carl Bridenbaugh, *Cities in the Wilderness: The First Century of Urban Life in Amer-ica 1625–1742* (London: Oxford University Press, 1966), p. 19.
16. A. H. Carding, "The Significance and Dynamics of Stray Dog Populations with Specific Reference to the U.K. and Japan," *Journal of Small Animal Practice* 10 (1969):419–46.
17. Victor E. F. Solman, "Aircraft and Wildlife," in *Wildlife in Urbanizing Environment*, ed. Noyes and Porgulske, p. 138.
18. Ibid.
19. David A. Manski, Larry W. Van Druff, and Vagn Flyger, "Activities of Gray Squir-rels and People in a Downtown Washington, D.C. Park: Management Implications," in *Transactions of the Forty-Sixth North American Wildlife and Natural Resources Conference* (Washington, D.C.: Wildlife Management Institute, 1981):439–54.
20. Tommi L. Brown, Chad P. Dawson, and Robert L. Miller, "Interests and Attitudes of Metropolitan New York Residents about Wildlife," in *Transactions of the Forty-fourth North American Wildlife and Natural Resources Conference* (Washington, D.C.: Wildlife Management Institute, 1979): 289.

Chapter 11. Designing Wildlife Habitats

1. Warren R. Winter and John L. George, "Role of Feeding Stations in Managing Non-Game Bird Habitats in Urban and Suburban Areas," in *Transactions of the Forty-Sixth North American Wildlife and Natural Resources Conference*, ed. Kenneth Sabol (Washington, D.C.: Wildlife Management Institute, 1981), p. 414.
2. Daniel J. Witter, David L. Tilka, and Joseph E. Werner, "Values of Urban Wildlife in Missouri," in *Transactions of the Forth-sixth North American Wildlife and National Resources Conference* (Washington, D.C.: Wildlife Management Institute, 1981), p. 424.
3. Richard M. DeGraaf and Gretchin M. Witman, *Trees, Shrubs, and Vines for Attract-ing Birds: A Manual for the North East* (Amherst: University of Massachusetts Press, 1979); Alexander C. Martin, Herbert S. Zim, and Arnold L. Nelson, *American Wildlife and Plants: A Guide to Wildlife Food Habits* (New York: Dover, 1951).

4. This and many of the subsequent recommendations are taken from Daniel L. Leedy, Robert M. Maestro, and Thomas M. Franklin, *Planning for Wildlife in Cities and Suburbs* (Washington, D.C.: Fish and Wildlife Service, 1978).

5. Michael Hounsome, "Bird Life in the City," in *Nature in Cities*, ed. Ian C. Laurie (Chichester, England: Wiley, 1979), p. 189.

6. Ibid.

7. Richard T. T. Forman, "Interaction among Landscape Elements: A Core of Landscape Ecology," in *Regional Landscape Planning: Proceedings of Educational Sessions, American Society of Landscape Architects*, 1981, p. 45.

8. Jack Ward Thomas and Ronald A. Dickson, "Cemetery Ecology," in *A Symposium on Wildlife in an Urbanizing Environment*, ed. John H. Noyes and Donald R. Porgulske (Amherst: University of Massachusetts Cooperative Extension Service, 1974), p. 107.

9. Ibid., p. 108.

10. Robert D. Williamson, "Birds in Washington, D.C.," in *Wildlife in Urbanizing Environment*, ed. Noyes and Porgulske, pp. 134–35.

11. DeGraaf and Witman, *Attracting Birds*, p. 42.

12. Don Gill and Penelope Bonnett, *Nature in the Urban Landscape: A Study of Urban Ecosystems* (Baltimore: York Press, 1973), pp. 78–79.

13. Ibid., pp. 129–31.

14. Brown et al., 290.

15. Ibid.

16. Witter et al., pp. 429–30.

Chapter 12. The City as an Infernal Machine

1. C. S. Holling and Gordon Orians, "Toward an Urban Ecology," *Ecological Society of America Bulletin* 52 (1971):5.

2. Abel Wolman, "The Metabolism of Cities," *Scientific American*, March 1965, p. 180.

3. Ibid.

4. U.S. Council on Environmental Quality, *Environmental Quality—The Tenth Annual Report of the Council on Environmental Quality* (Washington, D.C.: U.S. Government Printing Office, 1979), p. 256.

5. U.S. Council on Environmental Quality, *Environmental Quality—The Eighth Annual Report of the Council on Environmental Quality* (Washington, D.C.: U.S. Government Printing Office, 1977), p. 50

6. City of New York, *From Landfill to Park: An Experiment in Construction Waste Management at the Pennsylvania Avenue Landfill Site* (New York: Department of City Planning, 1974), p. 7.

7. U.S. Council on Environmental Quality, *Eighth Annual Report*, p. 56.

8. U.S. Council on Environmental Quality, *Eighth Annual Report*, p. 50.

9. The account of the Love Canal tragedy is based upon the description in Samuel S. Epstein, Lester O. Brown, and Carl Pope, *Hazardous Waste in America* (San Francisco: Sierra Club Books, 1982), pp. 89–132. This volume documents many other instances of water and earth contaminated by hazardous waste.

10. Ibid., pp. 448–49.

11. U.S. Council on Environmental Quality, *Environmental Quality—The Ninth Annual Report of the Council on Environmental Quality* (Washington, D.C.: U.S. Government Printing Office, 1978), p. 160.

12. U.S. Council on Environmental Quality, *Eighth Annual Report*, p. 46.

13. Wolman, "Metabolism of Cities," p. 182.

14. Nelson M. Blake, *Water for the Cities: A History of the Urban Water Supply Problem in the United States* (Syracuse, N.Y.: Syracuse University Press, 1956), p. 132.

15. Gary B. Griggs and John A. Gilchrist, *Geologic Hazards, Resources, and Environmental Planning* (Belmont, Calif.: Wadsworth, 1983), p. 303.

16. Ibid.

17. Ibid.

18. M. Richard Nalbandian, "Some Public Health Aspects of Physical Planning for Human Settlements." Mimeographed, 1982.

Chapter 13. Designing the Urban Ecosystem

1. Stanley K. Schultz and Clay McShane, "To Engineer the Metropolis: Sewers, Sanitation, and City Planning in Late Nineteenth-Century America," *Journal of American History* 65 (1978):403.
2. George Waring, "The Disposal of the City's Wastes," *North American Review* 160 (July 1895):52.
3. Schultz and McShane, "To Engineer the Metropolis," p. 395.
4. C. S. Holling and Gordon Orians, "Towards an Urban Ecology," *Ecological Society of America Bulletin* 52 (1971):6.
5. William E. Cooper and Raymond D. Vlasen, "Ecological Concepts and Applications to Planning," in *Environment: A New Focus for Land Use Planning*, ed. Donald M. McAllister (Washington, D. C.: National Science Foundation, 1973), p. 199.
6. Frederick Law Olmsted, *Public Parks and the Enlargement of Towns* (Cambridge, Mass.: Riverside Press, 1870), p. 8.
7. Granville H. Sewell, *Environmental Quality Management* (Englewood Cliffs, N. J.: Prentice-Hall, 1975), p. 152.
8. Milton F. Pikarsky, "Chicago's Northwest Incinerator," *Civil Engineering*, September 1971, p. 55.
9. The description of Arcata's experiment is based on Robert Weireter, "Waste Not Wastewater: West: The Arcata Experiment," *American Forests* 88 (1982).
10. William J. Marrazzo, "The Selling of Waste," *EPA Journal* 7 (August 1981):26.
11. Ibid., p. 27.
12. Ibid.
13. Robert K. Bastian, "Natural Treatment Systems in Wastewater Treatment and Sludge Management," *Civil Engineering* (May 1982), p. 65.
14. Ibid.
15. Ibid., p. 63.
16. Wallace McHarg Roberts and Todd, *Environmental Resources of the Toronto Central Waterfront* (Philadelphia, Pa.: WMRT, 1976).
17. City of Dallas, *The Dallas Ecological Study* (Dallas: Department of Planning and Urban Development, 1973).
18. City of Dallas, *Natural Open Space Plan*, (Dallas: Department of Urban Planning, 1979); City of Dallas, *The Escarpment Report: Environmental Assessment and Development Guidelines for the White Rock Escarpment* (Dallas: Department of Planning and Development, 1982).

BIBLIOGRAPHY

A Note on the Sources

Over the past three decades, natural scientists have amassed considerable data on urban, as distinguished from rural, ecosystems, and have described the characteristics of urban climate and air quality, urban geology and soils, urban hydrology and water quality, and urban vegetation and wildlife. Unfortunately, much of this now considerable literature has been published only in specialized scientific journals and is written in the technical language of the individual academic disciplines. The information is therefore not readily available to design and planning professionals or laymen, nor is it tailored to their needs.

This bibliography lists books and articles that will permit the interested reader to pursue a topic further, as well as sources upon which the present volume relied for documentation. To facilitate its use, the bibliography is divided into eight sections, corresponding roughly to the parts of the book. A short review of the literature introduces each section and identifies the most useful sources.

Excellent, comprehensive monographs exist for certain areas of the urban physical environment, like climate, geology, and hydrology, but are lacking in others. Readers wishing to pursue a further interest in the city's biological environment, its soil, vegetation, and wildlife, for example, must read a selection of articles and books, each of which treats only a small part of the subject. Articles in professional and scientific journals are available in most large university libraries, but papers collected in conference proceedings are often difficult to obtain. Many case studies are described only in technical reports and papers intended for limited distribution. To date, there are no indices of the literature that cover the field adequately or comprehensively.

The Background: History and Theory

The literature on the history of cities and urban form is extensive; the following sources merely provide an introduction. Mumford's *The City in History* traces the evolution of the city from its origins to the twentieth century and is an excellent introduction to the subject. Morris's *History of Urban Form* is well illustrated and provides a valuable overview of urban form as it developed from ancient cities through the nineteenth century. Many other sources document the history of cities by looking at a particular period, a single country, or a specific city. Reps's *Making of Urban America,* which is lavishly illustrated with historic plans and views, provides a particularly good introduction to the history of city planning in the United States. Carcopino's *Daily Life in Ancient Rome* and Bridenbaugh's *Cities in the Wilderness* and *Cities in Revolt* give a vivid picture of the life and layout of ancient Rome and colonial North American cities respectively. An abundant literature portrays the development of urban form in individual cities; examples include Rasmussen's book on London, Poète's books on Paris, and Whitehill's, Warner's, and Zaitzevsky's books on Boston. Such books as these permit an appreciation for how urban form expresses the natural setting and cultural values of a particular place or time and how common activities of the human community were accommodated. Lynch's *Theory of Good City Form* reviews how urban settlement patterns have responded to social values and how they influence the health and welfare of all city residents. The histories of specific elements of urban form have also been treated separately. Rasmussen's *Towns and Buildings,* for example, is a lively book about city buildings and the streets and squares between them, and Chadwick's *The Park and the Town* describes the new role that parks began to play in the cities of nineteenth- and twentieth-century Britain.

The conflict between city and countryside is an old one. "Of Cyvile and Uncyvile Life" (Hazlett, ed.) is a sixteenth-century dialogue on the virtues of city versus country life. Williams puts that dialogue into perspective in a survey of how English literature has romanticized the countryside and criticized the city. Weimer and the Whites document an anti-urban strain in American culture and literature. Berry's articles yield an insight into the modern conflict between city and countryside and the implications that conflict has today for urban form. Utopian literature often provides both a criticism of the contemporary city and a vision of what the city might be; More, Howard, Bellamy, and Richardson all offered alternative urban forms.

Abercrombie, Patrick. "Ideal Cities, No. 2 Victoria." *The Town Planning Review* 9 (September 1921):15–20.

Alberti, Leone Battista. *Ten Books on Architecture.* Edited by Joseph Rykwert. New York: Transatlantic Arts, 1966.

Appleyard, Donald. *Livable Streets.* Berkeley and Los Angeles: University of California Press, 1981.

Atkinson, William. *The Orientation of Buildings, or Planning for Sunlight.* New York: Wiley, 1912.

Bellamy, Edward. *Looking Backward: 2000–1887.* Boston: Houghton Mifflin, 1888.

Benevolo, Leonardo. *The Origins of Modern Town Planning.* Cambridge, Mass.: MIT Press, 1967.

Berry, Brian J. L. "The Urban Problem." In *The Farm and the City: Rivals or Allies?* Edited by Archibald M. Woodruff. Englewood Cliffs, N. J.: Prentice-Hall, 1980.

_____. "Urbanization and Counterurbanization in the United States." In *Changing Cities: A Challenge to Planning. Annals of the American Academy of Political and Social Science* 45(September 1980):13–20.

Blumenfeld, Hans. *The Modern Metropolis: Its Origins, Growth, Characteristics, and Planning.* Edited by Paul D. Spreiregen. Cambridge, Mass.: MIT Press, 1972.

_____. "Theory of City Form, Past and Present." *Journal of the Society of Architectural Historians* 8 (July–December 1949):7–15.

Branch, Melville C., ed. *Urban Planning Theory.* Community Design Series, no. 15. Stroudsberg, Pa.: Dowden, Hutchinson, and Ross, 1975.

Braun, George, and Hogenberg, Franz. *Old European Cities.* Edited by Arthur Hibbert and Ruthardt Oehme. London: Thames and Hudson, n.d.

Bridenbaugh, Carl. *Cities in Revolt: Urban Life in America 1743–1776.* London: Oxford University Press, 1971.

_____. *Cities in the Wilderness: The First Century of Urban Life in America 1625–1742.* London: Oxford University Press, 1971.

Burke, Gerald L. *The Making of Dutch Towns.* London: Cleaver-Hume Press, 1956.

_____. *Towns in the Making.* London: Edward Arnold, 1971.

Carcopino, Jérôme. *Daily Life in Ancient Rome.* New Haven: Yale University Press, 1941.

Chadwick, Edwin. *Report on the Sanitary Condition of the Labouring Population of Great Britain.* London: W. Clowes and Sons, 1842.

Chadwick, George F. *The Park and the Town.* London: Architectural Press, 1966.

Cosgrove, J. J. *History of Sanitation.* Pittsburgh: Standard Sanitary Manufacturing Co., 1909.

Cranz, Galen. *The Politics of Park Design.* Cambridge, Mass.: MIT Press, 1982.

Creese, Walter L., ed. *The Legacy of Raymond Unwin: A Human Pattern for Planning.* Cambridge, Mass.: MIT Press, 1967.

_____. *The Search for Environment.* New Haven: Yale University Press, 1966.

De La Croix, Horst. *Military Considerations in City Planning: Fortifications.* New York: George Braziller, 1972.

Doxiadis, C. A. *Anthropolis: City for Human Development.* New York: Norton, 1974.

Eliot, Charles. *A Report upon the Opportunities for Public Open Spaces in the Metropolitan District of Boston, Massachusetts.* Boston: Wright & Potter Printing Co., 1893.

Fabos, Julius Gy.; Milde, Gordon T.; and Weinmayr, Michael. *Frederick Law Olmsted, Sr.: Founder of Landscape Architecture in America.* Amherst: University of Massachusetts Press, 1968.

Fein, Albert. *Frederick Law Olmsted and the American Environmental Tradition.* New York: George Braziller, 1972.

————. *Landscape into Cityscape.* Ithaca, N.Y.: Cornell University Press, 1967.

Firey, Walter. *Land Use in Central Boston.* Cambridge, Mass.: Harvard University Press, 1947.

Fisher, Robert Moore, ed. *The Metropolis in Modern Life.* Garden City, N.Y.: Doubleday, 1955.

Fitch, James Marston. *American Building: The Environmental Forces That Shape It.* New York: Schocken, 1975.

Frankfort, Henri. "Town Planning in Ancient Mesopotamia." *Town Planning Review* 21 (July 1950):98–115.

Galantay, Ervin Y. *New Towns: Antiquity to the Present.* New York: George Braziller, 1975.

Gallion, Arthur B., and Eisner, Simon. *The Urban Pattern: City Planning and Design.* 4th ed. New York: Van Nostrand Reinhold, 1983.

Geddes, Patrick. *Cities in Evolution.* London: Williams and Norgate, 1915.

Glaab, Charles N. *The American City: A Documentary History.* Homewood, Ill.: Dorsey, 1963.

Glikson, Artur. *The Ecological Basis of Planning.* Edited by Lewis Mumford. The Hague: Martinus Nijhoff, 1971.

Gothein, Marie Luise. *A History of Garden Art.* Edited by Walter P. Wright. 2 vols. New York: Dutton, 1928.

Haller, William. *The Puritan Frontier: Town-planting in New England Colonial Development 1630–1660.* New York: Columbia University Press, 1951.

Handlin, Oscar, and Burchard, John, eds. *The Historian and the City.* Cambridge, Mass.: MIT Press, 1963.

Hazlett, W. C., ed. "Of Cyvile and Uncyvile Life." In *Inedited Tracts: Illustrating the Manners, Opinions, and Occupations of Englishmen during the Sixteenth and Seventeenth Centuries.* Roxburgh Library, 1968.

Heckscher, August. *Open Spaces: The Life of American Cities.* New York: Harper & Row, 1977.

Hill, Leonard, and Campbell, Argyll. *Health and Environment.* London: Edward Arnold, 1925.

Howard, Ebenezer. *Garden Cities of To-Morrow.* Edited by F. J. Osborne. Cambridge, Mass.: MIT Press, 1965.

Howe, M. A. DeWolfe. *Boston Common: Scenes from Four Centuries.* Cambridge, Mass.: Riverside Press, 1910.

Huth, Hans. *Nature and the American: Three Centuries of Changing Attitudes.* Berkeley and Los Angeles: University of California Press, 1957.

Jacobsen, Thorkild, and Adams, Robert M. "Salt and Silt in Ancient Mesopotamian Agriculture." *Science* 128 (1958):1251–58.

Jowett, Benjamin, and Twining, Thomas, trans. *Aristotle's Politics and Poetics.* New York: Viking, 1957.

Lampl, Paul. *Cities and Planning in the Ancient Near East.* New York: George Braziller, 1968.

Lynch, Kevin. "The Pattern of the Metropolis." In *The Future Metropolis,* edited by Kevin Lynch. New York: George Braziller, 1961.

————. *A Theory of Good City Form.* Cambridge, Mass.: MIT Press, 1981.

Marx, Leo. *The Machine in the Garden.* New York: Oxford University Press, 1964.

McHarg, Ian. *Design With Nature.* New York: Natural History Press, 1969.

Meller, Helen E., ed. *The Ideal City.* Leicester: Leicester University Press, 1979.

More, Sir Thomas. *Utopia.* Edited by Edward Surtz, S. J. New Haven: Yale University Press, 1964.

Morris, A. E. J. *History of Urban Form: Prehistory to the Renaissance.* London: George Goodwin, 1972.

Mumford, Lewis. *The City in History.* New York: Harcourt Brace Jovanovich, 1961.

Nash, Roderick. *Wilderness and the American Mind.* New Haven: Yale University Press, 1967.

Olmsted, Frederick Law. *Public Parks and the Enlargement of Towns.* Cambridge, Mass.: Riverside Press, 1870.

Olmsted, Frederick Law, Jr., and Kimball, Theodora, eds. *Frederick Law Olmsted: Landscape Architect, 1822–1903.* 2 vols. New York: Putnam, 1922–28.

Pinkney, David H. *Napoleon III and the Rebuilding of Paris.* Princeton, N.J.: Princeton University Press, 1958.

Poète, Marcel. *Formation et évolution de Paris.* Paris: Société d'Édition et de Publications, 1910.

————. *La promenade à Paris au XVII siècle.* Paris: Librairie Armand Colin, 1913.

————. *Une vie de cité Paris,* vol. 3. Paris: Éditions A. Picard, 1931.

Pundt, Hermann G. *Schinkel's Berlin: A Study in Environmental Planning.* Cambridge, Mass.: Harvard University Press, 1972.

Rasmussen, Steen Eiler. *London: The Unique City.* Cambridge, Mass.: MIT Press, 1967.

————. *Towns and Buildings.* Cambridge, Mass.: MIT Press, 1969.

Reps, John W. "The Green Belt Concept." *Town and Country Planning* 28 (1960):246–51.

————. *The Making of Urban America: A History of City Planning in the United States.* Princeton, N.J.: Princeton Unversity Press, 1965.

————. *Town Planning in Frontier America.* Princeton, N.J.: Princeton University Press, 1969.

Richardson, Benjamin Ward. *The Health of a Nation.* London: Dawsons of Pall Mall, 1965.

————. *Hygeia: A City of Health.* London: Macmillan, 1876.

Robinson, Charles Mulford. *The Improvement of Towns and Cities.* New York: Putnam, 1901.

————. *The Width and Arrangement of Streets: A Study in Town Planning.* New York: Engineering News Publishing Co., 1911.

Roper, Laura Wood. *A Biography of Frederick Law Olmsted.* Baltimore: Johns Hopkins University Press, 1973.

Saalman, Howard. *Haussman: Paris Transformed.* New York: George Braziller, 1971.

————. *Medieval Cities.* New York: George Braziller, 1968.

Scientific American. *Cities.* New York: Knopf, 1966.

————. *Cities, Their Origin, Growth and Human Impact.* San Francisco: W. H. Freeman, 1973.

Shurtleff, Nathaniel B. *A Topographical and Historical Description of Boston.* Boston: Rockwell and Churchill, 1890.

Stalley, Marshall. *Patrick Geddes: Spokesman for Man and the Environment.* New Brunswick, N.J.: Rutgers University Press, 1972.

Stein, Clarence S. *Towards New Towns for America.* Cambridge, Mass.: MIT Press, 1973.

Strauss, Leo. *The City and Man.* Chicago: Rand McNally, 1964.

Sutton, S. B. *Civilizing American Cities: A Selection of Frederick Law Olmsted's Writings on City Landscapes.* Cambridge, Mass.: MIT Press, 1971.

Thorpe, H. *Report of the Departmental Committee of Inquiry into Allotments.* London: Her Majesty's Stationery Office, 1969.

Thomas, Keith. *Man and the Natural World; A History of the Modern Sensibility.* New York: Pantheon, 1983.

Tunnard, Christopher. *The City of Man.* New York: Scribner, 1953.

Vigier, François, and Serageldin, Mona. "Urban Needs of Modernizing Societies: New Directions in Planning." Paper delivered at the Symposium on the Arab City: Its Character and Islamic Cultural Heritage, Medina, Saudi Arabia, March 1981.

Vitruvius. *The Ten Books on Architecture.* Cambridge, Mass.: Harvard University Press, 1914.

Warner, Sam Bass, Jr. *The Private City.* Philadelphia: University of Pennsylvania Press, 1968.

————. *Streetcar Suburbs: The Process of Growth in Boston, 1870–1900.* 2nd ed. Cambridge, Mass.: Harvard University Press, 1978.

————. *The Urban Wilderness: A History of the American City.* New York: Harper & Row, 1972.

————. *The Way We Really Live: Social Change in Metropolitan Boston since 1920.* Boston: Boston Public Library, 1977.

Weimer, David R., ed. *City and Country in America.* New York: Appleton-Century-Crofts, 1962.

White, Morton, and White, Lucia. *The Intellectual versus the City.* New York: New American Library, 1964.

Whitehill, Walter Muir. *Boston: A Topographical History.* 2nd ed. Cambridge, Mass.: Harvard University Press, 1959.

Williams, Raymond. *The Country and the City.* New York: Oxford University Press, 1973.

Wingo, Lowdon, Jr. *Cities and Space: The Future Use of Urban Land.* Baltimore: Johns Hopkins University Press, 1967.

Woodruff, Archibald M., ed. *The Farm and the City: Rivals or Allies?* Englewood Cliffs, N.J.: Prentice-Hall, 1980.

Wycherly, R. E. *How the Greeks Built Cities.* London: Macmillan, 1949.

Zaitzevsky, Cynthia. *Frederick Law Olmsted and the Boston Park System.* Cambridge, Mass.: Harvard University Press, Belknap Press, 1982.

General Sources on Nature in the City

Marsh's *Man and Nature* is a pioneering nineteenth-century study that treats the impact of human activities on the natural environment. Few authors since Marsh have attempted to write an overview of the topic. Most recent literature consists of anthologies or books by multiple authors. *Man's Role in Changing the Face of the Earth*, edited by Thomas, remains a classic compilation. Detwyler's *Man's Impact on Environment* provided an update to that earlier anthology. Both treat not only the city, but human impact on nature in general. *Urbanization and Environment*, edited by Detwyler and Marcus, and *Nature in Cities*, edited by Laurie, deal specifically with the natural environment of the city; in both volumes, some aspects of the urban natural environment are described in great detail, others are neglected. The *Annual Report* of the U.S. Council on Environmental Quality has, since 1970, provided a valuable summary of information on air, water, and soil pollution and on energy resources and waste disposal problems in the United States.

Berry, Brian J. L., and Horton, Frank E. *Urban Environmental Management.* Englewood Cliffs, N.J.: Prentice-Hall, 1974.

Burton, Ian; Kates, Robert W.; and White, Gilbert F. *The Environment as Hazard.* New York: Oxford University Press, 1978.

Dansereau, Pierre, ed. *Challenge for Survival: Land, Air, and Water for Man in Megalopolis.* New York: Columbia University Press, 1970.

Detwyler, Thomas R., ed. *Man's Impact on Environment.* New York: McGraw-Hill, 1971.

Detwyler, Thomas R., and Marcus, M. G., eds. *Urbanization and Environment: The Physical Geography of the City.* Belmont, Calif.: Duxbury Press, 1972.

Epstein, Samuel S.; Brown, Lester O.; and Pope, Carl. *Hazardous Waste in America.* San Francisco: Sierra Club Books, 1982.

Laurie, Ian C., ed. *Nature in Cities: The Natural Environment in the Design and Development of Urban Green Space.* Chichester, England: Wiley, 1979.

Marsh, George Perkins. *Man and Nature.* 1864. Reprint, Cambridge, Mass.: Harvard University Press, Belknap Press, 1974.

Massachusetts Institute of Technology. *Man's Impact on the Global Environment: Assessments and Recommendations for Action.* Cambridge, Mass.: MIT Press, 1970.

Matthews, W. H.; Smith, F. E.; and Goldberg, E. D., eds. *Man's Impact on Terrestrial and Oceanic Ecosystems.* Cambridge, Mass.: MIT Press, 1971.

Melosi, Martin V. "Urban Pollution: Historical Perspective Needed." *Environmental Review* 3 (Spring 1979):37–45.

Sewell, Granville H. *Environmental Quality Management.* Englewood Cliffs, N.J.: Prentice-Hall, 1975.

Spirn, Anne Whiston. "The Role of Natural Processes in the Design of Cities." In *Changing Cities: A Challenge to Planning.* In the *Annals of the American Association of Political and Social Scientists* 451 (September 1980):98–105.

Thomas, William L., Jr., ed. *Man's Role in Changing the Face of the Earth.* 2 vol. Chicago: University of Chicago Press, 1956.

U.S. Council on Environmental Quality. *Environmental Quality—The First Annual Report of the Council on Environmental Quality.* Washington, D.C.: U.S. Government Printing Office, 1970.

U.S. Council on Environmental Quality. *Environmental Quality—The Second Annual Report of the Council on Environmental Quality.* Washington, D.C.: U.S. Government Printing Office, 1971.

_____. *Environmental Quality—The Third Annual Report of the Council on Environmental Quality.* Washington, D.C.: U.S. Government Printing Office, 1972.

_____. *Environmental Quality—The Fourth Annual Report on the Council on Environmental Quality.* Washington, D.C.: U.S. Government Printing Office, 1973.

_____. *Environmental Quality—The Fifth Annual Report of the Council on Environmental Quality.* Washington, D.C.: U.S. Government Printing Office, 1974.

_____. *Environmental Quality—The Sixth Annual Report of the Council on Environmental Quality.* Washington, D.C.: U.S. Government Printing Office, 1975.

_____. *Environmental Quality—The Seventh Annual Report of the Council on Environmental Quality.* Washington, D.C.: U.S. Government Printing Office, 1976.

_____. *Environmental Quality—The Eighth Annual Report of the Council on Environmental Quality.* Washington, D.C.: U.S. Government Printing Office, 1977.

_____. *Environmental Quality—The Ninth Annual Report of the Council on Environmental Quality.* Washington, D.C.: U.S. Government Printing Office, 1978.

_____. *Environmental Quality—The Tenth Annual Report of the Council on Environmental Quality.* Washington, D.C.: U.S. Government Printing Office, 1979.

U.S. Forest Service. *Children, Nature, and the Urban Environment: Proceedings of a Symposium Fair.* Upper Darby, Pa.: Northeastern Forest Experiment Station, 1977.

White, Gilbert F., and Haas, Eugene J. *Assessment of Research on Natural Hazards.* Cambridge, Mass.: MIT Press, 1975.

Urban Air

The characteristics of urban climate are well documented, and there are excellent reviews of the literature: Peterson in 1968, Chandler in 1968, and Oke in 1974. Landsberg's *The Urban Climate* provides an overview of the subject and incorporates the most recent research in urban climatology. Chandler's *Urban Climatology and Its Relevance to Urban Design* is particularly useful to urban planners and designers. The volumes edited by Stern are standard texts on air quality and its management. Rydell and Schwarz's review article on air quality and urban form is a good survey of the issues and of work done prior to 1968. Hutchinson et al. and Knowles address how urban form and urban climate influence energy consumption. Both Olgyay and Givoni apply principles of climatology to the form of settlements and buildings and discuss the variables that affect human comfort; Plumley examines the factors that influence human comfort in urban open spaces. Penwarden and Wise, Gandemer and Guyot, and Durgin and Chock demonstrate the problems and varieties of urban wind conditions.

Altshuller, A. P. "Composition and Reactions of Air Pollutants in Community Atmospheres." In *Urban Climates*, Technical Note 108. Brussels: World Meteorological Organizations, 1968.

Arens, Edward. "On Considering Pedestrian Winds During Building Design." In *Proceedings: International Workshop on Wind Tunnel Modeling Criteria and Techniques in Civil Engineering Applications*, Gaithersburg, Md., April 1982. Ed. Timothy A. Reinhold. Cambridge: Cambridge University Press, 1983.

Arens, Edward, and Ballanti, Donald. "Outdoor Comfort of Pedestrians in Cities." In *Proceedings: Metropolitan Physical Environment*, U.S. Forest Service General Technical Report NE-25. Upper Darby, Pa.: Northeastern Forest Experiment Station, 1977.

Arnold, George, and Edgerley, E., Jr. "Urban Development in Air Pollution Basins: An Appeal to the Planners for Help." *Journal of the Air Pollution Control Association* 17 (1967):235–37.

Beuchley, Robert W.; Van Bruggen, John; and Truppi, Lawrence E. "Heat Island = Death Island?" *Environmental Research* 5 (1972):85–92.

Bidwell, R. G. S., and Fraser, D. E. "Carbon Monoxide Uptake and Metabolism by Leaves." *Canadian Journal of Botany* 50 (1972):1435–39.

Bove, John L., and Sienenberg, Stanley. "Airborne Lead and Carbon Monoxide at 45th Street, New York City." *Science* 167 (1970):986–87.

Brice, Robert M., and Reosler, Joseph F. "The Exposure to Carbon Monoxide of Occupants of Vehicles Moving in Heavy Traffic." *Journal of the Air Pollution Control Association* 16 (1966):597–600.

Carpenter, Alan B.; True, Douglas K.; and Stanek, Edward J. "Leaf Burning as a Significant Source of Urban Air Pollution." *Journal of the Air Pollution Control Association* 27 (1977):574–76.

Cermak, J. E. "Applications of Fluid Mechanics to Wind Engineering—A Freeman Scholar Lecture." *Journal of Fluids Engineering* 97 (1975):9–38.

Chandler, T. J. "Absolute and Relative Humidities in Towns." *Bulletin of the American Meteorological Society* 48 (1967):394–99.

_____. "Night-Time Temperatures in Relation to Leicester's Urban Form." *Meteorological Magazine* 96 (1967):244–50.

_____. *Selected Bibliography on Urban Climate.* Geneva: World Meteorological Organization, 1968.

_____. *Urban Climatology and Its Relevance to Urban Design,* Technical Note 149. Geneva: World Meteorological Organization, 1976.

_____. "Urban Climatology: Inventory and Prospect." In *Urban Climates,* Technical Note 108. Brussels: World Meteorological Organization, 1968.

_____. "Wind as a Factor of Urban Temperatures: A Survey in North-East London." *Weather* 15 (1960):204–13.

Clairborne, Robert. *Climate, Man, and History.* New York: Norton, 1970.

Clarke, John F. "Some Climatological Aspects of Heat Waves in the Contiguous United States." *Environmental Research* 5 (1972):76–84.

_____. "Some Effects of the Urban Structure on Heat Mortality." *Environmental Research* 5 (1972):93–104.

Clarke, John F., and Bach, W. "Comparison of the Comfort Conditions in Different Urban and Suburban Microenvironments." *International Journal of Biometeorology,* January 1971, pp. 41–54.

Daines, Robert H.; Motto, Harry; and Chilko, Daniel M. "Atmospheric Lead: Its Relationship to Traffic Volume and Proximity to Highways." *Environmental Science and Technology* 4 (1970):318–22.

Davidson, Ben. "A Summary of the New York Urban Air Pollution Dynamics Research Program." *Journal of the Air Pollution Control Association* 17 (1967):154–58.

Deering, Robert B. "Technology of the Cooling Effect of Trees and Shrubs." *Housing and Building in Hot Humid and Hot Dry Climates.* Washington, D.C.: National Academy of Sciences, 1953.

DeWalle, David R. "Manipulating Urban Vegetation for Residential Energy Conservation." In *Proceedings: National Urban Forestry Conference, Washington, D.C., November 13–16, 1978,* edited by George Hopkins. Syracuse: State University of New York, College of Environmental Science and Forestry, 1980.

Durgin, Frank H., and Chock, Alfred W. "Pedestrian Level Winds: A Brief Review." *Journal of the Structural Division, Proceedings of American Society of Civil Engineers* 108 (1982):1751–67.

Evans, Martin. *Housing, Comfort, and Climate.* London and New York: Architectural Press and Wiley, 1980.

Evelyn, John. *Fumifugium: Or the Inconvenience of the Aer and Smoake of London Dissipated.* Oxford: Old Ashmolean Reprint, 1930.

Everett, Michael D. "Roadside Air Pollution Hazards in Recreational Land Use Planning." *AIP Journal* 40 (March 1974):83–89.

Federer, C. A. "Effects of Trees in Modifying Urban Microclimates." In *Trees and Forests in an Urbanizing Environment.* Planning and Resource Development Series, no. 17. Amherst: University of Massachusetts Cooperative Extension Service, 1971.

Fennelly, Paul F. "The Origin and Influence of Airborne Particulates." *American Scientist* 64 (January–February 1976):46–56

Franke, Erhard, ed. *City Climate: Data and Aspects for City Planning.* Translated for EPA by Literature Research Company. TR-79-0795. FBW—A Publication of Research, Building, and Living, no. 108. Stuttgart, West Germany: Karl Kramer, 1976.

Fuggle, R. F., and Oke, T. R. "Infra-Red Flux Divergence and the Urban Heat Island." In

Urban Climates, Technical Note 108. Brussels: World Meteorological Organization, 1968.

Gajzago, L. "Variation of Global Radiation in Budapest." In *Urban Climates,* Technical Note 108. Brussels: World Meteorological Organization, 1968.

Gandemer, J., and Guyot, A. *Intégration du phénomène vent dans la conception du milieu bâti.* Paris: Ministère de la Qualité de la Vie, 1976.

Geiger, Rudolf. *Climate Near the Ground.* 2nd ed. Cambridge, Mass.: Harvard University Press, 1965.

Georgii, H. W. "The Effects of Air Pollution on Urban Climates." In *Urban Climates,* Technical Note 108. Brussels: World Meteorological Organization, 1968.

Givoni, B. *Man, Climate and Architecture.* 2nd rev. ed. London: Applied Science Publishers, 1976.

Godin, Gaetan; Wright, Geoff; and Shepard, Roy, J. "Urban Exposure to Carbon Monoxide." *Archives of Environmental Health* 25 (1972):305–13.

Haagen-Smit, A. J. "Carbon Monoxide Levels in City Driving." *Archives of Environmental Health* 12 (1966):548–51.

Hanna, Steven R. "A Simple Method of Calculating Dispersion from Urban Area Sources." *Journal of the Air Pollution Control Association* 21 (1971):774–77.

Heidorn, K. C. "A Chronology of Events in the History of Air Pollution Meteorology to 1970." *Bulletin of the American Meteorological Society* 59 (1978):1589–97.

Heisler, Gordon, and Herrington, Lee P. "Selection of Trees for Modifying Metropolitan Climate." *Better Trees for Metropolitan Landscapes Symposium Proceedings,* edited by F. Santamour, H. D. Gerhold, and S. Little. U.S. Forest Service General Technical Report NE-22. Upper Darby, Pa.: Northeast Forest Experiment Station, 1976.

Herrington, Lee P. "Urban Vegetation and Microclimate." In *Proceedings: National Urban Forestry Conference, Washington, D. C., November 13–16, 1978.* Edited by George Hopkins. Syracuse: State University of New York, College of Environmental Science and Forestry, 1980.

Herrington, Lee P., and Vittum, J. S. "Human Thermal Comfort in Urban Outdoor Spaces." In *Proceedings: Metropolitan Physical Environment.* U.S. Forest Service General Technical Report NE-25. Upper Darby, Pa.: Northeastern Forest Experiment Station, 1977.

Hill, A. Clyde. "Vegetation: A Sink for Atmospheric Pollutants." *Journal of the Air Pollution Control Association* 21 (1971):341–46.

Hoffman, U. "Problems of the City Climate of Stuttgart." In *City Climate: Data and Aspects for City Planning.* FBW—A Publication of Research, Building, and Living. Erhard Franke, ed. Translated for EPA by Literature Research Company. TR-79-0795. Stuttgart, West Germany: Karl Kramer, 1976.

House Beautiful. "The Climate Controlled House," October 1949–January 1951.

Hutchinson, Boyd A.; Taylor, Fred G.; Wendt, Robert L.; and the Critical Review Panel. *Use of Vegetation to Ameliorate Building Microclimate: An Assessment of Energy Conservation Potentials.* Environmental Sciences Division Publication no. 19103. Oak Ridge, Tenn.: Oak Ridge National Laboratory, 1982.

Jaffe, Louis S. "Carbon Monoxide in the Biosphere: Sources, Distribution, and Concentrations." *Journal of Geophysical Research* 78 (1973):5293–305.

Johnson, Warren B.; Ludwig, F. L.; Dabberdt, W. F.; and Allen, R. J. "An Urban Diffusion Simulation Model for Carbon Monoxide." *Journal of the Air Pollution Control Association* 23 (1973):490–98.

Kaufman, Werner. "Stuttgart Cleans the Air." *Landscape Architecture* 57 (1967):176.

Kleiner, Beth C., and Spengler, John D. "Carbon Monoxide Exposures of Boston Bicyclists." *Journal of the Air Pollution Control Association* 26 (1976):147–49.

Knowles, Ralph. "Solar Access and Urban Form." *The American Institute of Architects Journal* 46 (February 1980):42–49.

————. *Sun, Rhythm, Form.* Cambridge, Mass.: MIT Press, 1981.

Kopec, Richard J. "Daily Spatial and Secular Variations of Atmospheric Humidity in a Small City." *Journal of Applied Meteorology* 12 (1973):639–48.

Kuhn, Eric. "Air Flow around Buildings." *Architectural Forum* 107 (September 1957):166–68.

————. "Planning the City's Climate." *Landscape* 8 (1957):3.

Kupchik, George J., and Franz, Gerald J. "Solid Waste, Air Pollution, and Health." *Journal of the Air Pollution Control Association* 26 (1976):116–18.

Kurtzweg, Jerry A. "Urban Planning and Air Pollution Control: A Review of Selected Recent Research." *AIP Journal* (1973):82–92.

Landsberg, Helmut E. "The Assessment of Human Bioclimate: A Limited Review of Physical Parameters." In *Urban Climates*, Technical Note 108. Brussels: World Meteorological Organization, 1968.

_____. "Atmospheric Changes in a Growing Community: The Columbia, Maryland Experience." *Urban Ecology* 4 (1979):53–81.

_____. "Bioclimatology of Housing." *Meteorological Monographs* 2 (1954):81–98.

_____. "Climates and Urban Planning." In *Urban Climates*, Technical Note 108. Brussels: World Meteorological Organization, 1968.

_____. "Microclimatology." *Architectural Forum* 86 (March 1947):113–19.

_____. "Micrometeorological Temperature Differentiation through Urbanization." In *Urban Climates*, Technical Note 108. Brussels: World Meteorological Organization, 1968.

_____. *Physical Climatology*. 2nd. rev. ed. Dubois, Pa.: Gray Printing, 1958.

_____. *The Urban Climate*. New York: Academic Press, 1981.

Langewiesche, Wolfgang. "How to Fix Your Private Climate." *House Beautiful*, October 1949, pp. 150–55.

Lave, Lester B., and Seskin, Eugene P. *Air Pollution and Human Health*. Baltimore: Johns Hopkins University Press, 1977.

Lawson, T. V. *Wind Effects on Buildings: Design Applications*, vol. 1. London: Applied Science Publishers, 1980.

Lesiuk, Stephen. "Architectural and Environmental Horticulture: An Investigation into the Use of Vegetation for Energy Conservation." In *Proceedings of the Tenth Annual Conference of the Environmental Design Research Association*. Edited by Andrew D. Seidel and Scott Danford. Washington, D.C.: Environmental Design Research Association, 1979.

Loessner, G. Arno. "An Air Quality Program with Visible Results." *Practicing Planner* 9 (1978):35–37.

Lowry, William P. "The Climate of Cities." In *Cities: Their Origin, Growth, and Human Impact*. San Francisco: W. H. Freeman, 1973.

Ludwig, F. L. "Urban Temperature Fields." In *Urban Climates*, Technical Note 108. Brussels: World Meteorological Organization, 1968.

McDermott, Walsh. "Air Pollution and Public Health." In *Cities: Their Origin, Growth, and Human Impact*. San Francisco: W. H. Freeman, 1973.

Munn, R. E. *Descriptive Micrometeorology*. New York: Academic Press, 1966.

_____. "Airflow in Urban Areas." In *Urban Climates*, Technical Note 108. Brussels: World Meteorological Organization, 1968.

_____. "Urban Meteorology: Some Selected Topics." *Bulletin of the American Meteorological Society* 54 (1973):90–93.

Neiburger, M. "Air Pollution Considerations in City and Regional Planning." In *Urban Climates*, Technical Note 108. Brussels: World Meteorological Organization, 1968.

_____. "Diffusion Models of Urban Air Pollution." In *Urban Climates*, Technical Note 108. Brussels: World Meteorological Organization, 1968.

Oke, T. R. *Review of Urban Climatology, 1968–1973*, Technical Note 134. Geneva: World Meteorological Organization, 1974.

Oke, T. R., and Hannell, F. G. "The Form of the Urban Heat Island in Hamilton, Canada." In *Urban Climates*, Technical Note 108. Brussels: World Meteorological Organization, 1968.

Olgyay, Aladar. "Solar Control and Orientation to Meet Bioclimatic Requirements." *Housing and Building in Hot Humid and Hot Dry Climates*. Washington, D.C.: National Academy of Sciences, 1953.

Olgyay, Aladar and Olgyay, Victor. *Solar Control and Shading Devices*. Princeton, N.J.: Princeton University Press, 1963.

Olgyay, Victor. *Design with Climate: Bioclimatic Approach to Architectural Regionalism*. Princeton, N.J.: Princeton University Press, 1963.

Oliver, John E. *Climate and Man's Environment: An Introduction to Applied Climatology*. New York: Wiley, 1973.

Parry, M. "Sources of Reading's Air Pollution." In *Urban Climates*, Technical Note 108. Brussels: World Meteorological Organization, 1968.

Penwarden, A. D. and Wise, A. F. E. *Wind Environment around Buildings*. Department of the Environment, Building Research Establishment. London: Her Majesty's Stationery Office, 1975.

Peterson, James T. *The Climate of Cities: A Survey of Recent Literature.* Raleigh, N.C.: National Air Pollution Control Administration, 1968.

Plumley, Harriet. "Design of Outdoor Urban Spaces for Thermal Comfort." In *Proceedings: Metropolitan Physical Environment.* U. S. Forest Service General Technical Report NE-25. Upper Darby, Pa.: Northeastern Forest Experiment Station, 1977.

Rimsha, A. *Town Planning in Hot Climates.* Translated by A. Shvarts. Moscow: Mir Publishers, 1976.

Roberts, John J.; Croke, Edward J.; and Booras, Samuel. "A Critical Review of the Effect of Air Pollution Control Regulations on Land Use Planning." *Journal of the Air Pollution Control Association* 25 (1975):500–20.

Rydell, C. Peter, and Schwarz, Gretchen. "Air Pollution and Urban Form: A Review of Current Literature." *AIP Journal* (1968):115–20.

Schuck, E. A., and Locke, J. K. "Relationship of Automotive Lead Particulates to Certain Consumer Crops." *Environmental Science and Technology* 4 (1970):324–30.

Schwerdtfeger, P., and Lyons, T. J. "Windfield Studies in an Urban Environment." *Urban Ecology* 2 (1976):93–107.

Shellard, H. C. "Microclimate and Housing: Topographical Effect." *The Architect's Journal Information Library,* 6 January 1965, pp. 21–26.

_____. "Microclimate and Housing: Effects of Orientation." *The Architect's Journal Information Library* (13 January 1965) 81–84.

Simiu, Emil, and Scanlan, Robert H. *Wind Effects on Structures: An Introduction to Wind Engineering.* New York: Wiley, 1978.

Singer, T. A., and Smith, M. E. "A Summary of the Recommended Guide for the Prediction of the Dispersion of Air-Borne Effluents." In *Urban Climates,* Technical Note 108. Brussels: World Meteorological Organization, 1968.

Smith, William H. "Metal Contamination of Urban Woody Plants." *Environmental Science and Technology* 7 (1973):631–36.

_____. "Urban Vegetation and Air Quality." In *Proceedings of the National Urban Forestry Conference November 13–16, 1978,* edited by George Hopkins. Syracuse: State University of New York, College of Environmental Science and Forestry, 1980.

Smith, William H., and Staskawicz, Brian J. "Removal of Atmospheric Particles by Leaves and Twigs of Urban Trees: Some Preliminary Observations and Assessment of Research Needs." *Environmental Management* 1 (1977):317–30.

Spirn, Anne Whiston. *Plants for Passive Cooling: A Preliminary Investigation.* Cambridge, Mass.: Harvard Graduate School of Design, 1981.

Sterling, Elia. "The Impact of Air Pollution on Residential Design." In *Urban Climates,* Technical Note 108. Brussels: World Meteorological Organization, 1968.

Stern, Arthur C., ed. *Air Pollutants, Their Transformation and Transport.* 3d ed. New York: Academic Press, 1976.

_____., ed. *Air Quality Management.* New York: Academic Press, 1977.

_____., ed. *The Effects of Air Pollution.* 3d ed. New York: Academic Press, 1977.

_____., ed. *Engineering Control of Air Pollution.* New York: Academic Press, 1977.

_____., ed. *Measuring, Monitoring, and Surveilance of Air Pollution,* 3d ed. New York: Academic Press, 1976.

Terjung, Werner H. "Urban Energy Balance Climatology." *Geographical Review* 60 (1970):31–53.

Van Haverbeke, David F. "Trees in Urban Energy Conservation." In *Proceedings of the National Urban Forestry Conference, November 13–16, 1978,* ed. George Hopkins. Syracuse: State University of New York, College of Environmental Science and Forestry, 1980.

Wedding, James B.; Lombardi, David J.; Cermak, Jack E. "A Wind Tunnel Study of Gaseous Pollutants in City Street Canyons." *Journal of the Air Pollution Control Association* 27 (1977):557–66.

White, Robert F. *Effects of Landscape Development on the Natural Ventilation of Buildings and Their Adjacent Areas.* Research Report 45. College Station, Texas: Texas Engineering Experiment Station, 1954.

Wise, A. F. E.; Secton, D. E.; and Lillywhite, M. S. T. "Urban Planning Research: Studies of Air Flow around Buildings." *The Architect's Journal Information Library* (19 May 1965):1185–89.

World Meteorological Organization. *Proceedings of the Symposium on Urban Climate and Building Climatology, vol 1: Urban Climates,* Technical Note 108. Brussels: World Meteorological Organization, 1968.

Urban Land

The application of geology to urban design and environmental planning is well documented. Legget's *Cities and Geology* and Leveson's *Geology and the Urban Environment* are excellent, comprehensive introductions to the subject. Leveson assumes less knowledge and may therefore be more appropriate for those unfamiliar with principles of geology. Legget is especially valuable for the description of extensive case studies. The anthologies edited by Betz, Coates, and by Utgard et al. have assembled many important articles on urban geology which were previously far less accessible. Bolt et al.'s volume is an excellent introduction to geologic hazards and their mitigation. The United States Geological Survey has conducted many case studies of urban geology in American cities and is an important source of information on the application of geology to land use planning in metropolitan areas (useful studies include those of Fleming et al., Guy, Nichols et al., and Robinson and Spieker, among others). The state geological surveys of California and Colorado have also published reports useful to urban planning and design (Alfors et al. and Rogers et al.). There is no monograph on urban soils, nor are the articles and papers that do exist easily assembled. Most research in soil science has been directed to agricultural productivity and to the structural stability of soils. The U.S. Soil Conservation Service published its first urban soil survey in 1976. Studies in Russia (Zemlyanitskiy), Germany (Sukopp et al.), and the United States (Bockheim) suggest that urban soils share certain characteristics.

Alfors, John T.; Burnett, John L.; and Gay, Thomas E., Jr. "Urban Geology Master Plan for California—A Summary." In *Geology in the Urban Environment,* edited by R. O. Utgard, G. D. McKenzie, and D. Foley. Minneapolis: Burgess, 1978.

Bailey, Edgar H., and Harden, Deborah R. "Mineral Resources of the San Francisco Region, California: Present Availability and Planning for the Future." In *Geology in the Urban Environment,* edited by R. O. Utgard, G. D. McKenzie, and D. Foley. Minneapolis: Burgess, 1978.

Baker, Victor R. "Urban Geology of Boulder, Colorado: A Progress Report." *Environmental Geology* 1 (1975):75–88.

Barltrop, D.; Thronton, I.; Strehlow, C. D.; Webb, J. S. "Absorption of Lead from Dust and Soil." *Postgraduate Medical Journal* 51 (1975):801–4.

Bates, Robert L. "Mineral Resources for a New Town." In *Geology in the Urban Environment,* edited by R. O. Utgard, G. D. McKenzie, and D. Foley. Minneapolis: Burgess, 1978.

Berghinz, C. "Venice is Sinking into the Sea." *Civil Engineering* (March 1971):67–71.

Betz, Frederick, ed. *Environmental Geology.* Stroudsberg, Pa.: Dowden, Hutchinson & Ross, 1975.

Bockheim, James G. "Nature and Properties of Highly Disturbed Urban Soils: Philadelphia, Pennsylvania." Paper presented before Soil Science Society of America, 15 November 1974, in Chicago, Illinois. Mimeographed.

Bolt, B. A.; Horn, W. L.; MacDonald, G. A.; and Scott, R. F. *Geological Hazards.* New York: Springer-Verlag, 1975.

Botsai, Elmer E.; Goldberg, Alfred; Fisher, John L.; Lagorio, Henry J.; and Wosser, Thomas D. *Architects and Earthquakes.* Washington, D.C.: U.S. Government Printing Office, 1975.

Branagan, D. F. "Geological Data for the City Engineer: A Comparison of Five Australian Cities." *24th International Geologic Congress Proceedings,* 1972, pp. 3–12.

Briggs, Reginald P.; Pomeroy, John S.; and Davies, William E. "Landsliding in Allegheny County, Pennsylvania." In *Geology in the Urban Environment,* edited by R. O. Utgard, G. D. McKenzie, and D. Foley. Minneapolis: Burgess, 1978.

Buckman, Harry O., and Brady, Nyle C. *The Nature and Properties of Soils.* 7th rev. ed. New York: Macmillan, 1969.

Burgess, Peter J. "The Role of Engineering Geology in Developing Sydney's Environment—Past, Present, and Future." *25th International Geologic Congress Proceedings*, 1976, pp. 525–26.

Campbell, Russell H. "Soil Slips, Debris Flows, and Rainstorms in the Santa Monica Mountains and Vicinity, Southern California." *Professional Paper 851*. Washington, D.C.: U.S. Geological Survey, 1975.

Cargo, David N., and Malbry, Bob F. *Man and His Geologic Environment*. Reading, Mass.: Addison-Wesley, 1974.

City of New York. *From Landfill to Park: An Experiment in Construction Waste Management at the Pennsylvania Avenue Landfill Site*. New York: Department of City Planning, 1974.

Coates, Donald R., ed. *Environmental Geomorphology and Landscape Conservation*, volume 2: *Urban*. Stroudsberg, Pa.: Dowden, Hutchinson & Ross, 1975.

————. *Urban Geomorphology*. Special Paper 174. Boulder, Colo.: Geological Society of America, 1976.

Colcord, Joanna C., and Johnston, Mary. *Community Programs for Subsistence Gardens*. New York: Russell Sage Foundation, 1933.

Cratchley, C. R., and Denness, B. "Engineering Geology in Urban Planning with an Example from the New City of Milton Keynes." *24th International Geological Congress Proceedings*, 1972, pp. 13–22.

Craul, Phillip J., ed. *Urban Forest Soils: A Reference Workbook*. Syracuse, N.Y.: U.S. Forest Service and State University of New York, College of Environmental Science and Forestry, 1982.

Dobrovolny, E., and Schmoll, H. R. "Geology as Applied to Urban Planning: An Example from the Greater Anchorage Area Borough, Alaska." In *Environmental Geology*, edited by Frederick Betz. Stroudsberg, Pa.: Dowden, Hutchinson & Ross, 1975.

Flawn, Peter T. *Environmental Geology*. New York: Harper & Row, 1970.

Fleming, Robert W.; Varnes, David J.; and Schuster, Robert L. "Landslide Hazards and Their Reduction." *Geological Survey Yearbook*. Washington, D.C.: U.S. Geological Survey, 1978.

Folk, Robert L. "Geologic Urban Hindplanning: An Example from a Hellenistic Byzantine City, Stobi, Yugoslavian Macedonia." *Environmental Geology* 1 (1975):5–22.

Forrester, Frank. "Land Subsidence." In *Geology in the Urban Environment*, edited by R. O. Utgard, G. D. McKenzie, and D. Foley. Minneapolis: Burgess, 1978.

Friend, Gil. "Getting the Lead Out." *Self-Reliance* (June 1976):11–12.

————. "Poisoned Cities and Urban Gardens." *Elements* (January 1976):8–11.

Godfrey, Andrew E. "A Physiographic Approach to Land Use Planning." *Environmental Geology* 2 (1977):43–50.

Griggs, Gary B., and Gilchrist, John A. *Geologic Hazards, Resources, and Environmental Planning*. Belmont, Calif.: Wadsworth, 1983.

Grube, F. "Urban and Environmental Geology of Hamburg." In *Environmental Geology*, edited by Frederick Betz. Stroudsburg, Pa.: Dowden, Hutchinson & Ross, 1975.

Guy, Harold P. "Sediment Control Methods in Urban Development: Some Examples and Implications." In *Urban Geomorphology*, edited by Donald R. Coates. Geological Society of America, Special Paper 174. Boulder, Colo.: Geological Society of America, 1976.

Hansen, Wallace R. "Geomorphic Constraints on Land Development in the Front Range Urban Corridor, Colorado." In *Urban Geomorphology*, edited by Donald R. Coates. Geological Society of America, Special Paper 174. Boulder, Colo.: Geological Society of America, 1976.

Hart, Stephen S. "Potentially Swelling Soil and Rock in the Front Range Urban Corridor." In *Geology in the Urban Environment*, edited by R. O. Utgard, G. D. McKenzie, and D. Foley. Minneapolis: Burgess, 1978.

Hopke, Philip K.; Lamb, Robert E.; and Natusch, David F. S. "Multielemental Characterization of Urban Roadway Dust." *Environmental Science and Technology* 14 (1980):169–171.

Hornick, Sharon B.; Patterson, James B.; and Chaney, Rufus L. "An Evaluation of Urban Garden Soil, Vegetation, and Soil Amendments." Mimeographed.

Howard, Arthur D., and Remsen, Irwin. *Geology in Environmental Planning*. New York: McGraw-Hill, 1978.

Hulbert, Archer Butler. *Soil: Its Influence on the History of the United States*. New Haven: Yale University Press, 1930.

301

Inman, R. E.; Ingerson, R. B.; and Levy, E. A. "Soil: A Natural Sink for Carbon Monoxide." *Science* 172 (1971):1229–31.

Jacobsen, Thorkild, and Adams, Robert. "Salt and Silt in Ancient Mesopotamian Culture." *Science* 128 (1958):1251–58.

Johnston, Paul M. "Geology and Ground-Water Resources of Washington, D.C. and Vicinty." *Water Supply Paper 1776*. Washington, D. C.: U.S. Geological Survey, 1964.

Kaye, Clifford A. "Beacon Hill End Moraine, Boston: New Explanation of an Important Urban Feature." In *Urban Geomorphology*, edited by Donald R. Coates. Geological Society of America, Special Paper 174. Boulder, Colo.: Geological Society of America, 1976.

———. "Geology and Our Cities." In *Environmental Geology*, edited by Frederick Betz. Stroudsberg, Pa.: Dowden, Hutchinson & Ross, 1975.

Kellaway, G. A., and Taylor, J. H. "The Influence of Landslipping on the Development of the City of Bath, England." *23rd International Geologic Congress Proceedings*, 1968, pp. 65–76.

Kingsley, Charles. *Town Geology*. London: Daldy, Isbister & Co., 1877.

Legget, Robert F. *Cities and Geology*. New York: McGraw-Hill, 1973.

———. *Geology and Engineering*. 2d ed. New York: McGraw-Hill, 1967.

Leighton, F. Beach. "Urban Landslides: Targets for Land-Use Planning in California." In *Urban Geomorphology*, edited by Donald R. Coates. Geological Society of America, Special Paper 174. Boulder, Colo.: Geological Society of America, 1976.

Lerzu, Catherine. "Poisoned Gardens." *Elements*, September 1975, pp. 1–3.

Leveson, David. *Geology and the Urban Environment*. New York: Oxford University Press, 1980.

Loehnberg, Alfred. "Aspects of the Sinking of Mexico City and Proposed Countermeasures." *American Waterworks Association Journal* 50 (1958):432–40.

Mader, George G., and Crowder, Dwight F. "An Experiment in Using Geology for City Planning: The Experience of the Small Community of Portola Valley, California." In *Environmental Planning and Geology: Proceedings of the Symposium on Engineering Geology in the Urban Environment*, edited by Donald R. Nichols and Catherine C. Campbell. Washington, D.C.: U.S. Geological Survey and U.S. Department of Housing and Urban Development, 1969.

McGill, John T. "Growing Importance of Urban Geology." *Circular 487*. Washington, D.C.: U.S. Geological Survey, 1966

Mossman, R. W.; Heim, George E.; and Dalton, Frank E. "Seismic Exploration in the Urban Environment." *24th International Geological Congress Proceedings*, 1972, pp. 183–90.

National Center for Resource Recovery. *Sanitary Landfills: A State of the Art Study*. Lexington, Mass.: D. C. Heath, 1974.

Nichols, Donald R., and Buchanan-Banks, J. M. "Seismic Hazards and Land-Use Planning." In *Geology in the Urban Environment*, edited by R. O. Utgard, G. D. McKenzie, and D. Foley. Minneapolis: Burgess, 1978.

Nichols, Donald R., and Campbell, Catherine C., eds. *Environmental Planning and Geology: Proceedings of the Symposium on Engineering Geology in the Urban Environment*. Washington, D.C.: U.S. Geological Survey and U.S. Department of Housing and Urban Development, 1969.

Page, A. L., and Ganje, T. J. "Accumulations of Lead in Soils for Regions of High and Low Motor Vehicle Traffic Density." *Environmental Science and Technology* 4 (1970):140–42.

Parsons, Henry Griscom. *Children's Gardens for Pleasure, Health and Education*. New York: Sturgis & Walton Co., 1910.

Patterson, James C. "Enrichment of Urban Soil with Composted Sludge and Leaf Mold: Constitution Gardens." *Compost Science* 16 (1975):18–22.

———. *Planting in Urban Soils*. Ecological Services Bulletin No. 1. Washington, D.C.: U.S. National Park Service, 1974.

———. "Soil Compaction and Its Effects upon Urban Vegetation." In *Better Trees for Metropolitan Landscapes Symposium Proceedings*, edited by F. Santamour, H. D. Gerhold, and S. Little. U.S. Forest Service General Technical Report NE-22. Upper Darby, Pa.: Northeastern Forest Experiment Station, 1976.

Poland, J. F., and Davis, G. H. "Land Subsidence Due to Withdrawal of Fluids." *Reviews in Engineering Geology* 2 (1969):187–269.

Purves, D., and MacKenzie, E. Jean. "Trace-Element Contamination of Parklands in Urban Areas." *Journal of Soil Science* 20 (1969):288–90.

Robinson, G. D., and Spieker, Andrew M. "Nature to be Commanded . . . " *Professional Paper 950.* Washington, D.C.: U.S. Geological Survey, 1978.

Rockaway, John D. "Evaluation of Geologic Factors for Urban Planning." *24th International Geologic Congress Proceedings,* 1972, pp. 61–69.

Rogers, W. P.; Ludwig, L. R.; Hornbaker, A. L.; Schwochow, S. D.; Hart, S. S.; Shelton, D. C.; Scroggs, D. L.; and Soule, J. M. *Guidelines and Criteria for Identification and Land-Use Controls of Geologic Hazard and Mineral Resource Areas.* Special Publication No. 6. Denver: Colorado Geological Survey, 1974.

Schmitt, N.; Philion, J. J.; Larsen, A. A.; Harnadek, M.; and Lynch, A. J. "Surface Soil as a Potential Source of Lead Exposure for Young Children." *CMA Journal,* 8 December 1979, 1474–78.

Schuberth, Christopher J. *The Geology of New York City and Environs.* Garden City, N.Y.: Natural History Press, 1968.

Schuster, Robert L., and Krizek, Raymond J., eds. *Landslides: Analysis and Control.* Special Report 176. Washington, D. C.: National Academy of Sciences, 1978.

Spangle, William, and Associates; Leighton, F. Beach, and Associates; and Baxter, McDonald and Company. "Earth Science Information in Land-Use Planning—Guidelines for Earth Scientists and Planners." *Circular 721.* Washington, D.C.: U.S. Geological Survey, 1976.

Spears, F. W. "Vacant Lot Cultivation." *Charities Review* 8 (1868):74–107.

Spittler, Thomas M., and Feder, William A. "A Study of Soil Contamination and Plant Uptake of Lead in Boston Urban Gardens." Mimeographed.

Stauffer, Truman P. "Kansas City: A Center for Secondary Use of Mined-Out Space." In *Geology in the Urban Environment,* edited by R. O. Utgard, G. D. McKenzie, and D. Foley. Minneapolis: Burgess, 1978.

Suffolk County Extension Service. "Lead in the Soil: A Gardener's Handbook." Boston: University of Massachusetts, 1979.

Sukopp, Herbert; Blume, Hans-Peter; and Kunick, Wolfram. "The Soil, Flora, and Vegetation of Berlin's Wastelands." In *Nature in Cities,* edited by Ian Laurie. New York: Wiley, 1979.

U.S. Soil Conservation Service. *Soil Survey of District of Columbia.* Washington, D.C.: United States Department of Agriculture and United States Department of the Interior, 1976.

Utgard, R. O.; McKenzie, G. D.; and Foley, D., eds. *Geology in the Urban Environment.* Minneapolis: Burgess, 1978.

Wallwork, Kenneth L. *Derelict Land.* London: David and Charles, 1974.

Wilson, H. E. "The Geological Map and the Civil Engineer." *24th International Geological Congress Proceedings,* 1972, pp. 83–86.

Withington, C. F. "Geology: Its Role in the Development and Planning of Metropolitan Washington." In *Geology in the Urban Environment,* edited by R. O. Utgard, G. D. McKenzie, and D. Foley. Minneapolis: Burgess, 1978.

Yaalon, Dan H., and Yaron, Bruno. "Framework for Man-Made Soil Changes: An Outline of Metapedogenesis." *Soil Science* 102 (1966):272–77.

Zaruba, Quido, and Mencl, Vojtech. *Landslides and Their Control.* Translated by H. Zarubova and V. Mencl. New York: American Elsevier, 1969.

Zemlyanitskiy, L. T. "Characteristics of the Soils in the Cities." *Soviet Soil Science* 5 (1963):468–75.

Urban Water

No single book deals equally well with the problems of urban hydrology, water supply, and water quality, and their implications for urban planning and design. Dunne and Leopold's *Water in Environmental Planning* is an important text, but it is mainly concerned with geomorphological processes of river dynamics and drainage basins and deals relatively little with problems of water supply and quality. Tourbier and Westmacott's *Handbook of Measures to Protect Water Resources in Land Development* is a valuable resource on stormwater management for designers and planners. The United States

303

Geological Survey has issued many publications addressed to geologists and engineers, planning and design professionals, as well as to laymen (for example, the works by Leopold, Britton et al., Rantz, and Schneider et al.). Much of the recent work on urban water quality has been conducted under the auspices of the United States Environmental Protection Agency (for example, Field and Lager; Bastioan; Lager et al.). The United States Council on Environmental Quality addresses issues of water quality in its annual report (see General Sources section). Blake's *Water for the Cities* provides an excellent historical background to the water supply problems of modern cities.

American Society of Civil Engineers, Task Committee on the Effects of Urbanization, Low Flow, Total Runoff, Infiltration, and Groundwater Recharge of the Committee on Surface Water Hydrology. "Aspects of Hydrological Effects of Urbanization." *Journal of the Hydraulics Division, Proceedings of the American Society of Civil Engineers* 101 (1975):449–68.

Antoine, Louis H. "Drainage and Best Use of Urban Land." *Public Works* 95 (1964):88–90.

Ardis, Colby V.; Dueker, Kenneth J.; and Lenz, Arno T. "Storm Drainage Practices of Thirty-Two Cities." *Journal of the Hydraulics Division, Proceedings of the American Society of Civil Engineers* 95 (1969):383–408.

Baldwin, Helene L., and McGuiness, C. C. *A Primer on Groundwater.* Washington, D.C.: U.S. Geological Survey, 1963.

Bastian, Robert K. *Natural Systems in Wastewater Treatment and Sludge Management: An Overview.* Washington, D.C.: U.S. Environmental Protection Agency, 1981.

————. "Natural Treatment Systems in Wastewater Treatment and Sludge Management." *Civil Engineering,* May 1982, pp. 62–67.

Belt, C. B., Jr. "The 1973 Flood and Man's Constriction of the Mississippi River." *Science* 189 (1975):681–84.

Blake, Nelson M. *Water for the Cities: A History of the Urban Water Supply Problem in the United States.* Syracuse, N.Y.: Syracuse University Press, 1956.

Boston Metropolitan Park Commission, and the Massachusetts State Board of Health. *Report of the Joint Board Consisting of the Metropolitan Park Commission and the State Board of Health upon the Improvement of Charles River: From Waltham Line to the Charles River Bridge.* Boston: Wright & Potter Printing Co., 1894.

Boston Metropolitan Sewerage Commissioners. *Report of the Metropolitan Sewerage Commissioners upon a High Level Gravity Sewer for the Relief of the Charles and Neponset River Valleys.* Boston: Wright & Potter Printing Co., 1899.

Boston Park Commission. "Proposed Sanitary Improvement of Muddy River." Document 130, 1881.

Braids, Olin C., and Gillies, Nola P. "Groundwater." *Journal of the Water Pollution Control Federation* 49 (1977):1302–07.

Britton, L. J.; Averett, R. C.; and Ferreira, R. F. "An Introduction to the Processes, Problems and Management of Urban Lakes." *Geological Survey Circular 601-K.* Washington, D.C.: U.S. Geological Survey, 1975.

Bruer, W. J. "Economics of Urban Drainage Design." *Journal of the Hydraulics Division, Proceedings of the American Society of Civil Engineers* 88 (1962):93–114.

Burgh, John. "Saving Water Scenically." *Water Engineering and Management* 129 (March 1982):46–47.

Burton, Ian; Kates, Robert W.; and Snead, Rodman E. *The Human Ecology of Coastal Flood Hazard in Megalopolis.* Department of Geography Research Paper no. 115. Chicago: University of Chicago, 1969.

Butler, R. E. "The Buried Rivers of London." *London Naturalist* 41 (1962):31–41.

Camp, Dresser, and McKee, Inc. *Revised Discharge Plan Reflecting Addition of Tertiary Treatment: The Bishop's Lodge, Santa Fe, New Mexico.* Denver: Camp, Dresser & McKee, 1980.

The Charles River Basin as a Water Park and Playground. Boston: Wright & Potter Printing Co., 1928.

Charles River Watershed Association. "Better Days for the Charles River." *EPA Journal* 8 (1982):13–14.

Chemical and Engineering News. "Porous Asphalt Paving Developed." January 10, 1972. p. 40.

Civil Engineering. "What's New in Dallas and Texas? Woodlands—New Town is Planned around Ecology." March 1977, p. 64.

Claycomb, Elmer L. "Urban Storm Drainage Criteria Manual from Denver." *Civil Engineering,* July 1970, pp. 39–41.

Daily, Eugene J. "Storm Water Retention in Urban Areas." *Public Works* 92 (1961):146–47.

Dallaire, Gene. "EPA's 1/A Program Speeds Use of New Wastewater Treatment Methods." *Civil Engineering,* November 1981, pp. 62–64.

Denver, Colorado, Mayor's Platte River Development Study. *In Response to a Flood: Denver, Colorado.* City of Denver, 1966.

Denver, Colorado, Urban Drainage and Flood Control District. *Flood Hazard News* 10 (September 1980):1–9.

Denver Planning Office. *Denver 1985: A Comprehensive Plan for Community Excellence.* City and County of Denver, 1967.

Dinges, W. R. "Who Says Sewage Treatment Plants Have to Be Ugly?" *Water and Wastes Engineering* 13 (April 1976):20–23.

Doxat, John. *The Living Thames: The Restoration of a Great Tidal River.* London: Hutchinson Benham, 1977.

Dunne, Thomas, and Leopold, Luna B. *Water in Environmental Planning.* San Francisco: W. H. Freeman, 1978.

English, J. N., and Mitchell, T. M. "Water Reclamation and Reuse." *Journal of the Water Pollution Control Federation* 48 (1976):1174–80.

Environmental Science and Technology. "Deep Tunnel Storage May Solve City Storm Water Problem." Vol. 3, no. 3 (1969):209.

Fair, Gordon Maskew; Geyer, John Charles; and Okun, Daniel Alexander. *Water and Wastewater Engineering,* vol. 1. New York: Wiley, 1966.

Fairchild, Warren D. "Balancing Economic Development and Environmental Quality through the Water Resources Council's Principles and Standards." In *Transactions of the Forty-first North American Wildlife and Natural Resource Conference,* edited by Kenneth Sabol. Washington, D.C.: Wildlife Management Institute, 1976.

Fay, Christopher W. "Waste Not Wastewater: Wolfeboro Solution." *American Forests* 88 (1982):42–43.

Felton, Paul M., and Lull, Howard W. "Suburban Hydrology Can Improve Watershed Conditions." *Public Works* 94, no. 1 (1963):93–94.

Feth, J. H. "Water Facts and Figures for Planners and Managers." *Circular 752.* Washington, D.C.: U.S. Geological Survey, 1977.

Field, Richard; Bowden, Russell; and Rozgonyi, Kathy. "Urban Runoff and Combined Sewer Overflow." *Journal of the Water Pollution Control Federation* 49 (1977):1095–1104.

Field, Richard; Curtis, J.; and Bowden, Russell. "Urban Runoff and Combined Sewer Overflow." *Journal of the Water Pollution Control Federation* 48 (1976):1191–1206.

Field, Richard, and Knowles, Donna. "Urban Runoff and Combined Sewer Overflow." *Journal of the Water Pollution Control Federation* 47 (1975):1352–69.

Field, Richard, and Lager, John A. *Countermeasures for Pollution from Overflows: The State of the Art.* Cincinnati: U.S. Environmental Protection Agency, 670/2–74–090, 1974.

————. "Urban Runoff Pollution Control: State-of-the-Art." *Journal of the Environmental Engineering Division, Proceedings of the American Society of Civil Engineers* 101 (1975):107–25.

Field, Richard; Struzeski, Edmund J.; Masters, Hugh E.; and Tarfuri, Anthony N. "Water Pollution and Associated Effects from Street Salting." *Journal of the Environmental Engineering Division, Proceedings of the American Society of Civil Engineers* 100 (1974):459–77.

Field, Richard, and Weigel, Pauline. "Urban Runoff and Combined Sewer Overflow." *Journal of the Water Pollution Control Federation* 45 (1973):1108–15.

Forrest, Edward, and Aronson, Harvey G. "Highway Ramp Areas Become Flood Control Reservoirs." *Civil Engineering,* February 1959, pp. 35–37.

Franke, O. L., and McClymonds, N. E. "Summary of the Hydrologic Situation on Long Island, New York, as a Guide to Water Management Alternatives." *Professional Paper 627-F.* Washington, D.C.: U.S. Geological Survey, 1972.

Goddard, James E. "Flood-Plain Management Must be Ecologically and Economically Sound." *Civil Engineering*, September 1971, pp. 81–85.

Grava, S. *Urban Planning Aspects of Water Pollution Control*. New York: Columbia University Press, 1969.

Guy, Harold P. "Sediment Problems in Urban Areas." *Circular 601-E*. Washington, D.C.: U.S. Geological Survey, 1970.

Hart, J. L. "Swampy Site Turned into a Prize Winner." *Civil Engineering*, June 1973, pp. 82–84.

Hittman Associates. "Reusing Storm Runoff." *Environmental Science and Technology* 2 (1968):1001–5.

Jones, D. Earl, Jr. "Urban Hydrology: A Redirection." *Civil Engineering*, August 1967, pp. 58–62.

————. "Where is Urban Hydrology Practice Today?" *Journal of the Hydraulics Division, Proceedings of the American Society of Civil Engineers* 97 (1971):257–64.

Juneja, Narendra, and Veltman, James. "Natural Drainage in the Woodlands." *Environmental Comment*, November 1979, pp. 7–14.

————. "Natural Drainage in the Woodlands." In *Storm Water Management Alternatives*, edited by J. Toby Tourbier and Richard Westmacott. Newark, Del.: Water Resources Center, University of Delaware, 1980.

Katznelson, Eliyu; Buium, Itzhack; and Shuval, Hillel I. "Risk of Communicable Disease Infection with Wastewater Irrigation in Agricultural Settlements." *Science* 1974 (1976):944–46.

Koelzer, Victor A.; Bauer, William J.; and Dalton, Frank E. "The Chicago Area Deep Tunnel Project." *Journal of the Water Pollution Control Federation* 41 (1969):515–34.

Konuel, Thomas. *Quabbin: The Accidental Wilderness*. Lincoln, Mass.: Massachusetts Audubon Society, 1981.

Lager, John A.; Smith, William G.; Lynard, William G.; Finn, Robert M.; and Finnemore, E. John. *Urban Storm Water Management and Technology: Update and Users Guide*. Cincinnati: U.S. Environmental Protection Agency SPA-600 8-77-014, 1977.

Lazaro, Timothy R. *Urban Hydrology: A Multidisciplinary Perspective*. Ann Arbor, Mich.: Ann Arbor Science Publishers, 1979.

LeGrand, Harry E. "Management Aspects of Groundwater Contamination." *Journal of the Water Pollution Control Federation* 39 (1964):1133–45.

Leopold, Luna B. "Hydrology for Urban Land Planning—A Guidebook on the Hydrological Effects of Urban Land Use." *Circular 554*. Washington, D.C.: U.S. Geological Survey, 1968.

————. *Water: A Primer*. San Francisco: W. H. Freeman, 1974.

————.; Wolman, M. G.; and Miller, J. P. *Fluvial Processes in Geomorphology*. San Francisco: W. H. Freeman, 1964.

Li, C. Y. "Sewerage Plan Involves Open Space Preservation." *Civil Engineering*, January 1973, pp. 85–86.

Mahida, Vijaysinh U., and DeDecker, Frank J. *Multi-Purpose Combined Sewer Overflow Treatment Facility, Mount Clemens, Michigan*. Cincinnati: U.S. Environmental Protection Agency, 1975.

Mallory, Charles W., and Boland, John J. "A Systems Study of Storm Runoff Problems in a New Town." *Water Resource Bulletin* 6 (1970):980–89.

McPherson, M. B., ed. *Hydrological Effects of Urbanization*. Paris: Unesco Press, 1974.

Notardonato, Frank, and Doyle, Arthur F. "Corps Takes New Approach to Flood Control." *Civil Engineering* (June 1979):65–68.

Obrist, A. "Ponding against the Storm." *Landscape Architecture* 65 (1974):388–90.

Pailthorp, Robert E. "Alternatives to End-of-Pipe Treatment." *Civil Engineering*, February 1977, pp. 49–51.

Peixoto, Jose P., and Kettani, M. Ali. "The Control of the Water Cycle." *Scientific American* (April 1973):46–61.

Pham, C. H.; Halverson, H. G.; and Heisley, G. M. "Precipitation and Runoff Water Quality from an Urban Parking Lot and Implications for Tree Growth." *Forest Service Research Note NE-253*. Washington, D.C.: U.S. Department of Agriculture, 1978.

Poertner, Herbert G. "Better Storm Drainage Facilities at Lower Cost." *Civil Engineering*, October 1973, pp. 67–70.

————. "Better Ways to Finance Stormwater Management." *Civil Engineering*, April 1981, pp. 67–69.

_____. "Drainage Plans with Environmental Benefit." *Landscape Architecture* 65 (1974):391–93.

Rantz, S. E. "Urban Sprawl and Flooding in Southern California." *Circular 601-B.* Washington, D.C.: U.S. Geological Survey, 1970.

Reed, Sherwood; Bastian, Robert K.; and Jewell, William J. "Engineers Assess Aquaculture Systems for Wastewater Treatment." *Civil Engineering* (July 1981):64–67.

Rice, Leonard. "Reduction of Urban Runoff Peak Flows by Ponding." *Journal of the Irrigation and Drainage Division, Proceedings of the American Society of Civil Engineers* 97 (1971):469–82.

Rickert, David A., and Spieker, Andrew M. "Real Estate Lakes." *Circular 601-G.* Washington, D.C.: U.S. Geological Survey, 1971.

Robinson, Charles Mumford. *Proposed Plans for the Improvement of the City of Denver.* Denver: Art Commission, 1906.

Schaeffer, John R.; Ellis, Davis W.; and Spieker, Andrew M. "Flood Hazard Mapping in Metropolitan Chicago." *Circular 601-C.* Washington, D.C.: U.S. Geological Survey, 1973.

Schneider, William J. "Hydrologic Implications of Solid-Waste Disposal." *Circular 601-F.* Washington, D.C.: U.S. Geological Survey, 1970.

Schneider, William J., and Goddard, James E. "Extent and Development of Urban Floodplains." *Circular 601-J.* Washington, D.C.: U.S. Geological Survey, 1973.

Schneider, William J.; Rickert, David A.; and Spieker, Andrew M. "Role of Water in Urban Planning and Management." *Circular 601-H.* Washington, D.C.: U.S. Geological Survey, 1973.

Schneider, William J., and Spieker, Andrew M. "Water for Cities—The Outlook." *Circular 601-A.* Washington, D.C.: U.S. Geological Survey, 1969.

Searns, Robert M. "Denver Tames the Unruly Platte: A Ten-Mile River Greenway." *Landscape Architecture* 70 (1980):382–86.

Shoemaker, Joe, and Stevens, Leonard. *Returning the Platte to the People.* Denver: Greenway Foundation, 1981.

Sinton, John W. *Charles River: An Urban River in Its Changing Social Context.* Water Resources Research Center Publication No. 23. Amherst: University of Massachusetts, 1964.

Smith, Benjamin J. W. "Smoother Waters for the Next 110,000 Years." *Landscape Architecture* 65 (1974):382–84.

Stoner, J. D. "Water Quality Indices for Specific Water Uses." *Circular 770.* Washington, D.C.: U.S. Geological Survey and Department of the Interior, 1978.

Tarr, Joel A., and McMichael, Francis C. "Historical Turning Points in Municipal Water Supply and Wastewater Disposal, 1850–1932." *Civil Engineering* (October 1977):82–86.

Thomas, Harold E., and Schneider, William J. "Water as an Urban Resource and Nuisance." *Circular 601-D.* Washington, D.C.: U.S. Geological Survey, 1970.

Thomas, Richard E. "Land Disposal, II: An Overview of Treatment Methods." *Journal of the Water Pollution Control Federation* 45 (1973):1476–84.

Thorpe, Jim, Jr. "Water Reclamation Provides Room for Expansion at the Bishop's Lodge." *Resort Management* (November 1981):10–11.

Tofflemire, T. J. "Land Application of Wastewater." *Journal of the Water Pollution Control Federation* 48 (1976):1180–90.

_____. "Land Application of Wastewater." *Journal of the Water Pollution Control Federation* 49 (1977):1087–94.

Tofflemire, T. J., and Farnan, R. A. "Land Disposal of Wastewater." *Journal of the Water Pollution Control Federation* 47 (1975):1344–52.

Tourbier, J. P. Toby, and Westmacott, Richard. *A Handbook of Measures to Protect Water Resources in Land Development.* Washington, D.C.: Urban Land Institute, 1981.

Tourbier, J. P. Toby, and Westmacott, Richard, eds. *Storm Water Management Alternatives.* Newark, Del.: Water Resources Center, University of Delaware, 1980.

Tucker, Scott L., and Degroot, William G. "Regional Flood Plain Management." *Civil Engineering* (November 1976):46.

Uiga, Antz. "Let's Consider Land Treatment Not Land Disposal." *Civil Engineering* (March 1976):60–61.

U.S. Army Corps of Engineers. *Charles River, Massachusetts: Main Report and Attach-*

ment. Waltham, Mass.: Department of the Army, New England Division, Corps of Engineers, 1972.

————. *Natural Valley Storage: A Partnership with Nature.* Public Information Fact Sheet. Waltham, Mass.: Department of the Army, Corps of Engineers, Spring 1976, 1977, and 1978.

Wallace McHarg Roberts and Todd. *Woodlands New Community: Guidelines for Site Planning.* Philadelphia: WMRT, 1973.

————. *Woodlands New Community: An Ecological Inventory.* Philadelphia: WMRT, 1974.

————. *Woodlands New Community: Phase One: Land Planning and Design Principles.* Philadelphia: WMRT, 1974.

————. *Woodlands New Community: An Ecological Plan.* Philadelphia: WMRT, 1974.

Weibel, S. R.; Anderson, R. J.; and Woodward, R. L. "Urban Land Runoff as a Factor in Stream Pollution." *Journal of the Water Pollution Control Federation* 36 (1964):914–24.

Weireter, Robert. "Waste Not Wastewater West: The Arcata Experiment." *American Forests* 88 (June 1982):38–53.

Whipple, W., Jr., and Hunter, J. V. "Nonpoint Sources and Planning for Water Pollution Control." *Journal of the Water Pollution Control Federation* 49 (1977):15–23.

Williams, Garnett. "Washington, D.C.'s Vanishing Springs and Waterways." *Circular 752*. Washington, D.C.: U.S. Geological Survey, 1977.

Wrenn, Douglas. "Storm Water: Liability or Asset?" *Environmental Comment* (November 1979):3.

Wright, Kenneth, and Taggart, William C. "The Recycling of a River." *Civil Engineering* (November 1976) 42–46.

Urban Vegetation

The literature falls into five broad categories: the identification of common urban plants (Page and Weaver), the problems which beset urban plants (Roberts), the design and management of urban vegetation (Grey and Deneke, and the U.S. Forest Service publications), and the social and economic values of urban vegetation (for example, Schmid). Bernatzky's *Tree Ecology and Preservation*, perhaps the most comprehensive single volume, reviews common problems of urban trees and methods of management, and describes the effect of trees on urban climate and air quality.

Allen, Mea. *Weeds: The Unbidden Guests in Our Gardens.* New York: Viking Press, 1978.

Anderson, Edgar. "Man as a Maker of New Plants and New Plant Communities." In *Man's Role in Changing the Face of the Earth*, edited by W. L. Thomas. Chicago: University of Chicago Press, 1956.

————. *Plants, Man and Life.* Berkeley and Los Angeles: University of California Press, 1969.

Anderson, Edgar. *Landscape Papers.* Berkeley, Calif.: Turtle Island Foundation, 1976.

Andreson, John W., ed. *Trees and Forests for Human Settlements.* Toronto: Centre for Urban Forestry Studies, 1976.

Bangerter, E. B. "The Botany of the London Area." *London Naturalist* 40 (1961):6–16.

Barlow, Elizabeth. *The Forests and Wetlands of New York City.* Boston: Little, Brown, 1969.

Bates, J. M. "The Flora of a Neglected Door-Yard." *Asa Gray Bulletin* 8 (1900):58–63.

Bernatzky, A. *Tree Ecology and Preservation.* Amsterdam: Elsevier, 1978.

Bos, H. J., and Mol, J. L. "The Dutch Example: Native Planting in Holland." In *Nature in Cities*, edited by Ian C. Laurie. Chichester, England: Wiley, 1979.

Boston Redevelopment Authority. *Boston Urban Wilds.* September 1976.

Callahan, John C., and Bunger, Tom P. "Economic Cost of Managing Street Trees on a Crisis Basis." In *Trees and Forests for Human Settlements*, edited by John W. Andresen. Toronto: Centre for Urban Forestry Studies, 1976.

Cole, Lyndis, and Keen, Caroline. "Dutch Techniques for the Establishment of Natural Plant Communities in Urban Areas." *Landscape Design* 116 (1974):31–34.

Cox, Jenny A. "The Green Ways of Stuttgart." *Landscape Design* 110 (1975):11.

Daubenmire, Rexford. *Plant Communities.* New York: Harper & Row, 1968.
Daubenmire, Rexford. *Plants and Environment.* London: Wiley, 1959.
Falk, John Howard. "Energetics of a Suburban Lawn Ecosystem." *Ecology* 57 (1976):141–50.
Foster, Ruth S. "Roots: Caring for City Trees." *Technology Review* 79 (July/August 1977):29–34.
Goodwin, R. H., and Neiring, W. A. "The Management of Roadside Vegetation by Selective Herbicide Techniques." *Connecticut Arboretum Bulletin* 2 (1959):4–10.
Grey, Gene W., and Deneke, Frederick J. *Urban Forestry.* New York: Wiley, 1978.
Hammerschlag, Richard S., and Patterson, James C. "Constitution Gardens: The Making of an Urban Park." In *Manual of Site Management.* Reston, Va.: Environmental Design Press, 1978.
Hartmann, Frederick. "The Chicago Forestry Scheme." *Natural History* (November 1973):72–73.
Harris, Richard. *Arboriculture: Care of Trees, Shrubs, and Vines in the Landscape.* Englewood Cliffs, N.J.: Prentice-Hall, 1983.
Hill, H. Michael, and Chadwick, L. C. "Shade Tree Evaluation Project." In *Proceedings of the Forty-Third International Shade Tree Conference.* Wooster, Ohio: Collier Printing, 1967.
Holscher, Clark E. "City Forests of Europe." In *Natural History* (November 1973):52–54.
Hopkins, George, ed. *Proceedings of the National Urban Forestry Conference, November 13–16, 1978.* 2 vols. Syracuse: State University of New York, College of Environmental Science and Forestry, 1980.
Jewell, Linda. "Planting Trees in City Soils." *Landscape Architecture* 71 (1981):387–89.
Kay, Jane Holtz. "The City Tree." *Horticulture* (October 1976):22–30.
Kenfield, G. W. *The Wild Gardener in the Wild Landscape: The Art of Naturalistic Landscaping.* New York: Hafner, 1966.
Kozel, P. C.; Jansen, M. J.; and Hettel, G. P. "Which Trees Do Best in the City." *Ohio Report* 63 (January–February 1978):6–9.
Lanfair, F. O. "Urban Vegetation: Values and Stresses." *Hortscience* 6 (1971):332–34.
Larson, Joseph S. *Managing Woodland and Wildlife Habitat in and near Cities.* Amherst: University of Massachusetts Press, 1971.
Laurie, Ian C. "The Return of the Dutch Natives." *Landscape Architecture* 64 (1974):411–13.
Manning, Owen. "Designing for Nature in Cities." In *Nature in Cities,* edited by Ian C. Laurie. Chichester, England: Wiley, 1979.
Maxwell, Margaret. "The Fall of London's Trees." *Country Life* 152 (1972):382–84.
Miller, Howard C., ed. *Proceedings: Urban Forestry Conference.* Syracuse: State University of New York, College of Environmental Science and Forestry, 1973.
Myehlenbach, Viktor. "Along the Railroad Tracks, A Study of Adventive Plants." *Missouri Botanical Garden Bulletins* 57, no. 3 (1969):10–18.
Niering, William A. "The Ecology of Wetlands in Urban Areas." *Garden Journal* 18 (1968):177–83.
Niering, William A., and Goodwin, Richard H. "Creation of Relatively Stable Shrubland with Herbicides: Arresting 'Succession' on Rights of Way and Pastureland." *Ecology* 55 (1974):784–95.
Olmsted, Frederick Law. "Trees in Streets and Parks." *The Sanitarian Monthly,* September 1882, pp. 513–18.
Page, Nancy, and Weaver, Richard E., Jr. *Wild Plants in the City.* New York: Quadrangle, 1975.
Parker, Phillip A. "Planting Strips in Street Rights-of-Way: A Key Public Land Resource." In *Trees and Forests for Human Settlements,* edited by John W. Andreson. Toronto: Centre for Urban Forestry Studies, 1976.
Peets, Elbert. "Street Trees in the Built-up Districts of Large Cities." *Landscape Architecture Quarterly,* October 1915, pp. 15–31.
Powell, E. P. "Housetop Gardens." *Garden and Forest* 5 (1892):125–26.
Prost, J. H. "City Forestry in Chicago." *American City* 4 (1911):277–81.
———. "Reforestation of a Great City." *World Today* 19 (1910):735–40.
———. "What Chicago Is Doing for Its Trees." *Garden Magazine* 13 (1910):18–20.
Roberts, Bruce R. "The Physiology of Trees in and near Human Settlements." In *Trees*

and Forests for Human Settlements, edited by John W. Andresen. Toronto: Centre for Urban Forestry Studies, 1976.

Ruff, Allan R. *Holland and the Ecological Landscape.* Stockport, England: Deanwater Press, 1979.

Santamour, F; Gerhold, H. D.; and Little, S., eds. *Better Trees for Metropolitan Landscapes Symposium Proceedings.* Technical Report NE-22. Upper Darby, Pa.: U. S. Forestry Service, Northeastern Forest Experiment Station, 1976.

Schmid, James A. *Urban Vegetation.* Department of Geography Research Paper No. 161. Chicago: University of Chicago, 1975.

Shinstone, J. C. "The Flora of London Building Sites." *Journal of Botany* 50 (1912):117–24.

Sieberth, Hermann. "The 'Railway Track Triangle' Natural Park: When Will They Ever Learn . . . ?" *Anthos* 21 (1982):8–19.

Solotaroff, William. "The City's Duty to its Trees." *American City* 4 (1911):131–34.

Spears, F. W. "Vacant Lot Cultivation." *Charities Review* 8 (1868):74–107.

Stearns, Forest W. "Urban Botany: An Essay on Survival." *University of Wisconsin at Milwaukee, Field Stations Bulletin* 4, no. 1 (1971):1–6.

Sukopp, Herbert; Lume, Hans-Peter; and Kunick, Wolfram. "The Soil, Flora and Vegetation of Berlin's Wastelands." In *Nature in Cities,* edited by Ian C. Laurie. Chichester, England: Wiley, 1979.

Tregay, Rob. "Urban Woodlands." In *Nature in Cities,* edited by Ian C. Laurie. Chichester, England: Wiley, 1979.

U.S. Forest Service. *Proceedings of the Conference on Metropolitan Physical Environment.* General Technical Report NE-25. Upper Darby, Pa.: Northeastern Forest Experiment Station, 1977.

————. *Proceedings of the Symposium on the Role of Trees in the South's Urban Environment.* Athens: University of Georgia Center for Continuing Education, 1971.

Urban Wildlife

The literature on urban wildlife deals largely with the study of individual species in specific places: their occurrence, habitat, and behavior. The problems of urban wildlife, both pests and more desirable species, and broader issues of their management are seldom addressed. The slim volume by Gill and Bonnett is by far the best introduction to urban wildlife, the urban environment to which it must adapt, and its problems and management. Their recommendations for how wildlife habitats might be created in the city are of particular value to designers and planners. Recent work in biogeography (as exemplified by Forman's article) has benefited wildlife management (for example, Goldstein et al.). Fitter's *London's Natural History* (1945) is a classic study of urban wildlife in a single city. Its value lies not only in its description of individual species, but also in the definition of urban wildlife habitats from rubbish dumps to reservoirs and parks. Kieran's *Natural History of New York City* is less detailed, but it is especially readable and its description of urban wildlife is applicable to other American cities.

Beck, Alan M. *The Ecology of Stray Dogs.* Baltimore: York Press, 1973.

Beck, Alan M. "The Ecology of Urban Dogs." In *A Symposium on Wildlife in an Urbanizing Environment,* edited by John H. Noyes and Donald R. Porgulske. Amherst: University of Massachusetts Cooperative Extension Service, 1974.

Brown, E. P. "The Bird Life of Holland Park: The Effect of Human Influence." *London Bird Report* 26 (1963):60–87.

Brown, E. P. "The Bird Life of Holland Park 1962–1963." *London Bird Report* 28 (1964):69–78.

Brush, Robert O. "Wildlife Research Needed by Landscape Architects." In *Transactions of the Forty-first North American Wildlife and Natural Resources Conference,* edited by Kenneth Sabol. Washington, D.C.: Wildlife Management Institute, 1976.

Burgess, R. L., and Sharpe, D. M. *Forest Island Dynamics in Man-Dominated Landscapes.* New York: Springer Verlag, 1981.

Burton, John A. *The Naturalist in London.* London: Newton and Abbot, 1974.

Cauley, Darrell L., and Schinner, James R. "The Cincinnati Raccoons." *Natural History*, November 1973, pp. 58–60.

Dagg, A. I. "Wildlife in an Urban Area." *Naturaliste Canada* 97 (1970):201–12.

DeGraaf, Richard M., and Payne, Brian R. "Economic Values of Non-Game Birds and Some Urban Wildlife Research Needs." In *Transactions of the Forty-second North American Wildlife and Natural Resources Conference*, edited by Kenneth Sabol. Washington, D.C.: Wildlife Management Institute, 1977.

DeGraaf, Richard M., and Wentworth, James M. "Urban Bird Communities and Habitats in New England." In *Transactions of the Forty-sixth North American Wildlife and Natural Resources Conference*, edited by Kenneth Sabol. Washington, D.C.: Wildlife Management Institute, 1981.

DeGraaf, Richard M., and Witman, Gretchin M. *Trees, Shrubs and Vines for Attracting Birds: A Manual for the Northeast*. Amherst: University of Massachusetts Press, 1979.

Dubkin, Leonard. *Enchanted Streets*. Boston: Little, Brown, 1947.

Fitter, R. S. R. *London's Natural History*. London: Collins, 1945.

Forman, Richard T. T. "Interaction among Landscape Elements: A Core of Landscape Ecology." In *Regional Landscape Planning: Proceedings of Educational Sessions, American Society of Landscape Architects*, 1981.

Frankie, G. W., and Koehler, C. S., eds. *Perspectives in Urban Entomology*. New York: Academic Press, 1978.

Fuhriman, Jerry W., and Crozier, Edward S. *Planning for Wildlife and Man*. Washington, D.C.: U.S. Fish and Wildlife Service, 1976.

Gibbs, A. "The Bird Population of Rubbish Dumps." *London Bird Report* 26 (1963):104–10.

Giles, R. N. *Wildlife Management Techniques*. 3rd rev. ed. Washington, D.C.: Wildlife Society, 1969.

Gill, Don, and Bonnett, Penelope. *Nature in the Urban Landscape: A Study of Urban Ecosystems*. Baltimore: York Press, 1973.

Goldstein, Edward L.; Gross, Meir; and DeGraaf, Richard M. "Explorations in Bird–Land Geometry." *Urban Ecology* 5 (1980/81):113–24.

Goldstein, Edward L.; Gross, Meir; and DeGraaf, Richard M. "Wildlife and Green Space Planning in Medium Scale Residential Developments." *Urban Ecology*, in press.

Guth, Robert W. "Wildlife in the Chicago Area: The Interaction of Feeding and Vegetation." In *Transactions of the Forty-sixth North American Wildlife and Natural Resources Conference*, edited by Kenneth Sabol. Washington, D. C.: Wildlife Management Institute, 1981.

Hanke, Steve H. "Options for Financing Water Development Projects." In *Transactions of the Forty-first North American Wildlife and Natural Resources Conference*, edited by Kenneth Sabol. Washington, D. C.: Wildlife Management Institute, 1976.

Hathaway, Melvin B. "Ecology of City Squirrels." *Natural History*, November 1973, pp. 61–62.

Hounsome, Michael. "Birdlife in the City." In *Nature in Cities*, edited by Ian C. Laurie. Chichester, England: Wiley, 1979.

Jenkins, Robert. "Maintenance of Natural Diversity: Approach and Recommendations." In *Transactions of the Forty-first North American Wildlife and Natural Resources Conference*, edited by Kenneth Sabol. Washington, D.C.: Wildlife Management Institute, 1976.

Kieran, John. *A Natural History of New York City*. New York: Fordham University Press, 1982.

Kinkead, Eugene. *A Concrete Look at Nature*. New York: Quadrangle, 1974.

Leedy, Daniel L.; Maestro, Robert M.; and Franklin, Thomas M. *Planning for Wildlife in Cities and Suburbs*. Washington, D.C.: Fish and Wildlife Service, Office of Biological Services, 1978.

Locke, Louis N. "Diseases and Parasites in Urban Wildlife." In *A Symposium on Wildlife in an Urbanizing Environment*, edited by John H. Noyes and Donald R. Porgulske. Amherst: University of Massachusetts Cooperative Extension Service, 1974.

Longrie, Dean P. "Wildlife Biologists' Involvement in the Planning Process." In *Transactions of the Forty-first North American Wildlife and Natural Resources Conference*, edited by Kenneth Sabol. Washington, D.C.: Wildlife Management Institute, 1976.

311

Noyes, John H., and Porgulske, Donald R., eds. *A Symposium on Wildlife in an Urbanizing Environment*. Amherst: University of Massachusetts Cooperative Extension Service, 1973.

Nudds, Thomas D. "Theory in Wildlife Conservation and Management." In *Transactions of the Forty-fourth North American Wildlife and Natural Resources Conference*, edited by Kenneth Sabol. Washington, D.C.: Wildlife Management Institute, 1979.

Provost, Maurice W. "Relationships between Insect Control and Human Health." In *Transactions of the Forty-second North American Wildlife and Natural Resources Conference*, edited by Kenneth Sabol. Washington, D.C.: Wildlife Management Institute, 1977.

Reez, Gordon A., and Pierce, Dale A. "Flood Control and Wildlife Preservation in the Los Angeles Water Projects." In *Transactions of the Forty-first Wildlife and Natural Resources Conference*, edited by Kenneth Sabol. Washington, D.C.: Wildlife Management Institute, 1976.

Rublowsky, John. *Nature in the City*. New York: Basic Books, 1967.

Schinner, James R., and Gauley, Darrell L. "The Ecology of Urban Raccoons in Cincinnati, Ohio." In *A Symposium on Wildlife in an Urbanizing Environment*, edited by John H. Noyes and Donald R. Porgulske. Amherst: University of Massachusetts Cooperative Extension Service, 1974.

Shafer, Elwood L., and Moeller, George H. "Wildlife Priorities and Benefits: Now, 2000, and Beyond." In *Transactions of the Thirty-ninth North American Wildlife and Natural Resources Conference*, edited by Kenneth Sabol. Washington, D.C.: Wildlife Management Institute, 1974.

Shaw, William W. "Meaning of Wildlife for Americans: Contemporary Attitudes and Social Trends." In *Transactions of the Thirty-ninth North American Wildlife and Natural Resources Conference*, edited by Kenneth Sabol. Washington, D.C.: Wildlife Management Institute, 1974.

Sheaffer, John R. "Living with a River in Suburbia." In *Transactions of the Fortieth North American Wildlife and Natural Resources Conference*, edited by Kenneth Sabol. Washington, D.C.: Wildlife Management Institute, 1975.

Shoesmith, Merlin W., and Koon, W. H. "The Maintenance of an Urban Deer Herd in Winnipeg, Manitoba." In *Transactions of the Forty-second North American Wildlife and Natural Resources Conference*, edited by Kenneth Sabol. Washington, D.C.: Wildlife Management Institute, 1977.

Shomon, J. J. "More Wildlife for Urban America." *The Conservationist*, February–March 1970, pp. 2–7.

Siderits, Karl, and Radtke, Robert E. "Enhancing Forest Wildlife Habitat through Diversity." In *Transactions of the Forty-second North American Wildlife and Natural Resources Conference*, edited by Kenneth Sabol. Washington, D.C.: Wildlife Management Institute, 1977.

Solman, Victor E. F. "Aircraft and Wildlife." In *A Symposium on Wildlife in an Urbanizing Environment*, edited by John H. Noyes and Donald R. Porgulske. Amherst: University of Massachusetts Cooperative Extension Service, 1974.

Stearns, Forest W. "Wildlife Habitat in Urban and Suburban Environments." In *Transactions of the Thirty-second North American Wildlife and Natural Resources Conference*, edited by Kenneth Sabol. Washington, D.C.: Wildlife Management Institute, 1967.

Thearle, R. J. P. "Urban Bird Problems." In *The Problems of Birds and Pests*. Symposia of the Institute of Biology, no. 17. Edited by K. K. Murton and E. N. Wright. London: Academic Press, 1966.

Thillman, John H., and Monasch, Walter J. "Wildlife as Inputs to Comprehensive Planning." In *Transactions of the Forty-first Wildlife and Natural Resources Conference*, edited by Kenneth Sabol. Washington, D.C.: Wildlife Management Institute, 1976.

Thomas, Jack Ward, and Dickson, Ronald A. "Cemetery Ecology." In *A Symposium on Wildlife in an Urbanizing Environment*, edited by John H. Noyes and Donald R. Porgulske. Amherst: University of Massachusetts Cooperative Extension Service, 1974.

Wheeler, Alwyne. "Fish in an Urban Environment." In *Nature in Cities*, edited by Ian C. Laurie. Chichester, England: Wiley, 1979.

Williamson, Robert D. "Birds in Washington, D.C." In *A Symposium on Wildlife in an Urbanizing Environment*, edited by John H. Noyes and Donald R. Porgulske. Amherst: University of Massachusetts Cooperative Extension Service, 1974.

Williamson, Robert D. "Birds—and People—Neighborhoods." *Natural History* (November 1973):55–57.

Winter, Warren R., and George, John L. "Role of Feeding Stations in Managing Nongame Bird Habitats in Urban and Suburban Areas." In *Transactions of the Forty-sixth North American Wildlife and Natural Resources Conference*, edited by Kenneth Sabol. Washington, D.C.: Wildlife Management Institute, 1981.

Zisman, S. B. "Urban Open Space." In *Transactions of the Thirty-first North American Wildlife and Natural Resources Conference*, edited by James B. Trefethen. Washington, D.C.: Wildlife Management Institute, 1966.

Urban Ecosystems

In the early 1970s the National Science Foundation supported numerous studies on the modeling of ecosystems, on the interaction of land use and the environment, and on the urban ecosystem specifically. Many of the following sources are outgrowths of that support. Stearns and Montag's *The Urban Ecosystem* presents the findings and recommendations of an interdisciplinary group of natural and social scientists and planning and design professionals. McAllister's *Environment: A New Focus for Land-Use Planning* is an NSF publication consisting of task-group reports on the relation between environment and land use. Cooper and Vlasen's chapter in that volume is a particularly useful summary of the application of ecological concepts to urban planning. Elsewhere, Holling and Orians summarize the potential contribution of ecologists to urban planning and identify future research needs. Much work on environmental modeling and decision making has been accomplished in the past two decades. The Holcomb Research Institute has summarized the United States experience, and the volume edited by Ott contains numerous examples of these models.

Blum, S. L. "Tapping Resources in Municipal Solid Waste." *Science* 191 (1976):669–75.

Brady, R. F.; Tobias, Terry; Eagles, Paul F. J.; Ohrner, R.; Micak, J.; Veale, Barbara; and Dorney, R. S. "A Topology for the Urban Ecosystem and Its Relationship to Larger Biogeographical Landscape Units." *Urban Ecology* 4 (1979):11–28.

Calkins, Hugh H.; Marble, Duane F.; and Peuquet, Donna J. "Information System Support of Regional Environmental Analysis." In *Regional Environmental Systems*. University of Washington, Department of Civil Engineering, 1976.

Civil Engineering. "Chicago Reclaiming Strip Mines with Sewage Sludge." September 1972, pp. 98–102.

Cooper, William E., and Vlasen, Raymond D. "Ecological Concepts and Applications to Planning." In *Environment: A New Focus for Land-Use Planning*, edited by Donald M. McAllister. Washington, D.C.: National Science Foundation, 1973.

Dorney, R. S. "Role of Ecologists as Consultants in Urban Planning and Design." *Human Ecology* 1 (1973):183–99.

Evans, Francis C. "Ecosystem as the Basic Unit in Ecology." *Science* 123 (1956):1127–28.

Ferguson, Francis. *Architecture, Cities and the Systems Approach*. New York: George Braziller, 1975.

Friedmann, John. "The Future of the Urban Habitat." In *Environment: A New Focus for Land-Use Planning*, edited by Donald M. McAllister. Washington, D.C.: National Science Foundation, 1973.

Gilman, Edward F.; Flower, Franklin B.; and Leone, Ida A. *Standardized Procedures for Planting Vegetation on Completed Sanitary Landfills*. Cincinnati: Municipal Environmental Research Laboratory, U.S. Environmental Protection Agency, 1982.

Godron, Michel, and Forman, Richard T. T. "Landscape Modification and Changing Ecological Characteristics." In *Disturbance and Ecosystems*, edited by H. A. Mooney and M. Godron. New York: Springer-Verlag, 1982.

Holcomb Research Institute, Butler University. *Environmental Modeling and Decision Making: The United States Experience*. New York: Praeger, 1976.

Holling, C. S., and Orians, Gordon. "Toward an Urban Ecology." *Ecological Society of America Bulletin* 52 (1971):2–6.

Marcus, Melvin G., and Detwyler, Thomas R. "Urbanization and Environment in Perspective." In *Urbanization and Environment*, edited by Thomas R. Detwyler and Melvin G. Marcus. Belmont, Calif.: Duxbury, 1972.

Marrazzo, William J. "The Selling of Waste." *EPA Journal* 7 (August 1981):26–27.

McAllister, Donald M., ed. *Environment: A New Focus for Land-Use Planning*. Washington, D.C.: National Science Foundation, 1973.

Meier, Richard L. "A Stable Urban Ecosystem." *Science* 192 (1976):962–67.

Morris, David. *Self-Reliant Cities: Energy and the Transformation of Urban America*. San Francisco: Sierra Club Books, 1982.

Nalbandian, M. Richard. "Some Public Health Aspects of Physical Planning for Human Settlements." Mimeographed, 1982.

National Science Board. *Patterns and Perspectives in Environmental Science*. Washington, D.C.: U.S. Government Printing Office, 1972.

Odum, Eugene P. *Fundamentals of Ecology*. Philadelphia: Saunders, 1971.

Ott, Wayne R., ed. *Proceedings of the Conference on Environmental Modeling and Simulation*. Washington, D.C.: U.S. Environmental Protection Agency, 1976.

Pikarsky, Milton F. "Chicago's Northwest Incinerator." *Civil Engineering*, September 1971, pp. 55–58.

Schultz, Stanley K., and McShane, Clay. "To Engineer the Metropolis: Sewers, Sanitation, and City Planning in Late Nineteenth-Century America." *Journal of American History* 65 (1978):389–411.

Smith, William H. "Lead Contamination of the Roadside Ecosystem." *Journal of the Air Pollution Control Association* 26 (1976):753–66.

Stearns, Forest, and Montag, Tom, eds. *The Urban Ecosystem: A Holistic Approach*. Stroudsburg, Pa.: Dowden, Hutchinson & Ross, 1974.

Thomas, William A., ed. *Indicators of Environmental Quality*. New York: Plenum, 1972.

University of Washington, Department of Civil Engineering. *Regional Environmental Systems*. Seattle: University of Washington, 1976.

Waring, George E., Jr. "The Disposal of a City's Waste." *North American Review* 161 (July 1895):49–56.

Wolman, Abel. "The Metabolism of Cities." *Scientific American* (March 1965):178–90.

Woodwell, George M. "Toxic Substances and Ecological Cycles." *Scientific American*, (March 1967):24–31.

LIST OF ILLUSTRATIONS

INDEX

acid rain, 264

Acropolis (Athens), 109

aerial photography, 3–4, 258

aesthetics, landscape, 179–83

Ailanthus altissima (tree-of-heaven), 182–83, 186, 198, 199

air conditioning, 41–42, 55, 85

air movement: comfort and, 66–67; relationship of ground surface and obstacles to rate of, 64–65; in Stuttgart, 82–85; *see also* wind

airplane crashes, 212

air pollution, 10, 41–52, 229–30, 295*n*–300*n*; "acceptable" levels of, 67; average city dweller and, 231; cities compared for, 47, 48, 49; in colonial cities, 28; distribution of, 47, 56, 63–66; fragmented approach to, 235; improvement of, 41, 60–61, 62–87, 281*n*; inversions and, 47–50, 64, 74; major sources of, 44, 64; in street canyons, 56–58; along streets and highways, 67–74, 84; wildlife and, 208; wind conditions and, 50, 51–52, 56, 57, 64–66, 73, 82

airports, as bird habitats, 212, 217

Alabama, sinkholes in, 100

Albany, N.Y., wildlife projects in, 224

Alfors, John T., 300*n*

algae, overproduction of, 137

allées, 189

Allegheny County, Pa., landslides in, 97

American Institute of Architects, 115

Amstelveen, Netherlands, 197

Amsterdam, Netherlands, 20, 73, 197

Anchorage earthquake (1964), 94, 95

ancient cities: climatic adaptations of, 62; decline of, 91; as model for modern cities, 263–64; modern cities compared to, 5, 12–13, 61–63; nature incorporated into, 109; waste problem of, 102; water systems of, 142–43

animals, *see* wildlife; *specific animals*

Annual Report (Council on Environmental Quality), 294

Anona (celestial city), 274

apartments, high-rise, 77–78, 94, 105

Aphrodiasias, waste problem in, 102

Appleton Street (Boston), 70

apple trees, birds' reliance on, 221–22

appliances, water use and, 140–41

aqueducts, 142–43; construction of, 24–25

aquifers, 144, 163, 164; *see also* groundwater

Arcata, Calif.: reconstructed wetland in, 251–52; water restoration in, 151

area source, of air pollutants, 64

Aristotle, 143

Army Corps of Engineers, U.S., 23, 154–57

Arnold Arboretum (Boston), 26, 172

arterial streets, 68, 70–73, 74

asphalt, 16, 77, 81–82, 84, 101

Aswan Dam fiasco, 237

Atlantic City, N.J., 138

Audubon Society, 174

Austin, Tex., sewage treatment in, 151

automobiles: air pollution and, 41, 42, 46, 56, 61, 64, 67, 231, 236, 238; alternatives to, 85; in arterial streets, 70–71; in celestial city, 270; in development of suburbs, 35, 36; ecosystem polluted by, 236, 238; in local streets, 68–69; social cost of, 238

avenues, 189

Back Bay (Boston), 22, 28, 147, 173; filling of, *16, 18, 20*

bacteria levels, in drinking water, 137

Baltimore, Md., 25, 50; dog owners in, 209; neighborhood study in, 68; wildlife problem in, 208, 211

Bath, England, landslides in, 115

Beacon Hill (Boston), 15, 18, 19, 177

Bellamy, Edward, 291*n*

Bendall's Cove (Boston), 17

Beneluxlaan (Amstelveen highway right-of-way), 197

Berlin, West Germany, 140; parks in, 215; plant life in, 27, 199

ures against, 105, 112–15, 273; principal zones of, 111; reconstruction after, 115

East Coast cities, repetitive patterns in, 11–12

Ecological Services Laboratory, U.S., 202–4

economic crisis, air quality in times of, 60–61

"Ecorock," 252, 253

ecosystem, urban, 13, 227–62, 313n–14n; in celestial city, 274; "closed" vs. "open," 245; complexity of, 229, 235, 246; comprehensive management of, 260–62; designing of, 242–62, 289n; dynamics of, 244–46; efficient energy use in, 246–50; energy and materials flow in, 243–46; exploitation of wastes in, 250–53; physical structure of, 244–45; resilience of, 245; as tool for understanding urban environment, 244; unforeseen consequences in, 235–41, 246

Egypt, problem of technology transfer in, 237

elm trees, 178, 180, 202, 206

Emerald Necklace (Boston), 147, 172–73

energy, 66, 230, 231; conservation of, 55, 64, 85, 281n; in design of urban ecosystem, 243–50; efficient use of, 246–50; transportation and, 248

Environment (McAllister, ed.), 313n

environmentalists, disputes of, 174–75

environmental problems: attitudinal factors in, 5; collection of successful solutions to, 259; comprehensive vs. modest solutions to, 85–87; "crisis response" to, 264; fragmented approach to, 231, 235–41; incremental change and, 10, 85–86, 87, 230–31; in nineteenth vs. twentieth century, 262; as societal problems, 265–68; tools to cope with, 10–11, 63, 243, 254–60; understanding vs. solution of, 10; *see also* specific problems

Environmental Protection Agency (New York), 211

Environmental Protection Agency, U.S. (EPA), 121, 136, 137, 233, 234, 252, 304n

epidemics, 134–36, 234–35

erosion, 16–17, 131, 237

Evelyn, John, 43, 44, 63

expressways, *see* highways

Fairbanks, Richard, 27

fall-line, 12

family streets, 68

Faraday, Michael, 134–35

fault zones, 95, 112

feces, dog, 211–12

Fens (Boston park), 22–23, 32, 146–48, 149, 172, 173, 263; parking lot in, 173; plan for, 146, 147

fires, after earthquakes, 115

First National Bank (Boulder), 150

fish, 252; killing of, 137, 210, 264

fisheries, urban, 224–25

Fitter, R. S. R., 310n

Fleming, Robert W., 300n

floodplains: building on, 132, 133–34, 145; dynamics of, 131–32; in Woodlands, 164–65

floods, 10, 19, 22, 91–92, 129, 283n–84n; increase of, 130–34; prevention of, 10, 22–23, 130, 132–33, 143, 145–50, 154–66, 236, 250, 259, 273

food chain, 216

food storage, pests and, 207, 209, 213

food web, 216

Foothill College (Los Altos), 153

forester, city, 174

forests, 10, 185; in celestial city, 271–72; colonial depletion of, 26; urban, 172, 174, 185, 188, 202–204

Forest Service, U.S., 81, 308n

Forman, Richard T. T., 310n

France, street trees in, 189

Frankfurt, West Germany, 10, 71–72

Franklin, Benjamin, 139

Franklin Park (Boston), 26, 172, 181, 182

Frog Hollow Park (Denver), 161

Gandemer, J., 295n

garbage, 15, 102–103, 232–33, 242–43; as landfill, 18, 100–101; pest problem and, 207, 209–210, 213

garden cities, 33–34

"Gardenlife," 252, 253

gardens, 5, 29–32, 73, 120–22, 269; allotment, 121; in ancient and medieval cities, 29–30, 120, 184; in celestial city, 269; courtyard, 152–53; Islamic, 153; lead in soil of, 104, 121–22, 283n; roof, 84, 194–95, 269; selection of vegetables to grow in, 121–22; watering of, 140; wildlife attracted to, 209